WILD ITALY

BY

TIM JEPSON

SIERRA CLUB BOOKS

SAN FRANCISCO

Published in the United States by Sierra Club Books,
San Francisco, 1994

Designed and produced by
Sheldrake Press,
188 Cavendish Road,
London SW12 0DA

Copyright © 1994 Sheldrake Publishing Ltd

Jepson, Tim.
    Wild Italy / by Tim Jepson.
    224p. 21.0 x 14.9cm.
    Includes index.
    ISBN 0-87156-478-5
    1. Natural history—Italy—Guidebooks.
    2. Natural areas—Italy—Guidebooks. 3. Italy—
Guidebooks.   I. Title.
QH152.J46   1994
508.45—dc20   93-28770
                                         CIP

Printed in Spain by Imago

EDITOR-IN-CHIEF: Simon Rigge
Editor: Malcolm Day
Picture Editor: Karin B. Hills
Art Direction: Ivor Claydon
Book Design: Ralph Sandoe
Assistant Editors: Mandy Greenfield, James Harpur,
Chris Schüler
Editorial Assistants: Charlotte Cox, Nikki Macmichael,
Aileen Reid, Tracey Stead
Picture Researcher: Elizabeth Loving
Line Illustrations: Syd Lewis
Production Manager: Geoff Barlow
Maps: Swanston Publishing Ltd
Index: Sandra Hobbs

THE AUTHOR

TIM JEPSON was educated at Oxford
University where he read English Literature.
He has written six books about Italy and has
a particular interest in Tuscany and Umbria.
He lived in Italy for five years and wrote for
The Sunday Telegraph as their Rome-Italy
correspondent. He has written widely on
other areas of the world in *Train Journeys of
the World*, *Mediterranean Wildlife* and the
Rough Guides to Canada and the Pacific
Northwest.

THE GENERAL EDITOR

DOUGLAS BOTTING was born in London
and educated at Oxford University. He has
travelled to the Amazon, South Yemen, the
Sahara, Arctic Siberia, to many parts of
Africa and to many European wild places.
    Douglas Botting's travel books include *One
Chilly Siberian Morning*, *Wilderness Europe*
and *Rio de Janeiro*. He has also written a
biography of the great naturalist and explorer
Alexander von Humboldt, entitled *Humboldt
and the Cosmos*. He has recently returned
from a second expedition to the rarely-visited
Arabian island of Socotra.

THE CONSULTANT

TERESA FARINO is an ecologist with a
Master's degree in Conservation from
University College, London. She has
travelled widely in southern Europe and has a
detailed knowledge of the habitats, flora and
fauna of the area. She is the author of several
books on wildlife, including *The Living
World*, *Sharks — the ultimate predators*
and the *Photographic Encyclopedia of
Wildflowers*. Having lived in northern
Spain since 1986, she contributes regularly
to *BBC Wildlife* magazine about the
environmental problems of that country and
is also joint author of *Wild Spain* in the Wild
Guides series.

CONTENTS

About the Series   4

Wild Italy: An Introduction   5

The Key to Wild Italy   7

Chapter 1: The Western Alps and Italian
Riviera 10
Valgrande 15 / Alta Valsesia 16 / Parco Nazionale
del Gran Paradiso 18 / Gran Bosco di Salbertrand
24 / Orsiera-Rocciavrè 25 / Alpi Marittime 26 /
Monte di Portofino 33 / Cinque Terre 35

Chapter 2: The Dolomites and Central
Alps 38
Gruppo di Tessa 44 / Parco Nazionale dello
Stelvio 46 / Adamello-Brenta 50 / Sciliar 54 /
Paneveggio-Pale di San Martino 55 / Puez-Odle
57 / Fanes-Sennes-Braies 59 / Dolomiti di Sesto 60

Chapter 3: The Venetian Plain and Eastern
Alps 62
Monte Baldo 66 / Monte Lessini and Pasubio 69 /
Parco Nazionale delle Dolomiti Bellunesi e
Feltrine 69 / Foresta del Cansiglio 72 / Alpi
Giulie-Carniche 73 / Laguna di Caorle 77 /
Laguna di Marano and Laguna di Grado 78 /
Carso 80

Chapter 4: The Po Basin and Northern
Apennines 82
Delta Padano 87 / Torrile 90 / Sassi di Rocca
Malatina 91 / Abetone and Monte Cimone 92 /
Foreste Casentinesi 93 / Monte Conero 96 / Parco
Nazionale dei Monti Sibillini 99 / Torricchio 104

Chapter 5: Tuscany and Umbria 106
Alpi Apuane 111 / Migliarino-San Rossore-
Massaciuccoli 117 / Bolgheri 119 / Maremma
120 / Monte Argentario, Laguna di Orbetello
and Lago di Burano 124 / Parco Nazionale

d'Arcipelago Toscano 125 / Monte Cucco 127 /
Valnerina 128

Chapter 6: Abruzzo 130
Monti della Laga 133 / Gran Sasso d'Italia 136 /
Monte Velino and Monte Sirente 139 / Parco
Nazionale d'Abruzzo 141 / Bosco di
Sant'Antonio 148 / La Maiella 149 / Alto
Molise 153

Chapter 7: The Mediterranean Coast . . . 154
Lago di Vico and Monti Cimini 158 / Monti
Simbruini and Monti Ernici 160 / Posta Fibreno
162 / Parco Nazionale del Circeo 164 / Monti
Picentini 166 / Tirone-Alto Vesuvio 167 / Vallone
delle Ferriere 168 / Oasi di Serre Persano 170 /
Cilento 171

Chapter 8: The South of Italy 174
Gargano and Foresta Umbra 177 / Isole Tremiti
181 / Salina di Margherita di Savoia 182 / Cesine
182 / Le Gravine Pugliesi 183 / Massiccio del
Pollino and Monti Orsomarso 184 / Parco
Nazionale della Calabria 187

Chapter 9: Sicily and Sardinia 190
Sicily: Etna 195 / Nebrodi 197 / Madonie 198 /
Zingaro and Monte Cofano 200 / Isola Marettimo
200 / Isola di Pantelleria 201 / Isole Pelagie 202
Sardinia: Monti del Gennargentu 204 / Giara di
Gesturi 207 / Molentargius 208 / Monte Arcosu
209 / Sinis 209 / Monte Limbara 213 / Isola di
Asinara 213

Useful Addresses & Further Reading . . . 214

Glossary 215

Index 216

Picture Credits & Acknowledgements . . . 224

ABOUT THE SERIES

What would the world be, once bereft
Of wet and of wilderness? Let them be
left,
O let them be left, wildness and wet;
Long live the weeds and the wilderness
yet.

Gerard Manley Hopkins: Inversnaid

These books are about those embattled refuges of wildness and wet, the wild places of Europe. But where, in this most densely populated sub-continent, do we find a truly wild place?

Ever since our Cro-Magnon ancestors began their forays into the virgin forests of Europe 40,000 years ago, the land and its creatures have been in retreat before *Homo sapiens*. Forests have been cleared, marshes drained and rivers straightened. Even some of those landscapes that appear primordial are in fact the result of human activity. Heather-covered moorland in North Yorkshire and parched Andalucian desert have this in common: both were once covered by great forests which ancient settlers knocked flat.

What then remains that can be called wild? There are still a few areas in Europe that are untouched by man — places generally so unwelcoming either in terrain or in climate that man has not wanted to touch them at all — and these are indisputably wild.

For some people, wildness suggests conflict with nature: a wild place is a part of the planet so savage and desolate that you risk your life whenever you venture into it. This is in part true but would limit the eligible places to the most impenetrable bog or highest mountain tops in the worst winter weather — a rather restricted view. Another much broader definition considers a wild place to be a part of the planet where living things can find a natural refuge from the influence of modern industrial society. By this definition a wild place is for wildlife as well as that portmanteau figure referred to in these pages as the wild traveller: the hillwalker, backpacker, birdwatcher, nature lover, explorer, nomad, loner, mystic, masochist, aficionado of the great outdoors, or permutations of all these things.

This is the definition we have observed in selecting the wild places described in these books. Choosing them has not been easy. Even so, we hope the criterion has proved rigid enough to exclude purely pretty (though popular) countryside, and flexible enough to include the greener and gentler wild places, of great natural historical interest perhaps, as well as the starker, more savage ones where the wild explorers come into their own.

These are not guide books in the conventional sense, for to describe every neck of the woods and twist of the trail throughout Europe would require a library of volumes. Nor are these books addressed to the technical specialist — the caver, diver, rock climber or cross-country skier; the orchid-hunter, lepidopterist or beetle-maniac — for such experts will have reference data of their own. They are books intended for the general outdoor traveller — including the expert outside his own field of expertise (the orchid-hunter in a cave, the diver on a mountain top) — who wishes to scrutinize the range of wild places on offer in Europe, to learn a little more about them and to set about exploring them off the beaten track.

One of the greatest consolations in the preparation of these books has been to find that after 40,000 years of hunting, clearing, draining and ploughing, Cro-Magnon and their descendants have left so much of Europe that can still be defined as wild.

Douglas Botting

WILD ITALY: AN INTRODUCTION

The Italy of popular imagination is scarcely a wild country at all. Its familiar landscapes are those of Tuscany and Umbria – pastoral vignettes of vines, olives and cypress-topped hills melting into the haze of a summer afternoon. Its countryside is the ordered work of centuries, tilled and tamed by peasants since the dawn of history. Yet behind this benign veneer lie vast areas of wilderness, from the glacier-carved cirques of the Dolomites to the sun-scorched plains of the Sardinian interior. Vultures and eagles wheel in Sicily's skies, lynx pad the Tarvisian forests and wolves still roam the mountains of the Apennines.

Italy's natural heritage is, however, one of Europe's most threatened; damaged not so much by the draining of wetlands, felling of woodlands and cutting of grasslands, as elsewhere, but by the effects of industrialization, which in the last forty years has turned Italy from an agricultural backwater into one of the world's leading economic powers. In the course of this transformation the Italian coast has been ravaged, the Po poisoned by the effluent of northern cities and the countryside blighted by building projects that proceeded virtually unhindered by planning controls.

Progress in halting the environmental carnage has been slow. Although many national parks have been planned, only eight have been created in the last seventy years and only 3 per cent of the country enjoys a measure of protected status. Compare this with the United Kingdom (21 per cent), Germany (21 per cent) and countries like Kenya and Venezuela, both of which manage to extend some form of protection over 10 per cent of their territory.

Even when protection exists it often remains woefully inadequate in practice. Birds and mammals, whether protected or not, are still annihilated by hunters from 17 August to 11 March, and illegal practices such as the netting of birds, though in decline, are still frequently reported. Referendums and campaigns to limit hunting have failed in the face of opposition from one of the world's most powerful hunting lobbies. The thunder of guns on a Sunday morning remains a fact of rural Italian life.

If this sounds depressing, take heart, for much of Italy remains free from both hunters and developers. Flora and fauna are as varied as anywhere in Europe. Italians are invariably friendly and hospitable, especially in the rural areas. Although many will find it strange that you should want to explore their countryside, particularly if you are on foot, few are likely to mind you tramping across their land. Fewer still are likely to join you. Hiking is still a pleasure unknown to most Italians, except in the Alps.

Do not be surprised to find yourself addressed in a language other than Italian; Italy is less a country than a federation of independent regions. Walkers in parts of Piedmont will find themselves confronted with a French patois; in the mountains of the central Alps they will find themselves dealing in German; and in the Dolomites they might come across Ladin. In Sardinia the Sard language is rivalled in its impenetrability only by Welsh, and in Sicily and Naples the dialects are so strong they might as well be from another continent.

Foreigners wishing to explore the wilder parts of Italy are likely to find themselves hamstrung by lack of information on paths, areas of natural interest and regional flora and fauna. *Wild Italy* is the first guide of its type to offer such information, describing Italy's finest walks and landscapes, as well as its immense natural variety and scarcely known protected places. It cannot be encyclopaedic, but it will give you a taste of the country's wild places and, I hope, a desire to explore them for yourself.

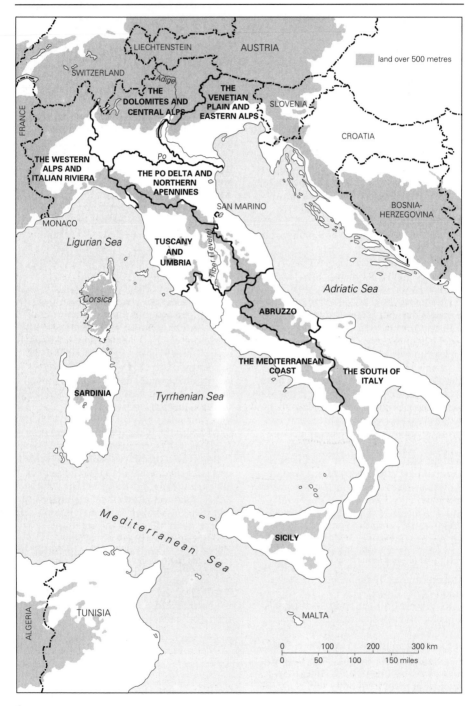

land over 500 metres

LIECHTENSTEIN

AUSTRIA

SWITZERLAND

Adige

THE DOLOMITES AND CENTRAL ALPS

THE VENETIAN PLAIN AND EASTERN ALPS

SLOVENIA

CROATIA

FRANCE

THE WESTERN ALPS AND ITALIAN RIVIERA

Po

THE PO DELTA AND NORTHERN APENNINES

BOSNIA-HERZEGOVINA

SAN MARINO

MONACO

Ligurian Sea

TUSCANY AND UMBRIA

Tiber (Tevere)

Adriatic Sea

Corsica

ABRUZZO

SARDINIA

Tyrrhenian Sea

THE MEDITERRANEAN COAST

THE SOUTH OF ITALY

Mediterranean Sea

SICILY

ALGERIA

TUNISIA

MALTA

| 0 | 100 | 200 | 300 km |
| 0 | 50 | 100 | 150 miles |

THE KEY TO ITALY'S WILD PLACES

WILD HABITATS

An appreciation of habitats is useful for anyone interested in experiencing wild species in their natural environment. In turn, to understand the variety of habitats it is necessary to look at the major influences, climate and geology. What follows is a thumbnail sketch of the forces that have shaped the Italian landscape.

Geology: In a nutshell, Italy divides into the Alps, Apennines and Po Valley (with a separate mountain system in Sardinia). The Alps were formed as a result of continental drift, when a fragment of Africa collided with the European land mass. They are essentially eroded Hercynian rocks, dating from the Carboniferous or the Permian periods (345–225 million years ago). The Apennines are generally older and more weathered, and consist mainly of sandstone and limestone marl (clay) in the north, limestone in the centre and limestone and Hercynian granite in the south. On either side of the Apennines' main ridge are the sub-Apennines, lower ranges built up of generally softer and more recent rocks. The Po Valley is a mixture of loams, gravels, permeable sands and silts brought down by glacial meltwaters after the Ice Ages. All over Italy, however, small geological anomalies intrude on these structures; the most famous are the seismic and volcanic zones around Etna, Vesuvius and the Campi Flegrei.

Soils: Rock type has a profound influence on soils and, in turn, on vegetation. In Italy differences in climate, altitude and geology have produced a wide variety of soils. Most common are the dark-brown podzols, typical of mountains with a lot of flint and heavy rainfall, such as the Alps. Similar soils occur in the Apennines, together with *rendzinas*, humus-carbonate soils characteristic of limestone mountain pastures and of many Apennine meadows and beech forests. Red earth, the famous *terra rossa*, derives from limestone rocks: after weathering, only the clay minerals are left. This distinctive residue occurs most notably in Puglia and the Veneto, where it is the favoured soil of vineyards and olive groves.

Drainage: Italy's rivers are relatively short: the longest is the Po which drains the western Alps but runs for only 650 kilometres (400 miles) before emptying into the Adriatic. The country's second river, the Adige, which drains the eastern Alps and the Dolomites, only stretches some 400 kilometres (250 miles). Other rivers flowing into the Adriatic from the Apennines, the peninsula's main watershed, tend to be even more modest. Those flowing west into the Tyrrhenian Sea are the more complex, including the Tiber, which flows through Rome, and the Arno, Florence's great river. Southern rivers are often dry in the summer but experience sometimes devastating flash floods in spring and autumn.

Climate: Italy lies essentially in a temperate zone, but because it is affected by the rest of Europe in the north and by the Mediterranean in the south it has at least four principal climate zones and experiences a huge range of weathers.

Peninsular Italy and Sardinia are characterized by hot dry summers and mild short winters, and are occasionally influenced by a moister and cooler Atlantic climate. The Alps, like the Apennines, produce complex micro-climates, and partially shield the peninsula from the colder and wetter weather of the north and west. Generally, though, the Alps experience a continental mountain climate of cold snowy winters and short mild summers. Cooler and wetter "Balkan" weather is felt in the east as a result of more marked continental effects, which include the *bora*, a summer wind which blows across the Adriatic from the north-east at up to 160kph (100mph). In Sicily and the south, North African weather often prevails, most obviously in the droughts and high summer temperatures which may be intensified by the fierce *scirocco* wind blowing up from the Sahara.

Mountains and uplands: Italy is largely mountainous: 35 per cent of its area is covered by ranges of over 700 metres (2,500 feet), 42 per cent by hills and only 23 per cent by plains. The Alps and Apennines are the two main mountain ranges, their vast extent producing a variety of landscapes that range from Arctic ice and tundra in the north to hot Mediterranean slópes in the south. Between these two extremes, more temperate conditions allow a wide range of flora and fauna to flourish in habitats that run the gamut of European upland environments.

Forest and shrubland: The largest remnants of Italy's great primeval forests, most of which have been cleared by centuries of cultivation, survive in the Sila, in Calabria and in the Casentini forests of Tuscany and Emilia-Romagna. Elsewhere, precious relics testify to long-vanished areas of former woodland, in Piedmont's Gran Bosco di Salbertrand, the Abruzzo's Bosco di Sant'Antonio and the Gran Bosco di Mesola on the edge of the Po Delta.

The Alps support magnificent fir forests, with larch and Norway spruce giving way at higher altitudes to green alder and dwarf varieties of pine, willow and juniper. Great forests of beech and sweet chestnut blanket much of the Apennines; holm oak, aleppo pine and olive are notable at lower levels. In the higher parts of southern Italy, the Apennines also support clumps of ancient mountain forest, boasting trees such as oriental plane, chestnut and flowering ash. Harsher, cooler parts of the range in the Abruzzo and Calabria also support various kinds of pine.

In lower lying areas of the peninsula, and especially in Sicily and Sardinia, trees typical of the Mediterranean flourish, principally cork oak and holm oak. In such areas, and where the original vegetation has been partially cleared, a vigorous layer of thick scrub, known as maquis, is common. This is typically between two and four metres (seven and fourteen feet) high. Drier stunted shrubland only half a metre (18 inches) in height, known as *garrigue*, may also develop, often on limestone or extremely thin soils. Steppes of tough drought-resistant plants and feather grasses now grow in Puglia, replacing olive trees and shore vegetation which have been cut down, and in Sardinia, where the removal of carob forests has had the same effect.

Wetlands: The wetlands, including lakes, swamps, marshes and rivers, are of great interest for the richness of their plant and bird life. The delta of the River Po, among Italy's best birdwatching areas, is the most famous. Some of the country's great areas of ancient marsh, such as Tuscany's Maremma and Lazio's Pontine, have been drained, but small slivers of wetland such as the Circeo National Park still offer rich rewards. Italy also has some 1,500 lakes, from glacially scoured tarns in the Alps to coastal saline lagoons, such as Lesina and Varano.

Coasts and islands: Where it is free of commercial development, the Italian coast offers a spectacular variety of sea shores — cliffs, estuaries, deltas and coastal dunes. In addition Italy has 32 islands, ranging from Sardinia to the coronet of wild islands around the north of Sicily, an archipelago which includes the naturalist's haven of Marettimo and the volcanic islets of Stromboli and Vulcano.

Along the Ligurian coast close to the French border, the littoral is a mixture of level shores and high cliffs. Moving south through Tuscany as far as Campania, long sandy beaches and dunes predominate along the Tyrrhenian Sea, interrupted by bold promontories. Calabria's coast is again high and rocky, whilst Sicily's is mainly flat. Around most of Puglia, however, and almost all the way up Italy's eastern Adriatic coast, the shore remains either flat or slightly terraced. Only the Po delta and the craggy spur of the Conero peninsula disturb its ruler-straight line. Lagoons characterize the area around Venice, before the coast picks up the limestone uplands of the Carso, close to Trieste.

ITALY'S NATURE CONSERVATION AREAS

Italy's system of environmental protection is one of the most confusing and slipshod in Europe. In many of the designated parks and reserves conservation is nominal. Bureaucratic wrangling and vested interests prevent the bodies charged with enforcing environmental standards from carrying out their responsibilities.

Parchi Nazionali: Italy has just eight national parks: Gran Paradiso (created in 1922), Abruzzo (1923), Circeo (1934), Stelvio (1935), Calabria (1968), Arcipelago Toscano (1989), Dolomiti Bellunesi (1990) and Sibillini (1990). They are administered by the State and all but the tiny Circeo and Arcipelago Toscano embrace large mountain regions. Another 18 major parks have been mooted for years, but only two have progressed to the planning stage: Pollino and Golfo di Orosei.

Parchi Internazionali: Like the stillborn national parks, Italy's international parks exist only on paper. Conservation and environmental protection will eventually be administered by park authorities whose powers will extend across national borders. The only international park so far up and running is Monte Bianco (Mont Blanc) in north-west Italy, realized in 1989. Other planned collaborations are the Stelvio and Engadina parks (with Switzerland), the Argentera and Mercantour (France), Gran Paradiso and Vanoise (France) and Tarvisio and Triglav (Slovenia).

Parchi Naturali Regionali: Currently numbering about 70, but covering only about 2% of the country, regional nature parks provide far less environmental protection than do national parks. They are administered by one or other of Italy's twenty regions, which differ greatly in their enthusiasm for the parks and their approach to their administration.

Riserve Naturali dello Stato: Usually tiny in extent and covering areas of outstanding natural interest, nature reserves run by the State currently number 137 (with a combined area of 80,000 hectares/200,000 acres), together with another 44 specially designated wetland zones (54,000 hectares/133,000 acres). Many are contained within larger protected areas, such as national parks. Environmental protection is generally rigidly enforced.

Riserve Naturali Regionali e Provinciali:
Provincial and regional reserves generally enjoy less protection than the State's nature reserves. Regions differ in their attitude to the reserves no less than to the regional nature parks. Piedmont, with 41 parks and reserves, and Lombardy, which has 73, are outstanding. By contrast, Umbria, Calabria, Puglia, Trentino-Alto Adige and several others have barely a handful of reserves between them.

Oasi Naturali: By far the smallest but also the best protected of Italy's wild places, the so-called *rifugi faunistici*, or nature oases, are a fairly new environmental initiative. Most are run, and often owned, by private bodies, of which the World Wildlife Fund for Nature (WWF) is the most notable; it has 32 *oasi* covering 12,000 hectares/ 30,000 acres. Similar reserves are administered by Italia Nostra and by LIPU, the national organization for the protection of birds, which has 15 sites. (For details of Italy's nature conservation bodies, see the Glossary at the end of the book.) Most oases have excellent trails and viewing facilities, though access is usually restricted to one or two days a week.

EXPLORING WILD ITALY

Italy is criss-crossed with ancient paths and mule-tracks. Only a tiny proportion of trails are marked as official footpaths, and good maps for large areas of the country, especially in the south, are difficult to obtain and invariably out of date. Marked long-distance paths are found mainly in the north, notably *Alta Vie* in the Dolomites and the *Grande Traversata delle Alpi* in Piedmont. Friuli in the north-east has the *Traversata Carnica*. The Alpi Apuane have two long paths, *Apuane Trekking* and *Garfagnana Trekking*, and Liguria boasts the *Alta Via Monti Liguri*. The *Grande Escursione Appenninica* (GEA) runs through Tuscany and Emilia-Romagna as far as Umbria, and there are plans eventually to extend it to the southern tip of the peninsula.

Local paths in the Dolomites and throughout the best-known parts of the western and central Alps are clearly marked and may be followed on several excellent series of maps. Planning and

executing a hiking trip is probably made easier in these areas than anywhere else in Europe.

Liguria and Tuscany's Alpi Apuane regions are also well served by maps and trails, while new maps in the Kompass series are opening up parts of Tuscany, Umbria and the Monti Sibillini to the walker. South of Rome, however, and especially in Calabria, Sicily and Sardinia, you must rely on the old military maps produced by the Istituto Geografico Militare (IGM). The complete series can be found at Viale Strozzi 44, Florence.

Often the best way of exploring more remote areas is to take an organized trip. The British firm, Alternative Travel Group, 69–71, Banbury Road, Oxford, T: (0865) 310 399, probably runs the best trips and organizes the most interesting itineraries. It is also an organization committed to conservation and environmental protection.

TO THE READER

Eagle symbols: The eagle symbols used at the head of some entries in this book indicate the wildness quality of the place to which they refer. This rating is based on a number of factors, including the remoteness, ruggedness, spaciousness, uniqueness, wildlife interest and the author's subjective reactions. Three eagles is the highest rating, no eagles the lowest.

Glossary: Nature conservation bodies are frequently referred to in the text by their common abbreviations. The glossary at the end of the book gives their full names and describes their activities. It also defines the abbreviations used for maps and official footpaths.

Rules of the Wild: Advice about mountain climbing and safety is given at the end of Chapter 2; a universally recognized country code of behaviour is given at the end of Chapter 9.

Updating: While everything possible has been done to ensure the accuracy of the facts in this book, information does gradually become outdated in the ever-changing countryside. For this reason we would welcome readers' corrections and comments for incorporation in revised editions. Please write to The Editor, Wild Traveller's Guides, Sheldrake Press, 188 Cavendish Road, London SW12 0DA.

Non-liability: Both the author and the publishers have gone to great pains to point out the hazards that may confront the traveller in certain places described in *Wild Italy*. We cannot under any circumstances accept any liability for any mishap, loss or injury sustained by any person venturing into any of the wild places listed in this book.

The Western Alps and Italian Riviera

The great arc of the Alps sweeps across northern Italy in a protective embrace that reaches from France to the Slovenian border. Europe's highest and most extensive mountains, they have nonetheless been spoiled in some parts by centuries of human habitation. Their valleys are often threaded with roads and railways, or blotted with towns and industrial plant. The unguided traveller may easily come across ski resorts and hydro-electric schemes on the higher slopes which were once the domain of bears and wolves, since harried and hunted to virtual extinction. So popular are these mountains that in summer the tracks and trails may be thronged with walkers, whether pushing through meadows ablaze with flowers or braving the remoter citadels of ice and rock. You have to choose carefully when and where to go to appreciate the wilderness of the Alps of old.

Bar a few stretches of Ligurian coastline, however, it is the Alps which yield north-west Italy's finest natural rewards. The greatest concentration of the glorious sites is in the Valle d' Aosta, one of Italy's smallest administrative regions, yet home to its most spectacular scenery and Europe's three highest mountains: Mont Blanc (Monte Bianco), Monte Rosa and the Matterhorn (Monte Cervino). The best of the rest are spread across Piedmont ("foot of the mountains"), whose mountainous borders with France and Switzerland are chequered with numerous parks, including Europe's highest protected area (the Valsesia) and one of its finest national parks (the Gran Paradiso).

Pine forests frame the peaks and glaciers at the end of the Valnontey, one of the loveliest valleys in Piedmont's Gran Paradiso National Park.

Yet for a first visit, leave these beautiful but busy areas for later and experience instead the Alpi Marittime, a pristine corner of solitude and wilderness in south-west Piedmont. Here you will find landscapes of spectacular and primordial beauty, where wilderness is still uncompromised. If you are intimidated by the Alps' numberless walking possibilities there is perhaps one walk you should tackle in these mountains if you tackle no other.

The hike in question follows part of the *Grande Traversata delle Alpi* (GTA), a long-distance footpath that meanders from the Alps' border with France to their climax in the Gran Paradiso. Head for the little hamlet of Sant'Anna, close to Valdieri, and drive to the Terme di Valdieri, a lonely windblown hotel built around the hunting lodge once owned by the Savoys, dukes of Piedmont and later Italy's first royal family. The road leading to the hotel eventually becomes a well engineered and beautifully scenic mule-track, created to allow royal parties a graceful approach to the hunting grounds beyond.

The track climbs along the side of a valley, looking down on to an ice-clear river fringed by stands of fir and pine. At the head of the valley, on the horizon high above, stand the pinnacles of the main alpine crest. Beyond that lies France and miles of wilderness. Sunlight filters through trees shading the track which hairpins ever higher and tests your lungs, just as the higher, more precipitous paths will test your nerve. This steep, early morning climb is typical of virtually all excursions in the Alps: most walkers will climb their looming glaciated valleys before finding the flower-strewn meadows hidden at greater heights.

Pausing for breath, as I did one

October morning made in heaven, I caught a glimpse of the wildlife for which these mountains are renowned. In this case it was the face of a startled chamois, and a little later, the contented nibbling figure of a marmot basking in the sunshine. Later still was to be the first time I heard the marmot's warning whistle, a piercing high-pitched shriek that echoed around the mountains as if from another world.

The reward for this climb, if reward were needed, is the appearance of the Valle di Valasco, perhaps the Alps' most idyllic upland meadow. After the path has wended its way round boulders and yellow-tinted larches, a series of waterfalls heralds this vast natural amphitheatre. Mountains gird it on three sides, craggy and snow-capped, and a lazy stream meanders through its centre. The mule-track picks its way towards a single stone building, the *Casa di Caccia*, a ruined hunting lodge, now quiet and overgrown, with no hint of the days when it sheltered the Savoys in all their splendour.

Beyond its tumbled stones and timbers the track peters out into a marshy stream-side path. A little later it picks up, curving round the head of the meadow to resume its climb towards the high ridges now crowding the skyline. On its way above the tree-line the hike continues through a typically alpine setting, encountering splintered pinnacles and plunging rock walls. Often this stage of a trek is cut short, interrupted by sheer rock-faces, glaciers and other impenetrable armour of the high Alps. Here, though, you can crest the mountains, should you wish, by scrambling up to a knife-edge ridge that looks down into France and a sweep of pastoral countryside that stretches to the Riviera.

As all too often in the Alps, however, you will probably find the terrain limits your options, leaving you no choice but to retrace your steps. On this occasion, I decided to forgo the ridge and head for a beautiful and unexpected trio of lakes, each cradled in a dramatic cwm and linked by a tortuous path that threads its way back to the meadow way below. The only sign of life up here was a tiny refuge, the Rifugio Questa, shuttered and forlorn, but one of dozens dotted all over the Alps, usually open only in summer, invaluable for longer excursions into the high mountains.

A leisurely return to the Terme marked the easy end to a perfect day's walk, the sun catching the snow as it set behind the mountains. Any one of hundreds, perhaps thousands, of alpine walks offers similar experiences: the slog from the valley, the stroll across upper meadows and the drama of the high country above the treeline.

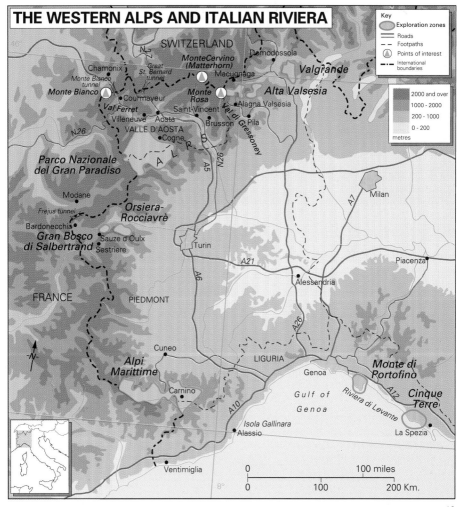

THE WESTERN ALPS AND ITALIAN RIVIERA

GETTING THERE

By air: international charter and scheduled flights operate to Genoa (for Liguria) and Turin (for Piedmont and the Valle d'Aosta).

By car: the main approaches from France are from Chamonix via the Mont Blanc tunnel (N26 and A5 motorway); the Frejus tunnel from Modane to Bardonecchia and the A10 to Genoa from Ventimiglia and the French Riviera. From Switzerland use the N21/27 and Great St Bernard tunnel.

By rail: main-line services to Paris and Turin via Modane, Genoa and the Riviera, Turin and Aosta.

WHEN TO GO

Climate makes the Piedmont and the Valle d'Aosta primarily summer destinations: July and Aug can be crowded in the Gran Paradiso and better-known parks. June is usually OK for walking, though snow can linger on higher ground; Sept and Oct are often excellent months for hiking.

WHERE TO STAY

There are plenty of hotels in the towns, villages and ski resorts of Piedmont and Valle d'Aosta. Mountain refuges, usually open June–Sept and Dec–Apr, are also dotted over the popular hiking areas.

Outdoor living: Most official campsites are near the sea (Liguria); in the mountains they tend to be near lakes. Most open between June and Sept.

ACTIVITIES

Walking: numerous marked paths in most of the alpine parks and mountains; there are also several excellent long-distance paths. The best-known is the 55-day *Grande Traversata delle Alpi* (GTA) from Carnino on the Ligurian border, which strikes north through the Alpi Marittime to the foothills of the Gran Paradiso. There are also two famous high level routes in the Valle d'Aosta: the 10-day *Alta Via Due* from Val di Gressoney to Val Ferret under the Mont Blanc massif (via large areas of the Gran Paradiso park). Other trails include a 4-day tour of Monviso and the *Tour du Mont Blanc*, an 11-day loop (with 2 stages in Italy).

Skiing: many well-known resorts, including Courmayeur, Breuil-Cervinia, Saint-Vincent, Brusson, Pila and Cogne (Valle d'Aosta) and Sestriere, Sauze d'Oulx, Alagna Valsesia and Macugnaga (Piedmont). Summer glacier skiing is also available in most resorts.

Fishing: sea fishing from boats or the shore is possible almost everywhere without a permit; to fish in freshwater you need an annual permit from FIPS offices; they will advise on local conditions and restrictions.

FURTHER INFORMATION

Tourist information: the main EPT provincial tourist offices are: (Piedmont) Turin, Via Roma 222, T: (011) 535 181; Cuneo, Corso Nizza 17, T: (0171) 693 258; (Valle d' Aosta) Aosta, Piazza Chanoux 8, T: (065) 35655; (Liguria) Genoa, Via Roma 11, T: (010) 591 407; La Spezia, Viale Mazzini 47, T: (0187) 36000.

CLUB ALPINO ITALIANO (CAI)

The Italian Alpine Club was founded in 1863. It now has a quarter of a million members, 280 branch offices and nearly 400 local groups. The club's activities include mountaineering, climbing, caving, hiking, trekking, survival and mountain rescue. In addition to some 470 refuges and 140 bivouacs, it runs 200 rescue stations, 150 avalanche, rescue and research centres, employs 400 instructors and recognizes 1,000 registered guides.

You can join the club at any branch office. Many branches are listed in the Fact Pack sections of this book. Often these offices are open for only a couple of hours each week, so call in advance or check with the local tourist office for opening times. Take two passport photographs for registration.

Membership entitles you to insurance cover, access to local CAI groups, the use of club equipment and a discount of up to fifty per cent on overnight fees in their refuges. Remember, however, that not all refuges are owned by the club. Private huts are about twice as expensive. CAI huts are also open to non-members.

Do not expect much for your money: bunks in unheated rooms and one cold tap are the norm in more spartan outposts. Most huts have a bar and serve meals, on which members receive a discount of 10 to 15 per cent. The great majority of huts are open only in July and August (June to October in a few cases) and over winter weekends. For a full list of CAI huts write to CAI, Via Ugo Foscolo 3, Milan. Local lists are often available from tourist offices. Finally CAI groups offer invaluable advice on local walks, climbs, mountains and their dangers; and, of course, a shared love and respect for wild places.

Valgrande

One of Italy's largest State nature reserves (3,383ha/8,360 acres), north-west of Lago Maggiore

The Valgrande reserve is one of Italy's last true wildernesses. This circle of peaks surrounded by deep ravines is the largest uninhabited area in the Alps. No buildings or cars, and few tourists, intrude on the landscape. The valleys are solitary and mysterious, the peaks barren, the ancient tracks that cross the reserve overgrown with vegetation.

The Valgrande's mountains are low compared with the peaks of Monte Rosa ranging across the skyline to the west. Properly speaking, they are only pre-Alps, with their ring of summits at Togano, Pizzo Mottac, Pizzo Proman and Cima della Laurasca barely rising above 2,000 metres (6,500 feet). Nevertheless, they present impressive views of alpine scenery.

At the heart of the reserve is the course of the Valgrande river itself. Rising among high rock walls at the head of the valley, where golden eagles and fleeting chamois can be spotted, it twists southwards through immense coniferous forests. Steep-sided gorges bubbling with streams and waterfalls join the upper valley, while chestnut, beech and maple trees, as well as the occasional yew, adorn the lower slopes. A plentiful supply of spring water also gives rise to many alpine flowers, including the tulip, martagon lily, gentian and edelweiss, with the rare white alpenrose outstanding.

One of the most arduous of alpine treks follows the valley, a three-day assault course from Malesco in the Val Vigezzo to the village of Cicogna outside the reserve. The challenge should be considered only in the best weather. This means early spring, before summer's rampant vegetation blocks your way. Those looking for a gentler outing usually depart from Cicogna, going via Casletta to the Ponte di Velina.

BEFORE YOU GO
Guidebooks: *Val Grande Ultimo Paradiso* and T. Valsesia, *Val Grande, Parco Naturale* (Alberti 1985).
Maps: IGM 1:25,000 *Verbania, Monte Zeda, Primosello Chiovenda* and *Ornavasso*.

GETTING THERE
By car: A8 from Milan and Novara, and then SS33 to Arona, Stresa and Domodossola. Minor road access from the S and Lago Maggiore; in the N from Santa Maria Maggiore and the SS337.
By rail: to Domodossola (Milan–Brig line) and from Locarno in Switzerland. A scenic line runs from Domodossola to Locarno across the northern edge of the Valgrande, with useful stations

at Malesco and Santa Maria Maggiore (10 trains daily).
By bus: all round Lago Maggiore to the S, and from Domodossola into the Val Vigezzo and N to the Val Formazza.

WHERE TO STAY
At many points on Lago Maggiore, or Domodossola (try the Piccolo Hotel, T: (0324) 42351; and Santa Maria Maggiore, La Jazza, T: (0324) 94471.
Outdoor living: campsites on the lake shore, with free camping in the Valgrande except for the integral reserve.
Refuges: spartan huts and bivouacs in the Valgrande and adjacent mountains; ask at tourist offices and CAI, Via Capis, Domodossola.

ACTIVITIES
Walking: though maps indicate tracks, many in the interior can be hard to locate. This said, there are plenty of hiking possibilities, many long and demanding. Among the more straightforward walks try: the climb to the Rif. Cavallone from Miazzina in the S, and the traverse from the Valle Loana to In La Piana via the Bocchetta di Scaredi.

FURTHER INFORMATION
Tourist offices: Via Romita 13 bis, Domodossola, T: (0324) 81 308; Via Domodossola 3, Santa Maria Maggiore, T: (0324) 9091; Piazzale Europa 3, Stresa, T: (0323) 30150; Corso Zannitello, Pallanza (Verbania), T: (0323) 42976.

Alta Valsesia

Piedmont's most spectacular small nature park (6,435ha/15,902 acres); a high, heavily glaciated alpine habitat

So wild are some parts of the Alta Valsesia that you can almost believe the legends associated with them: that hidden lakes brimmed over with liquid silver, and spring waters above Macugnaga issued from a "lost valley", which yielded the Valle d'Aosta's earliest tribes. Other parts, however, have lost some of their mystery, as skiing enthusiasts have taken advantage of the wonderful snow-covered mountainscape.

The highest nature conservation area in Europe, Alta Valsesia only once drops below 2,000m (6,500ft) and reaches 4,559m (14,958ft) at its western end, part of the Rosa mountain complex that straddles the Swiss–Italian border. Europe's second highest mountain after Mont Blanc, Monte Rosa is a little piece of the Himalayas in the Alps; an Italian folk-song goes as far as to call it "the most beautiful mountain in the world". To look at the colossal rock wall on its east face you might agree. This awe-inspiring collection of high peaks and glaciers, together with the Matterhorn (4,478m/14,691ft) immediately to the west, is the icy heart of the Alps.

Rosa's name comes not from its colour — though it glows rosy-pink under a sinking sun — but from *roese* or *roisa*, which in the local patois means "ice-covered". The park allows you an unparalleled close-up of such glacial features as cirques, moraines and tarns as well as its present glaciers, the Sesia, Vigne, Locce and Piode.

The park covers a disjointed area from the Rosa glaciers in the west to the lower ridges that lie to the east across the heads of the Valgrande, Carcoforo

---

The majestic golden eagle, with its 2m (6ft) wingspan, can be seen soaring over alpine meadows and forests in search of unwary ptarmigan or mountain hares.

and Valsesia valleys. Now one of the showpieces of Piedmont's fine conservation work, the park boasts 57 recorded species of rare high-altitude plants *above* the snowline, and many more below it. Animals are abundant at the lower altitudes, but are ill-suited to the upland tundra of ice, scree and boulder-covered pasture that characterizes much of Alta Valsesia.

If you should venture into the rocky terrain above the tree-line, though, you will no doubt be stricken with a sense of terrible inadequacy by the sheer agility of chamois racing down precipitous slopes at breakneck speed as you approach. Perhaps the easiest of all creatures to encounter in the high mountains today, they were once hunted relentlessly for their soft skins (much prized as shammy leathers), as well as for meat and marksmen's trophies. Marmots too can be found here, although you are more likely to see only the black tips of their tails disappearing into their burrows. Among the more predatory creatures of Alta Valsesia are stoats and foxes, while several pairs of golden eagles rear their young in the more inaccessible crags.

The Alta Valsesia has a superb network of paths and 11 well-equipped refuges, including Europe's highest, the Rifugio Regina Margherita at 4,559m (14,958ft). The paths are crowded in the summer, especially those from Macugnaga to the Rifugio Zamboni-Zappa, where you find the best views of the colossal walls of the Gnifetti (4,554m/14,940ft), the eastern flank of Monte Rosa.

A short stroll above Alagna (towards the Rifugio Pastore) brings you to the Acqua Bianca waterfall, with stunning views on to the massif and across the River Sesia's mighty canyon. To be alone, head for the lower and more solitary peaks in the east, such as Cima Lampone, Cima Tignaga, Pizzo Montevecchio, and their tranquil valleys, the Rima and Carcoforo.

Despite a proliferation of ski-lifts, much of the area has kept its traditional appearance, including the park's centres at Macugnaga and Alagna (both busy resorts). Wooden, geranium-hung houses, surrounded by flower-filled meadows, hark back to the area's famous *Walser* traditions. The *Walser* were medieval settlers who drifted here from other alpine valleys further north, bringing their language and customs with them. Today, most of the villages in this area speak the predominant *Walser* language, German. At Alagna, you can visit a museum, situated in a 1628 *Walser* house, which records the ways of this old mountain life.

Before you go: the park centre is at the Comunità Montana Valsesia, Via Franzani 2, Varallo Sesia, T: (0161) 51555. *Maps:* Kompass 1:50,000 *Monte Rosa* (Sheet 88); IGC 1:50,000 *Alagna–Macugnaga* (Sheet 10) — both detailed, excellent maps. *Guidebooks:* F. Fini, *Il Monte Rosa* (Zanichelli 1979); P. Carlese, *Sentieri Intorno al Monte Rosa* (a walkers' guide) (Tamari, 1986). **Getting there** *By car:* to Biella (A6/SS230) between Milan and Turin, and then SS142/SS299 to Varallo. From here the SS290 runs the length of the Sesia valley to Alagna. The approach to Macugnaga is more circuitous: A6 to Novara, SS32/33 via Arona and Lago Maggiore and then branch right on the SS549 along the Valle Anzasca.

In Italy the stoat is confined to the Alps, where it is supremely well adapted to the high mountain habitat. At the onset of winter, its coat turns pure white, serving as camouflage for ambushing prey and also preventing valuable heat escaping.

By rail: 7 trains daily to Varallo on the branch line from Novara (Milan–Turin line), with a bus service to Alagna from Novara and Varallo. Nearest station to Macugnaga at Piedimulera (30km/18 miles) on the Novara–Domodossola line. **Where to stay:** plentiful accommodation at Alagna, Macugnaga, Rima, Carcoforo and Riva Valdobbia. *Outdoor living:* prohibited in the park, but opportunities to pitch tents outside its limits; organized sites at Alagna and Macugnaga. *Refuges:* the Rifugio Pastore can be contacted direct, T: (0163) 91220; otherwise enquire at tourist offices or CAI, Via Durio 14, Varallo, T: (0163) 51530. **Activities** *Walking:* many options, but some stretches involve ice-traverses (even in summer) or rock climbs; check carefully with map or tourist offices. Cable cars and ski-lifts (summer and winter) provide a helping leg-up to ridges from Alagna and Macugnaga; one at Alagna climbs to Punta Indren (3,260m/10,695ft). Long-distance traverse of park

possible (unmarked, 2/3 days); noted walks include: ascent to Rif. Barba Ferrero from Rif. Pastore (4hr); for a view of Rosa's east face the classic walk is from Belvedere above Macugnano (chair lift from Pecetto) to Rif. Zamboni-Zappa, onwards to Lago di Locce (red-white markings) and back to Burki (4hr) via Rosareccio (blue markings). *Guides:* available for non-experts who wish to climb more challenging high peaks involving ice-traverses; the most famous, open to even average hikers, is the ascent of Punta Gnifetti from Punta Indren cable station via Mantova and Gnifetti refuges. Details, T: (0163) 91310 (Alagna); and T: (0324) 65549 (Macugnaga). *Skiing:* cross-country, alpine and summer glacier skiing options at Alagna and Macugnaga. **Further information** *Tourist offices:* Piazza della Chiesa, Alagna, T: (0163) 91118; Piazza del Municipio, Staffa (Macugnaga), T: (0324) 065119; Corso Roma 41, Varallo, T: (0163) 51280.

Parco Nazionale del Gran Paradiso

High alpine massif and valleys, 70,000 ha/ 173,000 acres

G ran Paradiso is just what it purports to be: a great paradise. Breathtaking views of distant snow-capped peaks appear at almost every turn in this landscape graced with 57 glaciers. The mountain after which the park is named is over 4,000 metres (13,000 feet) high, surrounded by dozens of other peaks of over 3,000 metres (10,000 feet). Forests of firs, mountain tarns, deep blue beneath a cloudless sky, and snow-bound upland plateaux, provide the typical settings for the abundant wildlife for which the park is famous.

In relation to the Alps, the Gran Paradiso massif acts like a huge hinge. The ridges of the western Alps swing round it northwards and eastwards taking the French and Swiss borders with them. Within the park itself, valleys run north and south from a central ridge, as they do with the great massifs of Mont Blanc and Monte Rosa. This arrangement divides the park neatly in two: the more open and developed valleys that feed into the Valle d'Aosta to the north (Rhêmes, Savarenche, Valnontey, Cogne), and the narrower valleys of Piedmont (Locana, Orco, Piantonetto, Eugio and Soana) to the south.

Received wisdom has the northern valleys as the more beautiful. While their grandeur is indisputable, it is unfortunate that commercialization has spread up the valleys. Hotels and refuges located in the heart of the mountains are convenient, but in places have turned the area into more of a playground than a wilderness. Part of the reason for this is its position, close to

Turin and, more importantly, to the Valle d'Aosta, which, since the opening of the Mont Blanc tunnel and associated motorways, has become one of Europe's busiest crossroads. The southern valleys are not so popular because the scenery is less dramatic and the mountains are generally lower. As a result these valleys have remained wilder and offer quieter, and still very beautiful, walks.

Gran Paradiso is the oldest of Italy's eight national parks. A royal ordinance forbade hunting in these mountains as early as 1821. By 1856 the Gran Paradiso had joined King Victor Emmanuel II's long list of personal game reserves. In 1919 the House of Savoy ceded 2,000 hectares (4,940 acres) to the State, a nucleus from which the park was born three years later. It has grown since then to cover an area of 70,000 hectares (173,000 acres).

The game reserve was set up for the purpose of hunting and husbanding the ibex. Now the symbol of the park, this hefty

mountain goat with its massive saw-toothed horns can be seen among craggy heights at over 3,000 metres (10,000 feet). Quick and agile despite its bulk, it is able to feed on plants found at the very edge of glaciers and moraines, though it prefers the shelter of the lower slopes in winter.

Once common throughout the Alps, ibex have been threatened with extinction since the eighteenth century. The animals were hunted not only for food and for their horns, but also to get at a little bone near their hearts reputed to have magical properties. As a result their numbers had declined to only a hundred by the advent of royal protection. After a revival, numbers fell again during World War II. Since then, concerted efforts have taken the population up to about 3,000. Indigenous herds survive only in the Gran Paradiso; all other existing colonies (in Italy's Stelvio and Tarvisio parks, in France and the former Yugoslavia) have been bred from the park's original nucleus.

The present population is too large, claim some authorities, arguing that as the ibex now lacks predators, bar the inevitable poachers, the herds' instinct for survival has been affected. Partly to rectify this imbalance, an attempt was made in 1975 to reintroduce lynx into the park. This large spotted cat, sometimes more than one metre in length, would make a glorious addition to the wildlife of the Alps, but the attempt was a half-hearted and less than scientific affair: only two animals were released, and both were male. Neither was heard of again.

The 10,000-strong army of marmots — again considered too many — is a further argument for reintroducing the lynx. The park's only other large predators, the fox and golden eagle, cannot keep them in check. Pressure to bring in the hunters instead, which the authorities know would be the thin end of the wedge, has so far been resisted. The chamois, numbering an estimated 5,000 to 6,000, is similarly wide-

The summit peaks around Monte Gran Paradiso (4,061m/13,068ft) are seen in this view from the Nivolè lakes to the west.

The ibex lives in remote craggy habitats. Larger than the Spanish ibex, it can be up to 1½m (5ft) long and nearly 1m (3ft) high to the shoulder.

spread on the upland slopes. It can be seen in summer grazing the more succulent grass of the high pastures, while in winter it descends to the forests and warmer south-facing slopes.

A wide range of butterflies flourish in the apparently inhospitable environment of rock, ice and snow. The apollo is unmistakable for the large red "eyes" on its grey hindwings. It uses them to flash warnings at predators and thrives at up to 2,000 metres (6,500 feet). Fluttering even higher, at up to 3,000 metres (10,000 feet), is *Parnassius phoebus sacerdos*, especially common in the mountains above Cogne.

There are some 1,500 plant species in the park, including many Ice-Age relics which have evolved in isolation and are unknown elsewhere. This magnificence has a variety of causes: partly the area's varied geology, a mixture of schists, gneiss and limestone; partly the variety of habitats ranging from moist meadow to Arctic tundra, and partly the enormous altitude range of more than 3,000 metres (10,000 feet).

Trees are mainly pines, and though the forests are comparatively thin, there are enough to swathe the lower valley sides in a cloak of green, thus completing the classic alpine trinity of colours: white of snow, green of tree and blue of sky. Autumn, and the turning of the larch, adds an equally vivid flash of yellow to nature's palette.

Whether expert botanist or interested layman, you should visit the "Paradisa" botanical garden at Valnontey. It contains many former alpine and pan-European species, as well as hosting a collection of the rare plants of Gran Paradiso. One of the most famous is the twinflower, *Linnaea borealis*, the only plant named after the great Swedish taxonomist Carl Linnaeus. Its pale pink petals and delicate perfume belie the harsh environment of its origin in the Arctic circle. The Gran Paradiso is now its southernmost limit.

Many of the rare species are also distant from their genetic forebears. One legume, the central Alps milk-vetch (*Astragalus centralpinus*), has Asian origins, while the cinquefoil *Potentilla pennsylvanica*, as its name suggests, has its nearest relative in Pennsylvania.

Walking is generally no problem, thanks to the network of mule-tracks made for the Savoys and the several hundred kilometres of marked trails. Most walks should reward you with an ibex — trek from Valnontey to the Cresta Lauson if you want to make sure. The ascent of the Gran Paradiso itself is the least arduous 4,000-metre (13,000-foot) climb in the Alps, and for trekkers the *Alta Via II* crosses the park from east to west. Cogne is probably the best base for first-time visitors, being close to some fine walks, to the park's most awesome glaciers and to the beautiful Valnontey valley.

BEFORE YOU GO
The park's administrative centre is in Turin: Via della Rocca 47, T: (011) 871 187. **Maps:** excellent Kompass 1:50,000 *Gran Paradiso — Valle d'Aosta* (Sheet 86); IGC 1:50,000 *Gran Paradiso* (for the S).

Guidebooks: R. Chabod, *Gran Paradiso — Parco Nazionale* (CAI-TCI); *Il Parco Nazionale del Gran Paradiso* (2 vols IGC); 2 walking guides: M. Bovio, *Escursioni in Gran Paradiso* (Tamari 1980); F. Brevini, *Gran Paradiso — Itinerari* (Musumeci 1982). Also R.

Mantovani, *Sci di Fondo in Valle d'Aosta* (cross-country ski-routes, De Agostini 1988).

GETTING THERE
By car: A5 from Turin to Aosta, and then SS507 to Cogne, or one of 3 unclassified roads from Aosta to the

Grisenche, Rhêmes and Savarenche valleys. Access to the southern valleys on SS460 from Turin via Rivarolo-Canavese and Pont.

You may reach the southern valleys from the N, crossing the Gran Paradiso's main ridge, using the Savarenche road from Aosta and the spectacular Nivolet pass (Colle del Nivolet, 2,612m/8,569ft).

By rail: regular services to Aosta from Turin, and from Milan (change at Chivasso). Trains also run from Turin to Pont (for the southern valleys) with connecting buses to Locana and Noasca.

By bus: SVAP run extensive services from Piazza Narbonne in Aosta, though some routes are suspended or reduced outside July and Aug. 5/7 buses daily to Cogne, Cerellaz, Pont, Valsavarenche and villages *en route*. Details, T: (0165) 41125.

Summer minibus services from Cogne to Lillaz, Valnontey and Gimillian.

WHEN TO GO

Best from May to Oct, though snow can linger until July, and reappear as early as Oct. Snow is permanent, of course, on the glaciers and highest ridges. In winter most of the park is out of bounds to the casual walker. Best to avoid mid-summer weekends when main paths and refuges can be crowded.

Come in June and July to see the flowers at their best, and from Nov to Dec to see male ibex and chamois doing battle.

WHERE TO STAY

Usually you can arrive and find something to suit, or let the tourist office do the arranging for you. Only in Aug might it be wise to book. Standards are generally high, and prices reasonable.

Even the smallest hamlets have rooms; there is no need to stay in Aosta. Cogne and

Valnontey are the busiest bases; Lillaz is quieter, and near relatively untramped country. Degioz is the key village in the Val Savarenche, with hotels also at Pont and Eau Rousse. Rhêmes-Nôtre-Dame is the main centre in the Val di Rhêmes.

Accommodation in the southern valleys at Ceresole-Reale, Noasca, Loana Campiglia and Valprato Soana. **Outdoor living:** no free camping, but numerous campsites. Cogne has 7 sites, with further pitches for tents at Valnontey, Lillaz, Epinel, Rhêmes-Saint Georges, Rhêmes-Nôtre-Dame and the Val Savarenche.

Refuges: 12 refuges and 15 bivouacs, ranging from stone huts to high-altitude hotels. The Aosta tourist office publishes a detailed list of all huts, with size, contact numbers and opening times.

ACTIVITIES

Walking: with 450km (280 miles) of trails, the permutations of walks are endless. Some of the best include: Valnontey to Rif. Vittorio Sella (2½ hr), onwards to Herbetet (3,778m/12,395ft) via the Lauson lakes, and return to the village (5hr) along the Valnontey valley (wildlife, and stunning views of mountains and the Tribolazione glaciers); Valnontey to the Alpe Money for great views of the main ridge of Gran Paradiso (4hr); Cogne to Lillaz, a gentler walk with view of the Lillaz waterfall (1hr); Pont to Rif. V. Emanuele (2½ hr) and onwards to Gran Paradiso (5hr); from Introd in the Valsavarenche to Orvieilles (3hr, views to the Gran Paradiso); the southern valleys of Valsoera and Piantonetto.

Climbing: excellent

(Overleaf) A chamois braves the perpetual snow that lies in the high alpine cwms throughout Piedmont and the Valle d'Aosta.

everywhere, with mainly rock and ice itineraries in the northern valleys (especially the Becco della Tribolazione), and rock walls in the Piedmont valleys (on the Caporal, Sergent and Becco di Valsoera).
Birdwatching: LIPU, Via Petigat 9, Aosta, T: (0165) 32992/96116; and Via Montagnayes, Aosta, T: (0165) 41047. Both run courses and birdwatching trips to the park.
Ballooning: trips over the mountains in hot-air balloons; contact Nello Charbonnier, Aosta, T: (0165) 40205/35818.
Skiing: modest pistes at Cogne and Rhêmes-Nôtre-Dame, but numerous cross-country runs (indicated on maps), hundreds of traverses and the GHRV long-distance route for alpine skiers (*Grande Haute Route Valdotaine*).
Guides: Unione Guide, Via Vevey 17, Aosta, T: (0165) 34983.

FURTHER INFORMATION
Tourist offices: Piazza Chanoux 8, Aosta, T: (0165) 35655; Piazza Chanoux, Cogne, T: (0165) 74040; Rhêmes-Nôtre-Dame, T: (0165) 96114; Valsavarenche, T: (0165) 95703; Ceresole Reale, T: (0124) 95186.

Gran Bosco di Salbertrand

Nature park of broadleaf and conifer forest in the Valle di Susa covering 2,005ha (5,000 acres)

"As grand, beautiful and mysterious as the hand of God," says a local ballad of Salbertrand's great wood, one of four reserves in the Valle di Susa, Italy's western gateway into France.

Easily accessible from Turin, the park covers the valley's southern flanks between Oulx and Salbertrand, the largest forest in Piedmont, and one of the most important areas of primeval woodland in the Alps. Some 700ha (1,700 acres) make up the forest, lying as an arboreal mantle over a shallow basin in the side of the valley above Salbertrand village.

The best route through the park is to follow the old military road, which hairpins up through the west of the wood to reach the park's high pastures and summit ridges. Five

minutes on, you might leave this for the *Sentiero Sersaret*, part of the GTA long-distance path. It takes you through the wood and round the head of the basin before rejoining the military road on the summit ridges. Myriad other tracks dip and weave through the forest, the eastern parts less dense and interspersed with meadows of flowers.

The natural panorama as you climb changes from the broadleaved trees of the valley bottom — ash, beech, birch — to the predominant pines and larches of the upper forest. Dozens of tiny streams accompany your panting ascent, splashing over mossy rocks, and watering glades that offer excellent cover for wildlife.

Red deer were introduced in 1962 from the Triglav park in Slovenia, in exchange for ibex from the Gran Paradiso. The experiment was almost too successful. There are now 600 deer in the park, too many for its size, though culling (not to mention poaching) is under way to bring numbers down. This does mean, however, that you will be able to see the animals easily. The best chance of a sighting is at dawn on the high pastures.

Chamois and marmots are also visible at the highest altitudes, along with roe deer, recently reintroduced and a comparative stranger to the Western Alps. Other typical forest creatures, such as badgers and wildcats, are also found here, although they are largely nocturnal and thus much more elusive. Wildcats mate in early March, giving birth to between two and four kittens in early May. At this time of year adult wildcats may be seen in broad daylight. Presumably the need to find food quickly so as not to leave their young undefended for too

The large azure flowers of the trumpet gentian (*Gentiana acaulis*) are a feature of rocky pastures in the Alps appearing in late summer.

long makes them less wary of people.

Such thick ancient forests are also home to a large number of birds, including the magnificent black woodpecker, much the largest of the region at 45cm (18in) from head to tail. Clothed in funereal black, at first sight this bird might be mistaken for a crow; however, the distinctive undulating flight and scarlet crown will soon clarify its identity. Middle spotted woodpeckers are also found here, the adults being easily distinguished from the similar greater spotted woodpecker by their red crowns and white cheeks.

Half a dozen pairs of eagle owls also inhabit these forests, along with breeding short-toed eagles, honey buzzards and goshawks. Above the tree-line it is not unusual to spot golden eagles soaring on high, but rock partridges and black grouse are less visible, spending most of their time foraging around on the ground. In winter you might be lucky enough to catch a glimpse of a merlin, Europe's smallest bird of prey, although most sightings consist of a blurred kestrel-like silhouette, dashing erratically past at ground level in pursuit of dragonflies and small birds.

Autumn is an obvious time to enjoy the Gran Bosco, but early summer is also rewarding as the high meadows yield their intense tapestry of wild flowers; not rich with rarities, but gloriously coloured with yellow mountain saxifrage, deep-purple, yellow and white pasque-flowers and countless others.

Before you go *Map:* IGC 1:50,000 *Valle di Susa–Val Chisone.*
Guidebooks: M. Vaschetto, *Il Gran Bosco di Salbertrand* (Cavalieri 1983); G. Valente, *Sui Sentieri del Piemonte* (CDA 1988).

Getting there *By car:* SS24 from Turin along the Val di Susa to Salbertrand.
By rail: frequent trains to Salbertrand (Turin–Modane line).
Where to stay: in Salbertrand, Oulx and Sauze d'Oulx. Campsites at Salbertrand, Oulx and Pragelato.
Activities *Walking:* for walk suggested above (6hr), follow the GTA (red–white dashes) on the ascent (850m/2,800ft) from the village, the orange forest signs for the return (on the military road). The circuit can be extended using the GTA to include Monte Gran Costa and Colle Blegier (2,381m/ 7,812ft). Itineraries from Salbertrand's tourist office.
Further information *Tourist offices:* Salbertrand's tourist office doubles as the park centre: Via Terras 1, T: (0122) 844 527; also the office at Oulx: Piazza Garambois, T: (0122) 831 596.

Orsiera-Rocciavrè

Nature park of alpine mountains and meadows on the watershed between Susa and Chisone valleys (8,250ha/20,400 acres)

Just 30km (20 miles) from Turin this area is, nevertheless, a microcosm of the Alps. Nicknamed the *Parco di pietra*, "park of stone", it is a wilderness of mountain peaks and glacier-tortured crests high above the bustling valleys of the Rivers Susa and Chisone. Remote alpine meadows are watered by a network of gurgling springs, waterfalls and streams; and twelve lakes dot the mountains, of which the highlight is Ciardonnet, appearing as a mirror of rock and sky clasped among Orsiera's jagged ridges.

Located around the pyramid peaks of Monte Orsiera (2,878m/9,442ft) and Monte Rocciavrè (2,778m/9,114ft), this reserve is the largest of those in the Susa and Chisone vicinity. Forest cover accounts for about a fifth of the reserve, but is patchy by contrast to the Gran Bosco di Salbertrand (which is an easy morning's walk to the west). Flowers, however, are prolific in most parts of the reserve in spring and summer, mainly mountain lilies, edelweiss, narcissi and trumpet gentian. They have persuaded local people of the value of the reserve and, as a result, a business enterprise has been set up at Usseaux to cultivate aromatic and medicinal plants for export.

The park's name bears sad witness to wild animals that are no longer in evidence. Orsiera refers to the *orso*, or brown bear, and Rocciavrè to the "mountain of goats", a nod to long-vanished herds of ibex. Red deer and wild boar, however, reach here from the woods of Salbertrand, and golden eagles are known to patrol the highest hunting grounds. Chamois, too, are present, but in small numbers, along with the Alps' typical lesser mammals: badgers, foxes, mountain hares, squirrels, marmots and stoats.

A network of paths now supplements the few ancient mule-tracks that once served working farmsteads, making exploration easy; and a smattering of refuges saves going down to the valleys for accommodation.
Before you go: the new park centre, an ideal departure point for walkers, is at Pro Catinat,

8km/5 miles N of Fenestrelle, T: (0121) 83757.
Guidebook: G. Valente, *Sui Sentieri del Piemonte* (CDA 1988).
Maps: IGM 1:25,000 *Monte Orsiera* and *Perosa Argentina.*
Getting there By car: SS25 from Turin to Susa and then dramatic road to Fenestrelle over the Finestre pass (2,176m/ 7,139ft). Minor road access to park's eastern fringes from Giaveno, Forno and Alpe Colombino. SS23 from the Chisone valley and the S. *By rail:* frequent trains to Bussoleno on Turin–Modane

line, with branch line connection to Susa (trains hourly). Buses from Turin to Susa, and Pinerolo to Fenestrelle.
Where to stay: hotels in Susa, Pro Catinat, Fenestrelle and many points in the Valle di Susa. Camping permitted outside park, with Serre Marie the nearest official site, T: (0121) 83982 (all year).
CAI operate 4 refuges in the park: Selleries, Gravio, Toesca and Il Colletto. Details from tourist offices and CAI, Via Sommmeiller 26, Pinerolo.

Activities *Walking:* often long, demanding tramps, but many of them; details from tourist offices and park centre. Area is crossed by the GTA long-distance path (*Grande Traversata delle Alpi*). The Valle di Susa has the *Sentiero dei Franchi* trail. Details from GTA Promotion, Via Barbaroux 1, Turin, T: (011) 514 477.
Further information *Tourist offices:* Corso Inghilterra 39, Susa, T: (0122) 2222; Via San Giuseppe 39, Pinerola, T: (0121) 77361.

Alpi Marittime

Alpine massif containing Parco Naturale dell' Argentera (25,000ha/62,000 acres), reserves of Palanfrè (1,050ha/2,590 acres) and Alta Valle Pesio (2,700ha/6,670 acres); proposed national park (30,000ha/74,000 acres)

I once hitched a lift with three pensioners, on their way to walk in the Alpi Marittime. Did they know these mountains well? "Yes, very well, too well," they replied, with some unease. We drove on, admiring the scenery and discussing the prospects of a fine day's walking. Then the car slowed and the old people fell silent. After a pause one old lady pointed to a snow-covered peak and said, *"Quella è la montagna dov'e morto mio figlio"* — "That is the mountain where my son died." After another pause we drove on. The remark now beats a salutary tattoo whenever I walk in the high wilderness.

Despite this touch of doom, the Alpi Marittime are probably my favourites among all the alpine massifs. If you have been to the south of France you will have seen them. Straddling the French border,

they form a spectacular backdrop to the sun-drenched shores of the Riviera.

The Italian flanks, though, are quite different from their tourist-ridden French counterparts. Tucked away in Piedmont's south-west corner they are some of the wildest and least known mountains in the Alps. Though the first and westernmost link in Europe's greatest mountain chain, they lack nothing in splendour, with peaks over 3,000 metres (10,000 feet), the Alps' most southerly glaciers, high meadows, crystal-clear streams, thick forests — in short, the whole panoply of alpine landscapes.

At the heart of the Alpi Marittime lies the Parco Naturale dell' Argentera centred on the 3,927-metre (10,800-foot) peak of the same name. To the east are the smaller reserves of Palanfrè, thick with primeval forest, and the Alta Valle Pesio, the only valley in the western Alps with a north–south orientation. The whole region, however, is so patently deserving of protection that plans for a 140,000-hectare (346,000-acre) park on both sides of the border have been afoot since 1948. The French have already created the huge Parc National du Mercantour (70,000 hectares/173,000 acres) on their side, but the Italians are still dilly-dallying, bogged down in bureaucracy.

It takes no special skill to spot the features that set the Alpi Marittime apart

from the icy grandeur of the central Alps. Their proximity to the warming Mediterranean lends a distinctly southern flavour to the lower slopes, dotted with pockets of Phoenician juniper, while the higher slopes are a jumble of jagged peaks, narrow valleys and chaotic rock formations, clothed with alpine meadows and dark green clumps of contorted mountain pines.

The three small reserves of the Alpi Marittime together play host to over 3,000 species of plants and 1,000 species of mammals and birds. Such a wealth of wildlife is the result not only of climatic range, but also of geological variation, the crystalline granites of the Argentera contrasting sharply with the limestones of the Valle Pesio. At Pesio, the Marguareis (2,651 metres/8,697 feet) boasts precipitous walls of pallid limestone, often described as "dolomitic" in their splendour. They tower dramatically over the huge karstic plain of the Conca delle Carsene, which is riddled with yawning sinkholes and caves as much

An ice-clear mountain stream meanders through dulcet meadows in the Valle di Valasco in the Alpi Marittime.

as 500 metres (1,600 feet) deep.

In these mountains the maritime influence brings ample and refreshing rain, a bounty squandered by the eastern limestone (except for one splendid waterfall, the Pis del Pes), but utilized to wonderful scenic effect in the Argentera. I remember an idyllic day I spent walking to the alpine meadow of Valle di Valasco, accompanied by the constant rippling and gushing of water. It flowed from cracks, from rocks, cascaded down waterfalls, ran in tree-shaded streams, lay mirror-still in lakes; all under a blazing sun and cloudless sky. I drank and drank, scooping up handfuls at every turn, unable to resist water which seemed to me the iciest and most wonderful I had ever tasted, what Byron had called "the purest god of gentle waters . . . the sweetest wave of the most living crystal".

27

ALPINE BUTTERFLIES

A wealth of butterflies can be found in the flower-filled meadows and high mountain pastures of the Alps. Among the better known species, identifiable even without the use of a net, are the small apollo, with its marbled grey wings bearing beautiful scarlet "eyes"; the mountain clouded yellow whose dark grey upper wings contrast vividly with its bright yellow underside; and the alpine grayling, a large pale yellow butterfly which has small, white-centred black "eyes" on the upper wing.

Dozens of ringlet butterflies inhabit the high pastures above the tree-line, but they need to be examined at close range to distinguish between them. The blind ringlet, characteristic of the Dolomites, is medium brown with conspicuous yellowish arcs on the wings, while de Pruner's ringlet, more typical of the Trentino Alps and Alto Adige, has rich chocolate-brown wings, each with an orange band containing small *ocelli* (eyelets). Among the species which occur only in the Alps are Mnestra's ringlet, with orange-brown unmarked wings, and the sooty ringlet, the males of which have velvety black wings.

Among the smaller, jewel-like Lycaenidae butterflies (of which most are blues, coppers or hairstreaks) it is the males which are generally the more eye-catching, the females for the most part being drab, brown and almost impossible to tell apart. In July and August the high Alpine meadows are resplendent with the shimmering violet-blue wings of the Osiris blues and the pale greenish-blue of the Glandon blues; and the almost luminous turquoise wings of the Eros blues, bordered by a narrow black band. The vivid blue wings of the alpine argus provide a perfect reflection of the summer sky.

You will need a full day for this walk. The climb starts at Terme di Valdieri on a mule-track that winds through rocky outcrops and cool verdant forests, with the snow-dusted peaks along the French border to lure you on. A steep haul past a shady

The small apollo butterfly of the Alpi Marittime is easily identified by its red "eyes", or ocelli. These are prominent markings designed to deter potential predators.

waterfall and you reach the Valasco plain, the glacier-scraped bed of an ancient lake set in an amphitheatre of huge mountains that now stand revealed in their full glory. A renewed attack on the rocky trail brings you to the Lago di Valscura at 2,300 metres (7,500 feet), magnificently lonely and lovely; just one of the Argentera's dozens of rock-cradled tarns.

This walk forms part of the *Grande Traversata delle Alpi*, a long-distance path that utilizes one of Victor Emmanuel's road-like tracks, constructed when the Argentera was declared a hunting reserve in 1857. If this route seems rather tame, the region is also criss-crossed with hundreds of less engineered trails. All are well marked and backed up by excellent maps and refuges that are superbly situated. Further exploration of the GTA will lead you eastwards into the Palanfrè and Valle Pesio reserves. Other tracks lead into France, where you might make for the cultural highlight of the Gallic park, the 3,000-year-old rock paintings of Mont Bego and the Vallons des Merveilles.

In both granite and limestone areas, the botanist will be spoiled for choice. In the Palanfrè reserve alone, 650 species of wild flowers can be found. The glistening crimson flowers of the red lily adorn the rocky areas, while the limestone woodlands shelter such specialities as Christmas roses, cyclamens and lady's slipper orchids.

Among the botanical riches of the Argentera, the star must be the ancient king (*Saxifraga florulenta*), a bizarre long-lived plant which is found only in rock crevices high in the granite cliffs of the central Alpi Marittime. Because of the paucity of nutrients and the climatic extremes of the high mountains the many-leaved rosettes of this saxifrage grow very slowly, taking up to 50 years to accumulate the strength to reproduce. Finally, at the very end of its life, a spike of salmon-pink flowers appears, after which the whole plant dies.

The Valle Pesio is renowned for its extensive forests of ancient pines, firs and broadleaves, all of which have benefited from centuries of care by the valley's Cistercian monks. Its alpine meadows teem with wild flowers and contain a good number of the reserve's 1,300 plant species. Orange lilies, with their upright, cup-shaped flowers of fiery vermillion, contrast spectacularly with the dull magenta "turk's-cap" bloom of the closely related martagon lily, while great yellow and spotted gentians stud the grass-

lands with spikes of gold in summer. The presence of species such as alpine pasqueflowers, alpine clematis, alpenrose and alpine toadflax testifies to the similarities between these mountains and the Alps proper. Three quite different species of fritillaries are found here: the three-bracted snakeshead (*Fritillaria involucrata*) has large jade-green bells, heavily chequered with purple; the slender-leaved snakeshead (*F. tenella*) has large greenish-yellow, drooping lanterns with faint purple markings; and an uncommon race of the Tyrolean fritillary (*F. tubiformis*, subspecies *moggridgei*), unique to this region, has brown-specked, yellow bells.

The Alpi Marittime are a good place to see some of the alpine columbines. Among the more attractive species are Bertoloni's columbine (*Aquilegia bertolonii*), with its dark violet-blue flowers, the purplish Einsel's columbine (*A. einseleana*) and the dark columbine (*A. atrata*), distinguished from all others by its velvety deep purple flowers with protruding yellow stamens.

The fauna is equally abundant, although large carnivores are few and far between. The lynx has not been seen here for decades, the last definite record being of

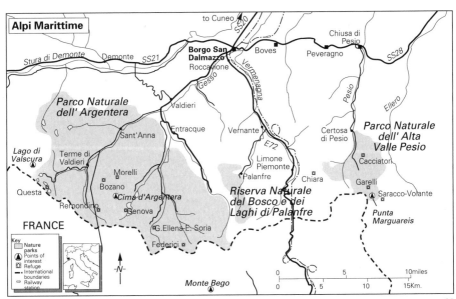

an animal which was shot near Sant'Anna di Valdieri more than 40 years ago; the presence of a small group of wolves, however, is suspected by the local people.

With only a limited number of predators, large herbivores such as chamois and ibex are able to flourish. About 3,500 alpine chamois haunt the rugged uplands, easily distinguished from the larger ibex by their small, backwards curving horns set close together between the ears; one of the best places to see these graceful creatures is from Tetti Niot above Sant'Anna. Ibex, with their robust curling horns, were introduced in 1920 from their stronghold in Gran Paradiso and the population now numbers a healthy 650 individuals.

Alpine marmots abound above the tree-line, their piercing alarm whistles notifying the walker of their presence even if they dive too quickly into their burrows for visual confirmation. Far more elusive are the mouflon. Although not native to the Alpi Marittime, these heavy-set sheep have been introduced to the French park and frequently stray across the border to nibble at Italian grass.

Among the hardened inhabitants of the harsh world above the tree-line are the classic alpine birds of the region: rock partridges and ptarmigan. Golden eagles, by far the largest birds of prey to stray within range of binoculars, soar above the peaks, while black grouse forage among the rocks, the males unmistakable in the breeding season with their glossy black plumage and lyre-shaped tails. Flocks of choughs are also a common sight, their wheeling antics and rifle-shot calls as distinctive as their scarlet beaks and legs. If you are extremely lucky you might spot a wallcreeper, fluttering up one of the sheer rock walls of the region and looking as much like a huge grey and crimson moth as a bird.

The forested valleys of the Alpi Marittime are the haunt of quite a different fauna. Black woodpeckers and eagle owls, both the largest European representatives of their families, breed in these forests, as do nutcrackers, honey buzzards and short-toed eagles. Wild boar, now rare in the Alps, can occasionally be seen snuffling through some of the lower woodlands at dusk or dawn.

BEFORE YOU GO
Map: IGC 1:50,000 *Alpi Marittime e Liguri* (Sheet 8).
Guidebooks: P. Rossi, *Parco Naturale dell'Argentera* (Priuli-Verlucca 1986); *Valli Cuneesi: Pesio, Gesso e Stura* (CAI-TCI).

GETTING THERE
By car: to Cuneo on A6/SS564 from Genoa and the Ligurian coast, A6/SS231 from Turin and the N. For Argentera from Cuneo take SS20 SW to Roccavione (8km/5 miles) and minor road to Valdieri, where small lanes diverge to major valleys within the park. For Palanfrè follow SS20 beyond

Roccavione to Vernante and take the lane to Palanfrè village. For Valle Pesio follow minor roads via Boves to Chiusa di Pesio, and take valley road S to Certosa di Pesio.
By rail: frequent trains from Turin to Cuneo (1hr), with connections to Vernante (for Palanfrè), Nice and the French coast. Information, T: (0171) 3681.
By bus: 5 buses daily from Cuneo station to Valdieri and Entracque; 1 weekly to Sant'Anna, with extra summer services, including a connection to Terme di Valdieri. Sporadic services to Chiusa di Pesio and Vernante.

WHERE TO STAY
Accommodation is concentrated in Cuneo and the skiing resort of Limone

Piemonte, but more central bases include the Terme di Valdieri, with an (ugly) luxury hotel open June–Sept, T: (0171) 97106, and the more intimate 1-star Turismo (summer only).

In Sant'Anna di Valdieri (best base for those on foot) try Verde Vivo hostel, Strada Provincia 60, T: (0171) 97389; and the 2-star Reginal (June–Oct). Rooms also in Valdieri, Entracque, Certosa di Pesio and Borgo S. Dalmazzo. For help in finding rooms call CIT at Cuneo, T: (0171) 698 749.
Outdoor living: prohibited in park and reserves, but camping ground at Valdieri (summer only). CAI bivouacs in the Argentera (see IGC map).
Refuges: 6 refuges and 10 bivouacs in the Argentera, 4 refuges in or close to the Valle

Pesio (most refuges are open June–Sept). For general details contact CAI, Via Allione 1, Cuneo, T: (0171) 67998; for Garelli and Valle Pesio huts, T: (0171) 738 019; for Argentera, CAI in Sant'Anna (next to the post office), T: (0171) 97199.

ACTIVITIES

Walking: (Argentera) Terme di Valdieri to Piano del Valasco (3hr), and onwards to Valscura lakes and Rif. Questa; Terme di Valdieri to Lourousa (3hr); (Palanfrè) from Palanfrè village on the GTA to the Laghi degli Alberghi (4hr); (Valle Pesio) the walk to the foot of the Marguareis rock walls is an alpine classic: start from the head of the road above Certosa and walk to the Rif. Garelli (red and white markings, trail H8), continue on the GTA S to the Laghi di Marguareis, and descend on H1 to your starting point (5hr); to the Pis del Pes (path H10) from the road above Certosa (2½hr); to Punta Pellerina and/or Cima Cars from Certosa (5hr, trails H4/5).
Birdwatching: LIPU, Corso Nizza 94, Cuneo, T: (0171) 693 153.
Guides: guides for rock and ice climbing, walking, cross-country skiing, nature and photography excursions: Cooperativa Guide Alpi Marittime, Corso Marconi 8, Cuneo, T: (0171) 54896.
Skiing: at Limone Piemonte, with more modest facilities at Entracque. Cross-country routes from Entracque, and on the Valle di Valasco (contact Lou Baus co-operative, details below).
Caving: excellent opportunities around the Marguareis (Valle Pesio) in some of Piedmont's deepest caverns; contact CAI Speleogia, Piazza Galimberti 13, Cuneo.
Canoeing: Italian canoeing federation local branch: Corso IV Novembre 29, Cuneo,

T: (0171) 54529.
Fishing: FIPS local branch: Corso Dante 21, Cuneo, T: (0171) 61422.
Ecology: the WWF organizes volunteer summer work camps in the Argentera; details, WWF Piemonte, Corso Regina Margherita 139, Turin, T: (011) 534 255.

FURTHER INFORMATION
Tourist offices: The main office

ALPINE GRASSLANDS

Meadows and grasslands are among Italy's most common mountain habitats, both in the Apennines and the Alps, and vary hugely according to soil, climate and altitude. Many are very interesting for their rarities and endemics, and in spring most have breath-taking displays of wild flowers. They can be divided broadly into calcareous and acid grasslands.

Calcareous meadows thrive on rocky and exposed slopes at altitudes of between 2,000 and 2,800 metres (6,500 and 9,000 feet). One grass is dominant, *Kobresia myosuroides*, found also in the Arctic and thus a relic of tundra plant communities that were once more widespread. Associated species include: snowy cinquefoil (*Potentilla nivea*); black alpine sedge; glacier pink (*Dianthus glacialis*); unbranched loveage (*Ligusticum mutellinoides*); and the delightfully named one-flowered fleabane (*Evigeron uniflorus*).

On lower and south-facing slopes the blue moor-grass *Sesleria albicans* predominates, found alongside milk-vetches, avens and that most famed of alpine flowers the edelweiss (*Leontopodium alpinum*). Two common sedges find favour in damper soils between about 1,700 and 2,000 metres (5,500 and 6,500 feet): *Carex ferruginea*, found on fresher slopes, and *Carex firma*, concentrated on steeper and stonier ground. With the first you might commonly find the alpine pasque flower (*Pulsatilla alpina*), alpine thistle (*Carduus defloratus*), leafy lousewort (*Pedicularis foliosa*) and the mountain hawk's-beard (*Crepis pontana* or *C. montana*). The second hawk's-beard keeps company with moss campion (*Silene acaulis*), blue saxifrage (*Saxifraga caesia*), gentians, alpine bistort (*Polygonum viviparum*), orchids and alpine rockrose (*Helianthemum alpestris*).

The acid grassland spreads over slopes at anything between 1,400 and 3,000 metres (4,500 and 10,000 feet). It develops well even in the face of heavy grazing, the key elements being the mat-grass *Nardus stricta*, and, at greater height, the sedge *Carex curvala*. Alongside thrive species such as tormentil (*Potentilla erecta*), golden cinquefoil (*Potentilla aurea*), trumpet gentian (*Gentiana acaulis*), arnica (*Arnica montana*), bearded bellflower (*Campanula barbata*), feast primrose (*Primula minima*), pale sedge (*Luzwa campestris*), field wood-rush (*Carex pallescens*) and alpine meadow grass (*Poa alpina*).

---

for the whole exploration zone is at Corso Nizza 17, Cuneo, T: (0171) 693258. Argentera park centre is at Corso Dante Livio Bianco 5, Valdieri, T: (0171) 97937. Also the tourist co-operative Lou Baus, Entracque, T: (0171) 978 458; Valle Pesio office: Via Sant' Anna, Chiusa di Pesio, T: (0171) 734 021. Palanfrè office: Vernante, T: (0171) 920 220.

Monte di Portofino

Nature park of coastal promontory with dramatic cliffs and coves noted for its varied flora (1,150ha/ 2,840 acres)

One of Italy's most fabulously beautiful stretches of coastline, the Portofino promontory still has parts untouched by the local commerce that serves the yachts of the rich and famous. For the naturalist it is the most important habitat between La Spezia and the French border. Sailing is the best way to explore this most romantic of coasts. Failing that you should take a boat trip from Portofino to the aptly named Golfo Paradiso, an unforgettable odyssey of high cliffs, turquoise seas, silver olives, green pines and rock-perched pastel villages.

From *terra firma* the views of the coastline are almost equally stunning. A spine of limestone hills separates the promontory's valleys and rises to a summit at Monte di Portofino (610m/2001ft). On warm herb-scented days the walking here is gentler and more pleasurable than any you will find on the Ligurian coast. Tracks start from most of the villages on and around the promontory, namely Portofino, Camogli and Santa Margherita Ligure, and push into an interior still without roads.

There are 700 different species of plant, courtesy of mild temperatures, a complex geology of marls, limestones and conglomerates, and the dividing ridge of hills, which creates opposing micro-habitats of Mediterranean,

montane and middle-European vegetation.

This combination yields peculiar inversions: chestnut trees reach down to the sea, and coastal maquis can be seen sprouting on hill tops. Though species are bizarrely mixed, the north-facing slopes tend to support trees and shrubs associated with a more continental climate, while the southern slopes which face sun and sea give rise to the more usual Mediterranean types.

One of the more interesting plants of the Portofino is the white-flowered saxifrage (*Saxifraga cochlearis*, the Latin epithet referring to its spoon-shaped leaves). Its lime-encrusted rosettes are found on shady rock walls, usually of limestone, in a small section of the Alpi Marittime. Remarkably, a few of these plants occur on the Portofino peninsula, some 130km (80 miles) further east.

Growing in similar habitats is the knapweed *Centaurea apoplepa*, a pink-flowered species found only in western Italy and on a few small islands in the Tyrrhenian Sea. There are numerous subspecies of this plant, many of which are confined to a very small area; here on the coast around Portofino it is *Centaurea apoplepa*, subspecies *lunensis*.

The promontory is also on a major bird migration route between Europe and Africa, a key resting place for spring and autumn travellers, situated between the urban bleakness of Genoa and La Spezia. Colourful migrants include great spotted cuckoos, conspicuous with their ash-grey crests and long white-edged tails, bluethroats, which rather resemble robins but have a series of blue, black, white and red bands about the throat, and collared flycatchers, the males of which boast striking pied

plumage with a stark white stripe around the back of the neck.

Breeding birds include wrynecks, small brownish woodpeckers whose mocking song truly heralds the onset of spring, as well as many more typically Mediterranean species: black and black-eared wheatears, golden orioles and four shrikes — great grey, lesser grey, red-backed and woodchat. The shrikes are commonly known as the butcher birds on account of their habit of impaling their prey — large grasshoppers and even small lizards — on thorn bushes to provide a "larder" for later consumption. Hobbies, too, find rich pickings along this coast, swooping on scythe-like wings after the swifts, swallows and martins on which they prey.

Also found in the Portofino maquis is the beech marten, distinguished from the very similar pine marten by its whitish, rather than yellow, throat, as well as red squirrels and foxes. There are plans afoot to reintroduce the crested porcupine, as well as the ocellated lizard, last seen on the promontory in 1958.

The area is a proposed marine park; the sea and its confines are reputed to support virtually every form of Mediterranean aquatic life. It is also a proposed national park; the power of local vested interests means that neither is likely to see the light of day.

Before you go: the park authority is the Servizio Beni Ambientali, Viale Brigate Partigione 2, Genoa, T: (010) 5485. Also contact the WWF, Via Colombo 1, Portofino. *Map:* IGM 1:25,000 *Chiavari* and hiking maps from tourist offices.

Guidebooks: A. Bariletti, *Il Monte di Portofino* (Sagep 1982); A. Desio, *Guida*

Naturalistica del Monte di Portofino (Agis).
Getting there *By car:* A12 from Genoa and La Spezia (exits Rapallo, Recco or Chiavari). *By rail:* to Camogli or S. Margherita Ligure (Pisa– Genoa line), both, like Portofino, excellent exploration bases.
Where to stay: plenty of accommodation at Portofino, Camogli, Recco, Paraggi and S. Margherita. Some hotels, especially in Portofino, are extremely busy and overpriced in summer.
Outdoor living: tents forbidden on the promontory; nearest campsite is the Rapallo at S. Margherita del Campo,

T: (0185) 60260.
Activities *Walking:* dense network of marked and well-kept paths. Most popular hike is the easy stroll from Portofino to San Fruttuoso (2hr, red markings). The next coastal stretch, Torretta–Punta Chiappa, the littoral's most spectacular, requires expertise and a head for heights.

From San Fruttuoso you could also cross the impressive little gorge of Pietre Strette and climb to Monte di Portofino and the summit ridge.

The full traverse of the promontory (4hr) is best undertaken from Camogli, finishing at Portofino. From Portofino another fine path

runs to S. Margherita via Olmi and the ruins of Madonna di Nozarego (2½hr).
Boat trips: Tiguello boats: S. Margherita–Portofino–San Fruttuoso (and return), T: (0185) 265 712; *Battelli* trips: Camogli–Chiappa–San Fruttuoso, T: (0185) 722 091.
Further information *Tourist offices:* Via Roma 35, Portofino, T: (0185) 269 024; Via XX Settembre 33, Camogli, T: (0185) 771 066; and Via XXV Aprile 2b, S. Margherita Ligure, T: (0185) 287 485.
Ecology: WWF, Via Columbo 1, Portofino.

Cinque Terre

Area of loosely protected zones totalling 5,500ha/13,600 acres; proposed national park

The *cinque terre,* or "five lands", are five pretty villages (Monterosso al Mare, Vernazza, Corniglia, Manarola and Riomaggiore) dotted along a stretch of Ligurian coastline between Levanto and Portovenere. Each village is surrounded by terraces of vines at the base of steep wooded valleys that dissect the cliffs. Beautiful and occasionally wild countryside forms the backdrop to this picturesque setting.

Once the villages were accessible only by sea or on foot, and known only for a wine, the Vernaccia delle Cinqueterre, quaffed and praised in verse by Dante, Petrarch and Boccaccio. Early man carved terraces or *ucian* here, reaping the benefits of a mild local climate to grow vines, figs, olives and capers. These terraces are still cultivated,

and are thought to be some of the oldest in the Mediterranean.

Sadly, however, the difficult terrain of the mountainous hinterland, described by one medieval writer as too steep not only for goats, but even for the flight of birds, has in part been breached by modern development and tourism. With Portofino, however, the Cinque Terre still form the wildest parts of the Ligurian littoral, especially noteworthy around Punta Mesco and Portovenere. Here the mountains fall to the sea in the great rock walls of the Muzzerone (favourites of La Spezia's climbing fraternity).

The best way to see the region is to walk the coastal path that links the villages, the *Sentiero Azzuro,* an extremely popular excursion that will take a robust pair of legs about eight hours. The best-known section lies between Riomaggiore and Manarola, the so-called *Strada dell'Amore,* or honey-mooners' "road of love". Undoubtedly beautiful, it is unfortunately overcrowded, and lined with handrails and concrete balconies. More solitary are the sections of the walk from Vernazza to Corniglia, and the other way from Vernazza to Mon-terosso (where the terracing is especially impressive, and where the path turns into a series of steep stone-cut steps).

Aleppo pines are characteristic of the steep promontories at Portofino.

CHAPTER 1: THE WESTERN ALPS AND ITALIAN RIVIERA

These sections will present you with varying scenery of sun-drenched headlands, rugged cliffs, lush vegetation, tree-shaded coves, cultivated slopes and consistently lovely seascapes. Even the villages filled with tourists have retained their charm, tiered on the cliffsides and riddled with mazes of tiny alleyways. While you walk, look for the alternation of sandstone and variegated limestones unique to the local geology. Most famous is the *Portoro* marble, found at Portovenere and on Isola Palmaria, renowned for its gold veining and grey lustre.

La Spezia's CAI branch has seen to it that all of the Cinque Terre is criss-crossed by marked trails. The most popular route after the coastal walk follows the mountain ridge that runs parallel to the sea. Taking in ten peaks — the highest Monte Malpertuso at 812 metres (2,664 feet) — the path crosses the entire summit ridge between Portonovo and Levanto, a haul of about 12 hours.

An exceptionally mild climate has allowed the survival of a specialized flora and fauna in Cinque Terre, also found on Palmaria Island and its outliers, Tino and Tinetto, to the south. Indeed, the islands have not suffered from the cultivation that has occurred on the mainland since they are mostly uninhabited.

Perfumed belts of maquis and garrigue, and great stands of aleppo pines have flourished alongside a wide range of wild flowers. Orchids such as the common spotted (*Dactylorhiza fuchsii*), burnt-tip (*Orchis ustulata*) and toothed orchid (*Orchis tridentata*) are common. A rare

The secretive, largely nocturnal, leaf-toed gecko has distinctive splayed feet with adhesive climbing pads only at the tips of the toes. It is the smallest of all European geckoes, usually measuring only about 6cm (2½in) from head to toe.

butterfly, the gloriously coloured two-tailed pasha (*Charaxes jasius*), can be seen, as well as a lizard not found elsewhere, the Tinetto lizard (*Podarcis muralis tinettoi*), numbering only about 200.

Rare species found only on the mainland include the freshwater crab (*Potamon edulis*), celebrated on coins minted by the people of Agrigento in southern Sicily and thought to be the crab represented in the constellation of Cancer; and the Italian cave salamander (*Hydromantes italicus*) which is found at the Portovenere promontory. The coastal margins from Punta del Mesco to Montenero have been designated a marine park, rich in all subterranean life and distinguished by rarities such as black coral.

BEFORE YOU GO
For general information visit the Comunità Montana, Levanto, T: (0187) 807 290.
Maps: CAI 1:40,000 *Carta dei Sentieri delle Cinque Terre* available in local shops or from CAI at La Spezia.
Guidebook: *Cinque Terre* (Regione Liguria).

GETTING THERE
By sea: sailings from La Spezia

to Palmaria and the coastal villages, T: (0187) 817 28066. Also an expensive crossing over the 400 metres of water separating Portovenere and Palmaria.
By road: to Portovenere (best southern base) on SS530 from La Spezia, and to Levanto and Monterosso (the most commercialized villages) from A12 (Carrodano) N of La Spezia. Connecting roads are

long and laborious, though a controversial new road is blasting its way to Monterosso, Riomaggiore and Manarola.
By rail: a better option than road, with stations on the La Spezia–Genoa line at all the Cinque Terre villages (except Portovenere). Frequent connections from La Spezia.
By bus: regular buses leave La Spezia's Piazza Chiodo for Riomaggiore and Manarola.

36

WHERE TO STAY

Levanto and Monterosso have the biggest accommodation range. Manarola has 1 hotel, the 2-star Marina Piccola, T: (0187) 920 103. Other centres with rooms available for renting include Portovenere, Levanto, Corniglia and Riomaggiore. **Outdoor living:** pressure of numbers means the area is out of bounds to campers, but there are organized sites at La Spezia, Levanto and Spiaggione di Corniglia. One option is to return nightly from walks to Levanto's Albero d'Oro site, T: (0187) 800 400.

ACTIVITIES

Walking: the coastal path, involving a hefty 1,200m (4,000ft) of climbing, is marked in red from Levanto to Punta del Mesco, blue to the Telegrafo above Riomaggiore, and in red onwards to Portovenere. Minor tracks descend to the sea at several points, or link to the trail along the interior ridge. Contact Levanto's tourist office and CAI, Via Carpenino 43, La Spezia.

Skin-diving: considerable scope around the islands, and from hired boats along the coast. Consult tourist offices, or the local subaqua club at the FIPS address below.

Fishing: FIPS local branch, Via V. Veneto 173, La Spezia, T: (0187) 511 026.

Cycling: for routes and information contact Cycling Club, Corso Roma 1, Levanto, T: (0187) 808 297.

FURTHER INFORMATION

Tourist offices: Via Fegina 38, Monterosso, T: (0187) 817 506; Piazza C. Colombo 2, Levanto, T: (0187) 807 175; Piazza Bastreri, Portovenere, T: (0187) 900 691; and Viale Mazzini 47, La Spezia, T: (0187) 36000.

MEDITERRANEAN REPTILES

Italy boasts a great selection of reptiles which are found only on the sun-baked Mediterranean coast. Perhaps the most characteristic are the tortoises, of which three species are found in Italy; all favour scrub-covered rocky hillsides in areas with hot summers. Hermann's tortoise is the smallest, its domed shell rarely exceeding 20 centimetres (8 inches) in length (see page 116). The similar spur-thighed tortoise has pronounced tubercles, or "spurs", on the thighs and is slightly larger. The marginated tortoise may reach 30 centimetres (12 inches) in length and has a flatter shell, flared at the rear.

Much larger, but closely related to tortoises, are the marine turtles. The only species seen regularly in Italian waters is the loggerhead, with its unmistakable heart-shaped horny carapace up to 110 centimetres (3½ feet) long and a proportionately massive head. Nowadays the loggerhead rarely comes ashore to lay eggs on Italian beaches because of the large numbers of tourists. Nevertheless, a few isolated coves may still be used by nesting loggerheads in the Golfo di Orosei in Sardinia, on the small island of Lampedusa south of Sicily and along the southern Sicilian coast.

Outstanding among Italy's lizard fauna are the geckoes; all four European species are found here. They are small soft-skinned creatures with large heads and, unlike other lizards, eyes with vertical pupils. All except the leaf-toed gecko have tubercles on the upper part of the body and all are nocturnal, except in cooler weather when they occasionally emerge during the day. Kotschy's gecko is the only species to lack adhesive pads on the toes, instead having characteristically kinked digits, but it is an agile climber nevertheless. Both the dark, flattened Moorish geckoes and the pale, almost translucent, Turkish geckoes are common on most of Italy's coasts. The leaf-toed gecko, on the other hand, is largely confined to islands in the Tyrrhenian Sea, Corsica, Sardinia and the north-western coast of the mainland.

Other typically Mediterranean reptiles include the eyed, or ocellated, lizard, now confined in Italy to the north-west coast. It is the largest European lacertid — some individuals are reported to be over 80 centimetres (2½ feet) long. The males are magnificent creatures, with massive broad heads and vivid green bodies, frequently with prominent blue "eyes" along the flanks. A rather different creature is the ocellated skink, a fat, almost snake-like, lizard with small limbs which can burrow rapidly into loose sand if threatened.

Several species of snake are also found on the coastal lowlands, such as the Montpellier snake, an aggressive creature up to two metres (six and a half feet) long which, although poisonous, has fangs set so far back in the upper jaw that it is unlikely to be dangerous to man unless it is picked up. The western whip snake of southern Italy and Sicily, although smaller, is a voracious predator with a diet of lizards, small birds, mammals and other snakes, even vipers. The southern smooth snake does not usually exceed half a metre in length and emerges mainly in the evening to prey on geckoes and other small lizards, while the metre-long leopard snake feeds mainly on rodents, killing its prey by constriction.

CHAPTER 2

The Dolomites and Central Alps

Venture into the Dolomites and you will find yourself in one of the most surreal landscapes on the planet: a Gothic fantasy of crenellated spires and splintered peaks, saw-toothed ridges and fearsome chasms; of screes and steep rock faces to challenge the most experienced climber; of forests, streams, waterfalls and high meadows covered in wild flowers. Often these peaks look more like the work of a painter's imagination than of nature's seismic upheavals; and indeed Titian, born at Pieve di Cadore near Cortina, recalled the mountains of his boyhood in the backgrounds of his paintings.

The range we know as the Dolomites consists of some twenty individual but close-packed massifs, each with at least one peak over 3,000 metres (10,000 feet). They form one of the largest self-contained areas within the Alpine chain, about 100 kilometres (60 miles) north–south, and 90 kilometres (55 miles) east–west. Separated from the main body of the Alps by the valleys of the Adige, Isarco and Pusteria rivers, the Dolomites divide into two groups of massifs, the western and eastern. Each was formed and weathered under slightly different conditions. The characteristic rock from which they are composed was named — fortunately not in full — after Dieudonné Sylvain Guy Tancrède de Grâtet de Dolomieu, the French mineralogist who first identified it as calcium magnesium carbonate. He wrote his treatise on the margins of his Bible while languishing

The unmistakable jagged peaks of the Dolomites form a spectacular backdrop to the forests of larches around Cortina d'Ampezzo.

in prison at Messina on his way home from Napoleon's Egyptian campaign.

Over 200 million years ago, in the late Triassic, the whole region lay under a tropical sea. Huge banks of coral built up into islands which eventually fossilized to form the rock known as Sciliar Dolomite, of which the main western massifs (Sciliar, Catinaccio, Latemar, Odle, Pale, Sella, Putia and Pale di San Martino) are composed. Two volcanoes spewed lava into the sea, where it settled in the gaps between the islands. Today this rock can be seen in parts of the Siusi, the Val Gardena, the Val di Fassa, Predazzo and elsewhere. In the late Triassic, the area became a vast tidal flat. Layer upon layer of marine detritus compressed to produce the Dolomia Principale, which characterizes the eastern Dolomites of Cristallo, Sesto, Pelmo, Civetta, Tofano.

Some 60 million years ago, Africa and Europe crashed into each other. This cataclysm produced the uplifting and buckling that gave birth to the Alps, and with them the Dolomites. Not all the terrain reacted in the same way. The western Dolomites — supported by thick underlying layers of ancient rock — rose as a single block. In the east this protective substructure was missing, and the top layers bore the full impact of the uplift resulting in massive folding and faulting. Ice and water then eroded the newest sediments, which made their way down to cover the Po valley, and, over thousands of years exposed the original Triassic coral reefs.

The Dolomites cover a vast area, and in certain places in the right season, they are so deserted you can feel you have the mountains to yourself. Yet they are famous throughout the world, probably visited by more skiers,

walkers and coach parties than all the other Italian mountains put together. Their accessibility means that walkers must be prepared to meet other travellers, no matter how remote the country through which they plan to go.

This was brought home to me one autumn morning in the Dolomiti di Sesto, renowned as some of the quietest and most breathtaking of the eastern Dolomites. On a grey inauspicious day I set off to see the Dolomites as the wild windblown mountains they normally are, not as portrayed in the blue-skied pictures on the front of chocolate boxes. Mist swirled around the summits, and for a time I had the damp, dripping forest path to myself. A couple of hours passed in solitude until, turning a corner, I found three little old ladies sitting on a tree-trunk. Dressed in their Sunday best and chattering away like small birds, oblivious to me and to the mountains, they might well have been playing a hand of bridge. They could not have been more unexpected had they been sitting on their tree-trunk stark-naked.

When you have had your fill of the Dolomites, retreat to the Valle Aurina to the north. This is Italy's most northerly point, and if not its best-kept secret, one overlooked by most people who visit these mountains. It is a supremely peaceful area of the utmost splendour.

Alternatively, visit the other mountains of Alto Adige, the German-speaking heart of one of Italy's autonomous "problem" regions. Geology made this a frontier zone, and through the millennia of human occupation it has remained the meeting place of Central Europe and the Mediterranean. The Alpine passes were in use as early as the Neolithic. Amber from the

Baltic found its way through here to Italy. Strange "statue menhirs", flat slab-like human figures, have been found in the upper Adige valley. Nobody knows for sure who made them, or when, but they probably date from the early Bronze Age. The Celts invaded around 500 BC, and held out against the Romans until 15 BC. After the collapse of Rome, Germanic settlers pushed the Romano–Celtic inhabitants up into the remoter valleys, where their language, Ladin, survives to this day. In the Middle Ages the Hapsburgs took control of the region. It remained part of Austria until 1918, and its indigenous inhabitants still refer to it as the South Tyrol. The onion-domed churches, wooden houses, even the brown bell-clanging cows, are all thoroughly Teutonic.

West of the Adige are the two largest areas of natural protection in Italy: the Stelvio and Adamello-Brenta parks. Their administration is shared between the regional governments of Lombardy and Trentino, a conflict that does not result in the care these astounding areas deserve.

Lombardy is an industrialized and intensively farmed region that offers little by way of untouched territory. North of Milan, the lakes of Maggiore, Lugano, Como and outlying Garda still have their moments, though tourists and pollution have taken a heavy toll

ALPINE PLANTS OF ROCK AND SCREE

High Alpine flora is remarkably rich and hardy, given the extreme conditions under which it must survive. Often plants suffer exposure to wind, frost and snow, with varied moisture levels and terrain that may be no more than a slight fissure or rocky ledge. Although mosses and lichens are common, it is fascinating to note that it is the flowering plants which usually first colonize these upland haunts. This contrasts with the lowlands where lichens come first followed by bryophytes and only then the higher plants.

Many species are dwarf cushion-forming perennials, with buds close to, or even under, the ground. Others are herbaceous perennials which die away at the onset of the coldest weather. All sorts of variations occur, of course. Screes, moraines and streams have their own communities. Endemics and Ice Age relics are common, particularly on calcareous bedrocks. What follows is merely a handful of the plants you might encounter in the high Alps.

In the highest zones you might commonly stumble upon dwarf rampion (*Phyteuma humile*), yellow genipi (*Artenisia mutellina*), King of the Alps (*Eritrichiuma nanum*), white musky-saxifrage (*Saxifraga exarata*), kernera (*Kernera souxatilis*), auricula (*Primula auricule*) and various species of rock jasmines (*Androsace*). On the outwash plains of glaciers, or in alluvial river areas, the mountain sorrell (*Oxyria digyna*), which is also found in the Arctic, takes pride of place, joined by glacier crawfoot (*Ranunculus glacialis*), alpine rockcress (*Arabis alpina*), creeping avens (*Geum reptans*), Italian figwort (*Scrophularia Scopolii*) and alpine willowherb (*Epilobium Heischeri*). At the highest levels, up to 3,400 metres (11,000 feet), rock jasmines take precedence, alongside a wealth of plucky species, such as mossy saxifrage (*Saxifraga bryoides*), purple saxifrage (*Saxifraga oppositifolia*), moss campion (*Silene acaulis*), mossy cyphel (*Minuartia sedoides*) and Bavarian gentian (*Gentiana barvarica*).

Limestone soils add to the variety, as in the Dolomites, where round-leaved pennycress (*Thlaspi votundifolium*) pushes through scree after the melting of winter snow. With it appears alpine butterbur (*Petasites paradoxus*), bladder campion (*Silene vulgaris*), Herb Robert (*Geranium robertianum*), white stonecrop (*Sedum album*), tolpis (*Tolpis staticifolia*), fairy's thimble (*Campanula cochlearifolia*) and double barrelled large pink hemp-nettle (*Galeopsis speciosa*).

on their once legendary beauty. In the mountains above them, the Orobie and Retiche massifs of the Central Alps, the scenery can still make you catch your breath, as might some of the so-called Bergamo valleys to the east, the Val Seriana and Val Brembana.

The finest small area of natural interest, however, is Monte Baldo, on Lombardy's eastern border. This pre-alpine ridge offers superlative views over Garda, the largest and least spoiled of the lakes, as well as being one of the richest floral havens in all Italy. From its summit your gaze is drawn away from the shimmering azure of the lake to the peaks ranged across the northern horizon — the rose-tinted lines of the Dolomites which rise, as ever in this region, like seductive and irresistible sirens to tempt those with a love of mountains.

GETTING THERE
By air: international airports at Munich, Milan and Venice or smaller airports in Verona and Innsbruck.
By car: the A8 and A9 motorways link Milan to the Italian lakes. The A22 Verona–Bolzano–Brenner motorway serves the Dolomite massifs, and the Stelvio and Adamello parks. Cortina and the eastern Dolomites are linked by the A27 and SS51 to Venice.
By rail: with the main Verona–Bolzano–Munich line, and the Bolzano–San Candido branch line, rail gives rapid access to the Dolomite region. International services from Milan do the same for the lakes. There are also slow lines linking Venice to Belluno and Trento.
By bus: bus services in Trentino-Alto Adige are exceptionally good; most centres are served from either Bolzano or Trento.

WHERE TO STAY
For value and quality, accommodation in the Dolomites is almost unsurpassed in Italy. Rooms can be found in even the smallest hamlets. Often you can arrive and hope for the best, but it is always worth checking with tourist offices to see if hotels are open; many close Oct–Dec and Apr–June. Booking is strongly

advised July–Aug, and Jan–Mar. Half- or full-board is the usual practice.

The following provincial tourist offices will provide full lists of hotels and rooms: Piazza Walther 8, Bolzano, T: (0471) 970 660; Via C. Battista 12, Sondrio, T: (0342) 512 500; Via Alfieri, Trento, T: (0461) 983 880.

Outdoor living: prohibited in the parks, but such is the area of wild country outside their borders that you will have few problems pitching a tent. Most organized sites are open only during the summer.

Refuges: hundreds over the region, many privately owned and effectively run as hotels. Some are on trails, others can be reached by road or cable car.

Many Trentino huts operate through the Società degli Alpinisti Tridentini; contact them for a list of 200 huts (and general mountain information) at: Via Manci 57, Trento, T: (0461) 21522.

Otherwise contact tourist offices or the following local CAI branches: CAI, Piazza Erbe 45, Bolzano, T: (0471) 021 172; Alpine Information Office, Bolzano, T: (0471) 993 809.

ACTIVITIES
Walking: hiking in the Dolomites is almost unequalled

anywhere in the world, with thousands of well-worn and well-marked trails to suit all abilities. Most paths are extremely popular in the summer, for which reason late spring and Sept–Oct are the best periods to visit. Do not be deceived by pictures of good paths or mountains in fine weather — the Dolomites can turn as nasty as any wilderness; go as well-equipped as you would for any upland trek.

There are 7 high-level *Alte Vie*, or long-distance paths. None needs more than normal hiking experience. Most are between 120 and 180km (75 and 110 miles) in length, and are designed to take about 2 weeks, though allow for rests and diversions. All are separately marked on Kompass maps.

The trails are: Lake Braies to Belluno (the most popular); Bressanone to Feltre: Villabassa to Longarone (the "Chamois" trail); San Candido to Pieve di Cadore (the Grohmann); Sesto to Pieve di Cadore (the Titian); Pieve to Vittorio Veneto; Belluno pre-Alps to Alpago. A useful guide is the *High Level Walks in the Dolomites* by M. Collins (Cicerone Press).

Oft-overlooked long-distance trails in Lombardy include: *Via dei Monti Lariari*

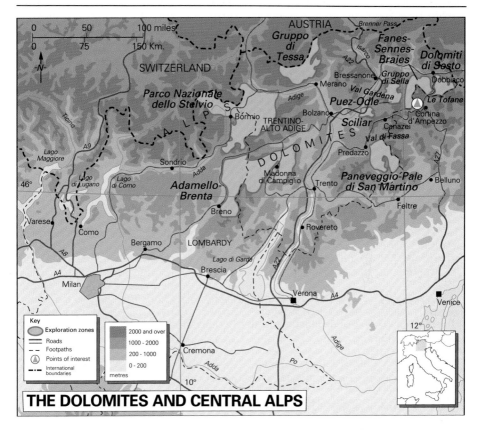

THE DOLOMITES AND CENTRAL ALPS

Key
- Exploration zones
- Roads
- Footpaths
- Points of interest
- International boundaries

2000 and over
1000 - 2000
200 - 1000
0 - 200
metres

on the W shore of Lake Como (130km/80 miles, 6 days); *Sentiero delle Orobie* (50km/31 miles, 6 days); *Sentiero Roma* (7 days) and *Alta Via della Valmalenco* (110km/68 miles, 10 days), both on the Badile and Disgrazia mountains. Details from CAI and the Federazione Italiana Escursionismo, Via Valtellina, Milan, T: (02) 688 2076.

Climbing: thousands of routes, with numerous *vie ferrate*, "iron paths" — fixed rope and ladder climbs. Consult *Classic Climbs in the Dolomites* by L. Dinoia (Cicerone) and *Vie ferrate: Scrambles in the Dolomites* by C. Davies (Cicerone).

Birdwatching: LIPU branches (for tours, advice and courses): Via Segantini 18, Bolzano,

T: (0471) 43170; Via Mantova 41, Trento, T: (0461) 31170; Via Settembrini 27, Milan, T: (02) 670 0353.

Skiing: choice is your only problem, with resorts throughout the regions. Numerous summer routes (Stelvio, Tonale, S. Caterina Valfurva, Marmolada, Val Senales); cross-country itineraries virtually everywhere, but notably in the Alpi di Siusi, Braies valleys, Dobbiaco, Anterselva and Canazei.

Canoeing: many fine runs on the Adige, Noce and minor rivers. Italian canoe federation office at Trento, Via Brescia 29, T: (0461) 21586, with clubs at: Via Portici 204, Merano, T: (0473) 32126; and Via B.

Minori 4a, Bressanone, T: (0472) 024 568.

Fishing: FIPS branches: Via Goethe 21, Bolzano, T: (0471) 975 332; Via A. da Trento 24, Trento, T: (0461) 983 083; Via Abruzzi 79, Milan, T: (02) 204 3952.

FURTHER READING
J. Goldsmith, *The Dolomites of Italy* (A & C Black) has hiking and skiing suggestions; also 2 guides in the *Sunflower* series, *Easy Walks in the Dolomites* and *Easy Walks in the South Tyrol* (Cicerone Press). A. Edwards, *Untrodden Peaks* (Virago) is a woman's account of travels in the Dolomites in the last century. G. Price, *Walking in the Dolomites* (Cicerone Press).

43

Gruppo di Tessa

High alpine massif (33,000ha/82,000 acres)

ЖЖЖ

High above the Adige valley on the border of Austria, the Tessa has some of the richest scenery in Trentino. There are dozens of peaks over 3,000 metres (10,000 feet), huge glaciers and moraines, mountain lakes and forest, and colossal rock walls that fall sheer to the valley floors. The park has an abundance of birds and mammals, and few visitors disturb its tranquillity. The local language is German, the culture Teutonic; characteristic castles and wooden houses are dotted amid the pine woods and vineyards of the lower valleys.

The lakes of the Tessa are famous. One of the park's loveliest spots is the Sopranes group of lakes which are individually named after their colouring, Nero, Latte and Verde (Black, Milky and Green). Also of special interest is the geology. Granite, gneiss and mica schists predominate, with rogue intrusions such as the ortogneiss on Monte Tschigat and the marble of the Cima Fiammante. A key area for exploration is the upper Val Seeber where a treasure of minerals can be found.

While the flora is limited by the ruggedness and acid bog of much of the area, there are some of the highest concentrations of animals in any of the Trentino parks. About 400 chamois roam the upper regions of the park. The young lambs, or kids, are born between April and June, some six months after the autumn rut, each female giving birth to a single offspring. Marmots too are plentiful, and red and roe deer inhabit the forests at lower levels. For the best view of the fauna of the Tessa you should visit the enchanting Val di Fosse in the west, an intimate valley where nature and scenery seem to be in perfect harmony.

Eagles and lesser raptors inhabit steep rock faces such as the Cima Bianca. One of the true alpine birds of the Tessa is the ptarmigan, a plump, short-winged bird with three distinct plumage phases: mottled brown above to blend with the vegetation, turning greyer in autumn and pure white in winter when the snow is thick on the ground. Other members of the grouse family found here include hazel hens, also known as hazel grouse, and black grouse. Both of these are more typical of forested areas and do not change their plumage for winter camouflage. The closely related capercaillie, the largest of the European grouse, is another species of the forest, resembling a clumsy turkey in flight. Both may be spotted in the Val Senales, the so-called "Valley of the Larches".

Hunting is still allowed in the Tessa, though restricted in theory to local inhabitants, a law that in practice is impossible to enforce. Otherwise, the park is well-tended and the wilderness kept intact.

BEFORE YOU GO
For hiking and climbing information enquire in Merano (best overall base) at the Alpine Association, Via Galilei 45 (weekdays 9am–12); Alpenvieren Südtirol, Heidenburger, Corso Libertà; and CAI, Corso Libertà 188.
Maps: Kompass 1:50,000 *Merano* (Sheet 55); IGM 1:25,000 4 III SO *Parcines* and 4 III NO *L'Altissima*.
Guidebook: G. Barducci, *Parco*

Naturale Gruppo di Tessa, available from tourist offices and park centre.

GETTING THERE
By car: SS38 from Bolzano runs the length of the Venosta valley, with stunning side roads into the Tessa (turn off at the junction at Naturno for Senales and the Val di Fosse) and the mountains along the Austrian border further W. The SS44

from Merano serves the park's eastern margin.
By rail: the Bolzano–Malles branch line also runs along the Venosta valley, but there are only 2 through trains daily (services are hourly to Merano).
By bus: buses offer a more comprehensive service than trains, serving most centres, including Santa Caterina and Ulfas, from Merano. T: (0473) 42002 for bus information.

THE MARMOT

The first time I heard the marmot's high pitched defensive whistle — an unearthly and extremely loud shriek — it had its desired effect. I was terrified out of my wits. I know of no sound in the animal kingdom more extraordinary.

Its scientific name, *Marmota*, is derived from the Latin for *muris*, "mouse", and *montis*, "mountain", though it is about the size of a bulky cat. It lives in the Alps above about 1,800 metres (6,000 feet) spending some five hours a day feeding off plants to give it enough fat to last through the winter hibernation. In the past it has been cruelly overhunted for its fur, meat and fat, the last purported to have medicinal qualities. It falls prey mainly after it emerges from hibernation when its senses are not fully alert and it cannot always detect predators quickly enough.

It is a diurnal animal, a lover of sunlight, gregarious in its habits and blessed with exceptionally acute eyesight. Like popes it has winter and summer residences, taking up winter quarters to undergo a prolonged period of sedation.

Marmots are one of the Alps' most characteristic mammals. In many places they are easily seen, despite a quite natural suspicion of man. Key locations are the Gran Paradiso and the Stelvio national parks, both areas where numbers of marmots are on the increase.

WHERE TO STAY

Merano is a large town with numerous hotels, but there are more central accommodation options in the Val Senales (Santa Caterina and Certosa) and in the valleys of the Plan (at Plan village), Fosse and Passiria.

Outdoor living: no free camping, but there are sites at Naturno and Merano; also 5 CAI and many private refuges. Contact Merano's tourist office for assistance.

ACTIVITIES

Walking: hundreds of walks, with many classic routes, some very busy. Walkers can cross the Tessa massif, choosing between high and low level sections of the *Meraner Hohenweg* long-distance path. Both legs start from Santa Caterina in the Val Senales, traversing eastwards to finish at Ulfas in the Val di Plan. The high level route takes in Val di Fosse, Monfert, Eishof, Stettiner, Rif. di Plan (11hr); the gentler low option is marked as trail 24, with many farms offering bed and breakfast *en route* (24hr).

Other fine walks include the ascent of L'Altissima (3,480m/ 11,417ft) on the marked *Hans Grutzmacher Weg*; the traverse of the Val di Fosse to the Rif. Petrarca (5hr); from Parcines to the Rif. Cima Fiammante (7hr), a walk that can be linked to hikes in the Val di Fosse; Velloi Plan traverse (12hr, using Riomolino chair-lift). **Skiing:** resorts in the Val Senales and at Merano 2000.

FURTHER INFORMATION
Tourist offices: Corso Libertà 45, Merano, T: (0473) 35223; Via della Stazione, Naturno, T: (0473) 87287.

Parco Nazionale dello Stelvio

Huge national park (148,271ha/366,378 acres) embracing the Ortles alpine massif, with glaciers, forests, lakes and valleys

O ne of Italy's eight national parks and the country's largest protected area, the Stelvio is a huge region of alpine wilderness. The principal summits, Ortles and Cevedale, are nearly 4,000 metres (13,000 feet) high and command views over dozens of lakes and more than 40,000 hectares (100,000 acres) of forests.

Called the park of rock, snow and ice, three-quarters of the Stelvio lies above 2,000 metres (6,500 feet) and one tenth is permanently covered in ice. Spectacularly vast are the hundred ice-sheets, of which the Ghiacciaio dei Forni, with an area of 2,000 hectares (5,000 acres), is the largest in Italy, and one of the largest in Europe.

Tucked up on the border with Switzerland, the Stelvio massif forms a key link between the central and eastern Alps. Nevertheless, it also forms a mountain kingdom in its own right. With 25 peaks over 3,000 metres (10,000 feet) and Europe's second highest pass, the Passo dello Stelvio, walkers will have no need to venture outside the park's network of over 1,500 kilometres (900 miles) of paths.

If this sounds daunting, a perfect introduction to the park's valley and high mountain environments is a walk that starts in the Val Zebrù, due east of Bormio. The dale cuts to the heart of the Ortles and

Cevedale massifs, with views of glaciers and, in the rutting season, a good chance of seeing the courting antics of red deer. Other glorious valleys lie on the northern fringes of the park; one of the favourites for climbers and trekkers is the Val Martello above Silandro. Many trails and cross-country ski routes start from the cluster of refuges at the head of the valley.

If you are seduced by the faintly ominous appeal of glaciers, the huge Forni ice-sheet beckons. Take a bus from Bormio to Santa Caterina and then hike up the Val di Forni. After an hour of passing streams, lakes and forests you will clamber on to the wasteland of the glacial moraine and eventually reach the Branca refuge, from where you can view the deeply fissured mountain of ice. More macabre are the remnants from World War I which was fought out in these mountains up to heights of 3,000 metres (10,000 feet).

In many cases guns, shell-casings, barbed wire and miscellaneous detritus have been preserved in the glaciers.

There is always some fly in the ointment in Italian reserves, and the Stelvio is no exception. This huge tract of territory straddles two administrative regions: Lombardy and Trentino-Alto Adige. The latter authority, now semi-autonomous, has abhorred the park almost since its inception in 1935. From 1948 it has actively encouraged the building of ski resorts and hydro-electric power stations, and now makes no bones about its wish to abolish the park altogether. Hunting is still allowed, resulting in the wanton massacre of red and roe deer, chamois, even marmots and rare birds.

The Lombardy authorities are more environmentally friendly. Hunting is controlled in their half of the park, and with their help in 1976 the park was extended up to the Swiss border. This action has linked the Stelvio to the Engadina National Park in Switzerland, continuing the international conservation initiatives of the Gran Paradiso-Vanoise, and Mercantour–Alpi Maritime parks in Piedmont.

Despite the hunting, there are exceptionally large numbers of mammals in both halves of the park. Ibex were introduced from the Gran Paradiso in 1967 and now number 200, most in the Val Zebrù. Red deer drifted across from Switzerland to form the nucleus of a colony of some 800. Chamois are more numerous still, with 1,800 individuals, while roe deer exceed 1,300. Most exciting of all has been the appearance of the brown bear, thought to have crossed from the nearby Adamello reserve.

All these animals except the bears can be seen easily, but if you are unlucky you can go to the deer reserve at Santa Caterina Valfurva, 12 kilometres (8 miles) from Bormio. Animal observation points are distributed through the park, their locations available from the visitors' centres.

Razor-sharp arêtes and hanging valleys are common features in the central Alps.

An entirely nocturnal bird of Italy's coniferous forests, the long-eared owl is distinguished from other owls by its vertical "ear" tufts. The ears proper are concealed lower down on each side of the head.

For birdwatchers Stelvio National Park is an absolute paradise, with 130 species recorded, almost one hundred of which breed in the park. The secret lies in the vast array of habitats, from the lowland meadows and scrublands to the thick alpine forests and bare windswept slopes above the tree-line.

Owls and woodpeckers are among the more interesting of the species found in the vast forests of the Stelvio, ranging from pygmy owls to eagle owls, the smallest and largest respectively in Europe; and both just as likely to be spotted by day as by night. Pygmy owls measure only 16cm (6in) in length and nest in old woodpecker holes, while the massive eagle owl can be anything up to 70cm (27in) from head to tail. Only a little larger than the pygmy owl is Tengmalm's owl, a genuinely nocturnal species with raised brows that give it a rather quizzical expression. Equally unmistakable are the elongated face and conspicuous ear tufts of the long-eared owl.

No fewer than five species of woodpecker breed here. The lower levels support wrynecks, so called because of their supposed ability to twist their heads through 360

degrees, and the great spotted woodpecker, probably the commonest member of the family in Europe. The dense montane forests are home to grey-headed woodpeckers, similar to green woodpeckers but with much less red on the crown, and the large black woodpecker. Perhaps the most distinctive is the three-toed woodpecker. It is the only one with no red in its plumage; instead the black-and-white barred males sport yellow crowns.

Above the tree-line you will find a wealth of small birds such as alpine accentors and snow finches, as well as rock thrushes, the males resplendent in blue and chestnut plumage; and ring ouzels, similar to the blackbird except for the broad white loop across the chest. Flocks of alpine choughs wheel through the sky, dwarfed by the silhouettes of golden eagles, of which no less than 22 pairs breed here, evidence indeed of how wild most of this mountain region still is. Sparrowhawks, goshawks, honey buzzards, kestrels and peregrines are present, too.

Botanists will also be spoiled for variety. The park's census, yet to be completed, has so far recorded 1,200 species of flora. The variety stems from a rich mixture of soils, which in turn correspond to a jumble of rock-types: ancient dolomites and other limestones in the east; crystalline schists rich in quartz, mica and feldspar in the west. The most striking of the flowers are deep azure trumpet gentians, which bloom at the height of summer, and smaller gentians with violet-blue fringes which come out in autumn. Equally spectacular are the red and martagon lilies, sweet-scented black vanilla orchids, mountain avens (also a plant of the arctic tundra) and alpine clematis, whose large purplish flowers would look familiar on any garden trellis.

Lurking in the depths of Stelvio's conifer woods is the rather unassuming, but nevertheless extremely attractive, chickweed wintergreen (*Trientalis europaea*). A member of the primrose family, this plant has a single whorl of smooth, shiny green leaves near the top of the stem, from which emerges a solitary, star-like white flower. Apart from the Alps, chickweed wintergreen is found in Great Britain, Scandinavia and northern Asia, but nowhere is it common. One site that is especially known for its meadows of flowers is the right bank of the Adige, in the north-west of the park. There is also a botanical garden at Bormio.

Finally, geologists will find interest beneath the soils that have produced such a richness of flora. Amid the folded lime-stones and granites lie twisted strata of metamorphic rock, and a glittering wealth of minerals. Magnetite occurs on the slopes of Monte Peio, with deposits of manganese in the Val Solda. Thermal springs are common, and in 1987 there were huge land-slips in the Valtellina (or Adda) valley. Many lives were lost in this tragic episode in the park's history.

BEFORE YOU GO
The park's headquarters are in Bormio: Via Monte Braulio 56, T: (0342) 901 582; try also the provincial visitors' centres: Servizio Parchi, Piazza Dante 15, Trento, T: (0461) 895 831; Cogolo, T: (0463) 74186; Bagni di Rabbi, T: (0463) 95190; Malè, T: (0463) 92155; Silandro, T: (0473) 70447; Prato allo Stelvio, T: (0473) 76140.

The main CAI office for the Lombardy area of the park is at Bormio; Via dei Simoni 42.
Maps: Kompass 1:50,000 *Ortles-Cevedale* and *Livigno-Crona di Campo*. IGM 1:25,000 9 III NO *Gran Zebrù*.
Guidebooks: *Alta Valtellina da Grosio allo Stelvio* (TCI-CAI), the definitive climbers' handbook; W. Frigo, *Parco Nazionale dello Stelvio: 50 Itinerari*; A. Gogna, *A Piedi in Valtellina* (De Agostini 1986).

GETTING THERE
By car: no approach to the Stelvio is particularly quick. For the northern access use A22 to Bolzano, and then SS38 to Malles (via Merano). Minor roads lead into 2 wonderful valleys from the SS38: the Val d'Ultimo (from Lana, S of Merano) and Val Martello (from Laces, near Silandro).

From Trento and the S follow SS42 and take lanes at Malè, Pellizzano and Ponte di Legno for the park's southern fringes. From Brescia, Silandro and the W — all long hauls — use the SS38 and SS42.

By rail: Bolzano–Malles branch line for the N of the park (3 trains daily); useful stations at Laces, Silandro and Sluderno. Brescia–Edolo line (10 daily) for access to the S.
By bus: more practical than trains, with services to most centres from Morano or Bormio. Winter schedules are more restricted.

Useful routes from Merano–S. Gertrude (5 daily, excellent for the Val d'Ultimo); Merano–Silano (8 daily); Silano–Genziana, in the Val Martello (2 daily); Sondrio–Bormio (1 daily); Bormio/Merano–Passo di Stelvio (summer only); Bormio–S. Caterina.

WHERE TO STAY
Many hotels in Bormio, Solda, Val Martello, Val d'Ultimo, Peio, S. Caterina, Trafoi, Bagni di Rabbi and scores of minor hamlets everywhere.

CAI and private refuges number about 30, the most popular at Pizzini, Branca, Mantova, Alpini and Payer, the last, above Solda, a base for climbs of Ortles, T: (0473) 75410.

ACTIVITIES
Walking: scope for exploration and trekking is vast; some of the most promising areas are outlined above. There are also comparatively easy hikes over ice if you are properly equipped. Certain areas (Val di Solda, Passo di Stelvio and Peio) have chair lifts high into the mountains.

Recommended routes

Parco Nazionale dello Stelvio

include the traverse of the Val di Zebrù to the Rif. Alpini; Val di Zebrù to Rif. Pizzini via the Passo dello Zebrù (and on to the Val dei Forni, 8hr/2 days); San Nicolo to Alpe Solaz, dropping to the Val di Zebrù; Passo di Gavia on the *Alta Via Camuna* (3/4 days).
Climbing: many routes, especially on snow and ice. Simple ascents of Cevedale open to hikers with ropes and crampons; Ortles and Gran

Zebrù are more demanding propositions.
Skiing: pistes at Bormio, S. Caterina, Valfurva, Peio, Rabbi, Solda, Trafoi and Ponte di Legno. Though cross-country options are limited, summer and alpine skiing possibilities are excellent.

FURTHER INFORMATION
Tourist offices: (Lombardy) Via Stelvio 10, Bormio, T: (0342) 903 300; Piazza

Migliavacca, S. Caterina Valfurva, T: (0342) 935 598; Corso Milano, Ponte di Legno, T: (0364) 91122; Via Vanoni 32, Sondalo, T: (0342) 801 127.
  (Trentino) Via Marconi, Malè, T: (0463) 91280; Via Principale 123, Silandro, T: (0473) 70155; Laces, T: (0473) 73109; Via Nazionale, Prato allo Stelvio, T: (0473) 76034; Malles Venosta, T: (0473) 81190.

Adamello-Brenta

Major alpine and Dolomite massifs (61,864ha/152,866 acres); proposed national park

One of the largest protected areas in the Alps, the Adamello-Brenta park is a meeting point of two great mountain chains. The central Alps reach their easternmost limit with the Adamello, while the Brenta is the most westerly of the Dolomite massifs. The park bridges the two ranges, marrying the crystalline rock of the Alps with the magnesium limestone of the Dolomites by means of a thin corridor of reserve north of Madonna di Campiglio.

Beneath this town runs the so-called Giudicarie Fault, a major alpine fracture that accounts for the striking disparity between the two areas. The Adamello's granite, formed 30 million years ago, is more recent than the rock of the Brenta, which consists of a unique formation of *Dolomia principale* overlaid with 300 metres (1,000 feet) of Rhaetic black shale. Oddly, the absence of Sciliar limestone makes the Brenta similar in appearance to the sawtooth mountains of the eastern Dolomites; an anomaly that underlines the complexity of the Alps' movements over the millennia.

For anyone seeking wilderness there is no question of which area to make for: the

Adamello. Its rich variety of scenery and huge proportions make it one of Italy's key alpine enclaves. At its heart rises the Adamello itself, 3,539 metres (11,611 feet) high, a massif of colossal peaks and glaciers, girdled by a further dozen summits each exceeding 3,000 metres (10,000 feet). The Val di Fumo divides two massive ridges running south from this heartland, and to the north an outlying wall of mountains, the Presanella, raises six more peaks of over 3,000 metres.

Between the Adamello and the Presanella lies the beautiful Val di Genova. Italia Nostra have described this ice-scoured valley as "the Alps' ultimate paradise". It is a small nook of delightful scenery with fine walks and numerous opportunities for encountering wildlife. The main attraction is a fairytale waterfall, the Cascata di Nardis, five kilometres (three miles) above the village of Carisolo. Two parallel streams drop 100 metres (350 feet) guarded by a pair of granite slabs which, according to legend, are two demons turned to stone. Similar falls farther up the valley crash over four successive rock steps, known locally as *scale*, "ladders", which descend the valley's snaking course.

Scenery at the head of the valley is breathtaking, with high snow-covered mountains and deeply fissured glaciers which in places have been compared to the landscapes of Alaska. Devils are said to wander the woods here, supposedly the spirits cast out by the Council of Trent (the Roman Catholic congress of the Counter-Reformation); so too is the legendary

King of Genova, a huntsman of bear and chamois, who can be heard howling on nights when the moon is full.

The plunging rock walls and soaring pinnacles of the Dolomiti di Brenta catch the sun's dying rays above Madonna di Campiglio.

Other noises in the woods may come from the three types of owl found here, the eagle, pygmy and Tengmalm's; or from the woodpeckers, the grey-headed, black and three-toed, which signal their presence to one another with their distinctive rhythmical drumming. Amongst the trees are a range of firs and pines, along with hazel, beech, birch, even cherry. Wonderful colours clothe the mountainsides in autumn, complemented by the distinctive crimson hue of the local lichen that covers the granite boulders of the valley.

Fauna typical of the Alps can be found, including chamois, deer, marmots and, remarkably, the alpine brown bear, of which perhaps a dozen survive in the Adamello and the Brenta. All you are likely to see of the bear, however, is evidence of their passage: droppings, disturbed bees' nests and scarred trees. Attempts to introduce bears from captivity have all failed.

The record of conservation in the park has been patchy. Some initiatives have been successful, such as averting the hydro-electric scheme for the Val Genova, but others have failed, for instance the attempt to prevent the development of uranium mines in the Val Rendena. Special reserves have been set up, as at Matterot on the Vedretta della Lobbia glacier, to study and

51

protect the recolonization by plants and animals of land newly exposed by the ice. Similar glacial retreats are protected around the peri-glacial lakes of Dinares and Pozzini, and around the Laris and Nardis waterfalls.

Moving over to the Brenta is like crossing the Great Divide of the Rocky Mountains, tumbling into a still more spectacular world, but one whose wilderness is compromised by the sheer number of visitors. The scenery, however, is likely to prove an unregrettable experience for any outdoor enthusiast. Immense rock faces and towering pinnacles are all served by refuges linked by excellent paths. The most famous of Italy's *vie ferrate*, the *Via delle Bocchette*, is here, one of the world's ultimate footpaths; unforgettable for those with the equipment, and heads for heights, who follow it.

The central ridge in the Brenta is lower than that of the Adamello, running at about 2,400 metres (7,900 feet) and peaking on Cima Tosa at 3,159 metres (10,364 feet), not that you will be able to reach any of the isolated turrets that are the "summits" in the Brenta. They are just a scenic backdrop for all but the most experienced climbers. There are many highlights, including the Crosson, a vast wall of grey rock, and the Campanile Basso, a perfect squared tower 400 metres (1,300 feet) high, the grandest in the Dolomites.

In summer, the central area around the Brentei and Tuckett refuges (Tuckett was one of several Englishmen to pioneer climbs in the Brenta in the 1860s) is perhaps the busiest region in the Alps. Local fauna are thinner on the ground as a result, though in the northern parts there are still a handful of bears. Alpine flora, on the other hand, is abundant, including rare mountain varieties such as edelweiss, lady's slipper orchid, Rhaetian poppy and black vanilla orchid. There are also more unusual species such as the spectacular primrose (*Primula spectabilis*), staining the rocks with its large pinkish red flowers; the scarce *Paederota bonarota* of the figwort family; and devil's claw (*Physoplexis comosa*), a fantastic blackish violet rampion with tear-shaped flowers arrayed in hemispherical clusters and surrounded by shining leaves.

Pressure of visitors, not to mention pollution, unfortunately threatens the Lago di Tovel, the most famous of the Brenta's natural landmarks. For years, under certain conditions, the lake took on a deep red tint, coloured by the presence of a rare alga, *Glenodinium sanguineum*. The effect was unknown anywhere else in the world, at least with such intensity. Sadly pollution has upset the lake's delicate natural balance and the intensity of the colour is waning.

The lady's slipper orchid (*Cypripedium calceolus*) is an extremely beautiful and increasingly scarce plant. Its petals form the shape of a ballerina's slipper, and may be found in European montane woods and thickets; it is protected by law in most countries.

BEFORE YOU GO
Guidebooks: For walkers and climbers, several books from the Cicerone Press; also G. Buscaini, *Dolomiti di Brenta* (TCI-CAI 1977), L. Visentini, *Dolomiti di Brenta* (Athesia 1987) and *A Piedi in Lombardia II* (Iter 1988).

Trento's tourist office issues an English guide to the Brenta, with details of walks and *vie ferrate*.
Maps: Kompass 1:30,000 *Gruppo di Brenta* and *Adamello-Presanella*.

GETTING THERE

By car: the SS42 is the main artery for the Adamello from Brescia, Bergamo and the west. The Brenta is easily reached from Trento (A22) via the SS43/42, and then SS239 to Madonna di Campiglio (the SS239 bisects the Park's 2 sections). Summer-only road to the Val di Genova from Carisolo, 12km (7 miles) S of Campiglio on the SS239.

By rail: to Trento on the main Verona–Brenner line, and then a short branch-line to Malè, 22km (17 miles) N of Campiglio (10 trains daily). For western access to the Adamello there is a slow branch line from Brescia to Edolo (10 trains daily).

By bus: from Trento to main villages and Campiglio via Stenico and Tione (4 daily, 2hr); from Milan to Campiglio; from Brescia to Breno, Edolo and western centres. Bus details at Trento, T: (0461) 983 627.

WHERE TO STAY

Hotels of all grades in virtually all centres, with Campiglio, or nearby Pinzolo, the best bases for exploration of both massifs. Molveno is good for the eastern Brenta, though path access to the high peaks is more limited.

Refuges: numerous (26 in the Brenta alone). The Città di Trento hut at the head of the Val di Genova is invaluable for the Adamello, T: (0465) 51193; the Brentei is popular in the Brenta, T: (0465) 41244.

Outdoor living: is permitted, and all but essential in much of the Adamello, with many organized sites (at Campiglio, Molveno, Pinzolo, Andalo, Vigo Rendena, Edolo and Sant'Antonio).

ACTIVITIES

Walking: hikes to suit every ability, with some 20 ski lifts to take you to starting points high in the mountains. Most walks in the Brenta from Campiglio are classics. The best known takes the Grosté chair lift from Campiglio to the Rif. Grosté (2,442m/8,000ft) and proceeds first to the Rif. Tuckett (trail 316) and then to the Rif. Brentei (trails 328/318). Here you can descend to Vallesinella and Campiglio (trail 317) or press on to the Rif. Pedrotti (7hr). There are endless variations to follow.

Routes in the Adamello tend to be longer. Well known are the hikes in the Val di Genova, especially those to the foot of the glaciers at the valley head. Also a long trek from the Val Caffaro to Ponte di Legno (6 days).

Skiing: large and popular resorts at Campiglio, Passo del Tonale and Val di Sole. Full range of pistes, and extensive alpine and cross-country opportunities.

Mountain-biking: Campiglio is rapidly becoming the Italian capital of this sport. Bikes can easily be hired in the town, and the tourist offices will advise on the many possible routes throughout the Adamello-Brenta park.

Ponytrekking: centres in Campiglio and the Val di Sole.

Windsurfing: facilities on Lago di Molveno.

FURTHER INFORMATION

Tourist offices: Via Alfieri 4, Trento, T: (0461) 983 880; Centro Rainalter, Madonna di Campiglio, T: (0465) 42000; Via del Sole, Pinzolo, T: (0465) 51007; Tuenno (for Lago di Tovel), T: (0463) 31149; Piazza Marconi 1, Molveno, T: (0461) 586 924; Corso Milano, Ponte di Legno, T: (0364) 91122; Piazza M. della Libertà 2, Edolo, T: (0364) 71065.

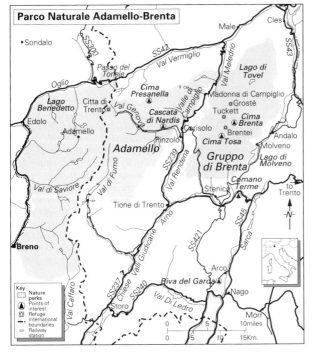

Parco Naturale Adamello-Brenta

Sondalo
Passo del Tonale
Oglio
Lago Benedetto
Edolo
Adamello
Val di Saviore
Val di Fumo
Breno
Val Caffaro

Key
Nature parks
Points of interest
Refuge
International boundaries
Railway station

Male
Val Vermiglio
Cima Presanella
Citta di Trento
Val Genova
Cascata di Nardis
Carisolo
Pinzolo
Adamello
Val Rendena
Gruppo di Brenta
Tione di Trento
Chiese
Val Giudicarie
Arno
Storo
Val Di Ledro
Riva del Garda
Nago
Arco

Cles
SS43
Val Meledrio
Lago di Tovel
Madonna di Campiglio
Grosté
Tuckett
Cima Brenta
Brentei
Cima Tosa
Lago di Molveno
Andalo
Molveno
Comano Terme
Stenico
to Trento
Sarca
SS45
SS421
Morr

-N-

0   5   10miles
0   5   10   15Km.

Sciliar

Dolomite mountain massif and high karstic plateau, the Alpe di Siusi (5,850ha/ 14,450 acres)

Rising in a huge wall that towers over Bolzano, the splintered peaks of the Sciliar are one of the classic sights of the Dolomites. Alongside stand the rock pinnacles of the Dente dello Sciliar, the so-called "Teeth of the Sciliar".

Unseen from the town, though, is the Alpe di Siusi, an undulating plateau of meadows that mingle with the peaks. At 2,000m (6,500ft), and extending over 5,000ha (12,000 acres), this green jewel set in a casket of mountains is one of the largest and most beautiful areas of meadow upland to be seen in Italy.

Once the snows have melted, the plains are soon covered in wild flowers. Fields of orchids, gentians, white crucifers and buttercups come into bloom in June and July; equally glorious are the marshes, particularly those near Ladinser.

Some of the Siusi plains have been spoiled by ski resorts and roads, both of which have appeared despite protests from conservationists. Most of the development is concentrated in the north, while wilder scenery remains in the southern Val di Tires.

The rocks of the Sciliar are the oldest in the Dolomites and have an abundance of fossils and minerals, the fruits of past volcanic activity. Near Cima di Terrarossa (2,655m/8,710ft) in the east the Denti di Terrarossa, "Teeth of Red Earth", form bizarre towers of volcanic rock. Areas like Ciapit and the Gola di Fromm enjoy worldwide renown for their mineral resources.

If the Sciliar's tableland and the plains of the Siusi sound tame by Dolomite standards, the views and walks to the nearby massifs of the Sella, Sasso Lungo and Catinaccio are superb if more pastoral than elsewhere. Spectacular, too, are the gorges that scythe down towards the villages of Fie and Siusi.

The Sciliar is also a massif of historical interest, known locally as "the mountain of destiny". Populated since ancient times, prehistoric remains have been found in its caves (most interesting is the Buco dell'Orso) and on Monte Castello, probably a site of pagan worship.

Before you go: *Maps:* Kompass 1:50,000 *Bolzano.*
Guidebook: Parco Naturale dello Sciliar, available from tourist office and park centre in Bolzano.
Getting there *By car:* A4 to Bolzano Nord, and then SS12 and minor roads into the park. Access also from Val Gardena and the north (SS242), and from the Val Fassa and the E (SS48). Several ski-lifts operate to the Siusi from the N.
By rail: station at Bolzano, also the terminus for local buses.
By bus: services to Siusi, and from Siusi to Saltaria in the heart of the Alpe wetlands. T: (0471) 975 117 for bus information.
Where to stay: wide choice of hotels in central locations at Siusi, Castelrotto, Tires, Fiè, Alpe di Siusi, Saltaria and many isolated hamlets. Check off-season opening with tourist offices.

Many opportunities for *agriturismo* and several refuges; most used is the

Grasses and delicate Alpine flowers find shelter from the elements in the weathered limestone of the Parco Naturale di Fanes-Sennes-Braies.

Bolzano, T: (0471) 72952 (open June–Sept).

Outdoor living is prohibited within the park, but there is a site near Fiè at San Constantino, Alpe di Siusi, T: (0471) 71459 (open all year). **Activities** *Walking:* the classic 2-day hike over the Siusi to the summit of the Sciliar (Monte Pez, 2,563m/8,408ft) starts from Hotel Frommer above Siusi (trail 5). The path climbs to the Rif. Bolzano, with a wide choice of ascents and return routes (12hr).

Other climbs to the summit, often busy in summer, can be made from Tires, Siusi and Fiè (using the nearby lift at Ums

cuts out 1,000m/3,200ft of climbing). Hikes over the Siusi are all extremely simple and straightforward, with many refreshment points.

For a full-blown traverse of the park start at the Bellavista Hotel in Alpe di Siusi, climb to the Rif. Bolzano and descend to Fiè (6hr). Enjoy wilder hikes near Tires in the Valle Orsara and Valle Ciamin. Five paths are marked by the park authorities as nature trails. *Climbing:* climbs are rare by the Dolomites' high standards. Most routes are W of the Sciliar: Punta Santner, Punta Euringer and Piccolo Sciliar. *Ponytrekking:* centres

throughout, with the chance to hire horse-pulled sleds in winter. Contact tourist offices. *Skiing:* most centres are on the Alpe di Siusi, less crowded than some areas, with numerous lifts (a major one at Ortisei) plus skating and sled-run possibilities. Some 80km (50 miles) of renowned and spectacular cross-country routes, with downhill skiing on Monte Pez and the Sciliar plateau.

Further information *Tourist offices:* Piazza Walther 8, Bolzano, T: (0471) 970 660; Castelrotto, T: (0471) 71333; Fiè, T: (0471) 72047; Siusi, T: (0471) 71124.

Paneveggio-Pale di San Martino

Remote Dolomite massif and tract of primary forest (19,097ha/47,189 acres)

Lying south of the main Dolomite massifs, this enchanting park is divided into two contrasting areas near San Martino di Castrozza: Paneveggio, a huge area of primeval forest, and the Pale, some of the Dolomites' most desolate mountains.

Of Paneveggio's 2,690ha (5,500 acres), only 10ha (25 acres) are covered in roads and cultivated woodland. The rest is a wilderness of larch, silver fir, arolla and mountain pines, and Norway spruce. From its sombre expanse came the timber for the Venetian fleet of the seventeenth century, and the wood which Stradivarius and fellow Cremonese craftsmen turned into violins. Commercial pressure on these woodlands has been relieved

by a separate plantation that produces 120,000 trees a year.

The forest is an alpine miniature, with an abundance of streams and waterfalls (many well stocked with trout) and comparatively modest mountains, dominated by the rounded heights of Colbricon (2,603m/8,539ft). Away to the west stretch the granite ridges of the Lagorani, an immense emptiness which visitors overlook in favour of the Dolomites further north.

Larger mammals have been hunted to virtual extinction, though red deer reintroduced 30 years ago have formed a viable colony, and smaller mammals, including pine martens, have recovered ground since the park's inception in 1967. Unfortunately birds of prey have all but vanished.

Paths and surfaced bridleways are ideal for walking, mountain biking and cross-country skiing. Walks around Tognola (with a chair lift to 2,177m/7,145ft) are especially appealing, confined to easy meadow and woodland tracks.

A constant backdrop to the

forest walks of the Paneveggio are the stupendous jagged peaks of the Pale, one of the most breathtaking of all the Dolomite massifs. Distinct from neighbouring groups, its upper ridges and karstic plateaux are a barren wilderness, a landscape where comparisons with the surface of the moon are for once apposite. So pallid is the rock here that it glows even in the pale light of dawn.

Hiking itineraries vary greatly in degrees of difficulty. Although all paths are well marked, some are extremely challenging, with much scrambling and the occasional *vie ferrate*. Plan your walks and know your strength before setting out.

A little to the south of the main peaks of Vezzana and Cimon della Pala (both over 3,000m/10,000ft) lies the Val Canali, a more intimate and accessible area. Reached from Fiera di Primiero, it embraces Sass Maor and the Cima d'Oltro. A nineteenth-century traveller described the area as the most "lonely, desolate and tremendous scene . . . to be found this side of the Andes".

The yellow daisy-like flowers of arnica (*Arnica montana*) have long been used in country medicine by central Europeans, both externally for bruises, wounds and sprains and internally as a stimulant and febrifuge.

Alpine choughs are the walker's constant companion in the higher mountains, their yellow beaks and high-pitched whistling calls distinguishing them from the closely-related red-billed choughs. Golden eagles may also be spotted soaring high above the peaks, their size alone serving as identification.

The montane pastures are an absolute delight, with many of the classic alpine species. The star-like silvery flower-heads of edelweiss nestle side by side with the tiny dark purple spikes of the black vanilla orchid, while the orange-yellow flowers of arnica contrast with the pale lemon blooms produced by swathes of Rhaetian poppies. Lady's slipper orchids thrive in the seclusion of the least disturbed woodlands, while globeflowers flourish in the wetter grasslands.

Rarities of these mountains include the lilac-flowered primrose *Primula tyrolensis*, a plant confined to the Dolomites, and devil's claw (*Physoplexis comosa*), a bizarre member of the bell-flower family known only from limestone and dolomitic rock crevices in the southern Alps.

Before you go: park centre at Paneveggio village: T: (0462) 51934.

Maps: Kompass 1:50,000 *Pale di San Martino*; Tabacco 1:50,000, Sheets 4 and 7.

Guidebooks: G. Franceschini, *Pale di San Martino* (Ghedina 1978); L. Visentini, *Andar per Sentieri in Trentino-Alto Adige*, (De Agostini 1988, a walkers' handbook). Also leaflets and trail itineraries from park centre and tourist offices.

Getting there *By car:* SS48 from Trento and W via Predazzo (leave A22 at Egna-Ora exit); the scenic SS50 (from Feltre and the S) bisects the park, reaching 1,980m (6,495 feet) at the Passo Rolle.

By rail: stations at Feltre and Ora.

By bus: direct buses from Venice to San Martino; twice weekly from Milan (summer only); thrice daily from Trento to San Martino (3hr); once daily from Bolzano (4hr). Local

services to Fiera and Passo Cerada.

Where to stay: mainly at San Martino, with alternatives in Paneveggio, Fiera, Bellamonte and Cant del Gal.

Outdoor living: prohibited outside sites, but fine sites at Lago Paneveggio: Calavise, Imer, T: (0439) 67468; Sass Maor, San Martino, T: (0439) 68347.

Refuges: most useful are Treviso in the Val Canali, T: (0439) 62311; Pedrotti-Rossetta on the the Pale plateau, T: (0439) 68308/62567; and Pradidali, T: (0439) 67290.

Activities *Walking:* recommended walks in Paneveggio include Passo Rolle–Colbricon lakes–Rif. Malga Ces–San Martino (3hr); Tognola (use chair lift from San Martino)–Punta Ces–San Martino (7hr);

In the Pale: a classic hike from Rif. Rossetta (cable car from San Martino) to Rif. Pradidali (6hr, trails 701/702); Malga Fossa–Col Rif. Verde–San Martino (3hr, descend by lift or trail 701).

Guides: guided walks into the Pale during July and Aug from the Gruppo Guide Alpine in San Martino, T: (0439) 68795/ 68620.

Skiing: San Martino is the main resort S of Cortina d'Ampezzo, and a favourite with Italians. Lifts and piste at Tognola-Punta Ces and Passo Rolle. Most cross-country routes at Passo Rolle.

Outing: A worthwhile excursion might be made to see the fossil and mineral collection at the Museo di Etnologia, Via Molini, Predazza, T: (0462) 51237 (open summer 5–7pm).

Further information *Tourist offices:* San Martino, T: (0439) 68101/68352; Fiera, T: (0439) 62407; Piazza della Chiesa, Predazzo, T: (0462) 51237; Via F. Bronzetti 4, Cavalese, T: (0462) 30298.

Puez-Odle

Twin mountain massifs of the Dolomites (9,210ha/ 22,758 acres)

The fact that Reinhold Messner, one of the world's greatest climbers, chose to live in the Puez-Odle mountains suggests that they are above the common run of Dolomite massifs. He came for the climbing, following the enthusiasts who pioneered some of Italy's most difficult routes in the 1930's.

The scenery is also a powerful draw. A microcosm of Dolomite landscape, the skyline of Puez-Odle is as spectacular as any, dominated by the huge saw-toothed peaks of the Odle and the massive block-like Puez to the south. Many are the highlights: the wild Vallunga in the south, noted as the most unspoiled glacially carved valley in the Dolomites; the yawning natural arch of the Stelvia; the tiny ice-cold lakes of Crespeina and Campaccio; and the immense forests on the skirts of the Odle, which once grew much higher up the mountain, as fossilized trunks in local glaciers testify.

The park has been called an El Dorado for geologists, partly because the Val Badia marks a boundary between the eastern and western Dolomites (see page 40 for explanation of structural difference), and partly because there is evidence of Quaternary glaciation and Tertiary folding. There are also notable works of natural erosion, such as the Stelvia arch, the Col della Sone (shaped like a volcanic cone), the Worndle caverns, and any number of bizarre atriums, towers and pinnacles. In the Val Badia south of Pedraces lies a famous outcrop of strata, the San Classiano Formation, a seam rich in fossils that attracts collectors from all over Europe.

The comparative seclusion of the Puez-Odle Nature Park, created in 1977, has been a greater factor in the welfare of the park's wildlife than any protection afforded by the authorities. Hunting is still allowed, as it is in most of the reserves controlled from the major centre of Bolzano.

However, if fauna is a mite scarcer than in other regions, there is still much to be seen. Marmots are common in the Alpe di Cisles and golden eagles are known to breed regularly on the Forcella Mont da l'Ega. Chamois have been protected by a voluntary society of enthusiasts for 20 years, with about 100 recorded individuals, most of them in the Vallunga. There is also a fenced reserve for red and roe deer at Zanseralm in Messner's own valley, the Val di Funes.

This valley provides the best views in the entire park, and is the starting point for many peaceful walks. Certainly it is remoter than the Val Gardena, along the southern edge of the park, where crocodiles of walkers crowd the slopes and caterpillar coach tours grind along the the so-called "Road of the Dolomites". Instead, the verdant mix of meadows, huge larch forests and tranquil wooden hamlets of the Val di Funes will take you back to the Dolomites of a century ago.

Before you go *Maps:* Kompass 1:50,000 *Sella-Marmolada*; Tabacco 1:50,000 *Val Gardena*; 1:25,000 *Val di Funes* is available from tourist offices in

---

The western Dolomites (left) rose as an undeformed block. The eastern Dolomites (right), on the other hand, underwent severe buckling and folding when the European and African continents collided during the Tertiary period and rose as elongated humps. These subsequently weathered to produce the saw-toothed appearance for which the Dolomites are famous. See page 38 for geological history.

The mountains of Tofane, south of Parco Naturale di Fanes-Sennes-Braies, have the massive folded-block appearance typical of the eastern Dolomites.

the valley; IGM 1:25,000 11 II NO *S. Maddalena* (for Val di Funes).
Guidebooks: Parco Naturale Puez-Odle from tourist offices and Bolzano park authority; H. Menara, *Alti Sentieri delle Dolomiti* (high walks); P. Tirone, *I Parchi delle Alpi.*
Getting there *By car:* Val Gardena and Val di Funes are accessible from the A22 (Chiusa exit); Val Badia and the E from Brunico via the SS244 and from Cortina via the SS48, with limited minor road access to the interior from the Val Badia.
By rail and bus: there are

railway stations at Chiusa, Bressanone and Brunico, with bus services from these and other centres to most villages. Bus information can be obtained at Brunico, T: (0474) 85722.
Where to stay: rooms are available for renting in most centres, especially in the Val Gardena (S. Cristina and Selva) and Val Badia. There are also numerous high refuges, many in private hands.
Outdoor living: prohibited, but there are some potential pitches in the Val di Funes, with a camping site at Corvara in the Badia valley.

Activities *Walking:* the most noted hikes are the *Sentiero delle Odle* in the Val di Funes (with many variations); the *Sentiero dei Signori*, also in the Funes, with fine views of the Odle; the superb climb to the Rif. Puez from Selva Gardena via the Vallunga (5hr); traverse of the massifs on the *Alta Via 2 delle Dolomiti*; the Alpi di Gampen to Alpi Medagles (5hr); the ascent of the Sass de Putia (2,875m/9,000ft), from the Passo delle Erbe.

Various lifts climb into the S of the park from the Val Gardena. These can be used to start walks, but the paths, especially that from S. Cristina to the Rif. Firenze, are often crowded.

Climbing: many routes, some on poor and therefore dangerous rock, but less busy than most Dolomite playgrounds. The N face of the Furchetta on the Odle is the most difficult climb in the region.
Ponytrekking: in the Val Gardena at the Country Club S. Durich, Via Vidalong 2, Ortisei, T: (0471) 76904.
Skiing: extensive piste and facilities at Bressanone-Plose and the Val Gardena; more modest options in the Val di Funes and Val Badia. Excellent cross-country in the Odle forests.
Hang-gliding: Helmut Striker school at Pedraces in the Val Badia, T: (0471) 85770.
Further information *Tourist offices:* park centre in the Val di Funes at Malga Zannes, Via Stazione 9, T: (0472) 22401; Ortisei, T: (0471) 76328; S. Cristina, T: (0471) 76346; Selva Gardena, T: (0471) 75122; Badia, T: (0471) 849 422.

Fanes-Sennes-Braies

Three Dolomite massifs cut by deep valleys (25,680ha/ 63,455 acres)

The Fanes plateau is one of Italy's finest tracts of limestone scenery. Guarded by a ring of peaks, it nestles at the heart of three massifs in the eastern Dolomites. Pockets of beautiful scenery, such as the Lago di Braies trapped in a cwm high on the northern slopes, have kept a remoteness despite their share of summer coach parties.

The mountains offer stunning panoramas, especially around the Croda Rossa,

Conturines and Picco di Vallandro. Paths can be some of the Dolomites' loveliest and least travelled. The *Alta Via 1*, most famous of the high walks, starts at Braies, and for less energetic hikers there are the old military tracks of the *Prato Piazza*, also popular with mountain-bikers. Apart from Braies, lakes worth visiting are clustered around the Fanes refuge or the tiny Lago di Fanes, dwarfed by the huge crags of the Cima Scotoni.

Although hunting is permitted, shy groups of deer can still be seen on some of these walks, particularly on the long silent trails through the Val Foresta. In the high solitary wastes of the Croda Rossa (3,146m/10,322ft), sure-footed chamois leap up impossibly awkward crags, their flexible cloven hooves separating on landing, providing both shock

The craggy glaciated profile of Val Comelico contrasts with meadows and flowers in the Dolomiti di Sesto.

absorbers and the grip necessary to land on rock ledges only 30cm (12in) wide.

Another creature supremely adapted to life in these barren uplands is the mountain hare, also known as the blue, varying or arctic hare. Similar in appearance to the brown hare, but slightly stockier and with shorter ears, the mountain hare changes its coat with the seasons. During the summer its woolly fur is a brownish grey, but in the snowy conditions of winter the coat moults to a pure white — though the ears are still tipped black — helping to conceal the hare from predators.

Constant companions of the walker in the higher mountains are alpine choughs, their yellow beaks and high-pitched whistles distinguishing them from the closely related red-billed choughs. Golden eagles may also be spotted soaring high above the peaks, unmistakable for their size alone.

Before you go *Maps:* Kompass 1:50,000 *Brunico* and *Cortina d'Ampezzo*.
Guidebook: M. Mestre, *Sentieri delle Dolomiti* (De Agostini 1986) contains hiking itineraries in the Fanes.
Getting there *By car:* the Fanes is ringed by the SS244 from Brunico and SS51/48 from Cortina. Unclassified roads penetrate the park from several points on this ring.
By rail: stations at Brunico and Dobbiaco.
By bus: frequent buses between Brunico and Corvara on the W edge of the park, between Brunico and Dobbiaco for the N (and Lago di Braies), and between Dobbiaco and Cortina for the E (Croda Rossa and Prato Piazza).
Where to stay: at Valdoara, S. Vigilio di Marebbe, S. Cassiano, Pedraces, Villa S. Martino, Braies, and in centres along the Val Pusteria to the N.

60

Outdoor living: Free camping banned, but organized sites at Corvara and Armentarola.
Refuges: 15 CAI and private refuges. Most useful are: Fanes, T: (0474) 51097; and Lavarella, T: (0474) 51038. A jeep taxi service runs to both huts from San Vigilio (summer only).
Activities *Walking:* many choices, most relatively wild and untrodden; some of the best include trails in the rugged Valle di Lagazuoi; the traverse from Pederu to the hamlet of Armentarola via the Passo Tadega (2,157m/7,076ft); and ascents to the summits of peaks, accessible, unlike many in the Dolomites, to the normal walker.
Climbing: the massive rock walls of the Scotoni and the west face of the Conturines.
Skiing: exemplary cross-country trails in the Val Foresta and Valle di S. Vigilio.
Further information *Tourist offices:* Via Europa 22, Brunico, T: (0472) 85722; S. Vigilio di Marebbe, T: (0474) 51037; Braies-Prags (Lago di Braies), T: (0474) 78660; Valdoara, T: (0474) 46277.

Dolomiti di Sesto

Eastern Dolomite massif (11,635ha/28,751 acres)

The last of the Italian Dolomites before the Austrian border, the Sesto is a small but spectacular massif close to the razzmatazz of Cortina d'Ampezzo, one of Italy's foremost skiing resorts.

For those whose time is limited, the park provides a wide variety of Dolomitic scenery and habitats within a compact and self-contained area. Accessible by road and public transport, it makes a fine introduction to the Dolomites if you are starting in the east.

Its three-peaked mountain highlight, the Tre Cime di Lavaredo (2,998m/9,836ft), is one of the most photographed sights in the Dolomites. A road to the Auronzo refuge on its southern flanks, which conservationists want closed, delivers hordes of hikers to a mass of trails and some of the region's rockiest landscapes.

For more solitary exploration head for the Val di Sesto in the north-east, often claimed to be the prettiest in the Dolomites, and its two exquisite subsidiary valleys, the Fiscalina and Campo di Dentro. You can explore the mountains equally well from Sesto and Moso. The climb to the Locatelli refuge is exhilarating, while the view from the Comici refuge of the Cima Dodici ("the 12-peaked summit") is among the best in northern Italy.

Two of the Dolomites' high-level paths, the *Grohman* and *Titian* routes (numbers 4 and 5), start in the valley, from the villages of San Candido and Sesto respectively. Either of these, indeed any trail within the Sesto, quickly leaves civilization as it wends its way into the mountains. More pastoral spots are found in the west, around the steep-sided Rienza valley and the Lago di Misurina, one of the prettiest lakes in the region, noted for its shimmering colours.

The mountains of Sesto, incidentally, mark an evocative watershed: the Pusteria drains to the Adige and the Adriatic, the Drava to the Danube and the Black Sea. Given this position, it is no surprise to come across battle debris from World War I. Many walks — to Monte Piana, around the Tre Cime, and near the Cengia refuge — pass the scene of bitter fighting.

Before you go *Maps:* Tabacco 1:50,000 (Sheet 1) or Kompass 1:50,000 (Sheets 57/58). *Guidebooks:* L. Visentini, *Dolomiti di Sesto* (Athesia 1985); P. Ortner, *Parco Naturale Dolomiti di Sesto*, available from park office in Bolzano. For climbers, A. Berti, *Dolomiti Orientali* (CAI-TCI 1973).

Getting there *By car:* A22 from Bolzano (Bressanone exit) and then SS49 along the Val Pusteria to Dobbiaco and San Candido. From Cortina use SS51 to Dobbiaco, or SS48 for Auronzo refuge.
By rail: stations at Dobbiaco and San Candido on the branch line which leaves the main Bolzano–Brenner line at Fortezza (12 trains daily, with 7 direct from Bolzano).
By bus: bus services from Bolzano to Brunico, and from Brunico to Dobbiaco and Cortina (5 daily); San Candido, Sesto and Moso (8 daily). Bus information at Brunico, T: (0474) 85722.

Where to stay: Sesto and Moso are the best bases, with ample hotel and private-room accommodation. Other lodgings around Lago di Misurina, San Candido, Passo Monte Croce and Lago di Dobbiaco.
Outdoor living: free camping forbidden; organized sites: Sesto at Moso, T: (0474) 70444 (May–Oct); Olympia, 2km (1 mile) from Dobbiaco, T: (0474) 72147; and Lago di Dobbiaco and Lago di Misurina.
Refuges: there are 6 refuges within the park area.
Activities *Walking:* numerous

walks at every standard and length. The following routes are popular — avoid them in August when they get *too* popular: Valle Fiscalina–Rif. Comici (trail 103)–Rif. Locatelli (trail 101)–Valle Fiscalina (7hr, trail 102); Rif. Auronzo–Rif. Locatelli (trail 101)–Tre Cime–Auronzo (4hr, trail 105); Lago di Misurina–Rif. Fonda Savio (4hr, trail 115 and difficult 117 for descent); Lago di Landro–Monte Piana (2,324m/ 7,624ft), with superb views of the Cristallo and Sesto

massifs (4hr, trail 6).
Skiing: lifts and pistes at Sesto and Moso, and one of the Dolomites' most renowned cross-country routes, along the disused railway from Dobbiaco to Cortina (35km/28 miles); the Valle Fiscalina and Campo di Dentro provide further routes.
Further information *Tourist offices:* Via Canoncini, San Candido, T: (0474) 73149; Via Roma, Dobbiaco, T: (0474) 72132; Sesto/Moso, T: (0474) 70310.

The mountain hare is well-adapted to conditions in the Alps and Dolomites; its summer brownish grey fur turns to white at the onset of winter to conceal it from predators.

MOUNTAIN SAFETY

The Alps and the Dolomites are genuinely wild places and can present real dangers to those who venture into them without taking sensible precautions. The weather can change quickly in the mountains; even in summer, it is possible to get stranded by mist and fog, and exposure can be a serious hazard.

Always take a waterproof and some warm clothing; walking boots with moulded rubber soles (smooth soles can be lethal); food, map and compass; and a whistle to attract attention in case you get into difficulties.

Always tell someone where you are going and how long you intend to be, especially if walking alone.

CHAPTER 3

The Venetian Plain and Eastern Alps

Italy's north-eastern corner is a naturalist's dream and a politician's nightmare. The country's most extensive lagoons make the region a staging post for vast numbers of migratory birds, and the easternmost Alps are some of the wildest, most beautiful parts of Italy.

The area has been a crossroads of trade and peoples since prehistoric times. Italy, Austria and Slovenia meet at a point of passage used in the past by Celts, Romans, Avars, Istrians, Lombards, Slavs, Byzantines, Venetians, Friulians, Hungarians and, most unhappily for the Italians, by the Goths and Vandals who poured through a breach in the Eastern Alps to close the book on the Roman Empire.

All these peoples left their mark on the landscape, none more so than the Austrians in northern Veneto, which they ruled until 1918. During World War I the majestic Dolomite massifs of Cristallo, Marmolada and Civetta saw some of the most savage fighting ever to have taken place in an area of high wilderness. Traces of the front line are still visible along the highest ridges, and stories are still told of the extraordinary feats of men condemned to fight on rock and ice.

Veneto and Friuli-Venezia Giulia share a great arc of coastline, an almost unbroken belt of marsh and lagoon from the Po delta to the outskirts of Trieste. This flat, windswept landscape takes you across the famous Venetian

The chill waters of the Lago di Fusine lie amid the Tarvisian forests at the heart of the Alpi Giulie.

lagoons, through the lesser known and less-polluted Magnuno wetlands, and curves round the northern Adriatic before rising into the cliffs behind Trieste. More and more of this vast area is being lost to land reclamation and poisoned by industrial waste from the Po and the Veneto's huge urban hinterland. For birds in their millions, however, the lagoons and wetlands remain aquatic stepping stones on the Adriatic migration route that takes them — like peoples over the centuries — to the European heartlands.

This coastline has been sculpted by the great rivers which flow across the plains of both regions and into the Adriatic: the Po, Adige, Brenta, Piave, Tagliamento and Isonzo — all have their sources in the Alps. Mountains enclose both regions. Veneto claims the last and highest of the Dolomite massifs, while Friuli picks up the thread as the Dolomites give way to the lower and narrower chains of the Eastern Alps. The most extensive of these are the Carniche, a wall of mountains which runs for some 200 kilometres (120 miles) between Austria and Italy. The country's scenic finale is the Julian Alps, with massifs as spectacular as any in the entire Alpine range.

Between the mountains and the coast of both regions lies an area that is something of a vacuum for foreign visitors. Few people have any idea quite what happens between the evocative names of Venice and Trieste. Huge tracts of flat land lie there, of which the Friuli side has been compared to the plains of the American Midwest, whilst Veneto is one of the most densely populated parts of Italy.

In Friuli, some of the plains are desolate badlands, known locally as *magredis*. For the most part, though, they are monotonous prairies of corn,

seeded on reclaimed land and broken only by rows of poplars and church towers. In Veneto they support five million people, in an area that one Italian ecologist has described as "amongst the most naturalistically devastated regions in the world". Between the Alps and the plains, however, lies yet another area, the pre-Alps, a bland name that does little justice to the gorgeous and almost entirely overlooked pockets of wilderness in both regions. The most notable of these is the Carnia in upper Friuli, rippled with mountains over 2,000 metres (6,500 feet) and devoid of roads or habitation.

Veneto, too, for all the ecologists' gloom, has its brighter side, again in the pre-Alps. The Belluno Dolomites remain wild and quiet: lower than their northern counterparts, they have not been infested with ski resorts. Close by lie the Lessini mountains, a small botanical wonderland, and the Cansiglio plateau, the region's largest area of ancient woodland. All three areas now make up the region's only national park, the Parco Nazionale delle Dolomiti Bellunesi, giving much-needed protection to its fauna which is some of the most impoverished in the country. Veneto's hills have a nationwide reputation for being eerily silent, their birds annihilated by centuries of hunting.

For the most exciting wildlife you must go to the Julian Alps and the Tarvisio forests, in the farthest-flung corner of eastern Italy. The variety and richness of fauna here have less to do with Italy than with Slovenia, for it is from the wilderness over the border that most of the finest animals have strayed. Not only a few bears, but also lynx have found their way into the region's wild fir and pine forests. The same can be said of another tiny area in Friuli: the Carso. This tongue of limestone connecting Trieste with the rest of Italy provides a fantastically complex habitat for flora and avifauna that owe many of their characteristics as much to central Europe and the Balkans as to Italy.

GETTING THERE

By air: the area is well served by international airports at Venice: Marco Polo, T: (041) 661 111; and Trieste: Ronchi dei Legionari, T: (0481) 777 001; and other airports at Verona and Treviso.

By car: motorway links to Verona, Padua, Vicenza and Venice. For the northern, wilder parts of Veneto the main routes are the A27 Venice–Vittorio Veneto, and the SS51 to Belluno and Cortina. In Friuli the chief arteries are the A4 (Venice–Trieste) and A23 (Udine–Tarvisio). The SS52 joins the northern halves of the 2 regions.

By rail: fast main-line routes: Milan–Verona–Venice, Venice–Udine, Venice–Trieste and Udine–Tarvisio–Vienna. There is also a useful branch line from Venice to Belluno that serves northern Veneto.

WHERE TO STAY

You should have no accommodation problems, except in the remote areas of northern Friuli (Tarvisio) and the Carnia wilderness NE of Belluno.

Full lists of hotels and campsites can be obtained by writing to provincial tourist offices: Via Pesaro 21, Belluno, T: (0437) 22043; Piazza Pedrocchi 18, Padua, T: (049) 44711; Via Valverde 34, Verona, T: (045) 30086; Via Rossini 6, Trieste, T: (040) 60336; Via dei Missionari 2, Udine, T: (0432) 295 972; Galleria del Corso 100e, Gorizia, T: (0481) 83870.

Perhaps Europe's most famous alpine wild flower, the edelweiss (*Leontopodium alpinum*) grows in limestone pastures and screes up to 3,400m (11,000ft).

ACTIVITIES

Walking: numerous possibilities in both areas, the Friuli mountains especially being still largely undiscovered by hikers. Contact local CAI branches and tourist offices in relevant Exploration Zones for leaflets and guidance.

Birdwatching: LIPU offices: Corso del Popolo 29, Treviso, T: (0422) 361 094; Via Alpi Giulie 13, Trieste, T: (040) 828 709.

Caving: CAI speleology sections at: Verona, T: (045) 30555; Padua, T: (049) 22678; CAI Via Machiavelli 17, Trieste, T: (040) 60317.

Fishing: provincial FIPS offices: Via Cipro 13, Belluno, T: (0437) 24854; Via S. Ambrogio di Fiera 7, Treviso, T: (0422) 40695.

FURTHER INFORMATION

Tourist information: No state parks in either region have local headquarters, so for details of Veneto reserves contact relevant tourist offices or the Dipartimento Urbanistico, Cannaregio 99, Venice, T: (041) 792 111 (Veneto); and in Friuli, Direzione del Bilancio, Via Udine 9, Trieste, T: (040) 770 7266.

Ecology: regional WWF delegations: Via Chiodi 6, Verona, T: (045) 594 872; Via Odorico da Pordenone 3, Udine, T: (0432) 290 895.

FURTHER READING

J. Buckley, *The Rough Guide to Venice and the Veneto* (Penguin).

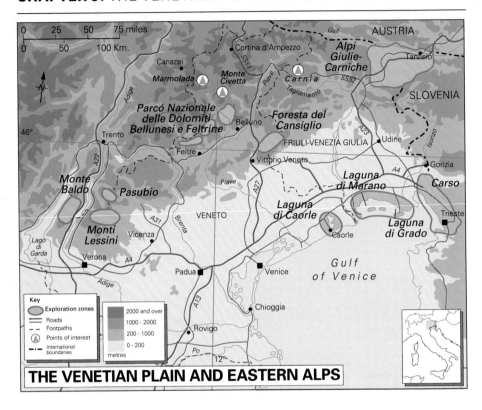

THE VENETIAN PLAIN AND EASTERN ALPS

Monte Baldo

Limestone range above Lake Garda renowned for flora and exceptional views; proposed regional park (10,000ha/24,700 acres)

Monte Baldo's ridges run for nearly 40 kilometres (25 miles) along the eastern coast of Lake Garda, cutting a fine profile as they rise sheer from the lake shore to Cima Telegrafa and Cima Valdritta over 2,000 metres (6,500 feet) up. The summits are a belvedere on to much of north-east Italy, with magnificent views across the lake (camp here just for the sunsets) to the distant Adamello massif and Brenta Dolomites to the north.

Yet it is not for these dramatic heights that the area is renowned, nor even for the shimmering plays of light over the lake, but for an immense botanical variety that as early as the sixteenth century had earned it the title *Hortus Italiae*, "Garden of Italy".

One of the finest floral hunting grounds in Europe, Monte Baldo's tremendous range of species is largely the result of wide geological and climatic variation. Baldo is mostly limestone, but this is broken up by basaltic lavas in the east, fossil-rich seams and more than 60 different types of marble, which have weathered to produce the famous soils of red, yellow and green around Brentonico in the north-east (protected by a 100-hectare/250-acre reserve).

Baldo's secret is its range of microclimates. The highest peaks have a distinctively alpine ambience, covered in snow in winter and scorched by the sun in summer.

The lower slopes, though, are subject to the influence of Lake Garda. The lake, which has only frozen over once in recorded history (in 1701), creates a natural greenhouse in which olives, palms, lemons, cypresses and cedars thrive.

Its morphology is also highly varied. The slopes facing east to the Adige are rounded and pastoral, whereas the lakeside slopes are steep and cut by glacial cirques. Monte Baldo's highest ridges remained out of reach of the huge Ice Age glacier that enveloped the area. As a result their plant populations survived, isolated from their nearest neighbours for several millennia. Not surprisingly, several endemic species have evolved, many of which bear the epithet *baldense* or *baldensis* to indicate their status: the bedstraw *Galium baldense*, the reddish-purple flowered scabious *Knautia baldensis* and the distinctive sedge *Carex baldensis*, whose flattish silvery heads are surrounded by leafy bracts.

Other plants are labelled with this specific name because they were first discovered on Monte Baldo, although later exploration revealed their presence elsewhere. Perhaps the best known of these is the Monte Baldo anemone (*Anemone baldensis*), whose blue-white flowers, up to 4cm (1½in) in diameter, are also found in other parts of the Alps and in the mountains of former Yugoslavia.

In spring, the grassy slopes of Monte Baldo are clothed in sheets of pheasant's-eye narcissi, to be replaced later in the year by clumps of narcissus-flowered anemones and alpine pasque-flowers. The rocky areas are strewn with the gorgeous pink cinquefoil with its silvery leaves and rose-coloured flowers, and interspersed with yellow mountain saxifrage, mountain avens and one-sided purple spikes of dragonmouth.

Other gems of Monte Baldo include the spectacular primrose (*Primula spectabilis*), easily identified even when not in flower by the white horny rim around each leaf, the single-flowered cushion saxifrage (*Saxifraga burserana*), with tiny cushions of pin-like, blue-green leaves and solitary white flowers up to 3cm (1 in) across, the beautiful reddish-purple blooms of large-flowered catchfly (*Silene elisabetha*) and the gracious, yellow-white spherical heads of rock bellflower (*Campanula petraea*).

The mountain also has many medicinal plants — a natural pharmacy attracting herbalists from all over the world — including the violet-flowered monk's hood *Aconitum compactum*, which contains many poisonous alkaloids that have found a use in homeopathic medicine to reduce fever and diminish the pain of neuralgia, lumbago and rheumatism, and mezereon (*Daphne mezereum*), whose bark has been used effectively in the treatment of snakebite, while chewing slices of the root is said to cure toothache.

The range of animal life to be found at Monte Baldo also reflects the variety of habitats. The summit is home to such typical montane birds as black grouse, rock partridges, alpine choughs, ravens and water pipits; recently, local naturalists have reported the return of the golden eagle. The thick maquis which clothes the sunnier slopes is alive with birdsong in the spring, its more notable occupants including melodious warblers, wrynecks, redstarts and red-backed shrikes. Conifer woods provide a haven for nutcrackers, nightjars and tawny owls, while thousands of swifts and alpine swifts gather over Lake Garda on migration, providing food for the occasional passing hobby.

Substantial herds of roe deer also inhabit the more thickly vegetated areas, while the brown bears occasionally stray into the region from the Trentino parks to the north. Plans are under way to reintroduce marmots and chamois to Monte Baldo's highest ridges, as well as red deer to the forest. Green lizards, wall lizards and slow-worms are typical denizens of the sunnier slopes, while small pools and slow-moving streams near the summit contain populations of alpine newts, distinguished from those found in the rest of Europe by their heavily spotted throats and red bellies.

For walkers Baldo is one of Veneto's most tantalizing pre-alpine chains, and busy as a result, especially around the Malcesine funicular which in summer brings hordes of tourists up from the lake shores. But if you

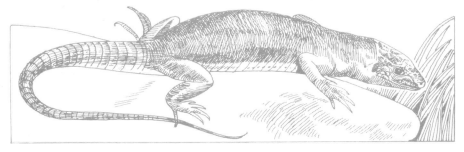

The large elegant green lizard is a sun-loving species which favours dense vegetation. It climbs expertly in search of large invertebrates, fruit and even the eggs and young of small birds. The bright green males are unmistakable, but the females are usually brownish.

come here off-season, you will have only the views and blustery wind for company. The most popular route is the well-worn ridge path, but there are quieter trails on Baldo's northern and eastern flanks.

Unfortunately, tourists and outdoor enthusiasts are disrupting Baldo's natural equilibrium. Some experts are adamant that the damage has already been done. A proposed park of 10,000 hectares (24,700 acres) is still some way off, which leaves two tiny reserves as Baldo's only environmental armour: the Lastoni-Selva Pezzi, which protects montane species, and the Gardesana, a sanctuary for Mediterranean relict plants on the lake shore.

BEFORE YOU GO
Maps: Kompass 1:50,000 *Lago di Garda-Monte Baldo* (Sheet 102).
Guidebooks: G. Corra, *Sui Sentieri del Monte Baldo* (walking guide, CAI 1983); E. Cipriani, *Il Monte Baldo* (Tamari 1987).

GETTING THERE
By car: A4 W from Verona (Peschieri exit) and SS249 on Garda's E shore to Malcesine (with minor roads for the interior). Entry to E flanks from SS12 (Verona-Trento) and unclassified lanes.
By rail: stations at Peschieri (Milan–Verona main line) and stopping trains (7 daily) on Verona-Bolzano line for stations in the Adige valley.
By bus: buses between all points on Garda, and in the Adige valley from Verona and Rovereto.

WHERE TO STAY
Vast accommodation and organized camping possibilities on Garda, with free camping allowed on Monte Baldo. More central rooms can be found in Prada, Brentonico and Ferrara.
Refuges: CAI run 5 refuges — Altissimo, Telegrafo, Chierego, Cornetto and Mondoni; contact tourist offices or CAI, Stradone Maffei 8, Verona, T: (045) 30555.

ACTIVITIES
Walking: steep routes from Garda can be avoided by using the lifts at Prada and Malcesine. Most popular walk is from the Rif. Chierego (at the top of the Prada lift) along the main Baldo ridge to the Telegrafo hut (5hr, red-white markings). You can also hike the ridge S to the Telegrafo (4hr) from the Malcesine lift via Cima Valdritta (2,218m/ 7,276ft).
    Walks from the E side leave from around Ferrara; to Bocchetto di Naole (2hr); from Novezzina to Telegrafo (3hr); from Avio in the Adige to the Telegrafo via Cavallo di Novezza (5hr).
Skiing: small resorts at Brentonico, Prada and above Malcesine. Cross-country routes around Prada and Ferrara.
Windsurfing: Torbole on Garda's N tip is the lake's main centre.
Mountain biking: whole area excellent, with many old military roads. The Furioli office in Malcesine rents bikes from the top of the lift, allowing a 4–6hr descent to the lake shore.
Ecology: the WWF at Caprino Veronese (at the southern end of the ridge) runs excursions and work-camps on Monte Baldo: Via Unità d'Italia 8.

FURTHER INFORMATION
Tourist offices: Via Capitanato, Malcesine, T: (045) 740 0044; Via 4 Novembre, Ferrara, T: (045) 722 0058; San Zeno (Prada 10km/6 miles), T: (045) 728 5076.

Monti Lessini and Pasubio

Small massifs north of Verona known for wild flowers and limestone scenery (3,650ha/9,000 acres)

I first saw the Lessini mountains, or *le piccole Dolomiti* ("little Dolomites") as they are nicknamed, while travelling north from Verona to Bolzano. Ready as you are to see the Dolomites towards the end of this journey, it comes as an interesting surprise to find the Dolomitic features of the Lessini while passing the eastern side of Lake Garda.

Of similar, though wilder, character is the adjoining massif of Pasubio to the north-east, reaching 2,235m (7,332ft). There are many who would like to see this extraordinary karstic landscape made into a national park; it is already a *zona sacra*, a sacred memorial to the dead of World War I — the territory was one of the most bitterly contested in Italy.

It is an area of tortuous ridge and valley relief, complex geology and mixed soils, and is far enough south to benefit from both alpine and Mediterranean influences. The resulting profusion of flowers is best seen around Lora, Val di Ronchi and Monte Summano (1,299m/4,261ft), the last a contender with Monte Baldo for the title of "Garden of Italy".

Alpine lilies — the red and the martagon — are here, while edelweiss occur not individually, but in entire meadows. Narcissi are also present but in smaller numbers. The great range of woodlands are home to such birds as the black woodpecker, pygmy owl, rock partridge, golden eagle and short-toed eagle, ptarmigan, black grouse, honey buzzard and the eagle owl.

Before you go: use tourist offices in the absence of park centres.
Getting there *By car:* SS12 from Verona to Rovereto; SS46 from Vicenza to Rovereto, with minor road access into both massifs (especially from Ala).
By rail: station at Ala on Verona–Bolzano line.
Where to stay: at Rovereto, Ala and Mas.
Activities *Walking:* many footpaths, old military roads and CAI marked trails; contact CAI, Stradone Maffei 8, Verona, T: (045) 30555; and CAI, Contra Reale 12, Vicenza, T: (0444) 545 369.
Further information *Tourist offices:* Via Roma 15, Folgaria, T: (0464) 71133; Via Dante 63, Rovereto, T: (0464) 30363; Piazza della Chiesa, Bosco Chiesanuova, T: (045) 705 0088.

Parco Nazionale delle Dolomiti Bellunesi e Feltrine

Southernmost Dolomite massif and national park (31,000ha/76,600 acres) formed from 4 main reserves: Vette Feltrine (2,764ha/6,830 acres), Piani Eterni (5,463ha/13,400 acres), Monti del Sole (3,500ha/8,600 acres) and the Schiara Occidentale (3,172ha/7,800 acres)

B elluno's Dolomites, the least known of these extraordinary mountains, are a disjointed group of massifs that form the last of the Alps before the Veneto plains to the south. A series of reserves have been made into a single national park in an area that has been described as a "living nature encyclopaedia".

The most important reserves run from west to east in an arc above Belluno and the Piave valley. In a coronet above Feltre lie the peaks of the Vette Feltrine, gathered around Monte Pavione (2,334 metres/7,657 feet). Moving north-eastwards we come to the upland plateaux and less lofty heights of the Piani Eterni, the "Eternal Plains"; and finally the highest and wildest areas, the Monti del Sole, the "Mountains of the Sun", and the Schiara Occidentale, dominated by Monte Schiara (2,563 metres/8,408 feet). Each reserve is divided from the next by one of a series of deep valleys, the Canale di Agordo, the Valle di Canzoi and the Canale del Mis.

The Bellunesi, though, are not a poor person's Dolomites. Some parts have the crowds of the northern playgrounds, around Monte Schiara's VII Alpi refuge, for example, but for the most part these mountains are wild and unvisited. Paths are long and lonely, and free of the route-marking of the other more popular parks. Roads rarely venture on to high ground, serving instead to link the little villages in the Piave valley below. Yet tracks are there if you want them, along with cosy refuges like the Feltrine's Dal Piaz hut, a throwback to the Dolomite hiking traditions of a century ago. And if you miss the refuges, you may always stumble across the *pendane*, ancient stone sheep pens, long-standing memorials to the area's pastoral tradition.

These paths and huts allow unlimited excursions into the remote and inspiring landscapes of the Bellunesi: to the wild valleys in the Schiara, for instance, for those with a passion for the worst nature can throw at them; or to the limestone wastes and glacial cirques (or *buse*) of the Vette Feltrine; to Monte Pizzocco below the cave-riddled Piani Eterni, a peak whose 800-metre (2,600-foot) ramparts have been compared to the Matterhorn; to the Gusela del Vescova, a rock needle below Pizzocco, beloved of many alpine climbers; the great gorges of the Ardo and Orrido di Val Clusa; or to the intimate, still Lago di Stua, hidden away in the Caorame valley.

Just an hour or so from the beautiful bedlam of Venice, all these make great escapes, not only for those in search of mountain respite, but also for botanists and naturalists. Whatever these Dolomites might lack in height when compared to their cold neighbours to the north, they make up for in warmth from their more southerly latitude. Protected from the harshness of the uplands, flora and fauna benefit from a mix of alpine and Mediterranean habitats.

Below the typical alpine forests of firs and pines lie the sunnier mixed woodlands of the south, interspersed with rich meadows, known as *malghe*. Spring heralds the appearance of such delightful flowers as *Iris pallida*, subspecies *cengialti*, endemic to north-east Italy and particularly abundant on Monte Cenglio and Monte Mauro; also its close relative the grassy-leaved iris (*Iris graminea*), with its distinctive peach-plum

perfume; and the beautiful, highly scented yellow lily *Hemerocallis lilioasphodelus*, known only in the foothills of the south-eastern Alps.

Two of the classic alpine amphibians, the alpine newt and the alpine salamander, are found here, together with several of peninsular Italy's 15 species of snake. Both adder and asp are known to occur, and are poisonous. However, there is no more chance of receiving a fatal snake-bite than of being struck by lightning. It goes without saying that you should never handle or provoke venomous snakes, and should avoid walking barefoot or in open shoes through areas where they occur.

Eagle owls and pygmy owls haunt the forests, together with capercaillie, hazel grouse and grey-headed woodpeckers, while the more open areas above the tree-line support black grouse and rock partridges. Birds of prey are also common, including up to seven pairs of golden eagles and five to six pairs of black kites, as well as a few honey buzzards. The lower slopes often attract short-toed eagles, the only large birds of prey (with a wingspan of around 1½ metres/5 feet) which hover like kestrels while searching for prey. They feed mainly on snakes and lizards and can some-times be seen flying along with the tail of one of these half-swallowed reptiles trailing from their beak.

Larger animals are enjoying something of a renaissance. Hunting, as ever, was the problem in the past, as you will gather if you visit Belluno's little church of San Stefano where a locally found Roman sarcophagus depicts a hunting scene involving deer and wild boar. Both animals still survive, though not, sadly, the bear or the wolf which were harried to extinction in the last century. Chamois and roe deer are both widespread, red deer a little less so, and the mouflon and fallow deer are being introduced. Ibex which had been intro-duced into the Parco Nazionale del Gran Paradiso have subsequently been moved to this region and are now already estab-lished around Cadore and Ampezzo valleys' lying just to the north of Bellunesi proper.

Lush vegetation thrives on the Pian del Gat in the Parco Nazionale delle Dolomiti Bellunesi.

BEFORE YOU GO
The body with responsibility for the reserves is the Azienda di Stato per le Foreste Demeniali, Via Gregorio XVI 8, Belluno, T:(0437) 24830.
Map: Kompass 1:50,000 *Alpi Bellunesi — Vette Feltrini.*
Guidebooks: P. Rossi, *Il Parco Nazionale delle Dolomiti* (Tamari 1970); C. Cima, *Andar per Sentieri in Veneto* (De Agostini 1989, a walker's guide); C. Lasen, *Guida Botanica delle Dolomiti di Belluno* (Manfrini 1977).

GETTING THERE
By car: routes to Belluno and Feltre which are connected by the SS50. Roads from this serve the reserves: SS203 to Monti del Sole and Schiara Occidentale; the SS50 winds round the western end of the Vette Feltrine; and a minor road from the SS203 gives access to the Piani Eterni.
By rail: there are 2 lines to Belluno and Feltre: from the Venice–Udine line (change at Sacile, 10 direct trains from Venice daily); and from the

Padua–Calalzo link (10 daily). Information, T: (0437) 25438.
By bus: services for local villages from Belluno and Feltre.

WHERE TO STAY
Feltre is one of the region's most delightful towns, with ample accommodation; other shelter available at Belluno, Agordo and Croce d'Aune.
Outdoor living: campers are not welcome in the reserves, but there is plenty of scope for pitching tents (on high ground if necessary) outside their confines.
Youth hostel: Ostello Feltre, Piazza Maggiore, Castello di Alboino, Feltre, T: (0439) 81188.
Refuges: contact CAI, Via Ricci 1, Belluno, T: (0437) 26841; and CAI, Porta Imperiale 3, Feltre, T: (0439) 81140.

ACTIVITIES
Walking: maps and trail details are available from tourist offices (and also marked on Kompass map). The most

popular walk is from Gioz to the Rif. VII Alpini in the Schiara; trails otherwise are some of the quietest in the Dolomites.
Birdwatching: LIPU, Via Feltre 17, Belluno, T: (0437) 212 423.
Ponytrekking: there are stables in many areas, with a centralized information centre: Associazione Turismo Equestre Feltrino at the tourist office in Feltre, T: (0439) 2540. Treks are also organized by the Comando Forestale at Cellarda, T: (0439) 89520.

FURTHER INFORMATION
Tourist offices: Belluno and Feltre offices are organized very much to serve the walker, with maps and assorted leaflets on the surrounding country: Via Pesaro 21, Belluno, T: (0437) 24854; Largo Castaldi 7, Feltre, T: (0439) 2540.

Parco Nazionale delle Dolomiti Bellunesi

black kite, sparrowhawk, buzzard and short-toed eagle at higher altitudes. Many warblers visit the forests of northern Italy, and one of the most common is the Orphean warbler. It can be recognized by its prominent white eye, dark cap, white throat and grey-brown plumage, if not by its loud, thrush-like song. Nests of the Orphean warbler will be hard to spot as they are tightly woven into the dense undergrowth for protection from predators.

Being karstic terrain, the region is also known for its caves, notably the Bus de la Lum (180m/590ft below ground) and Bus della Genziana (580m/1,902ft below ground). The latter has recently been made Italy's first speleological reserve.

Foresta del Cansiglio

Pastoral plateau and Veneto's largest ancient forest reserve

Travelling south from Belluno, the ancient forest of Cansiglio is the last area of wilderness before you reach the Venetian Adriatic. In between, the plains of the Veneto and Emilia-Romagna are unremarkable.

One of only a handful of big "historic forests", as the Italians call their relict woodlands, Cansiglio was once much bigger. To the Venetians it was the "Wood of Oars", the timber being used to make oars for the galleys of the Republic. From 1550 to 1830 its extent was reduced from 57,000ha (140,800 acres) to 14,000ha (34,600 acres). Under Austrian ownership it was further reduced to its present size of

6,600ha (16,300 acres). Though still run as a commercial forest, it enjoys a hunting ban and extensive conservation care.

Two-thirds of the trees are beech, the rest are pines, here unfortunately threatened by a pest called *Cephalia arvensis*. Forest agencies have resisted the use of insecticides, both to protect the forest's ecological balance, and because of the danger to the public.

Peace and wilderness can be found in the forest recesses, and more especially in the amphitheatre of dolomitic mountains, culminating in Monte Cavallo (2,250m/7,381ft), that cradle the plateau to the north. Over 1,000 roe deer share this tranquillity, along with red deer that have escaped forest reserves of "acclimatization" before their time. Plans are also afoot to try to introduce the lynx.

Long summer strolls should bring you in sight of many forest birds: the black woodpecker, black grouse and capercaillie being the most prized, and raptors such as the

Before you go: botanical garden, museum and visitors' centre in the hamlet of Pian di Cansiglio, T: (0438) 581 757.
Maps: IGM 1:25,000 *Bosco di Cansiglio* and *Puos d'Alpagao.*
Guidebook: G. Spada, *Il Cansiglio* (Tanmari 1984).
Getting there *By car:* A27 to Vittorio Veneto from the S, SS51 to Belluno from the N, and then minor road access from both towns.
By rail: station at Vittorio Veneto.
Where to stay: hotels at Pian di Cansiglio, Piancavallo, Belluno, Vittorio Veneto, Tambre and Pieve d'Alpago. Camping is allowed outside the reserves.
Activities: several nature trails, and large areas ideal for walking, ponytrekking and cross-country skiing. Ski-lifts and piste at Pian del Cansiglio, Nevegal and Tambre.
Tourist offices: Piazza di Popolo, Vittorio Veneto, T: (0438) 57243; Piazza dei Martiri 1, Tambre, T: (0437) 49193; Centro Servizi Turistici, Nevegal, T: (0437) 298 321.

Alpi Giulie-Carniche

*Mountain chains in the eastern Alps;
proposed Parco Nazionale delle Alpi
Tarvisiane (30,000ha/75,000 acres)*

𝄞𝄞𝄞

Italy's north-eastern corner is almost a peninsula jutting into foreign land; a remote mountainous frontier region where four cultures meet. Friulians, Slavs and Austro-Germans have fought the Italians ever since their ancestors first descended on the Roman Empire. As a result, perhaps, of this proximity to borderland, much of the forested uplands remains an uninhabited and wonderfully unspoiled wilderness.

An ineffable air of romance hangs over the region, where vast seas of firs, often laden with snow, evoke the wilderness of Russia in one of the coldest corners of the Alps. Walkers can expect the crisp crunch of snow underfoot. On average, four to five metres falls each year (10 metres/33 feet in 1951!), and permanent snow lies as low as 2,000 metres (6,500 feet), a thousand metres lower than in the Western Alps.

Still more, though, the romance comes from the proximity of the east, from the feeling you are on the threshold of a divide far greater than that created by international boundaries. Imagine you are standing on the bridge at Tarvisio, heart of this region and, except for Trieste, Italy's most easterly town. Drop a stick into the river and in one's imagination, at least, it will make its way via the Gail and

(Overleaf) An early morning mist lies over the Alpi Carniche, a mountain range that fills Italy's north-eastern corner.

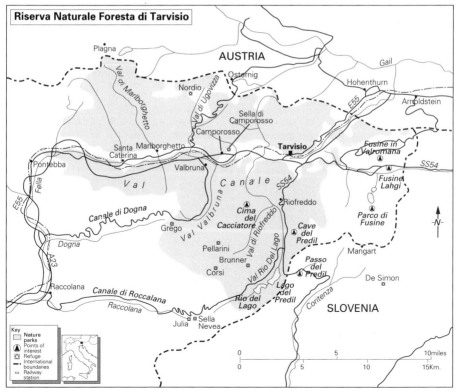

Riserva Naturale Foresta di Tarvisio

Plagna

AUSTRIA

Gail

Osternig

Hohenthurn

Val di Marlborghetto

Nordio

Val di Ugovizza

E55

Arnoldstein

Sella di
Camporosso

Camporosso

Santa Marlborghetto
Caterina

Tarvisio

Fusine in
Valromana

Pontebba

Valbruna

SS54

Fella

Val

Canale

SS54

Fusine
Lahgi

Canale di Dogna

Val Valbruna

Riofreddo

Cima
del
Cacciatore

Val di Riofreddo

Parco di
Fusine

-N-

Grego

Cave
del
Predil

Dogna

Pellarini

A23

Brunner

Passo
del
Predil

Mangart

Corsi

Raccolana

Canale di Roccalana

Val Rio Del Lago

Lago
del
Predil

De Simon

Rio del
Lago

Predil

Coritenza

Raccolana

SLOVENIA

Julia

Sella
Nevea

Key
☐ Nature parks
▲ Points of interest
◻ Refuge
- - - International boundaries
◻ Railway station

0		5		10miles
0	5	10		15Km.

Drava tributaries to the River Danube and eventually the Black Sea. Now walk a short way up the road and drop another stick into the River Fella. This small homage will float the other way, bobbing and weaving its way down the tortuous course of the River Tagliamento until it reaches the Adriatic Sea.

Up on the mountains, too, the landscape faces both ways. The barbarian route of invasion along the Val Canale naturally divides the region into the northerly Carnic Alps, running along the Austrian border, and the Julian Alps to the south of the valley. Both classified as pre-Alps, their heights, typically around 2,000 metres (6,500 feet), are generally lower than the Alps proper, though the Julian peaks rise to 2,753 metres (9,032 feet) at Iôf di Montasio. Whereas the lower Carnic mountains are rounded in appearance, the Julian Alps have the more familiar alpine profiles — jagged and glaciated.

In spite of the harsh winters, some marvellous varieties of flowers spring up. Alongside alpine staples such as edelweiss and gentians, there is the endemic product of its unique position, the *Papaver kerneri*, a yellow-flowered poppy. Others are the one-flowered cushion saxifrage (*Saxifraga burserana*), Einsel's columbine (*Aquilegia einseleana*), the carnic lily and, most famous of all, the dainty figwort *Wulfania carinthiaca*. This blue-flowered wonder is among Italy's rarest blooms, found above Pontebba on the flower-strewn meadows of the Passo di Pramollo (*pra-mollo*, "damp field"). To find it elsewhere you will have to visit Albania.

If Pramollo in the western Carnic range takes the floral honours, however, the Julian Alps have the edge when it comes to scenery. Their spectacular ridges bear the classic alpine imprint of glacial friction, with knife-edge ridges of splintered limestone, dolomitic in places, and towering rock walls like those on the north face of Mangart (some of the Alps' most demanding climbs). Elsewhere paths lead to the huge cwm at the head of the Valbruna, the moraines of Massa Pirona and Massa Marinelli (the Alps' biggest), and along the U-shaped valley of the Dogna.

These mountains are some of Italy's finest for larger fauna, thanks mainly to the lynx and brown bears that have strayed from their fecund families in the Triglav National Park of neighbouring Slovenia. Your best hope of spotting these shy creatures is to make for the highest reaches of the Val Uque, Val Bartolo or the windy bleakness above Cave del Predili.

Large herbivores are more readily seen, especially roe deer, of which there are some 2,000, and chamois, thought to number around 1,500. Red deer can muster 700, and ibex are growing in numbers on Monte Cacciatore ("Mountain of the Hunters"), of all places, having been introduced from Piedmont's Gran Paradiso. Hunting was banned in 23,000 hectares (57,000 acres) of State forest from 1980, a curb that benefited deer, as their numbers show, but also wild boar and lesser mammals such as stoat, red squirrels and badgers; all now multiplying at a prodigious rate.

The same is true of local avifauna, with birds now somewhat safer from hunters. The Julian Alps have the largest confirmed population of golden eagles in the Alps. Up to ten breeding pairs nest among the high mountain crags. Each pair has two or three nests which they use in rotation. Their soaring spirals during courtship are well-worth watching. Sometimes as they roll to dive earthwards they fly so close their talons appear to link. Sporadic visits from Balkan-based griffon vultures are also made to the region. Such abundance is a product of both a genuinely wild environment and, for once, of a park that seems able to look after the ecology.

At present the only fully protected area is the Fusine lakes, the sort of spot that for all its relative popularity (and this is still a region largely unknown, even to Italians) *must* be visited by any lover of the outdoors. A pair of glacial lakes picturesque beyond words, they are framed by Mangart's soaring mountain walls and virtually surrounded by forest stretching as far as the eye can see. Walks in the area, though short and simple, are some of Italy's most enchanting.

BEFORE YOU GO

For information on forests and the proposed park call at: Ufficio Forestale, Via delle Segherie, Tarvisio, T: (0428) 2039; also at the tourist office, Via Roma 10, Tarvisio, T: (0428) 2135.
Maps: Tabacco 1:50,000 *Alpi Giulie* (Sheet 8); IGM 1:25,000 14 III NE *Fusine in Valromana* (for the Fusine lakes walk).
Guidebooks: G. Buscaini, *Alpi Giulie* (CAI-TCI 1970).

GETTING THERE

By car: A23 Udine-Tarvisio from the S; SS52 from Cortina and the W. Handy lanes strike into the Valbruna, to the Val Raccolana, to Slovenia (SS54) and the Fusine lakes (access via the SS54 E of Tarvisio).
By rail: international main line Venice–Tarvisio–Vienna serves the area, with useful halts — as at Ugovizza — for walks in the Carnic mountains, Valbruna and Val di Ugovizza (5 stopping trains daily).
By bus: services to all centres in the Val Canale and Val Raccolana from Udine and Tarvisio.

WHERE TO STAY

Most hotels are in Tarvisio, with other options at Camporosso and the ski resorts of Pontebba, Valbruna and Sella Nevea.
Outdoor living: is permitted except in Fusine reserve; small site at Camporosso, the Da Cesco, T: (0428) 2254 (open all year).
Refuges: 16 refuges and bivouacs owned by CAI; the huts are open July–Sept and winter weekends. The most popular are: Zacchi (above the Fusine lakes), Nordio (Val di Ugovizza), Corsi ai Piedi (Iôf Fuart) and the Pellarini.

ACTIVITIES

Walking: the Fusine lakes trek is the most popular, taking in lake, forest and open mountain scenery; follow the tarmac road to the shore, the track to the Rif. Zacchi and then the path to the foot of the Mangart rock walls (with an optional side trail to the Nogara bivouac). Complete the circuit by descending to the lakes (3½hr, red-white marking).

Other fine walks in the Julian Alps include: the magnificent climb from Sella Nevea to the Corsi hut (5hr); from Lago del Predil (9km/6 miles E of Sella Nevea) to the Rif. Brunner (5hr); the traverse of the Valbruna and ascent to the Rif. Pellarini.

In the Carnic Alps: from the Rif. Nordio in the Val di Ugovizza to Monte Osternia; from Coccau (above Tarvisio) to Monte Goriane (4hr). You could also walk the last stage (2 days) of the long-distance *Traversata Carnica*, which runs the length of the Carnic range from Sesto in the Dolomiti di Sesto to Tarvisio.
Skiing: the area ranks as one of Italy's finest cross-country playgrounds, with 70km (43 miles) of routes around Tarvisio (and summer skiing above Sella Nevea). Main winter resorts are Sella Nevea, Valbruna and Pontebba, with nearby centres in Austria (Arnoldstein and Villacher Alpe).

Laguna di Caorle

Regional nature park of wetlands and lagoons east of Venice (8,500ha/21,500 acres)

Caorle is the most exemplary of the lagoons on the Gulf of Venice, far from the pollution and tourist disturbance that is destroying neighbouring natural habitats.

For years its four basins — Zignago, Perera, Grande and Nuova — were unknown except to hunters and fishermen. The Grande is the only one with a full complement of wetland birds and vegetation and, most tellingly, one of the last wetland habitats off the Venetian Gulf where the otter still thrives. Some 15,000 birds winter here, skimming over misty waters

77

Little egrets congregate on the Marano Lagunare, a natural oasis cradled in the broad arc of the Venetian lagoons.

that are rarely more than 50cm (20in) deep. Myriad species of duck (notably pochard), geese and coots predominate in winter, giving way to large numbers of breeding waterbirds in summer, such as night and squacco herons, little egrets, and marsh and Montagu's harriers.

Before you go: for information on the park and accommodation possibilities visit the tourist office at Caorle: Piazza Europa 3, T: (0421) 81085.

Getting there *By car:* Santo Stino or Portogruaro exits on the A4 from Venice and then minor road access to spots on the lagoons.

By rail: station at Santo Stino.

Where to stay: wide range of lodgings in Caorle, including 2 campsites: San Francesco, at S. Margherita, T: (0421) 81085; and the smaller Falconera at the mouth of the lagoon, T: (0421) 84282.

Laguna di Marano and Laguna di Grado

Italy's second largest lagoon complex; wetland of international importance and WWF oasis (1,400ha/ 3,460 acres)

The Marano and Grado lagoons, the most northerly in the Mediterranean, form a vast wetland complex between the Isonzo and Tagliamento rivers, with its centre at Marano Lagunare on the northern shore.

Some 32km (20 miles) long and 5km (3 miles) wide, they are second in Italy only to the Venetian lagoons to the west, and yet considerably freer of the pollution that is killing their more famous neighbours.

In the interest of their innumerable breeding and migratory bird populations, the whole area has been declared "of environmental concern" by the regional council, and of international ecological importance under the Ramsar Convention.

It is a major staging post on the Adriatic migration route to Central Europe, a refuge whose thick vegetation and marshy surrounds form a natural defensive cover, leaving birds safe from hunters and predators, if not from the increasing level of pollution, most of which comes from

scoters.

There is also an interesting range of wetland flora. The deeper parts of the lagoon are covered with eel-grass, the mud flats have cord-grass and tasselweed, and permanently exposed banks have glassworts. The dunes are bound by marram-grass and couch-grass, while the freshwater channels entering the lagoon have areas of reeds, bulrushes and willows.

Before you go: there is access by boat to the WWF oasis in organized groups 1 Nov–31 Mar (though you can see birds throughout the region). Details can be obtained from WWF, Via Oderico da Pordenone 3, Udine, T: (0432) 290 895.

Getting there *By car:* Take the A4 from Venice and exit at Latisana to the SS14 which lies parallel, from which lanes strike off to points on the lagoon.

By rail: frequent trains from Venice to stations at Latisana and Cervignano.

By bus: hourly buses from Udine to Grado (1hr), and every ½hr from Cervignano to Grado.

Where to stay: at the delightful resort of Grado, or Marano, Latisana or Aquileia. Campsites at Grado, Marano and Aquileia.

Activities *Boat-trips:* into the lagoon from Grado (7 daily to Barbana) and Marano (sometimes in the area's traditional flat-bottomed punts). To Trieste (4 weekly) and Venice (Fri). Details, Adriamare, Piazza Carpaccio 5, Grado.

Further information *Tourist offices:* Via D. Alighieri 72, Grado, T: (0431) 80035; Via Latisana 42, Lignano Sabbiadoro, T: (0431) 71821; Piazza Basilica, Aquileia, T: (0431) 91087.

either Venice or Trieste.

No fewer than eight rivers drain into the Marano, and it is at the estuary of the westernmost river, the Stella, that the WWF has created a wildlife oasis.

As well as safeguarding local birdlife, another motive for the reserve was to protect the Stella's otters, creatures not found in the polluted adjoining rivers of the Ausa and Corno.

Flocks of mallard, teal, white-fronted geese abound and black tern are common. Tufted ducks are also numerous, as are the rarer goldeneyes (*quattrocchi*, or "four-eyes", in Italian).

Pride of the reserve are the 10–15 pairs of breeding marsh harriers. Gulls, cormorants and waders of all descriptions are present, along with birds that it can be difficult to spot in other Italian wetlands, such as the eider, scaup, long-tailed duck and velvet and common

An autumnal kaleidoscope of colours descends upon the Tarvisio's mighty forests.

Carso

Among the most interesting areas for botany and geology in northern Italy; proposed national park (20,000ha/50,000 acres)

You need little etymological skill to extract *karst* from Carso. Thought to be a word of Celtic origin meaning "a rocky place", karst now denotes a brand of limestone scenery of which this region is a natural museum.

Carso is a slender ledge, a compressed finger of Italy that reaches down the east coast of the Adriatic to link Trieste to the mother country. Much of the hilly region is geologically, not to say socially, a part of Slovenia. This is its chief appeal, bringing a little piece of the Balkans within the naturalist's grasp. It is one of Europe's great environmental crossroads: a wild confusion of central European, alpine, Mediterranean and Balkan habitats, with a correspondingly diverse flora and fauna.

Plants must weather both the intense summer heat and the icy winter blast of the *bora*, a buffeting north-easterly wind so strong that ropes are sometimes strung along the steeper streets of Trieste for support. No surprise, then, to find that the Carso's flora is not only different from that elsewhere in Italy, with one of the country's highest tallies of endemics, but that it is also among the most diverse, harbouring no less than 1,600 distinct species. One of the

more remarkable endemics is the knapweed *Centaurea kartschiana*, whose solitary heads of tiny pink flowers refuse to grow anywhere but under a drenching sea spray along the Carso coast.

Every season brings its bounty: the delicate blossoms of hawthorn, plum and cherry herald the spring; wild roses, gentians and more than thirty species of orchid are spectacular in summer; and cyclamens add even more colour to the woodlands in autumn. Carso is perhaps at its most photogenic in the autumn, when entire hillsides of red sumac blaze with the intensity of a deep sunset; bushes tinted, so the locals say, with the blood of 100,000 soldiers who fell here during World War I.

The botanical garden at Sgonico has been attempting the Herculean task of collecting at least a portion of Carso's remarkable flora. The garden is divided into eight areas, each replicating a different local habitat.

Flowers alone would be enough to justify the Carso's proposed national park status, even in an area neither high nor wild. The plethora of limestone features provides a further rationale. The special features start on the coast which is fringed by low cliffs; an unusual sight on the Italian Adriatic which, except for the Conero and Gargano promontories, is mostly flat. Many of the cliffs are sculpted into strange shapes, almost waves of stone; the most interesting to see are at Duino, Sistiano and Miramare (which also has Italy's only underwater WWF oasis).

Inland, erosion of the soft local limestone has produced features almost as numerous as the flowers: more than 2,000 caves pit the landscape, with honeycombs of galleries and subterranean lakes, swallow-holes and dry valleys. The baffling Timavo river rises across the border and then flows 40km (25

Up to 25cm (10in) long, the cave-dwelling aquatic olm has an ivory-coloured cylindrical body with poorly developed limbs and obvious pink gills. It inhabits underground streams and lakes in the karst region of north-eastern Italy and the Adriatic coast.

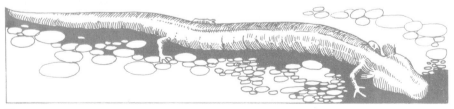

miles) underground to emerge in Italy with a volume 25 times as great as when it disappeared. Yet more mind-boggling is the Grotta Gigante, the largest cave in in the world open to the public — 107 metres (351 feet) deep and 208 metres (682 feet) broad — big enough to swallow St Peter's Cathedral in Rome.

The Val Rosandra is a microcosmic wilderness and magnet for local walkers and climbers. Birdwatchers cluster around three small adjoining areas of wetland on Lago di Doberdo, best known for its eight-metre (30-foot) changes in water level, a fluctuation that yields a rich variety of aquatic flora and fauna. Many hundreds of terns are the main attraction, but other birds inhabit this and other habitats of the Carso in large numbers all the year round. This is, after all, one of the stopping points on the Adriatic migration route.

Also of great interest to birdwatchers is the mouth of the River Isonzo, some 30 kilometres (20 miles) to the west of Trieste, where extensive mud flats and sandbanks attract breeding marsh harriers and purple herons, as well as large numbers of passage and wintering waterfowl, including red-throated and black-throated divers, red-necked and black-necked grebes; it is also one of the few sites in the Mediterranean region where eider duck can be seen in reasonable numbers in summer.

Compared with this wealth of birdlife, the Carso's other fauna may easily be missed. The range of climate and habitat yields scores of endemic invertebrates, as well as several typically Balkan reptiles which are unknown further west in Europe. These include the Balkan whip snake, the Dalmatian wall lizard and the Dalmatian algyroides (another lizard, the males distinguished by their orange-red bellies and blue throats), while Horvath's rock lizard is known from the karst region of north-eastern Italy and Slovenia.

The outstanding creature of the area is undoubtedly the olm, a cave-dwelling amphibian similar to the salamander, and the only member of its family in Europe; its nearest relatives occur in eastern North America. One unique feature is that the adults retain larval characteristics, including prominent external gills, but are nevertheless able to reproduce in this state — a feature known as neoteny.

Among alpine fauna, herds of roe deer are common in the remnant tracts of pine and oak forest and there have been sightings of bears in recent years.

BEFORE YOU GO
Map: IGM 1:25,000 53 I NE
S. Dorligo della Valle (for walks in the Val Rosandra).

GETTING THERE
By car: A4 Venice–Trieste motorway gives access to many minor roads along the coast N of Trieste.
By rail: frequent and fast trains on the main Venice–Trieste line.
By bus: buses recommended below leave from Trieste's Piazza Oberdan; for details, T: (040) 61080.

WHERE TO STAY
Hotels in Trieste cater for all tastes and budgets, with campsites at resorts along the coast and a youth hostel at Grignano: Ostello Tergeste, Via Miramare 331, T: (040) 224 102.

ACTIVITIES
Caving: (and climbing) information from CAI Commissione Grotte, Via Machiavelli 17, Trieste, T: (040) 60317.
Boat trips: boats ply the coastal route Mar–Sept (Pula–Trieste–Grado). Tickets from Via Duca degli Abruzzi, Trieste, T: (040) 69021.
Outings: the Carsanica botanical garden lies between Gabrovizza and Sgonico (46 bus). Open May–Sept, Sat 5–7pm, Sun 10am–12.30pm, T: (040) 820 002.

The land section of the WWF oasis at Miramare is open daily; for the underwater section (Apr–Oct, Sat only) contact the WWF in advance: Via F. Veneziano 27, Trieste, T: (040) 224 147.

Grotta del Gigante (45 bus half-hourly): guided visits Apr–Oct every ½hr, Nov–Mar hourly; closed Mon, T: (040) 227 312.

For the Val Rosandra take a 40 bus to S. Dorligo della Valle; for the Timavo river's re-emergence, a 43 bus to S. Giovanni del Timavo.

FURTHER INFORMATION
Tourist office: Castello di San Giusto, Trieste, T: (040) 309 298.

CHAPTER 4

The Po Delta and Northern Apennines

It was in the Marche, or Italian Marches, that I had my first taste of an Italian wilderness. Here I was taught three sharp lessons that could apply to almost anywhere in Italy: do not trust the maps; do not take a short cut through woods; and remember that Italy can be as cold, damp and miserable as any more desolate region of northern Europe.

Young, eager and chronically unhealthy, I had set off with a friend to see the Sibillini mountains in the south of the Marche. Plotting an easy course on the footpath, marked on our map with a thick red line, we headed towards the hills, keen to pitch our tent before what promised to be a storm of biblical proportions. Panting in the muggy air and mildly alarmed at my companion's observation that the colour of his sweat was brown, I soon realized that if the marked path had ever existed, it certainly did not now.

Paths that do exist in these parts are impermanent and were first mapped, it seems, from ancient hearsay or surveys carried out in the Mussolini era. A lot of vegetation can grow in fifty years, as we found out crashing through the woods in desperate search of our destination. Various tracks, either dry watercourses or eroded pathways, tempted us to follow them. But after a while they would peter out, leaving us to stagger blindly after the next false trail. At any other time I would have

The snow-streaked slopes of Monte Vettore loom over Castelluccio, at 1,452m (4,764ft) one of Italy's highest and most remote villages.

marvelled at nature's profusion, the densely packed trees, the thickness of the gorse bushes and, by contrast, the delicacy of the pink cyclamen among the yellowing grass. But right then I was too busy cursing, bleeding and wheezing.

Italian textbooks casually refer to this type of terrain as *sottobosco*, or undergrowth: an innocuous description on the page, but an impenetrable jungle on the ground and a challenge never to be undertaken lightly. In the way of these things, the promised storm broke some thirty seconds before the last tent peg had been hammered in. This was just long enough for us to get a fair old soaking and guarantee a long damp evening spent nursing wounds and cursing map-makers.

Our reward, though, came the next day as we gazed down into the mist-filled valleys of the Sibillini. Such mountain-top views are rare in the Marche and Emilia-Romagna, which are both predominantly low-lying areas. To find high wilderness you must go to their margins: almost to Umbria for the Sibillini, or to the border with Tuscany for the Casentini forests.

Emilia-Romagna, an area of rock-solid Communist voters, is the heartland of middle Italy. Like a vast flat corridor across the country, almost linking the Adriatic with the Mediterranean, it marks the division between the cold north of the Alps and the warm sunny south. Quiet pastoral hills stretch along the southern edge of its plain, gaining in height as you move further south until they break 2,000 metres (6,500 feet) and can safely be called the northern Apennines.

Emilia and Romagna were once separate Papal states. They were brought together during Italian unification but only given their present borders in 1947. Quite where one ends and the other begins is debatable. A local writer, Boldini, thinks it is a question of character not geography and has drawn up his own criterion for finding out where you are. Pull up at any house, he says, and ask if you might have a drink: while they give you water you are still in Emilia; when they give you wine you know you are in Romagna.

The first walkers to cross this area with any thought for route-making, of course, were the Romans, who drew a line on the map and built the Via Aemilia (nowadays spelt Emilia), a road running from north-west to south-east that has formed the region's axis ever since. In the Middle Ages Christian pilgrims travelled along it on their way to Rome, as did the Crusaders heading for Ravenna and thence the Holy Land. Agriculture thrived on the vast prairies on its flanks, earning it the titles of "bread basket" and "fruit bowl" of Italy. Pigs are still supposed to outnumber people here, and some of the famous Italian staples such as salami, Parma ham and Parmesan cheese help to make the regional capital, Bologna, the traditional culinary centre of Italy.

So much for the gourmet, but what is there to satisfy the wilderness-hungry traveller? Not very much is the answer, at least not when thinking of the tedious symmetry of the plains, fog-bound in winter and stifling in summer; but there is a great deal more in the Po delta, known as the "Italian Camargue" and one of Europe's great birdwatching areas.

The Po is Italy's longest river. However, despite its geographical importance separating the Alps from the Apennines, and the fact that its huge basin covers 15 per cent of Italy and supports a third of the country's population, it has few memorable landmarks. Unlike the Tiber, which is graced by Rome, the Po leads only to a bleak estuary on the Adriatic Sea and a view of the Balkans. Winding through the industrial lowlands it is now so full of nitrates that its aquatic wildlife is seriously threatened.

However, that is to be hard on a river which excites loyalty in writers and painters who are drawn to its subtle charms: rows of poplars across misty fields; long empty views over soft brown soils; and the mellow tints of autumn leaves promising winter evenings. Also, the Po is still a magnet for birds for whom the delta is a key stage on the migration route from Africa to Central Europe.

This route also takes them over the Marche which stretch south from the

COMACCHIO EELS

The bottle green waters of the Comacchio abound with fish but are noted, above all, for their eels. Fishing for them is an ancient craft, now fast vanishing, and best practised on the foulest and darkest of nights when storms rage in the Adriatic Sea.

European eels breed in the Sargasso Sea in the western Atlantic. Spawning takes place in spring, and in the summer the leaf-like larvae rise to the surface and catch the currents of the Gulf Stream. For up to three years they drift slowly eastwards until they arrive at the mouths of the European rivers where they undergo a transformation into elvers of between five and ten centimetres (two and four inches) long; they now have the recognizable shape of an eel.

The young female eels swim far upstream to the riverine headwaters, even making part of their journey over land to arrive in ponds and lakes not linked to the sea. Here they remain for anything up to 20 years, hiding by day and hunting by night, feeding on fish, carrion and even small water birds. The male eels, in the meantime, remain in the brackish lagoons and estuaries close to the sea.

Full-grown female eels may measure over a metre in length, but the adult males rarely reach half this size. As maturity approaches, the eels start to change in preparation for the 6,000-kilometre (4,000-mile) return journey to the Sargasso. Their bronze-green skins become coats of glistening silver to conceal them from predators in the open sea, their eyes enlarge for improved vision in the sunless ocean depths, and stores of body fat accumulate to sustain them on their journey (apparently they do not feed at all on the way). None will return, as they die after spawning.

Thus, in the autumn of their maturity the female eels travel back downstream to rejoin the males. The exceptionally high tides of the equinox bring a swell of salt water on to the lagoons and serve as a signal to the eels that the time has come to take to the open sea. But the exact moment of this mass exodus is carefully calculated by the Comacchio fishermen, and water-gates which date from Roman times are cranked into place. As the eels flood from the estuaries, the fishermen are waiting.

delta in a narrow strip of land that constitutes a large part of Italy's eastern coastline. "Marche" is derived from *marka*, the German for a boundary, and it is used here (as also in the case of the Welsh Marches), to describe a troubled frontier land. In ancient times it marked the border area disputed by early tribes such as the Umbrians, Picini, Sabines; and from about the tenth century AD it formed a border province of the Holy Roman Empire.

Apart from a rather drab coast, the Marche are a picture of beauty, the quintessence of pastoral Italy with olive groves, vineyards and green rolling hills as lovely as any of those in the more famous parts of Tuscany and Umbria. Undramatic as they are, the Marche combine one of the country's most civilized corners with pockets of Apennine wilderness where wolves, golden eagles and unspoiled walking country can still be found.

GETTING THERE
By air: Bologna's Guglielmo Marconi, T: (051) 311 576, handles major internal, and some international and charter, connections. Internal flights to Ancona's Falconara Marittima, T: (071) 56257. Summer charters to Rimini's Aeradria.
By car: Emilia-Romagna is the most important

communications centre in Italy, with major connections to all parts of the country. A1 Milan–Parma–Modena–Bologna–Florence–Rome, and access from Switzerland; A21 from Turin and France; A13 Venice–Bologna; A14 Bologna–Rimini–Adriatic coast; A22 Modena–Verona–Italian Lakes–

Dolomites–Austria.
In the Marche W–E routes are slow, the region's main axis being the A14 coastal link from Pesaro to Puglia. Motorway spurs run from the A14 to Urbino, Tolentino and Ascoli Piceno. Main trans-Apennine routes are the SS76 Ancona–Fabriano–Foligno and SS4 Ascoli–Rieti roads.

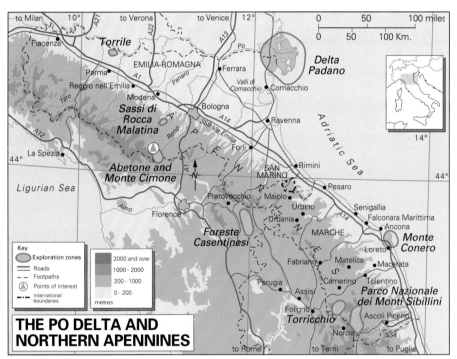

THE PO DELTA AND NORTHERN APENNINES

By rail: Bologna is the junction for national main lines: Rome–Bologna–Milan, Venice–Bologna, Bologna–Bolzano–Brenner and Milan–Bologna–Bari. The Marche's main route is the coastal line Rimini–Pesaro–Ancona, with a major link to Rome from Ancona via Fabriano, Foligno and Terni.

WHERE TO STAY
The main regional tourist offices are: Via Aldo Moro 38, Bologna, T: (051) 283 111 and Via G. Fabriano 9, Ancona, T: (071) 8061.
   For details of rural stays contact Agriturist, Via Lame 15, Bologna, T: (051) 233 321 and Agriturist, Corso Mazzini 107, Ancona, T: (071) 201 763.
ACTIVITIES
Walking: mainly low-level hill walking, except in the Sibillini and Cimone mountains. There is a long-distance path in 11 stages, the *Grande Escursione Appenninica*, along the Cimone group and a planned 8-stage path from the Conero promontory to the Sibillini.
Birdwatching: the Po delta is among Italy's finest birdwatching areas. LIPU

national headquarters are in Parma, Via S. Tiburzio 5, T: (0521) 33414, with regional branches at Pesaro, T: (0721) 452 734 and Bologna, T: (051) 244 552.
Skiing: the only organized facilities in Emilia-Romagna are around Cimone. In the Marche there are resorts in the Sibillini, which also offer excellent alpine and cross-country routes. Further modest centres are around Urbino and Macerata.
Ponytrekking: low hills and forests throughout both regions provide perfect trekking country. Contact tourist offices or the FISE regional committee for details: Via Padre Onorio 18, Parma, T: (0521) 38850. Riding centres in the Marche are at Fabriano, Macerata, Maiolo, Matelica, Senigallia and Urbania.
Fishing: The Po delta, the Adriatic and rivers of the Marche are a fisherman's paradise. For licences and information contact FIPS branches.

FURTHER INFORMATION
FIPS branches at Via Rizzoli 7,

The submerged leaves of the carnivorous greater bladderwort have small rounded bladders which catch tiny aquatic invertebrates by a trap-door mechanism.

Bologna, T: (051) 224 640; Via Settembre 3, Ascoli Piceno, T: (0736) 65292; WWF regional offices at Via Savenella 13, Bologna, T: (051) 332 233; and Via Marconi 103, Ancona, T: (071) 203 634.

Delta Padano

Major wetland habitat of lagoons, mud flats, marsh and islands at the mouth of the River Po; proposed national park of 30,000ha (75,000 acres)

The River Po crosses the entire breadth of northern Italy to feed an estuary that has become one of the most important river-lagoon habitats in Europe. Rising in the Alps near the border with France the river meanders along the southern edge of the plains of Lombardy before fanning out into the Adriatic Sea. Naturalists call the Po

delta's mosaic of marshes, dunes and islands the "Italian Camargue". Yet this is the last great European estuary that does not have environmental safeguards: Spain's Guadalquivir is protected by the Doñana National Park; in France the Rhône forms part of a 65,000-hectare (160,000-acre) regional park; and in Rumania the Danube estuary boasts reserves of 40,000 hectares (100,000 acres).
   A plan to turn the delta into a national park has been on the table for some twenty years. However, it has taken the growth of huge banks of algae in the Adriatic Sea, nurtured by the Po's contaminated discharge, to force the authorities to acknowledge what has long been known: that industrial and agricultural effluent has turned the Po into one of Europe's filthiest

rivers. Pollution is now being tackled, but the delta continues to be threatened in other ways. Drilling for natural gas proceeds unchecked while the commercial extraction of sand and gravel causes subsidence and adds to the already high risk of flooding along the river banks. Farmers press constantly for more marshland to be drained, as if the vast areas reclaimed since the 1950s were not enough. There is even a power station plumb in the middle of the delta, built only ten years ago despite widespread protests. Ecologists hope the clean-up campaign will help to realize the plan for a national park.

The park should extend from Chioggia, on the southern tip of the Venetian lagoon, to the woodlands of umbrella pine at Ravenna. If established, it will embrace a wide range of habitats: the woodlands of the Bosco della Mesola (already a reserve) and the *pinete*, or pine-woods, along the coast; the lagoons and marshes of Comacchio; the WWF oasis at Punte Alberete; and, dispersed throughout, thousands of hectares of shifting sand, islands and mud flats. In winter this vast flat landscape can be a breathtaking sight as chill winds sweep across grey scudding seas.

The Po has a delta which has evolved in textbook conditions. First, the Adriatic Sea is a long sheltered gulf fed by a sea virtually free of tides and currents. In any other place, the river's silt might have been dispersed, but here it has settled undisturbed at the river's mouth. Second, numerous tributaries add enormous volumes of silt gained from their upper reaches high in the mountains. The Po is estimated to deposit a ton of silt for every hundred tons of flowing water. Three other rivers, the Adige, Brenta and Reno, also empty into the sea nearby, adding their silt to the coastal waters.

Such is the scale of silt deposition that following the Po to its mouth becomes a difficult task. Having drifted and weaved through different courses over the centuries, the river has split into a leaf-skeleton of streams and channels, creating land one year, removing it the next. As it meanders seaward it loses its identity to such an extent that it is renamed several times: the Po della Pila, the Po di Goro, the Po di Venezia, the Po di Levante, the Po di Gnocca . . .

Just south of the Po delta lie the wetlands of the Valli di Comacchio, a paradise for waterfowl and birdwatchers. Thousands of birds pass through here on their migration route and spend the winter among its lagoons and marshes. Most noticeable, even to the casual observer, are the thousand or so bean geese, large grey geese with yellowish legs and bills, as well as a hundred or so greylag geese, distinguished by their pink legs. Up to 10,000 coot congregate here during the winter, accompanied by similar numbers of black terns, the commonest of the three European marsh terns. Rare species that are occasionally seen include great white egrets and broad-billed, marsh and curlew sandpipers.

Map: Delta Padano

Chioggia
Brenta
Foce del Brenta
Foce dell'Adige
Adige
Rosolina Mare
Foce del Po di Levante
to Rovigo
Rosolina
Foce del Po di Maistra
Contarina
Foce del Po di Maistra
Corbola
Taglio di Po
Ca' Venier
Pila
Porto Tolle
Scardovari
Mesola
Riserva Naturale Bocche di Po
Bosco Mesola
Goro
Codigoro
Delta del Po
to Ferrara
Bosco della Mésola
Grocchetta
SS309
A13
Comacchio
Foce del Reno
Valli di Comacchio
Reno
to Ferrara
Oasi di Punte Alberete
A14
Ravenna

Key
Nature parks
Points of interest
Refuge
International boundaries
Railway station

-N-

0   5   10miles
0   5   10   15Km.

Breeding birds are found in smaller numbers but in far greater variety. Garganey and shoveller, pochard and ferruginous duck represent the wildfowl; but it is the gulls and terns that are truly exceptional. Among the large colony of Mediterranean gulls, which are distinguished from the much commoner black-headed gulls by their "executioners' hoods" descending to the nape of the neck, you can spot small numbers of slender-billed gulls. Common terns and little terns are present in their thousands, interspersed with the much rarer (and somewhat larger) Sandwich and gull-billed terns. Bearded tits and purple herons raise their young in the shelter of the reed beds; while collared pratincoles prefer more exposed, often cultivated, land.

The islands in the Po delta also support breeding birds, in particular squacco herons, which have some sixty nests along the banks of the Po di Maistra. The brackish lagoons at Valle Bertuzzi, Lago delle Nazioni and Foce del Po di Volano have large numbers of Mediterranean gulls as well as wintering diving ducks, such as red-crested pochard, and black terns. As if anticipating the foundation of the national park, birds that had once vanished from Italy, such as the hen harrier and pygmy cormorant, are reported to have returned.

Mammals, by contrast, are scarce, with the exception of the red and fallow deer in the Mesola woodlands, the oldest populations in peninsular Italy. A few wild boar and perhaps a handful of otter prosper, along with hares, hedgehogs and weasels.

South of the Po delta there were once great forests on the coastal strip between Ferrara and Ravenna. Today, only the Mesola woodlands remain. Although man-made, they are known to be very old and were planted on reclaimed land, possibly by medieval monks or even by the Etruscans in pre-Roman times. After planting the woods were left alone and allowed to flourish. Mature oak, ash and holly rise above a lush forest floor, and through the sun-dappled glades roam several hundred head of deer. The beauty and tranquillity of these woods have been praised by generations of poets from Dante to Lord Byron.

BEFORE YOU GO
Maps: a variety of tourist maps of the delta is available within the park area.
Guidebooks: G. Ceruti, *Il Delta del Po, Natura e Civiltà*, (Signum 1983). *Zone umide del Delta del Po* and *Pinete di Ravenna* from the WWF in Ferrara. Numerous guides and leaflets from local tourist offices.

GETTING THERE
By car: the delta region extends 100km (60 miles) from N to S, with many access points. Take the SS309 from Venice and the N (this is the old *Via Romea*, or pilgrimage road to Rome). From Bologna and Ancona follow A14 to Ravenna, or A13 to Comacchio.
By rail: the Ravenna–Ferrara, Ferrara–Codigoro and Rovigo–Chioggia lines all serve the Delta region.
By bus: buses run to local towns from Padua, Ferrara, Rovigo and Ravenna.

WHERE TO STAY
Ravenna and Ferrara offer accommodation in every category. Locally, hotels may also be found in Rosolina Mare, Contarina, Porto Tolle, Goro, Comacchio and Sant'Alberto. There are numerous campsites along the entire coast (most open summer only).

The rare Italian spadefoot, or Padano toad, was discovered as late as 1873 near Milan, and occurs in the Padano-Venetian plain, Switzerland and Slovakia.

ACTIVITIES

Birdwatching: possible
virtually everywhere, though
the Comacchio, Argenta and
Campotto lagoons are
outstanding. For specialist
information and guided tours
contact LIPU, Via delle
Chiodare 3/5, Ferrara.

Boat-trips: in the summer there
are frequent small boat
excursions from a number
of centres. Traditional flat-
bottomed boats make trips into
the *valli* and canals. Key
departure points include Ca'
Tiepolo, Scardovari,
Pila, Ca' Venier and Taglio di
Po. Details from the Pro Loco
del Delta Padano at Porto
Tolle,
T: (0426) 660 531.

Fishing: for fishing trips at
sea and in the lagoons (and for
boat trips) contact: Cacciatori
Marino, Via Varsavia 10, Porto
Tolle, T: (0426) 81508; Gollino
Sullam, Ca' Vendramin, Taglio
di Po, T: (0426) 88019; Filli
Vicentini, Via Ponte in Ferro
8, Corbola, T: (0426) 95309.

Cycling: the flat terrain makes
ideal touring country, with
many embankment, forest and
canal-side routes. The TCI
publish cycle tours, available
from local bookshops, of the
following routes: Po di Levante
to Po di Maistra (starting at
Contarina), Po di Gnocca to Po
di Goro and Porto Tolle to Ca'
Tiepolo. There are also routes
within the Bosco della Mesola,
with bicycles available for hire.

FURTHER INFORMATION

The Pro Loco at Porto Tolle
(see above) has the most
comprehensive free
background material. Check
also local bookshops for
specialist pamphlets. The Po
Delta Group of Italia Nostra is
in Porto Tolle in Via Piazza.

Ecology: WWF at Contra Riela
12, Vicenza, T: (0447) 31777
and Via Mentana 19, Ravenna,
T: (0544) 35404.

90

Torrile

*Artificial wetland habitat
and LIPU reserve*

LIPU has created a refuge
for 175 species of birds by
returning cultivated fields to
their original marshland state.
This oasis, close to the banks
of the Po, has a variety of
environments, from canals,
islands and sand spits to lakes,
marsh and low-lying basins.
Alongside the oasis are nature
trails and observation towers
and, for the first time in an
Italian nature reserve, facilities
for the disabled.

The sanctuary supports
several species of heron and
numerous ducks and waders.
The waters are stocked with eel
and carp, and newts and lizards
have been introduced. Of
special interest is the rare
Pelobates fuscus insubricus,
a subspecies of the Italian
spadefoot toad, native to the
Padano-Venetian plain.

Freshly planted trees, such
as willow, oak, ash, alder, birch
and fruit trees, line the banks
and ditches. Introduced plants
include rarities such as the

carnivorous greater
bladderwort (*Utricularia
vulgaris*), which has bright
yellow flowers, and the floating
water-fern (*Salvinia natans*).

Before you go: LIPU's national
headquarters at Parma provide
a full range of information on
Torrile and most other Italian
birdwatching areas. They run
courses and visits to other local
reserves, including the Parco
del Tizzo (spring only) and the
Oasi del Cavaliere d'Italia at
Trescasali. The main office is
at Via S. Tiburzio 5, Parma,
T: (0521) 233 414. There is also
an office at the civic centre in
Piazza Garibaldi. For details
of courses and excursions,
T: (0521) 231 113.
Map: IGM 1:25,000 S. *Secondo
Parmense*.

Getting there: Take the N343
16km (10 miles) N of Parma to
Colorno; turn W on a minor
road to Torrile (4km/2 miles).

Where to stay: Parma offers
accommodation in every
category; for help contact the
tourist office: Piazza del
Duomo 5, Parma, T: (0521)
234 735. Ostello Cittadella is
a combined youth hostel and
campsite: Via Passo Buole 7,
T: (0251) 581 546.

Access: open daily 1 Sept–31
May.

Sassi di Rocca Malatina

Nature reserve with series of monolithic sandstone tors

Standing on one of the highest points in this reserve at 567m (1,900ft) you can gaze down the lovely Panaro valley spread out before you, or you can ponder the strange features of the area known as *sassi*, literally "stones". Representing nature at its most capricious, these are two groups of tors and rock outcrops that have been eroded into striking and often bizarre shapes amid the gently rolling hills south of Bologna.

The tors were formed by the weathering of soft surface sandstones, leaving more resistant rock beneath in the shapes of towers. Well-worn tracks weave among the *sassi* and the surrounding thickets of oak and chestnut, and just occasionally pass alongside violently bubbling pools of volcanic mud known as *vulcanelli*.

Italy's longest river, the Po, glides quietly to the Adriatic Sea between the marshes and islands of its complex delta.

The lower Sassi di Sotto are the most impressive, linked by ancient steps cut into the rock, and named after birds and animals.

The rocks are nesting places for many birds, in particular peregrine falcons. It was LIPU — very active in Emilia-Romagna — which pressed for the area to be declared a reserve, a status achieved in 1985. Sadly, there is some conflict between the organization and rock climbers who are accused of disturbing nests and scaring off potential breeding birds.

A well-known outcrop, the Pietra di Bismantova, a sacred place since prehistoric times and lauded by Dante, lies outside the reserve near Castelnovo ne' Monti. More spectacular even than the *sassi* is a high tableland of 1,000m (3,000ft) which rises sheer from the surrounding woodland. It is a landmark for miles around, popular with weekend trippers but nonetheless extraordinary enough to demand a visit.

Before you go: the park centre shares the town hall at Guiglia, T: (059) 792 412. The LIPU group at Modena has information and organizes guided tours of the park: Corso Grande 17, Modena, T: (059) 795 849.
Map: IGM 1:25,000 *Zocca* (Malatina); *Castelnovo* (Bismantova).
Guidebook: Valli dell'Appenninico Reggiano e Modenese, (CAI-TCI).
Getting there *By car:* Modena Sud exit on A1 for Rocca Malatina and then the SS623 via Vignola and Guiglia. From Bologna the SS569 to Vignola via Bazzano.
By bus: frequent bus services to Vignola from Modena and Bologna.
When to go: in spring, when the region around Vignola is covered with cherry trees in blossom.
Where to stay: at Zocca, 6km (4 miles) SE of the reserve, the 2-star Joli, T: (059) 987 429. Rooms also at Rocca Malatina, Guiglia and Vignola. No campsite within the reserve, but there is a year-round site near Zocca, the Montequestiolo, T: (059) 987 764.
Activities *Walking:* short strolls around the Malatina tors, and fine ascent of the Bismantova

(via Casale and Cornia) from the hermitage at the foot of the rock (3km/2 miles from Castelnovo).
Climbing: spectacular *via ferrata* on the Bismantova.
Further information *Tourist offices:* Palazzo Comunale, Zocca, T: (059) 987 073; Via Scudari 30, Modena, T: (059) 222 482.
Ecology: WWF, Corso Grande 17, Modena, T: (059) 222 161.

Abetone and Monte Cimone

Limestone mountains between Tuscany and Emilia-Romagna

Mountains make good boundaries, and few are as emphatic as the chain of ridges that marks the border between Tuscany and Emilia-Romagna. Known collectively as the Frignana, they curve gently eastward, gradually losing height to peter out in the modest hills above Florence.

They are the most westerly of three mountain groups that make up the northern Apennines, the two others being the Mugello and Montefeltro in the Marche. Away to the north stretch the hills of Emilia and beyond them the plains of the Po and Italy's industrial heartland. To the south lie the sunny hills of Tuscany — another country altogether.

The Frignana are the loftiest and most rugged of all the ranges in the northern Apennines. Heights of around 2,000m (6,500ft) match those of the more famous Abruzzi to the south.

These mountains have few visitors outside winter, when skiers crowd into Abetone and Cerreto. Monte Cimone, the highest point at 2,165m (7,102ft), is a favourite spot for skiing; a radio transmitter and a new road further increase the disturbance. Make instead for Monte Cusna, a long majestic crest north of the main ridge of Frignana, and connected to it by an outlier, the Lama Lite. Here you will encounter the simple delights of empty wilderness and fresh mountain air. Heavily wooded valleys, the Bargetana and the Abetina Reale, grace the slopes to the north and south.

Hikers should approach from the south, where the hamlet of Civago provides the most convenient starting base. Mountain huts are numerous and well distributed; the Battisti refuge on the Lama Lite (owned by CAI Reggio Emilia) is particularly welcoming. Ice-climbing and cross-country skiing are also possible on Cusna and nearby Monte Prato.

A distinguishing feature of the area is the Pistoiesi forests, the grandest of which are at Abetone, Maresca and Acquerino. Trees are mainly spruce, a species that enjoyed a huge expansion in Italy during the last Ice Age but has since retreated northwards. Fossils testify to the species' former southern extent at the Lago di Massaciuccoli near Pisa, nowadays an area of thoroughly Mediterranean character.

Wildlife, ravaged by hunting in the absence of any reserve authority, is scarce, though there are red and roe deer, mouflon and an estimated 50 marmots — survivors of a colony introduced by foresters in 1954.

As the mountains turn into hills towards Florence, so the forests become smaller, the main ones being the Alpe delle Tre Potenze in the south-east and the beech woods of Cantagallo in sight of the domes and spires of Florence.
Before you go *Maps: Sentieri dell'Appennino Modenese* (CAI Modena) and Multigraphic 1:25,000 (sheet 18) both indicate marked trails.
Guidebooks: A. Bietolini, *La Grande Escursione Appenninica,* (Tamari); *Valli dell'Appennino Reggiano e Modenese* (CAI-TCI 1984).
Getting there: from the N take A1 to Modena, SS12 to Pavullo and thence to Abetone — 50km (30 miles) of twists and turns.

From the S, exit A11 from Florence at Montecatini and use SS633 N to Abetone (60km/ 40 miles).
By rail: trains are of limited use. The nearest station is at Poretta on the Bologna–Pistoia line.
Where to stay: ample year-round accommodation in San Marcello, Abetone and Pievepelago. Pistoia is a good, albeit distant base.
Outdoor living: free camping is permitted. Campsites include Neve e Sol at Catigliano, T: (0573) 670 079; and Pinguino at Pian di Novello near Abetone, T: (0573) 673 008 (both open all year).
Refuges: numerous refuges, with the Battisti open July–Sept and winter weekends, T: (0522) 800 155. For information contact CAI, Via Ricasoli 7, Prato; CAI, Corso Garibaldi 14, Reggio nell' Emilia, T: (0522) 36685 and the Comunità Montana dell'Appennino at Pracchia, T: (0573) 630 7900. The only hostel is the Ostello Renzo Bizzarri in Abetone.
Walking: a long distance path, the *Grande Escursione Appenninica (GEA),* runs along the entire length of the ridge. The starting point is

92

Pracchia, which is 15km (9 miles) N of Pistoia on the SS632 (also situated on the Bologna–Pistoia rail line). The trail's most rewarding stretch, running through forests and marvellous Apennine scenery, is the long haul between Abetone and Cisa.

The most recommended of the shorter walks is the ascent of Monte Bondinaio (1,964m/ 6,443ft) from Lago Santo. This is 11km/7 miles S of Pievepelago and is accessible by road. Take trail 5 (marked red and white) to the Foce a Giovo, and then trail 7 W to the

summit, staying with the same path for the return to Lago Santo (4hr). **Further information** *Tourist offices:* Abetone, T: (0573) 60001; Gavinana, T: (0573) 66191; and Maresca, T: (0573) 64040.

Foreste Casentinesi

Forest reserves in the northern Apennines on mountain ridges between the Arno, Sieve and Savio valleys; proposed national park (10,600ha/26,200 acres)

I had hoped to catch the Casentini forests in their autumn splendour. As it turned out, I was a week early, with summer on the wane but still just holding out. The ground was a carpet of leaves and branches, wrenched from the trees by a late summer storm. Most were still green. But higher up the mountains where wintery winds were roaring off the Romagna plains, the leaves had started to turn. Their golden tints caught the evening sun, shining at last after a day of grey scudding clouds. Shiny new conkers and sweet chestnuts lay strewn on the ground; and squelching the fallen leaves underfoot released the distinctive wet smell of mulch from the forest floor.

Even as the forests clung to the last vestiges of summer, they were wild and chilly, their scale breathtaking. As I looked out from ridge-top eyries, no field or rock interrupted the mantle of sun-tinted trees. Views as far as the eye could see reached over line after line of wooded hills. All was breezy loneliness during a long solitary walk, my only human encounter a furtive couple bearing sacks of mushrooms.

These forests are the most important in the Apennines, if not in Italy. Straddling the border of Romagna and north-eastern

Tuscany, they contain a huge variety of woodlands, some pure and some mixed, dominated by firs, beech and mountain ash, but richly interspersed with chestnut, elm, lime, yew and oak. Most of the woods have been untouched for centuries, and even now are only felled to meet the minimum requirements of good husbandry.

Though you will be hard-pushed to find boundaries on the ground, the forests are loosely divided into a collection of reserves: Badia Prataglia, Campigna and Camaldoli, La Lamia and Sassofratino. They were acquired by the State in 1866 and 1914 and are subject to rigorous ecological supervision. Sassofratino, the first integral

The eagle owl, Europe's largest, lives in remote forested areas and hunts mainly at dawn and dusk. Although it feeds mostly on hares and game birds, such as capercaillies, the eagle owl is capable of taking prey up to the size of a young roe deer.

reserve in Italy (1959), is maintained as an ancient forest of immense scientific value. Entry here requires a special permit, but everywhere else access is free. Only the density of the woods will dampen your zeal for exploration.

The area's earliest settlers were twelfth-century Christian hermits, no doubt drawn by the woods' solitary and meditative tranquillity. Even today three important Franciscan monasteries — Camaldoli, Verna and Badia Prataglia — are the only human settlements.

Later the forests passed to the Grand Duchy of Tuscany, which used the biggest and straightest trees for its arsenal at Pisa. To qualify as masts for ships — the principal use for the trees — the trunks had to be 6 metres (20 feet) in girth and at least 28 metres (92 feet) high. You can still walk along the so-called *vie dei legni*, or "wood roads", which reached into the heart of the woods and along which the trees were transported. As many as 75 pairs of oxen were used to drag the biggest trunks to Pratovecchio on the Arno whence they were floated downstream to Florence. The journey took ten days, and another six if they were taken on to Pisa. Although the timber industry declined when supplies were exhausted by the building of railways and charcoal-burning (in Sassofratino alone there are ruins of 350 ovens), the local terrain, even in the forests' commercial heyday, was always too rugged for whole-sale exploitation.

The Apennines here are an unusual mixture of sandstone, schists and marls, creating the rich soils that nurtured the forests, but also producing steep bluffs and stratified outcrops, most marked on the highest northern margins. Given the scarcity of limestone, the more gentle slopes on the Tuscan side that ripple along as far as Vallombrosa reveal an unexpected play of streams and waterfalls in idyllic harmony with the woodland. Only the Ridracoli reservoir mars the surroundings,

set in the wildest area of the park north of the Romagna border. Roads have only begun to replace mule-tracks in the last few years. Even now they peter out in the higher mountains where tree cover is denser, such as on Monte Falco, Monte Falterona and Poggio Scali, all over 1,500 metres (5,000 feet). No doubt the inaccessibility of these forests has helped to preserve them to the present day. Although a national park has been promised, this is one place in Italy where such protection is unnecessary.

The careful management of foresters over the centuries has allowed not only trees but animals, plants and particularly birds to flourish. Among the communal chatter you may hear the desolate cry of the bullfinch or the bitter ring of the great spotted woodpecker and the near-hysterical laugh of the green woodpecker. Kingfishers dart over rocks splashed by streams, with kites and buzzards soaring above. Golden eagles once nested on Poggio Scali (1,520 metres/4,986 feet), between Camaldoli and Passo la Calla. Whether they still do is uncertain, for sightings are rare. Almost equally elusive are the goshawk, eagle owl and black woodpecker.

Many large mammals — rare in the Apennines — are found here, including 100 red deer and some 500 easily sighted roe deer. Numbers are increasing all the time. Wardens are concentrating on the Foresta della Lama, stocking the woods with mouflon and fallow deer, though not without some carping from purists who complain that they damage the trees and are not natural residents of the region. The otter is extinct here, but a candidate for reintroduction, given the abundance of water. Crested porcupines scratch the forest's low scrubby margins; but most remarkable is the recent reappearance of the Apennine wolf, its most northerly sighting to date.

The lattice of forest trails in the Casentini is ideal for easy strolls or mountain-biking and in winter provides perfect cross-country ski routes. Walks often follow mule-tracks and lumber roads or ancient paths between monasteries, whose lovely buildings complement a landscape the monks helped to

Musk thistles bring a touch of colour to the Val di Patino in the Monte Sibillini, a nesting site for a pair of Umbria's few golden eagles.

95

mould. If hikes among trees become too claustrophobic, high ridges and views are never far away. For dedicated yompers there is the *Grande Escursione Appenninica* (GEA), a 25-day long-distance route that includes a four-day traverse of the forests. With slight variations, ponytrekkers can also follow the trail.

Camaldoli has an alpine rescue call-out point, a salutary reminder that these are serious mountains, with disorientation a real danger if you lose the paths. This applies especially in winter, when snow lies in the valleys and on exposed ridges. Bear in mind, too, that in the dark depths of the forest, night falls early.

BEFORE YOU GO
Maps: IGM 1:25,000 *Pratovecchio, Monte Falterona, Badia Prataglia.* The tourist office at Poppi issues its own 1:25,000 *Carta turistica.* Other excellent, locally produced maps with paths and marked trails available from the bar at Camaldoli.
Guidebooks: A.Bietolini, *La Grande Escursione Appenninica*, (Tamari 1985) is a guide for walkers on the GEA long-distance footpath. Also M. Padula, *Sassofratino,* (Ministero delle Foreste 1982).

GETTING THERE
By car: there are many points of access to these extensive forests: from Florence and the W the SS67, SS556 and SS70; from Arezzo and the S the SS71 to Poppi and thence to Camaldoli; from Emilia-Romagna the SS67, SS310 and the SS310 (a beautiful N–S traverse of the region).
By rail: antiquated branch line from Arezzo to Stia. Ten trains daily, with useful halts at Bibbiena, Poppi and Pratovecchia.
By bus: services from Bibbiena to Stia, Bagno (via Badia Prataglia) and to Camaldoli, with summer-only link to the Eremo itself.

WHERE TO STAY
One of most easily reached bases is the 2-star Albergo Camaldoli at Camaldoli, T: (0575) 556 019. A fascinating

alternative is to stay in the monastery at Camaldoli itself: T: (0575) 556 021/556 044 or write c/o Foresteria dell'Eremo, 52010-Camaldoli. Badia Prataglia is also attractive, with cabins to rent in the woods themselves. Contact the tourist office (summer only), T: (0575) 509 054. More conventional farm accommodation is available near Badia at the Azienda Corsignano, T: (0575) 550 279.
Outdoor living: there is free camping in attractive wooded sites set aside by the forest authorities at Camaldoli and Castagno d'Andrea. Campsites are also located at Stia, Badia Prataglia and the Fonti del Menchino near Camaldoli, T: (0575) 556 075.

ACCESS
Free at all times, except for the *riserva integrale* at Sassofratino. For guided tours of this reserve contact the park centre at Pratovecchio.

ACTIVITIES
Walking: myriad possibilities for hikes of all lengths and standards. A 2-day portion of the GEA from Camaldoli to Castagno d'Andrea (red–white marking) crosses Monte Falterona and the best part of the forests. Favourite walks include the ridge circuit N of Badia via Passo dei Mandrioli and Passo dei Fangacci (5hr); the ascent of Monte Penna

(1,333m/4,373ft) from the Eremo via Prato alla Penna (2hr); the GEA section from Camaldoli to Passo della Calla, touching the Sassofratino reserve (4½hr).

FURTHER INFORMATION
The park headquarters are near Stia, at Pratovecchio, T: (0575) 58763. There are also forest ranger stations (Stazione Forestale) at Campigna, T: (0543) 980 174 and Camaldoli, T: (0575) 559 002. Camaldoli has a small museum devoted to the forests and their history.

Monte Conero

Mountainous promontory and rugged coastline (8,500ha/21,000 acres) with small nature reserve

While Italy's land mass was submerged during the Pliocene age, Monte Conero pushed up through the sea in splendid isolation. If you were stranded on its summit and you looked southwards across the vast expanse of sea, you would have seen the tips of the Gran Sasso and the Sibillini mountains appear as islands on the horizon.

This mighty promontory is still something of an island today, its jagged amalgam of marls, sandstones and limestone clearly visible from the sea and low hills of the Marche. As the most accentuated relief on Italy's east coast, it is the only headland to break the 500km (300 miles) of ruler-straight beaches that stretch from Ravenna to the distant Gargano peninsula.

In form Monte Conero resembles a cupola, thickly wooded in some places and barren in others, whose highest point of 572m (1,876ft) rears up spectacularly from the sea. To the south and west the promontory falls away in gentle slopes, most covered in dense, sometimes impenetrable, vegetation. To the north and east, dissected by ravines and gullies, rocky hills meet the sea as cliffs and headlands separated by tiny sandy coves.

Offshore, steeples of rock whose soft marls have been sculpted by the waves, stand out a brilliant white against the blue of the sea. Most striking are the Due Sorelle, the "two sisters", home to gulls and swallows, and peregrines poised to prey on migrating birds attracted by the tree cover of the promontory.

Only 1,000ha (2,500 acres) of the Conero are currently protected (park status has been requested for 20 years), and holiday homes have started to creep up the hillsides. Yet this still manages to be among the wildest of Italy's promontories.

The Conero is best known as an important refuge for flora, with many plants finding their southern or northern limits. More than a thousand species have been counted, including several extremely rare ones.

Among the rarest are *Bellevalia dubia* (found in grassy places, with greenish violet flowers in cylindrical spikes), *Fumana arabica* (of the rock rose family, with yellow flowers) and *Asphodeline liburnica* (of the lily family with yellow flowers, found in rocky or bushy places; it originates from the Balkan peninsula but has spread to Istra, Crete and south-east Italy). There are also examples of residual coastal vegetation, such as the grass *Ampelodesmos mauritanica*, along with a wide range of aquatic flora, including 62 species of algae, several of them endemic.

Conero is also one of the few spots on the Adriatic to retain remnants of maquis, including tree spurge (*Euphorbia dendroides*), among the more usual strawberry tree, oleander and lentiscus. Unusually for a rocky littoral, the north-east corner of the region around Portonovo contains an example of coastal marsh rarely found on the Adriatic; it harbours many ducks and is a favoured stopping point for migrating birds.

Before you go *Map:* IGM 1:25,000 Sheet 118 IV SE *Numana.*

Guidebooks: F. Burattini, *Guida del Monte Conero* (Aniballi); useful for non-Italian speakers, with photos and an excellent map.

Getting there *By car:* Conero is close to Ancona, with access via A14 (Loreto and Ancona Sud exits), SS16 and unclassified roads.

By rail: stations at Ancona, Osimo and Porta Recanati.

By bus: ATAM buses leave from Ancona's Piazza della Repubblica for Portonovo (½hr), Sirolo and Numana, all key exploration bases.

Where to stay: at Ancona, Portonovo, Camerano and Aspio Terme. Sirolo and Numana are convenient, but

crowded and expensive in summer. Try Numana's Gigli Eden, T: (071) 930 186.

Outdoor living: campsites at Torre, Portonovo, T: (071) 801 038; Numana Bluat Marcelli, T: (071) 930 863; also numerous summer-only sites on the coast to the S. Free camping is permitted, but good pitches are scarce.

Activities *Walking:* many easy, panoramic routes, though some paths have steep sections and can be blocked by vegetation. Dense scrub and a military zone make it difficult to explore off marked trails. 2 routes traverse the headland from N to S, both from the Hotel Internazionale at Portonovo. The better trail, initially marked by yellow–red– blue dashes via Badia di San Pietro to Sirolo (4hr), is well-worn. It forms part of an unmarked long-distance path from Portonovo to Visso in the Sibillini (8 days).

Ponytrekking: Conero's southern slopes offer gentle riding. Contact Centro Ippico del Conero, Via Buranico 199, Varano; or Riding Club le Azalee, Via della Molinella, Sirolo.

Boat trips: for boat trips and sea-fishing contact tourist offices or the Lega Navale, Via Mattei, Zippa, T: (071) 22506.

Skin-diving: the coastal waters are clean, rich in submarine life and designated as a marine park. There are two diving clubs in Ancona, Centro Attività Subaquee, Via Cialdini 24/b, T: (071) 50300 and Kamaros Club, Via Fortunato 5, T: (071) 26558.

Further information: *Tourist offices:* Via Thaon de Revel 41, T: (071) 33249; Piazza V. Veneto, Sirolo, T: (071) 936 141; Numana, T: (071) 936 142 (May–Sept).

Ecology: WWF, Via Marconi 103, Ancona, T: (071) 203 634; CAI, Via Cialdini 29A/B, Ancona.

Walking is a delight on the springy turf and open windy ridges of the Monte Sibillini.

Parco Nazionale dei Monti Sibillini

High Apennine limestone massif and upland plains (65,200ha/161,100 acres)

In all my walks in the Sibillini mountains I have met only one person, and that was on a wild autumn day as I tried to escape the freezing mist swirling on a high ridge. As

Sea stacks known as the Due Sorelle, "Two Sisters", form just a small part of the spectacular coast around the Conero peninsula, south of Ancona.

I made my way down from the summit, a shepherd's hut emerged from the murk and then its tattered owner appeared, an old weather-beaten man sporting a greasy white hat made from the raw wool of his sheep. A cross between a dishcloth and a nurse's bonnet, it gave him the appearance of a shambling madman.

The hut was his home. Dinner — half a sheep — hung inside. A small gas cylinder stood outside, the only visible concession to this century. His dogs, wolf-like, sat patiently, pure white and yellow-eyed. We were nearly 2,000 metres up (6,500 feet) on a windswept and exposed crest separating two deep valleys. In one of these mist

99

swirled and thunder rumbled in an ominous sky. In the other the view was clear, with patches of pale evening sunlight casting rocks and gullies into shadow. It seemed for a moment like a glimpse of the end of the world, with hell to one side and heaven to the other.

I could not help but let my mind drift through some of the superstitious and macabre tales associated with the mountains of the Sibillini which are named after one of the sibyls, or prophetesses, of classical antiquity. According to legend, the mythical harridan was chased here from the underworld, taking up residence on Monte Sibilla in the ominously named Grotta delle Fate, "Cave of the Furies". And Lago di Pilate, one of the loveliest lakes in the Apennines, with its deep dark waters lying in a glacial cwm below Monte Vettore, has acquired a reputation as a place of contemporary devil worship. Pontius Pilate was said to have been buried here after the oxen pulling his hearse refused to go any further. As though by way of warning, even the Kompass map to the area bears the number of the devil: 666.

It is not surprising the Sibillini have acquired such a sinister reputation. Mountain tarns set amid sharp glacial features can in a moment turn from the idyllic to the menacing. Monte Vettore, at 2,476 metres (8,123 feet), is a good example of the Janus-like quality of the landscape. The third highest mountain on the Italian peninsula, it gives an impression of huge size, of over-bearing, whale-backed immovability. Barren and smooth-sided on the west, it is marked on its eastern slopes with the savage scars of glaciation. Great rock walls with dolomitic pretensions rear up to impressive peaks, among them Pizzo del Diavolo, "the Devil's Beard". The Gole dell'Infernaccio, "Hell's Canyon", and the Ambro gorge, two of the most spectacular in the Apennines, carve through limestone mountains pitted with eerie caves and shadowy cirques.

Yet, by contrast, set between some of these mountains are the upland plains, or *piani*, the most celebrated natural feature of the Sibillini and one of Europe's most unusual landforms. Of the several in this region, the most impressive are Piano Perduto, Piano Piccolo, Piano dei Pantani and, most memorably, the Piano Grande.

Some 1,250 metres (4,100 feet) above sea level, eight kilometres (five miles) long and five (three) wide, the Grande is an enormous prairie without trees, hedges or houses, in fact with no individual features other than sheep and the odd haystack. The sheer faces of the Sibillini loom on all sides, creating a solemn amphitheatre that fills with mists rolling down the mountain sides. Gazing down on this from Castelluccio, a desolate shepherds' hamlet, as the weather turns, it is easy to imagine the danger that lurks for the unsuspecting traveller. In the past, Papal officials forbade the crossing of the plain during winter, and even today the bells of Castelluccio toll when there is mist, acting like a fog-horn to guide solitary shepherds wandering the plains.

Strange and compelling in any season, the *piani* are particularly splendid in spring, when they are ablaze with a feast of wild flowers. One week all 1,300 hectares (3,200

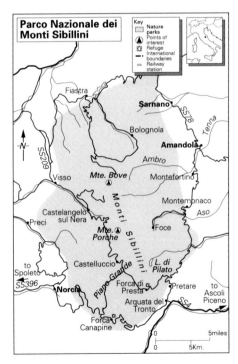

100

acres) of the Grande are covered with buttercups; the next, poppies spring up everywhere to give an intense flame-red spectacle. Snow-white daisies follow, dotted with wild tulips and alpine flowers such as the *Carex buxbaumii*.

Flowers are the glory of the Sibillini range. No wonder botanists have come to these slopes for more than two centuries. The Apennine edelweiss (*Leontopodion nivale*) grows on the summit of Vettore, and elsewhere only in very restricted areas of the Maiella and Gran Sasso. Other species include the martagon lily, bearberry, Apennine cinquefoil (with white flowers and silvery leaves) and the alpine buckthorn. Woodland is limited but beautiful, consisting mainly of beech found in little pockets up to 1,700 metres (5,600 feet).

Some of these woodlands support the roe deer, recently reintroduced. The conferring of national park status on the Sibillini in 1992 has facilitated the reappearance of the wolf, extinct like the brown bear since the eighteenth century. The fox and wildcat, though sadly not yet the bear or chamois, have also returned, as has the crested porcupine, once thought to have vanished for good. Among the raptors to be seen are buzzard, kestrel and sparrowhawk, as well as, in the rockier highlands, a handful of golden eagles. Breeding birds include the peregrine falcon (two or three pairs), rock partridge, eagle owl (three or four pairs), chough (100 pairs at most) and possibly the white-backed woodpecker.

As a curious footnote, it is worth mentioning a tiny endemic crustacean found at the Lago di Pilato. Pink and just half a centimetre (¼ inch) long, it is considerably smaller than its magnificent name, *Chirocephalus marchesonii*. The only living species that bear any relation to it are found in China and Turkey.

BEFORE YOU GO
Maps: Kompass 1:50,000 *Monti Sibillini* (Sheet 666) is the best single map. The new Universo 1:25,000 *Montevettore carta dei sentieri*, available locally, is extremely useful for the southern Sibillini.
Guidebooks: A. Alesi, *Guida dei Monti Sibillini* (for walkers and climbers, CAI Ascoli Piceno 1985); S. Ardito, *Piedi in Umbria* (for walkers, Iter 1989).

GETTING THERE
By car: western exploring bases are easiest to approach: SS395/209 from Spoleto for Visso, and SS396 to Norcia for Castelluccio and the Piano Grande. SS4 from Ascoli and the E for Arquata and the Forca di Presta (starting point for an ascent of Monte Vettore). Minor roads push into the eastern valleys from the SS78 between Ascoli and Amandola.
By rail: public transport is of limited use in this isolated area.

There is a station at Spoleto and a branch line from the east-coast line to Ascoli. Locals look kindly on hitch-hikers.
By bus: 4 buses daily from Spoleto to Norcia and Visso, and *one* bus a week, on Tuesdays, from Norcia to Castelluccio. Connections from Ascoli to Foce, Arquata, Amandola and Sarnano.

WHERE TO STAY
The simple Taverna at Castelluccio makes a perfect base for the Piano Grande and southern Sibillini, T: (0743) 870 158. Hotels also at Foce, Amandola, Bolognola, Sarnano, Arquata, Pretare, Forca Canapine. More choice further afield in Ascoli and Norcia.
Outdoor living: permitted everywhere, with many excellent pitches, but take plenty of water. Campsites at Bolognola, Castelsantangelo sul Nera, Fiastra, Montefortino, Preci, Sarnano and Montemonaco.

Refuges: sometimes at altitudes too low to be useful. The Zilioli hut (15 places) on Vettore is high, but in poor condition (details from the CAI, Ascoli). Roadside refuges include: Forca Canapine, T: (0736) 958 186 and Forca di Presta, T: (0736) 99165.

ACTIVITIES
Walking: some of the best hiking and backpacking in central Italy, with walks of all standards and, unlike many Italian uplands, opportunities for long ridge walks. There are 47 paths on Vettore alone, though few are marked and many are very minor tracks. CAI Perugia are currently marking trails; the linked trails 19/18/1, eventually to run the length of the range, are finished from Monte Pizzuto to Monte Porche. Updates are published with Universo map.

Classic hikes include: Forca di Presta to Vettore (4hr); traverse of the Gole dell'Infernaccio (3hr); the ridge

walks from Vettore to Foce (4hr) or Monte Porche; and Foce to Lago di Pilato (5hr) with spectacular views of the Valle del Tenna; Lago di Pilato is a favourite base for ascent of Monte Vettore.

Climbing: much-frequented and excellent routes with all degrees of difficulty on Monte Bove, the Pizzo del Diavolo above Lago di Pilato, and nearby Gran Gendarme. Also many excellent winter challenges. Details from the CAI clubs listed below.

Hang-gliding: Castelluccio has become one of *the* Italian centres for this sport. The smooth, open slopes of the western Sibillini offer perfect flying conditions.

Skiing: lifts and pistes at Frontignano, Forca Canapine, Monte Prata and Bolognana-Sarnano. However, this is an area where free-wheeling skiers seeking solitary runs are in their element. Superb cross-country possibilities everywhere, especially on the Piano Grande, with easy routes to Val Canatra (5km/3 miles) and Piano dei Pantani (8km/5 miles). Alpine skiing is also magnificent, with popular routes up Vettore from Foce and Forca di Presta.

FURTHER INFORMATION
Tourist offices: Amandola, T: (0736) 97291; Via Rimembranza, Sarnano, T: (0733) 667 144; Piazza XI Febbraio, Frontignano, T: (0737) 99124; Corso Mazzini 229, Ascoli Piceno, T: (0736) 51115; Piazza San Benedetto, Norcia, T: (0743) 816 165; CAI Corso Mazzini 81, Ascoli

The Sibillini's whaleback mountains cradle the Piano Grande, one of Europe's finest upland plains (1,200m/4,000ft). The spring burgeoning of buttercups, poppies, daisies and wild tulips add a blaze of colour.

Piceno; CAI Via della Gabbiaia 9, Perugia.
Ecology: for guidance on fauna contact the Società Botanica Italiana, Via la Pira 4, Florence, and the WWF, Via F. Crispi 113, Macerata, T: (0733) 40485.

Torricchio

Nature reserve of mountain ridges and the Val di Tazza WWF oasis (317ha/783 acres)

The Torricchio reserve is a tract of Apennine mountainscape lying between Camerino and the northernmost peaks of the Sibillini. Range after range of limestone hills form some of central Italy's least-known countryside. The rounded summits of Torricchio (1,444m/ 4,737ft) and Monte Fema (1,575m/5,167ft) are magnificent gaunt intrusions into the wide sweep of pastoral country, and belvederes for far-reaching views of the Sibillini and the long shadowy-grey ridges of the Valnerina.

St Francis Assisi tramped through this country, where high pasture alternates with conifer forests or mixed deciduous woodlands. In autumn, the russet and golden hues of extensive woods of wild cherry and beech, some trees 400 years old, make a glorious sight. Where woods have been cleared for grazing sheep, brought here from as far away as the Roman *campagna*, solitary beech trees have sometimes been left as shelter

for shepherds and their flocks.

The most interesting area for the naturalist is the Val di Tazza (850m/2,788ft), a narrow cave-pocked gorge on the flanks of Monte Fema. It contains a WWF reserve that keeps out the sheep, which used to nibble at the flowers. The flora is now rich and colourful, with white asphodels and orchids accompanying wild pear, wild strawberry, cyclamen and thickets of the unusual Neapolitan maple (*Acer obtusatum*).

This wealth of wild flowers attracts considerable numbers of butterflies, including metallic green hairstreaks, vivid orange scarce coppers and purple-shot coppers, whose vermillion wings have a distinctive iridescent violet sheen. Perhaps the most distinctive butterfly of the

reserve, however, is the *rebeli* race of the alcon blue (*Maculinea alcon*), although some naturalists consider it to be a separate species altogether. The males have bright-blue upper wings with chequered fringes, while the less conspicuous females are predominantly chocolate-brown.

Woodland is creeping forward on all fronts, giving refuge to wildlife that had been hunted to within a hair's breadth of extinction. Badgers, red squirrels and the occasional wolf from the Sibillini may be glimpsed, as may the elusive wildcat.

The greatest success has been the rehabilitation of the rock partridge which nests at Monte Fema. A major colony has been fostered from just two nesting sites present in 1970.

A rare subspecies of the alcon blue (*Maculinea alcon*, subspecies *rebeli*) is found in the Val di Tazza in the northern Apennines. Small isolated communities of the alcon blue are scattered across western Europe, but they have declined almost to the point of extinction.

THE WILDCAT

Closely resembling a large tabby, the wildcat can be recognized by its broad head and thick bushy tail with black rings. The largest can weigh as much as ten kilogrammes (twenty-two pounds). Although they feed mostly on small mammals, such as mice and rabbits, and ground-dwelling birds, they are also capable of bringing down animals as large as roe-deer fawn, using stealth and surprise rather than speed. Their hunting grounds are fields and meadows on the edge of woods in summer, whilst in winter they retire to the shelter of the forests.

Wildcats will normally stay in their individual territories to rear their young, but may travel long distances if a partner is not available. Once a suitable site in a hunting area is selected by the female, a litter of between two and four is born in April or May. At first the blind kittens are helpless but once their eyes have opened and they are strong enough on their short legs they will follow their mother on hunting expeditions. After about six months the mother will drive them out of her territory whereupon the young wildcats must fend for themselves.

Evidence suggests that wildcats rarely attack domestic livestock, although they may take a sick lamb or kid sometimes. However, people in rural areas are often convinced otherwise, and persecution of this magnificent feline persists in many parts of Europe.

minor roads branch off into the hills and provide excellent opportunities for further exploration. The WWF reserve is a short walk from the village of Pieve Torina, with a high-level entry point at the hamlet of Fematre.

Where to stay: Agli Scacchi at Preci, T: (0743) 99224; Tourist, Camerino, T: (0737) 3451. There is also perfectly good hotel accommodation at Visso and Muccia.

Outdoor living: campsites Il Collacio (Apr–Oct) at Castelvecchio near Preci, T: (0743) 99430 and at Ussita, 5km (3 miles) E of Visso. Camping permitted outside the reserve.

Activities *Walking:* many fine walks; the most noted is the ascent of Monte Fema from the Pian della Cuna (2hr) with superb views from the summit. Also appealing, the hike up and down the Val di Tazza (3hr), starting at Casale Picini, lower entrance to the WWF reserve.

Further information *Tourist offices:* Vico del Comune 4, Camerino, T: (0737) 2534; Piazza Umberto 1, Visso, T: (0737) 9239 (seasonal). *Ecology:* WWF, Via F. Crispi 113, Macerata, T: (0733) 40485.

Before you go *Map:* IGM 1:25,000 *Monte Fema.* *Access:* free at all times, except for WWF oasis. There is a warden at the site, but visits should be pre-arranged with *L'Istituto di Botanica* at Camerino University,

T: (0737) 40526.
Getting there *By car:* take the SS395 and then the SS209 from Spoleto along the Valnerina as far as Visso which is the best exploring base. From Camerino (14km/9 miles away) head S on the SS209. Many

CHAPTER 5

Tuscany and Umbria

For many people, Tuscany *is* Italy. One view of a cedar tree, vineyard or stone farmhouse moves us to that desire for the warmth of the south which Icelanders describe as the "need for figs". It is a huge region, however, and more complex than its beguiling popular image would suggest. The arc of the northern Apennines marks its northern and eastern borders, embracing the great Renaissance cities of Florence and Siena. Within this broad sweep lie the westerly Apuan Alps — jagged, marble-veined mountains that give the lie to the notion of Tuscany as a land of soft-centred pastoralism. Nothing to the east, in the high country of the Garfagnana, Mugello and Casentino, compares with their peculiar razor-like crests.

The naturalist's, though perhaps not the walker's, interest grows westwards as you cross the Tuscan heartland of the Chianti hills and Sienese badlands to arrive at Tuscany's coast and little-known offshore islands. This area has undergone a huge transformation in the last two hundred years, changing from a malaria-infested marsh and woodland to a drained and prosperous agricultural area of almost unremitting tedium. But it is precisely in the few remaining relics of the earlier landscape that the birdwatcher and naturalist will find their interests.

In the Maremma, for example, Tuscany can claim the finest piece of untouched coastline in the country: a pristine tract of maquis, hills, dune and

Cultivation over thousands of years has banished wilderness from much of Tuscany and Umbria. Today their vineyards, woods and gentle hills are a picture of pastoral harmony.

coastal pine woods (or *pinete*) that enjoys fierce protection and is one of only two proposed national parks in the region. Close by are the Orbetello and Burano lagoons, the finest birdwatching areas on Italy's western coast, and the WWF oasis at Bolgheri which is one of the few areas in Tuscany where minor mammals, particularly the indigenous boar, can roam safe from hunters' guns.

Guns are also trained on the birds and animals of Umbria, as I found out when I lived in a little hamlet on the region's borders. An ear-shattering fusillade of shots under my bedroom window would wake me every Sunday morning. You hear all sorts of things about Umbria: that it is the country's "green heart", that it is Tuscany's "gentler sister" or that it is the country's "mystical soul". All have more than a grain of truth. Umbria is an insular region, the only one in Italy without either a sea coast or a border with another country. Its timeless countryside and coronet of hill-towns are as beautiful and pastoral as anything in Tuscany. It is also a region steeped in religion. The *terra dei santi*, the "land of the saints", has given birth to Benedict of Norcia (Nursia) and Francis of Assisi, the fathers of Western monasticism, and to more minor saints than probably any other patch of ground in Christendom.

Some say that this preponderance of saints stems from a mystical quality inherent in the landscape. There certainly is an extraordinarily soft and misty light, as is shown, for example, in the paintings of Raphael, who was apprenticed in the region, which enhances your appreciation of the gentle beauty of its hills and woods.

But Umbria is not always a pastoral idyll. Prolonged periods of wind and rain can make it a desolate place. Brooding mountains rise above the rolling hills, plains and Tiber valley that make up the "green heart" side of the equation. Towards the eastern margins the Apennines become more rugged and soar to great heights. If the west is the domain of sheep and pasture, the east is that of wolf and wilderness.

These uplands, bordered by the Sibillini, mark the beginning of the central Apennines, where limestone replaces sandstone in Italy's mountainous spine. They are superb for walking, with their lines of 1,500-metre (5,000-foot) summits, and for caving, climbing and hang-gliding.

Any thought for wildlife in Umbria, however, soon reminds you of the Sunday morning hunters. Given the region's well-known associations with St Francis, noted for his love of nature and the famous sermon to the birds, it is ironic that Umbrian folk slaughter their birds, and that the regional authorities have one of the worst environmental records in the country.

The region came under the international spotlight in 1983, when a mass demonstration at Assisi called for action to stop not only the killing of local birds, but the huge slaughter that takes place all over Italy year after year. The guiding light behind the so-called Assisi Bird Campaign was an American ornithologist who came here expecting to see birds and instead was almost shot by a hunter's stray bullet. The campaign's immediate aim was to bring birdsong into the hills above Assisi and to force Umbria to create a reserve to keep the hunters out. That neither goal has been achieved is no reflection on the conservationists, but rather a sad comment on foot-dragging Italian bureaucrats.

Seekers of figs should expect to feel

a certain ambivalence about both Tuscany and Umbria. Although some of their scenery has a timeless quality, the modern world has crept in and factories and ugly new towns disfigure both regions. You find this development mostly in the basins of the main valleys, the Arno and the Tiber, both now pollution-filled and shadows of their former selves.

These are the buffer zones of central Italy, where the affluence and flavours of the north fade slowly to the relative poverty and Mediterranean manners of the south. Such meeting points have always brought friction — ever since the Romans dislodged the Etruscans. Today the battle is more insidious: that between progress and pastoralism.

THE BEE-EATER
Perhaps the most colourful of any summer visitor to central Italy, the bee-eater is distinguished by its plumage of orange, yellow, green and blue. This gregarious species breeds in tunnels in sandy banks, often several hundred to a colony. In flight it is easily identified by its pointed wings and central streamers, and its long tail. The bird feeds on insects, which it catches on the wing, and its long thin bill allows it to take stinging insects like bees and wasps from their nests.

GETTING THERE
By air: international and internal flights to Pisa's Galileo Galilei, T: (050) 28088. Alitalia, T: (050) 501 570. There are plans to upgrade Perugia's airport, which has flights only from Milan, to accommodate international aircraft.
Rome's Fiumicino is convenient for both Tuscany and Umbria, with good road and rail links to both regions.
By car: the A1 Rome–Florence motorway divides Tuscany and Umbria, with spurs to Viterbo, Siena, Arezzo, Perugia; and the SS3 from Orte serves Terni, Spoleto, Gualdo Tadino and thence Ancona and the Marche.
The SS2 (Via Cassia) runs from Rome through the heart of Tuscany to Siena and beyond. On the coast, the SS1 (Via Aurelia) from Rome

serves the entire western half of Tuscany; both SS1 and 2, however, are slow roads with few modern sections. Eastern Umbria and NE Tuscany have poor but scenic road systems.
By rail: the main coast line, Ventimiglia–Genoa–Rome, serves western Tuscany, with branch lines: Florence–Pisa, Grosseto–Siena, Florence–Siena, Lucca–La Spezia and La Spezia–Parma.
Umbria is extremely well-served, with the main Rome-Florence line in the W (Orvieto, Castiglione del Lago); the Rome–Ancona linking Orte, Spoleto, Foligno and Gualdo; and branch lines: Foligno–Assisi–Perugia–Terontola, Terni–Rieti and Terni–Perugia–Sansepolcro.

WHEN TO GO
Mid–Apr to late May for orchids, wild flowers and best

walking weather (late May to June in the higher parts of Apuan Alps and Valnerina).

WHERE TO STAY
Virtually all centres in both regions have ample, high-quality accommodation. For detailed hotel and campsite lists contact main tourist offices: Via Manzoni 16, Florence, T: (055) 247 8141; Via di Città 43, Siena, T: (0577) 280 551; Piazza IV Novembre 3, Perugia, T: (075) 6961; Piazza della Libertà 7, Spoleto, T: (0743) 49890.

ACTIVITIES
Walking: some of the country's loveliest hill-walking in both regions, with more strenuous mountain hikes in the Apuan Alps and Orecchiella (Tuscany) and in the Valnerina and around Monte Cucco (Umbria).

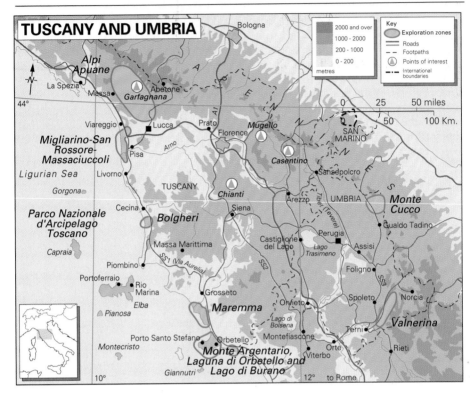

Long-distance paths: *Apuane Trekking* (4 days); the *Grande Escursione Appenninica*, from Pracchia along ridges of the Apennines to the Emilia-Romagna border (25 days); this path links to the *Alta Via dei Monti Liguri* at the Passo dei Due Santi. Short marked trails in the Parco Naturale della Maremma. No long paths in Umbria, but marked trails around Spoleto and Monte Cucco.

Useful contacts include: CAI, Via di Città 25, Siena; CAI, Via della Gabiaia 9, Perugia; and mountain centres at: Pracchia, T: (0573) 630 790; Passo dei Due Santi, T: (0187) 830 359. Other CAI contacts are given in the appropriate Exploration Zones.

Ponytrekking: there are probably more riding centres in Tuscany than in any other Italian region; apply to ANTE head office in Rome for a full list of approved establishments. Many organize all-day and week-long treks with overnight accommodation. See also local tourist offices.

Skiing: modest resorts at Abetone, Cutigliano and Monte Amiata (Tuscany) and around Norcia, Forca Canapine and Spoleto (Umbria).

Caving: the best in Italy, with main underground systems in the Apuan Alps and around Monte Cucco; see Exploration Zones.

Fishing: rivers (Arno, Ombrone, Nera, Tiber, Clitunno), lakes (Trasimeno, Corbara and Piediluco) and Tuscany's coast offer endless fishing possibilities. The main FIPS offices are: Piazza Tolomei 5, Siena, T: (0577) 41111; Piazza Sopra I Ponti 6, Arezzo, T: (0575) 24201; and Via Piaggia Colombata 2, Perugia.

Ecology: WWF, Via San Gallo 32, Florence, T: (055) 475 079; WWF, Delegazione Umbra, Via Cotogno 1, Perugia, T: (075) 65816; Italia Nostra, Via Gramsci 9a, Florence, T: (055) 247 9213.

The WWF branch at Todi in Umbria runs summer work camps to the Monti Sibillini and other areas of natural interest: WWF, Via delle Caselle 19c, Todi, T: (075) 882 078.

FURTHER READING
Buckley, Jepson and Ellingham, *The Rough Guide to Tuscany and Umbria* (Penguin).

Dante's *Divine Comedy* mentioned the Procinto, a dramatic pillar of rock seen here with the Alpi Apuane in the background.

Alpi Apuane

Nature park of dramatic mountain chain parallel to north Tuscan coast (60,000 ha/ 148,000 acres)

The first time I saw the Apuan Alps, dusk was falling on the Tuscan coast. Dark waves broke on the shore and, to the east, shadows were lengthening over the land. The last rays of the sun caught the crests of a jagged mountain chain making them shine with a creamy, almost luminous light against a sky tinted red. The forests below were already in darkness, twinkling with the lights of isolated farms; and long after they should have faded into the night, the mountains continued to display a strange unearthly glow.

It was marble that was catching the light — huge open mines of rock. The Apuan Alps, the most spectacular mountains of the northern Apennines, have for two thousand years been the marble capital of Italy.

111

Innumerable factories and workshops line the coast. Some 300 quarries in and around the mountains remove half a million tons of stone annually, making this the single largest marble-producing area in the world.

There are those who begrudge the quarriers' activities, claiming the landscape is being spoiled. I am not sure. Maybe the beauty and grandeur of this noble stone, even in open-cast mines, is so impressive along the seaward slopes that it seems to complement the lush hinterland of Tuscany; or perhaps it is simply because sculptors from Michelangelo to Henry Moore have always turned to Apuan marble. Whatever the reason, marble is an integral part of life in these mountains. Every shade and hue of stone is here, whether mined locally or imported. For although Apuan marble is mainly white, like that of Michelangelo's David, the skill of its craftsmen attracts the importation of unworked stone of different colours from all over the world.

The 50 kilometres (30 miles) of ridges that dominate the seaward side of the region fully merit the title of Alps, their jagged profiles as spectacular as any of their northern counterparts. Although the highest point at Monte Pisanino is under 2,000 metres (6,000 feet), these mountains can appear vast from their position close to the sea. Such relatively low heights also mean you can reach the summit ridges, often difficult in the Alps proper.

The scenery changes markedly towards the east, becoming more Apennine in character. More rounded and greener foothills drop down to the Garfagnana valley which separates the Apuan Alps from the Orecchiella mountains farther east. Although the eastern peaks tend to be lower, there are still some spectacular sights, especially the towering Monte Altissimo and the Pania della Croce, known as the "Queen of the Apuan Alps".

More unusual is the much-photographed *finestra*, or "window", of Pania Forata, an arched hole that looks like the huge eye of a Cyclops cut into the mountain crest. Myth has it that for one moment each year the setting sun shines through the hole to cast a menacing beam on the already darkened villages in the east. The single most impressive feature of the Apuan Alps, however, is the Procinto, an isolated rock tower straight out of the Yosemite National Park in California. The 200-metre (650-foot) rock walls that rise around this craggy pinnacle, along with those of the Pizzo d'Uccello to the north, are the finest of the many climbing areas in these mountains.

It was while marching back from this marvel, feeling rather self-satisfied after my walk, that I bumped into two cavers, exhausted and bedraggled after two days underground. They put my hike to Monte Nona into perspective. How far had I walked — 20 kilometres (12 miles) perhaps? Under these mountains there were an estimated 400 kilometres (250 miles) of caves and galleries. One cave, the Antro del Corchia, is the deepest in Italy. Its depth of 1,200 metres (nearly 4,000 feet) was not far off what I had *climbed* that day.

Not surprisingly, this is the undisputed caving centre of Italy, with some of the greatest challenges in European caving: the Tana dell'Olmo Selvatico, La Tano che Urla, the Abisso Roversi, the Grotta del Vento and many more. Although most of these caves are for experts only, some of them are open to the general public, notably the Grotta del Vento at Fornovolasco near Vergemoli.

These, and nearby caverns, are the dens of cave salamanders. Quite unlike other European tailed amphibians, they have partially webbed feet with short squarish toes which make them agile climbers. Only two species of cave salamander have so far been discovered in mainland Italy: *Speleomantes ambrosii*, recently classified, is confined to a very small area near Florence, while the Italian cave salamander *Speleomantes italicus* is more widespread. Because of their chosen habitat, however, populations tend to be isolated from one another and numerous endemic races have been identified; here in the Apennines they belong to the subspecies *gormani*.

Far more accessible to the average naturalist is the huge range of wild flowers. Because of their location and varied topography, the Apuan Alps contain a number of different habitats. Bleak upland moors resembling the Arctic tundra grade down to alpine meadows with wild flowers galore. Beech and chestnut form colossal expanses of woodland which must be as dense as any in the Apennine Mountains. Lower still, the dry Mediterranean grasslands are enlivened with orchids and lilies in early spring.

About one quarter of all the plants found in Italy are known to occur in the Apuan Alps, including species otherwise rare in Italy, such as the Irish spurge (*Euphorbia hyberna*), which thrives on the Apuan marble; or the Tunbridge filmy fern (*Hymenophyllum tunbridgense*), a native of the Valle d'Inferno near Montignoso, a botanical treasure house.

Centuries of hunting have left the larger fauna rather thin on the ground; and although snow voles and marmots are still found in the higher parts of the Apuan Alps, they are much less common in the Apennines than in the northern Alps. Snow voles, also known as alpine voles, are delightful pale grey rodents with long whiskers, found in most mountain ranges in central and southern Europe. Unusually for rodents, they can sometimes be seen basking in the sun on tussocks of grass, but more often than not, the only signs of their presence are the mazes of semi-circular tunnels which are revealed when the snow melts; the snow itself forming the top of each tunnel.

Just inland from the Apuan Alps lies one of Italy's best-kept secrets: the Garfagnana valley. Magnificent swathes of heather and rhododendron bloom near the craggy summits from which peregrines and golden eagles survey the green lower slopes for prey. Eagle owls, honey buzzards and goshawks are some of the 165 types of bird recorded in the area.

(Overleaf) Deciduous woods, mainly sweet chestnut, dominate the lower slopes of the Orecchiella and Alpi Apuane, otherwise known as Tuscany's highest and most rugged corner.

BEFORE YOU GO
Maps: the Alps are covered by a superb series of Multigraphic 1:25,000 maps, all widely available in local shops. Paths, long-distance trails and refuges (with contact numbers) are clearly marked.
Guidebooks: A. Nerli, *Alpi Apuane* (CAI-TCI 1979, for climbers and cavers); R. Marotta, *Attraverso Le Alpi* (Il Melograno 1987); *Garfagnana Trekking* (AA.VV) covers trails in both mountain groups.

GETTING THERE
By car: direct motorway access (A12/A11) to all western and southern areas of the Alps; A15 from Milan and Parma; A12 and SS1 (Aurelia) from Pisa and the S. Lanes thread into the park from points round its border; one, from Massa to Castelnuovo, crosses it from W to E.

Main access to the eastern Alps is by same roads; then

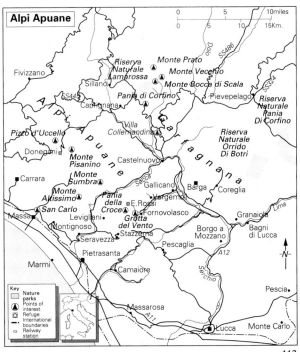

take the twisting SS445 from Lucca to Castelnuovo, which runs the length of the Garfagnano valley to Aulla.
By rail: the Rome–Genoa line has convenient stations at Pietrasanta, Massa and Carrara, and a charming and useful branch line runs the length of the Garfagnana from Lucca to Aulla (10 trains daily); details, T: (0583) 47013.
By bus: an extensive network of CLAP buses links most centres (including many remote villages) from Lucca, Massa, Carrara, Pietrasanta and Castelnuovo.

WHERE TO STAY
In the summer many small villages have *pensione* and private room accommodation; off-season you will have to settle for the uglier coastal centres — all otherwise perfectly good bases, such as Forte dei Marmi, Massa and Carrara — and then rely on the efficient bus network. The Garfagnana valley, and Castelnuovo in particular, has prettier locations.
Outdoor living: prohibited in the park, but numerous sites along the coast (summer only) and in the Garfagnana valley.
Refuges: 15 refuges, bivouacs and high-altitude hotels in the Alps, 8 run by the CAI local

branches at Lucca, Massa and Carrara. The most popular are: Del Freo (Apr–Oct), T: (0584) 778 007; Donegani (May–Nov), T: (0583) 610 085; and Carrara, T: (0585) 841.
Details from CAI branches and tourist offices.

ACTIVITIES
Walking: numerous routes and marked trails. The Alps' best walks are the climb to the Rif. Freo and Pania della Croce (1,858m/6,095ft) from Levigliani (4hr); to the Procinto from Seravezza (2hr); ascent of Pizzo d'Uccello rock walls from Seranaia (4hr). Long-distance paths include Apuane Trekking from Carrara (4 days, or 8 days with full variations) and Piglione Trekking, 3 days in the S, starting from Metato.
Garfagnana Trekking is a circular 10-stage walk from Castelnuovo through the Alps and the Orecchiella.
Climbing: some of the best on the Italian peninsula: rock climbs on the Pizzo d'Uccello, Procinto, Penna di Sumbra and Monte Nona; excellent snow climbs on Pania della Croce and the crests of Pisanino. Contact CAI branches for full details: Via Giorgi, Carrara, T: (0585) 76782; Piazza Mazzini 13, Massa, T: (0585) 488 081.

Also Comunità Montana Garfagnana, Castelnuovo, T: (0583) 65169.
Caving: for full details contact the CAI addresses above, plus CAI Gruppo Speleologico, Via del Proconsolo 10, Florence. Non-experts can descend the Grotta del Vento, located on the Garfagnana side of the Alps at Fornovalasco (17km/11 miles from Barga). In the summer there are 2 tours daily: 1 tour (1hr) leaves at 10am, noon, 3pm, 6pm; the other (2hr) at 11am, 3pm, 4pm, 5pm. In winter the cave is open on public holidays only. Further details from the cave office, T: (0583) 763 084; and the tourist office at Barga, Piazza Angelico, T: (0583) 73499.
Skiing: few runs in the ragged landscape of the Alps, bar brief cross-country routes on Campo Cecina and Campo Catino; better opportunities in the Orecchiella, with a resort at Foce delle Radici, and cross-country excursions on forest paths.
Botany: botanical gardens at Villa Collemandina, Pania di Corfino, T: (0584) 62994 (open all year); Orto Pietro Pellegrini, Pian della Fioba, Massa, T: (0585) 47801 (June–Sept). They have huge numbers of plants, including all local indigenous species.

HERMANN'S TORTOISE
One of southern Europe's most endangered reptiles, Hermann's tortoise is common along the Tuscan coast but can also be found a little way inland. It is equally at home in sand dunes, meadows and dense scrub. It feeds mainly on vegetation, but also eat carrion, molluscs and slow-moving insects. In the breeding season, male tortoises aggressively repel rivals and court their chosen females passionately. Females lay around a dozen eggs which take several weeks to hatch, depending on the weather: the warmer, the quicker.

FURTHER INFORMATION
Tourist offices: Piazza 2 Giugno 14, Carrara, T: (0585) 70894; Lungomare Vespucci 24, Marina di Massa, T: (0585) 240 063; Piazza Guidiccioni 2, Lucca, T: (0583) 41205; Rocca, Castelnuovo Garf., T: (0583) 62268.

For information on Garfagnana contact the excellent Comunità Montana Garfagnana, Piazza delle Erbe 1, Castelnuovo di Garfagnana, T: (0583) 65169.

Migliarino– San Rossore– Massaciuccoli

Nature park of mixed coastal habitats and large relict woodland near Pisa; proposed national park (30,000ha/74,000 acres)

Drab urban surroundings make this the most dubious of Italy's proposed national parks. The conservationists' motive here, however, is to protect at any cost the beach, dunes, maquis and woodland that form the largest surviving tract of traditional Tuscan littoral. Despite the effects of river pollution and building development there are parts that are still wild and beautiful.

The unspoiled area divides into three regions. In the north, squeezed between motorways, lies the Massaciuccoli lake, only 2m (7ft) deep but occupying an area the size of nearby Pisa. It is the lone survivor of many such lagoons long since lost to land reclamation. A LIPU oasis has been created here, and 80 breeding and 65 occasional species have been recorded. Among the former are the little bittern, squacco and purple herons, black-winged stilt, collared pratincole, marsh harrier and hundreds of moustached warbler; and, in spring, the lake is swarming with passage ducks, terns and gulls.

To the south lies the Macchia di Migliarino, the main body of the park. This runs in a 35-km (22-mile) coastal band from Viareggio to Livorno containing dune, marsh, mixed woodland and some of the most enchanting colonnades of trees in Italy. Although these long avenues of trees, lined across flat countryside, are plantations, they do provide one of the most elegant images of Italy. Pine, oak, ash, elder and poplar were planted in the eighteenth century to consolidate the littoral and shelter the fields from lashing winter storms. The best of the woods to visit, if you do not have much time, is the 300 hectares (740 acres) at Pineta di Levante between Versilia and the Bufalina river.

Most of the Tuscan coast was once forested, and few of the woods were as grand as San Rossore. The area now contains the remains of only two ancient woods, the *Silva pisana* and *Silva palatina*. With their protected colonies of red and roe deer, wild boar and smaller mammals, these woods are still enchanting. Numerous species of waterfowl migrate to San Rossore and Migliarino in spring, including the glossy ibis, greater flamingos, bean and greylag geese, garganeys, ferriginous ducks, cranes and black and white-winged black terns. Intensive shooting has, however, drastically reduced the colonies of wintering wildfowl. Among the smaller species to be seen here are penduline tits.

Before you go: the park headquarters organize group visits to restricted parts of the San Rossore reserve: Via C. Battisti 10, Pisa, T: (050) 43512/27271. For Migliarino, T: (050) 804 0361.

Maps: IGM 1:25,000 *Torre del Lago*, *Tirrenia* and *Marina di Pisa*.

Getting there *By car:* take A12 and A11 motorways to Pisa, then Pisa Nord exit for the lake and Pisa Sud for Migliarino. There is also minor road access from Viareggio and Livorno.

By rail: there is a train to Pisa or Livorno on the main Rome–Genoa and Florence–Pisa lines.

Where to stay: Pisa or Viareggio. *Outdoor living:* free camping is prohibited, but there are several sites dotted along the coast, two near Massaciuccoli: Burlamacco, T: (0584) 340 797; and Italia, T: (0584) 341 504.

Access: LIPU restrict entry to certain parts of Massaciuccoli, but minor roads lead to E and W shores, one by way of a lovely 6-km (4-mile) colonnade of lime trees (Via dei Tigli). The San Rossore woodland — including roads marked on maps — is closed except on public holidays.

Activities *Birdwatching:* from Mar–Sept LIPU local branch at Torre del Lago leads tours of Massaciuccoli: T: (0584) 975 186/975 567. Information also from LIPU at Pisa, T: (050) 65696.

Further information *Tourist office:* Piazza del Duomo, Pisa, T: (050) 501 761; and Via Carducci 10, Viareggio, T: (0584) 962 233.

Ecology: WWF, Via San Martino 108, Pisa, T: (050) 28302.

Bolgheri

Bird and wildlife sanctuary in classic Mediterranean marsh, scrub and woodland habitat; WWF oasis (2,700ha/6,700 acres)

This beautiful patchwork of habitats on the Tuscan coast north of Piombino was ceded to the WWF in 1962 by its nature-loving owner, thus becoming the first privately founded nature reserve in Italy.

The results have been remarkable. Huge numbers of birds can be seen throughout the year. In winter thousands of starlings wheel in the sky; the lapwing nests here, its southernmost breeding point; and the rare bluethroat and Blyth's reed warbler (its first sighting in Italy) are passage migrants. Grey herons, little egrets, knights of Italy (black-winged stilts), cranes, black storks, and hunters such as the osprey and the very scarce lesser spotted eagle can also be seen on migration here.

The list of rare birds is long, and increasing all the time, so much so that the oasis is recognized under the Ramsar Convention as a habitat of international importance. So successful was the reserve that with intense WWF pressure the area of protected marshland was enlarged to include a classic tract of Mediterranean seashore. As a result there are now few places in Italy where it is easier to see birds and animals in their natural habitat.

A damp autumn morning breaks over the Chianti hills, with the heights of the Pratomagno and Foreste Casentinesi in the far distance.

Its loveliest corners are the lakes and marshy grasslands, which brim with birds in winter, and are dry in summer, and emerald green with lush grass in spring. All the elements of the old Maremma are here: exquisite pine groves, relict tracts of juniper and mixed scrub forest.

Plants such as the spiny sea holly thrive on the dunes, together with the sea daffodil, whose flower of the purest white breaks out in July, casting its creamy perfume over the shingle and upper beaches. Beyond the dunes unfolds a succession of maquis, marsh and hills, all dominated by some of the most ancient stands of cypress in Italy.

Such is the Eden-like tranquillity of the reserve that many animals can be seen easily in broad daylight. Wild boar — the ancient Maremma breed — root in the undergrowth alongside equally pure-bred roe deer, one of only a few such relict colonies in Italy. The crested porcupine flourishes here, and there are hopes of reintroducing otters.

Before you go *Guidebook:* F. Pratesi, *Oasi d'Italia.*

Access: the reserve is open 9am–12 and 2–4.30pm each Fri and on the first and third Sat of the month 15 Oct–15 Apr. Information from the offices of the Vigili Urbani in the village of Donoratico, T: (0565) 777 125.

Getting there *By car:* SS1 to the hamlet of Bolgheri, 10km/6 miles S of Cecina. The reserve — set back 5km (3 miles) from the road — is on the small lane from the SS1 over the railway. *By rail:* station at Bolgheri on the main Rome–Pisa line, best reached on a stopping train from Cecina (7 daily). Details, T: (0564) 22366. *By bus:* buses to Bolgheri from Grosseto and Cecina. Details, T: (0564) 25380.

Where to stay: Cecina is a modern town with functional hotels, and nearby historic towns (Volterra, Massa Marittima) make more attractive bases.

Outdoor living: no camping in reserve, but many sites up and down the coast.

Further information *Tourist office:* Largo Cairoli 17, Marina di Cecina, T: (0586) 620 678. *Ecology:* WWF, Via XX Settembre 15, Piombino.

The adult osprey is a striking bird with a white head, a loosely-crested crown and dark stripe through the eyes. It is a fish-hunter, equipped with large feet and long powerful talons for grasping its prey.

THE CRESTED PORCUPINE

One of Italy's most eye-catching mammals, the crested porcupine is not a native of the country. The Romans probably introduced it from Africa. Now it is quite common on hill slopes that give adequate cover. Generally nocturnal, it occasionally appears during the day near its hole. Predators are deterred by its loud grunts and the erection of its bristly white hairs and needle-like quills. Although resembling giant-sized hedgehogs, porcupines are rodents, relatives of rats and mice, with teeth designed for gnawing.

Maremma

Nature park of traditional Tuscan littoral and 15km (9 miles) of original coastline; proposed national park (9,800 ha/24,200 acres)

The Maremma probably takes its name from the Spanish word *marisma*, or marsh, the linguistic legacy of two centuries of Spanish rule. Dante described the region as running from Cecina near Pisa down to Corneto on the present border with Lazio. In his day it was an inaccessible mixture of forest, dune, swamp and scrub made practically uninhabitable by malarial mosquitoes. All that has now virtually gone: the dunes have been levelled and the marshes drained, and the mosquitoes were vanquished in 1950. All that remains is a short strip of coast, saved largely by the authorities' refusal to sell out to tourism or agriculture.

It is impossible to overstate the importance, or for that matter the beauty of this area, which has been described as the last completely unspoiled stretch of coastline in the whole of Italy from Ventimiglia on the French frontier round to Trieste on the Slovenian border. Access is strictly controlled; no cars are allowed and entry is by bus only. Once you have bought your entry ticket, and have trundled through the hills and scrub, you are herded from the bus and left to your own devices.

The introduction to the Maremma begins not at the coast, but in the middle of the Monti dell'Uccellina, a long series of whale-backed hills that form the park's core. These come as a surprise as you travel along the Tuscan coast. They are only 400 metres (1,300 feet) high, but alongside the coastal plain seem much loftier. Old Spanish watch-towers add a romantic touch to the wooded hill-tops, except on cloudy days when, with the slopes in deep shadow, they seem like sinister outposts in what are already melancholy hills.

On sunny days, however, the uplands are a delight. The first of four marked trails weaves from the set-down point into the rocky green hills. This is by far the least-used of the paths, most people preferring the dunes and the sea. Be warned, however, that the paths' markings are not always reliable, so keep your sense of direction about you. With the sea as a constant reference it is difficult to get lost for long.

In the past the woods were exploited briefly by the Spanish and Sienese for cork and charcoal, one of the few occasions when this area has known even the most rudimentary population. Before that, monks inhabited San Rabano in the eleventh century and built a monastery, abandoning it around 1650. Its ivy-covered ruins lie in the hills and are reached by Trail 1. The only other signs of human habitation are the prehistoric remains discovered in caves on the north-west edge of the hills. These caves, the Scoglietto, Fabbrica and Galino, can be visited by following Trail 3.

If you are on a day trip and decide to explore the hills, you probably will not have time to cover the mosaic of coastal landscape that adjoins the park. If you are a first-time visitor you may well be tempted by this coastal option, since all nature's variety seems to have been compressed into this small area: the beaches, pine forests, dunes and maquis are so rich and lush that they seem artificial. It is as if they had started life as an ornamental park and then degenerated into wilderness.

It was the beach that drew me, but nature's design is such that you tramp through several habitats before seeing the open sea. Below the hills lay a stretch of meadows and groves of ancient olive trees, their trunks gnarled and twisted, sometimes fused together in smooth whorls of wood. Everywhere rosemary bushes were in bloom. Hillsides and pathsides were dotted with light mauve flowers, the air alive with the constant busy humming of bees. Beyond the olive groves came the park's crowning glory. I had seen pictures of the Maremma's pine forests, but climbing a low hill to look down on them for myself was one of the loveliest sights I have seen in Italy. A vast green panoply of umbrella pines, like tightly packed emerald mushrooms, stretched almost as far as the eye could see. Here and there a rogue juniper or foreign pine would interrupt the even canopy that was limited only by the blue borders of sea and sky.

Many of the pines were planted for particular purposes: the domestic variety for their pine nuts, which are still collected, and the maritime variety, now spreading rapidly, to consolidate the Maremma's vast area of dunes. To wander through these woods is a delight. The ground is a soft carpet of sand and dry needles, the branches alive with birdsong and the under-

growth rich with heathers and grasses. Occasionally you may even hear the rustle of a wild boar snuffling away as you approach. Elsewhere in Italy this small frugal creature has been replaced by the larger boar of central and eastern Europe.

You can roam for hours along the coast, your only limits the canals and areas of marsh at their fringes. These, too, are a joy, with their fringes of reeds and trees, the plopping sound of frogs and crystal waters full of darting fish. Otters are on the increase, and birds are numerous, especially migrating winter species. Tiny reptiles, invertebrates and larger mammals, such as roe deer, badger, fox and the crested porcupine, can also be seen. Together with the flowers and trees all this wildlife proves, as Italia Nostra claims, that the Maremma is "one of the last earthly paradises in Italy".

There are those who come here simply to

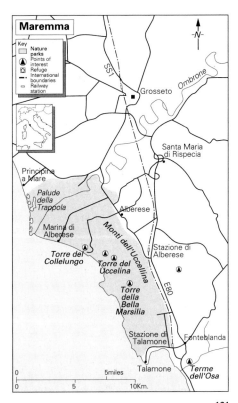

121

enjoy a beach without roads, bars or litter. You can walk for hours through sand and scenery that would be a credit to Treasure Island. The Uccellina hills and maquis hinterland provide a wonderful backdrop. To the south, dunes give way to cliffs and bays (Trail 4); to the north, they stretch empty and flat to the mouth of the Ombrone.

These extremes are the park's most deserted enclaves. Some of the cliffs and interior country can be approached from the fishing port of Talamone south of the park. Although access from here is less restricted than in the north, the best introduction remains along the beach, using Trails 2 and 4 as far as the headland at Cala di Forno (12 kilometres/7 miles). During the walk look out for the dwarf palm, Italy's only naturally growing palm. In the park it finds its most northerly natural home.

By contrast, the mouth of the Ombrone, Tuscany's second longest river, is a flat alluvial plain. In some areas dunes have been colonized by pine-woods creeping up from the south. The rest are a mixture of marsh (the Paludi di Trappola on the northern bank), cultivated fields and lakes behind dunes. Here you can see the rarest of the park's birds — the flamingo, osprey and peregrine — as well as the stone curlew, hobby, roller and bee-eater. Of particular note, too, are the oxen and semi-wild horses for which the Maremma is famous. Sadly, the Maremma's legendary horsemen are nearly all gone; although the rounding up of the horses, with 30 or more animals galloping through lake and marsh, is still a spectacular sight.

BEFORE YOU GO

For access to the park go to the village of Alberese and the park centre in its main square: T: (0564) 407 098. Tickets cost L5,000, with buses on the hour to take you into the park. You can also walk, but not drive, on the lanes that enter the park (10km/6 miles). Buses return hourly from the put-down point until dusk.

3 trails from Talamone give southern access to the coast and lower hills of the Uccellina. These are always open, as is the superlative beach at Marina di Alberese (accessible by road from Alberese).

Maps: the map provided by the park office is worse than useless: it will tend to lead you astray. IGM 1:25,000 sheets *Bocca d'Ombrone, Collecchio* and *Talamone* are very useful and comprehensive.

Guidebooks: A. Mazzolai, *Guida alla Maremma* (Arsuna

1982); M.P. Pruneti, *Il Parco dell'Uccellina* (Bonechi 1980); C. Guerrini, *Il Parco della Maremma* (Tellini 1982). Material is available at the park office.

GETTING THERE

By car: from the S (Rome) and N (Pisa) take the coastal SS1 towards Grosseto. Exit 15km (9 miles) S of the town at Santa Maria di Rispescia or Stazione di Alberese, and follow minor roads for 3km (2 miles) to Alberese.

By rail: plenty of connections to Grosseto on the Rome–Pisa line; Alberese's station is served by only 2 trains daily. Details, T: (0564) 25380.

By bus: infrequent service from Grosseto to Alberese, making a taxi from the station the best option if you are using public transport. Details, T: (0564) 22366.

WHERE TO STAY

Grosseto is the nearest centre, a modern, functional town with hotels to match. Rooms at Talamone are more picturesque; try the 3-star Capo

d'Uomo, T: (0564) 887 077 (closed Oct–Mar). Choices also at Albinia, Fonteblanda and Principina a Mare.

Outdoor living: strictly prohibited within the park, and difficult in the intensely cultivated surroundings, but many official sites on neighbouring coastline.

Access: the park is open Wed, Sat and Sun 9am–dusk, with visitors limited to 500 daily.

ACTIVITIES

Walking: 3 short trails from Talamone, and 4 from the bus set-down point at Pratini. All interconnect and can be abandoned at will in favour of freelance exploration.

Trail 1: to San Rabano abbey through woods and rocks of the Monti dell'Uccellina; most demanding, but one of the most rewarding walks, with superb views over Tuscan interior and the park's varied habitats (6½ km/4 miles, 4hr).

Trail 2: *Le Torri* — links several of the towers on lower hills, with views over the pine forests (from Torre Castel Marino), and can be linked

Great spotted cuckoos arrive in western Italy in early spring. They lay their eggs in magpie nests, thus avoiding the tiresome chore of raising their own young. With no parental duties the adults have usually left for Africa by June.

with Trail 1 to make a good day's walk (5½ km/3 miles, 2hr).

Trail 3: *Le Grotte* — visits prehistoric caves; flatter and more mundane than other walks, but follows a long stretch through the pine woods (8½ km/5 miles, 4hr).

Trail 4: *Cala di Forno* — long cliff-top, hill and coastal walk; good views and little-frequented (12km/7 miles, 5hr).

Birdwatching: the LIPU branch at Grosseto runs summer work camps and provides information on the park's birds, T: (0564) 21628.

Ponytrekking: many centres, with main trekking on the dikes and paths around the mouth of the Ombrone. Contact the excellent centre Le Canelle at Talamone, T: (0564) 887 020.

Outing: the castle overlooking Talamone houses a natural history museum with exhibits relating to the Maremma (9am–12, 4–7pm).

FURTHER INFORMATION
Tourist office: Via Monterosa 20b, Grosseto, T: (0564) 22534.
Ecology: WWF, Via Inghilterra 91, Grosseto. The WWF main branch in Florence runs summer work camps in the park: WWF, Via San Gallo 32, T: 055) 475 079.

Monte Argentario, Laguna di Orbetello and Lago di Burano

Mountainous promontory and lagoon habitats partly protected by WWF oases

Monte Argentario juts from the straight line of the Lazio and Tuscan coast, sheltering in its ample lee the largest lagoon on the Tyrrhenian seaboard, the Laguna di Orbetello. A little farther south is the Lago di Burano, acclaimed as the coast's most important habitat and one of Italy's most important bird sanctuaries.

The WWF oases protect 300ha (740 acres) at Burano and 870ha (2,150 acres) at Orbetello, including a specialized section of lagoon in the northern corner of Orbetello where fresh water enters from Albegna.

Argentario is as near to wilderness as southern Tuscany comes, with its rugged corners, quiet stretches of coast and a highest point of 635m (2,083ft). An island for thousands of

years, it was eventually joined to the mainland by the 3 sandspits that enclose the 2,600-ha (6,424-acre) Orbetello lagoon. This and the Burano lagoon constitute the birdwatching capital of Italy, claiming 200 of the estimated 450 species that inhabit or visit Italy every year.

Among those species that breed here are the little egret, stone curlew, Montagu's harrier, bee-eater and the knight of Italy (black-winged stilt), which otherwise breeds only in Sardinia and the lagoons of the Po delta. Other rare birds include goosanders, great white egrets, purple and grey herons, velvet scoters, bluethroats, smew and in spring, with luck, the rare great spotted cuckoo. Storks and grey herons arrive in large numbers in the autumn, while flamingos and garganey are common winter visitors. With the cold and damp also come wigeon, shovellers and pochard, with their bobbing chestnut red heads and golden eyes. On the iciest, freshest days you might see geese on their way to milder wintering quarters.

One reason for the variety of birds is the general lack of refuge elsewhere on Italy's western coast. Another is the modest 1-metre (3-ft) depth of both lagoons, which provides an accessible mulch of fish, molluscs, algae and crustaceans as food; and a variety of wood, marsh, maquis, dune and reed habitats for nest-building.

The lagoon should not blind you to the delights of the Argentario itself. Although a forest fire destroyed many valuable habitats some years back, there are numerous short walks, coves and shingle beaches. The higher crags are home to rapacious peregrines which, alongside ospreys and marsh harriers, hunt the rich feeding grounds of the lagoons.

Wildlife anomalies include the red-rumped swift, which breeds only here and in Puglia; a rare African butterfly, the two-tailed pasha (*Charaxes jasius*); and, especially on offshore rocks, a number of rare lizards, which include two subspecies of wall lizard, *Lacerta muralis beccarii* and the *Lacerta muralis marcuccii*, the latter distinguished by an extraordinary azure skin.

Before you go *Maps:* IGM 1:25,000 *Orbetello* and *Porto Ercole*.

Guidebooks: F. Pratesi, *Oasi d'Italia* (Musumeci 1987), and local guides available from the tourist office and bookshops in Orbetello.

Getting there *By car:* SS1 from Pisa and the W coast to Orbetello Scalo. The link road to Orbetello, and much of the Argentario, can be congested in July and Aug; the S of the promontory, with a 24-km (15-mile) circular road, is less hectic. Lago di Burano is ½km from the Capalbio Scalo exit off SS1.

By rail: station at Orbetello Scalo, with connections to Rome and Pisa, with 2 through trains to Siena and Florence daily. Station at Capalbio (Rome–Grosseto line) for Lago di Burano.

Where to stay: plentiful, popular and expensive accommodation at Orbetello, Porto Santo Stefano, Porto Ercole and at other spots on the coast (Capalbio and Ansedonia). Summer booking advised.

Outdoor living: several campsites on the coast near Orbetello, with 2 on the northern sandspit (the Gianella): Gianella-La Costa, T: (0564) 820 049; and Haway, T: (0564) 870 164. Also possible on the 20km (12 miles) of unbroken dunes behind the Lago di Burano oasis.

Access: WWF oasis at

Orbetello is open from 1 Sept to 30 Apr; at Burano from 1 Aug to 31 May; both at 10am and 2pm on Thurs and Sun. However, birds can be seen from many other points: for Orbetello go to the southern spit, known as the Feniglia (a 470-ha/1,160-acre state *riserva naturale* with free access); for Burano, take the minor road along the northern shore or walk along the dunes to see the western coastal shore.

Activities *Walking:* short walks on Argentario, including climb to summit (Il Telegrafo) via a choice of tracks from Porto Ercole. Also on the Tombola di Feniglia, from where you can make a simple coastal walk via Ansedonia to the WWF oasis at Burano (4hr). There is a planned long-distance path from Siena to the Argentario, as yet not fully marked.

Birdwatching: outstanding throughout, with hides and observation points in the Orbetello oasis (2km/1 mile east of Albinia on the SS1).

Further information *Tourist office:* Corso Umberto 55a, Porto S. Stefano, T: (0564) 814 208.

Parco Nazionale d'Arcipelago Toscano

Islands of Elba, Gorgona, Capraia, Pianosa, Montecristo and Giannutri; national park of 67,500ha (168,000 acres)

The seven islands in the Tuscan archipelago lie midway between the Tuscan mainland south of Livorno and the French island of Corsica. Three have penal colonies and two are uninhabited; of the remaining two, Giglio has many tourists (for which reason it is ignored here), and Giannutri is becoming commercialized.

You have to be selective, therefore, when choosing where to go. The reserves on Montecristo and Capraia, however, fully merit a visit, and Elba is a rich field for the mineralogist (and also the third largest of the Italian islands).

Among the summer visitors to Italy's wetlands is the black-winged stilt, a black and white wading bird distinguished by its enormously long crimson legs.

When Napoleon was exiled to Elba in 1814, it was doubtless a considerable wilderness. Today it is a holiday resort with one million visitors coming in August alone. However, there are still areas of untouched scrubland in the west, and the interior is green and pretty.

As with the other islands, Elba forms part of a submerged granite range, whose peaks are the islands, blessed with huge mineral wealth. Inhabited since 3,000 BC, Elba provided copper, bronze and iron for early mankind. The Greeks named the island *Aethalia*, or "sparks", after its many forges, and it was with Elban iron in their swords that the Romans forged an empire. Enthusiasts can pick over a range of minerals, from andalusite to zircon, and visit Rio Marina's geology museum by way of an introduction.

Wooded Montecristo (1,031ha/2,548 acres), home of Alexandre Dumas' fictional Count, was recently declared an integral nature reserve. Although visits are difficult, private boats and day-trippers are allowed to dock at Cala Maestra, one of many coves on the steep-sided coast. On the island you may see Bonelli's eagles and the majestic osprey, as well as the red-legged partridge, which is extinct in Italy except for pockets of Piedmont and Liguria. Be sure to take binoculars: this is one of the last refuges of the monk seal in the Mediterranean. It is also home to the Montecristo viper, a variant of the asp viper, with a wide brown dorsal stripe, and to numerous indigenous lizards and invertebrates.

Distant Capraia, which is unspoiled, varied and very beautiful, is the best of the islands. Since 1979 the local council, helped by young volunteers, has promoted a 1,926-ha (4,759-acre) *parco naturale*, now doing an admirable job of preserving the island's heritage.

The island's volcanic origin has given rise to spectacular coastal cliffs, some of black contorted lavas, others of bright red rock, as at Cala Rossa. Sea winds make the climate mild, and there are several springs, even an idyllic lake, La Stagnone, which keep the rugged interior green.

Tracks criss-cross the entire island, and there are simple walks to the highest point, Monte Castello (445m/1,459ft), as well as to the bay at Zuvletti and the headland at Punta dello Zenobito. Boats will also take you around the 40 or so kilometres (25 miles) of consistently spectacular

coastline (the western cliffs especially are pitted with caves).

Isolation has favoured specialized endemics on these islands, similar to species confined to Sardinia and Corsica. Plants include the Capraia toad flax (*Linaria capraria*), with purplish-violet flowers, and the campion *Silene salzmannii*. Birds are of exceptional interest, with 40 resident species and many migratory visitors. Breeding birds include 50–120 pairs of Audouin's gull (the rarest breeding gull in Europe), Manx and Cory's shearwaters, peregrines, gannets and warblers (notably Marmora's, spectacled and Dartford). Passage migrants include honey buzzards, Bonelli's and booted eagles, as well as ospreys.
Before you go *Map:* IGM 1:25,000 *Isola di Capraia.* Map

of hiking trails on Elba from the Comunità Montana, Viale Manzoni 4, Portoferraio, Elba. *Guidebook:* C. Serpel, *Traveller's Guide to Elba and the Tuscan Archipelago* (J. Cape). Also M. Lambertini's *Isola di Capraia*, produced by the park co-operative, which organizes nature rambles, birdwatching and botany courses, T: (0586) 905 071.
Getting there *By sea:* boats from Livorno to Capraia daily except Mon and Sun (3hr), and weekly from Portoferraio on Elba (2hr); details from Toremar Lines, T: (0586) 905 069.

Numerous ferries and hydrofoils to Elban ports (Portoferraio, Porto Azzuro and Rio Marino) from Piombino (1hr), T: (0565) 33031 and Livorno (3hr), T: (0565) 918 101.

Booking for cars in summer

highly recommended.

For Pianosa take boats from Elba (Porto Azzuro); for Montecristo, from Pianosa and Porto Azzuro. Half-day trips round Capraia can be arranged through the island's tourist office.
Where to stay: a great many camping and hotel possibilities on Elba, though many are open Apr–Oct only. Contact the main tourist office (address below).

Capraia has 1 hotel, the Milanao, T: (0565) 95032, 2 *pensioni* and a 3-star campsite, Sughere, Via delle Sughere 1, T: (0586) 905 066.
Activities *Walking:* marked trails on Elba, notably on and around Monte Capanne (1,018m/3,340ft); paths and tracks on Capraia.
Scuba-diving: excellent diving around coast of Capraia.
Further information *Tourist offices:* Via Roma 2, Capraia Town, T: (0586) 905 025; Calata Italia 26, Portoferraio, Elba, T: (0565) 92671.

Monte Cucco

Regional park of limestone massif in north-east Umbria popular with walkers, cavers and hang-gliders (8,400ha/20,800 acres)

Monte Cucco, one of the highest points in Umbria (1,566m/5,137ft), is a robust and rounded mountain quite different in character from the pastoral countryside for which

Seabirds wheel above the remote western coast of Capraia. Much of the island is under conservation order.

127

Umbria is renowned. However, what is famous in this instance is neither the countryside nor the mountain but what lies below: the deepest cave system on the Italian peninsula and the fifth deepest in the world.

It was first explored as early as 1889; but it has only recently been opened up by the hundreds of cavers that flock here from all over Europe. Known to be at least 920m (3,000ft) deep, with 40km (25 miles) of galleries, it was the inspiration for the formation of Italy's most energetic caving club at nearby Costacciaro. Only 40m (130ft) of the cave system are open to the public (entry is by means of a steep metal ladder), but the club organizes deeper sorties for enthusiasts and offers guidance for visiting experts. For the non-expert it coordinates pursuits both underground and on the surface.

If you do not want the high mountain challenges of the Abruzzo or the deep south, Cucco offers some of the loveliest medium-standard walking in central Italy. The area is accessible from Rome, with all the woods, meadows, gentle grass slopes and rounded summits typical of the Apennines. The caving club and local councils between them have marked 30 different paths in the area, all collected on a map available from Costacciaro; and the area has become a well-signposted destination for walkers and campers.

Botanists will find special joy in May and June amid the wild flowers of the high meadows. In the fresh, less exposed valleys of the Ranco and the Macinare, there are magnificent beech woods. The smooth terrain provides perfect piste and cross-country opportunities for skiers with

128

ample winter snow, despite Cucco's modest heights. The Pian delle Macinarie north-west of the summit is the best for skiing.

There are plenty of walks in the surrounding mountains, particularly from the resort of Valsorda. One of the most travelled is the trek made by thousands of pilgrims to the summit of the Serra Santa, "Holy Mountain" (1,421m/ 4,662ft). Car drivers should take the SS360 north from Costacciaro to the Gola del Corno, a magnificent gorge between Cucco and Catria.

Before you go: whatever your outdoor interest, a visit to the caving club, the Centro Nazionale di Speleologia, is essential: Corso Mazzini 9, Costacciaro, T: (075) 917 0236. They hire equipment and publish a 1:16,000 map of paths on and around Monte Cucco.

Maps: IGM 1:25,000 *Costacciaro* and *Fossato di Vico.*

Getting there *By car:* A1 to Orte (from Rome) and then SS3 to Costacciaro via Foligno and Gualdo Tadino. An unclassified road leads from Sigillo, 12km (7 miles) N of Gualdo, to the Val di Ranco, best departure point for walks in the area. Approaches from the E are more difficult, the best access being the SS76 via Fabriano and Fossato di Vico. *By rail:* station at Fossato di Vico on the main Rome–Ancona line. *By bus:* bus connections to Gualdo Tadino, Sigillo and Costacciaro from Perugia, Fano and Foligno.

Where to stay: Da Tobia at 1,048m (3,438ft), high in the Val di Ranco, is a fabled cavers', and hang-gliders, hotel, and the best base for walkers; try to book, T: (075) 917 194.

Nearby alternatives are at Sigillo, Costacciaro, Scheggia,

Sassoferrato and Fabriano, though you might prefer to stay in Gubbio, one of Umbria's prettiest hill-towns.

Nearest hostel is Centro Sociale Verde Soggiorno, Via del Bosco 5, Gualdo Tadino, T: (075) 916 263.

Outdoor living: camping is permitted, and there are organized sites at Costacciaro and Valsorda, T: (075) 913 261 (open May–Oct).

Activities *Walking:* 30 marked trails in the area; for the straightforward ascent of Cucco from the Val di Ranco (4hr) follow Trail 1 to the summit (via Pian delle Macinare) and Trail 2 for the descent (yellow–red markings). You might also try the walk from Casa il Sasso (near Pascelupo) through the Valle delle Prigioni to the Pian di Rolla (4hr); the short climb to Monte le Gronde from the Pian delle Macinare (1½hr); or the walk to the austere Riofreddo canyon.

Climbing: routes at Le Lecce and the Fossa Secca. Details: CAI, Via Piermarini, Foligno; and CAI, Via Pianciani 4, Spoleto, T: (0743) 28233.

Hang-gliding: main areas are S of Cucco in the Val di Ranco, where there are 2 organized take-off points. For instruction contact the school at Scirca, near Sigillo, T: (075) 917 185.

Caving: descent of the Grotta del Monte Cucco is for experts only. There are 20 separate pots, the largest, the Gizmo, 176m (577ft) deep. Non-cavers can explore the first pot with a guide from the caving centre. Other local caves, again for experts, include the Voragine Boccanera and Grotta Ferrata.

Further information *Tourist offices:* Piazza Calai 39, Gualdo Tadino, T: (075) 912 172; Porta Romana, Foligno, T: (0742) 60459.

Ecology: WWF, Via Pignattara 2, Foligno, T: (0742) 55181.

Valnerina

Regional park of deeply incised valley (40km/25 miles) between high limestone ridges in Umbria

Wilderness in Umbria can be discovered tucked away in a remote part of the region, east of Spoleto. This is the Valnerina, a long tributary valley of the Tiber, running from near Norcia through wild mountain scenery to Terni. All the vivid beauty of the Apennines is here: an unending succession of rocky crags and forests, with fortified villages, peaks and valleys, and the fast-flowing River Nera itself with trout, eels, even crayfish.

A road runs the length of the valley and serves side valleys that lead into isolated countryside. Passable tracks climb to pronounced ridges that rise to a high point at Monte Coscerno of 1,685m (5,500ft). Gloriously solitary to walk, the hills have wonderful views and meadows filled with wild flowers. Wild boar populate the clumps of beech forest, and wolves — the ultimate seal on any wilderness — are known to prowl the higher slopes.

Until a few years ago, a railway ran along most of the valley, linking Spoleto and Norcia. In its day it must have been one of the most beautiful in Italy. Now its trackless route forms the basis for an increasingly popular hike, a novel and gentle alternative to the mountain paths. The best section starts midway down the valley at the road junction for the village of Sant'Anatolia di Narco. From here the route winds through tunnels (take a torch) and over viaducts to Spoleto, a seven-hour walk

through whale-backed mountains and wooded gorges.

Farther down the Valnerina, close to Ferentillo, looms the ninth-century abbey of San Pietro in Valle, resplendent in its isolation, and one of the most important monasteries in central Italy. Also close to Ferentillo are crags and overhangs that together are fast becoming the free-climbing centre of Italy.

The famous waterfalls at Marmore are spectacular, though man-made. Created by the Romans for drainage projects in the southern hills, they can now be switched off in order to divert the water to hydro-electric turbines. The setting, however, is magical. Lush green foliage and marble, polished by cascading water, frame 165m (540ft) of falls. Standing alongside such a powerful sight, I was a little disheartened to know that this symphony of water rested on the flick of a switch.

Before you go *Maps:* IGM 1:25,000 *Campello sul Clitunno* and *Spoleto* (railway walk); *Ferentillo, Visso, S. Anatolia di Narco, Preci* and *Monte Femaul* (the Valnerina). Kompass 1:50,000 *Monti Sibillini* (no. 666)

Getting there *By car:* the SS209 runs the length of the Valnerina, reached from Terni and from Spoleto (on the picturesque SS395). Laborious approaches from the E (Ascoli Piceno) on the SS4/SS396 via Norcia.

By rail: station at Spoleto, with frequent connections to Rome, Perugia and Ancona; 4 buses daily from the station to Norcia and villages *en route*. Station at Terni for the southern valley with buses to Marmore, Ferentillo and Arrone. Also a halt at Marmore on the Terni–Rieti rail link.

By bus: details, T: (0744) 59541.

Where to stay: modest hotels at Norcia, Ferentillo, Triponzo, Preci, Visso, Sant'Anatolia; more luxurious options at Spoleto and Terni. There is a hostel at Ferentillo for climbers and naturalists. In Norcia try the 3-star Grotta Azzurra, T: (0743) 816 513, and in Scheggino the 2-star Del Ponte, T: (0743) 61131.

Outdoor living: free camping is possible, and there are sites at Spoleto, Terni and in the valley itself at Preci, T: (0743) 99430 (open Apr–Oct).

Activities *Walking:* the area is a dream for walkers, with plenty of unfrequented hills, good access and ample accommodation. Spoleto's tourist office publishes a free leaflet of local walks.

Apart from the recommended railway walk, appealing outings include the climb from Preci to Monte Fionchi (1,337m/4,400ft) (3hr), and the ascent of Monte Coscerno from Gavelli (4hr).

Climbing: for information on the new routes around Ferentillo contact: CAI, Via Piancini 4, Spoleto, T: (0743) 28233; and CAI, Via Roma 96, Terni.

Canoeing: lovely, straightforward runs with few changes in level.

Fishing: the Nera is heavily stocked and heavily fished; permits, conditions and information from tourist offices and the FIPS branch, Corso Tacito 84, Terni, T: (0744) 409 235.

Outing: the Marmore Falls are switched on at different times in the year. Contact the local tourist office for information.

Further information *Tourist offices:* Piazza San Benedetto, Norcia, T: (0743) 816 165; Viale C. Battisti, Terni, T: (0744) 409 201; Piazza Libertà 7, Spoleto, T: (0743) 28111/49890.

CHAPTER 6

Abruzzo

To come to the Abruzzo is to find some of the wildest and most beautiful country in Italy. You are just an hour from Rome's Via Veneto and famous Seven Hills, and yet you might be in a backwater from the last century. This is still a land that could provide settings for a dozen fairy tales, with its wolves and bears, sturdy country folk, woodsmen and shepherds. Villages on snow-dusted hills are wreathed in mist amid the wild mountains, deep valleys and dark forests; and ancient are crafts practised for their own uses, not for the tourists.

Most of all, though, it is a land of wilderness, the heartland of the Apennines and the Italian peninsula. It is the most completely mountainous region in the country. Only 23 of its 261 *comunes*, the Italian equivalent of a parish, are below 500 metres (1,600 feet). In the Gran Sasso it has the highest point on the mainland south of the Alps, and supports only about three per cent of the country's population. Except for a sandy coastal strip, all is upland, with hills rising quickly to mountains, of which there are three distinct groups — the Laga, the Gran Sasso and the Maiella.

For the most part the scattered inhabitants receive few visitors. The Abruzzo was for centuries the most isolated part of the country except for Calabria. Not many people made the effort to breach its natural defences. The English poet Henry Swinburne tried in 1779, and was forced back to Rome by "as outrageous a blast of snow as any I faced, even in my own

On high ground in the central Apennines, the limestone and cool climate provide perfect conditions for beech trees to flourish.

country". Many an Abruzzese village is still cut off for weeks in deep winter.

To some extent things are beginning to change. A motorway now runs across the region, ferrying hikers and skiers to the burgeoning resorts of the Gran Sasso. Rome has been as much a magnet for the dispossessed of the Abruzzo as it has been for the young of Sicily and the south. Emigration has left villages full of old people and old ways, and not rewarded many of those who escaped. Every wintertime-seller of roast chestnuts in Rome is from the Abruzzo, and in the way of these things the Abruzzese have become the butt of any Italian joke that requires a slow-witted dullard.

The break with the past has been most felt in sheep farming, the pastoral mainstay of Abruzzese life for centuries. Local pasture was too poor to support animals through the winter; and since Puglia's land was scorched by summer sun, landowners came up with a system of transhumance that made the best of both worlds. They organized twice-yearly migrations along ancient *trattari*, sheepways up to 20 metres (66 feet) wide and as often as not filled with animals 12 abreast and in flocks that could number many thousands. This army of grey wool moved forward in divisions, each flock led by a shepherd and an old ram, the *manso*, meaning "gentle" or "trained". Before the nineteenth century over a million sheep a year were moved in this way. Now the flocks are smaller, the roads abandoned, and movements, such as they are, made in articulated trucks. The old curse of the shepherds, however, the Apennine wolf, still prowls the Abruzzo's mountains. The huge white sheepdogs used to wear spiked collars to protect them from attack.

Today the focal point for wildlife is the Parco Nazionale d'Abruzzo, the most important natural reserve on the entire peninsula. The Apennines' last bears roam here and some of the tamest chamois you could hope to find. Excellent though the conservation in this park is, for the taste of real wilderness I prefer the untended heights of the Maiella or the endless forests of the Monti della Laga.

All of the Abruzzo, except for the Laga, is quintessential limestone scenery: high buckled massifs unrivalled in the Apennine landscape. Myriad species of plants enjoy the soils, and beech proliferates in huge mixed forests of montane and Mediterranean types. Yet this rugged natural beauty conceals an immense destructive power: the Abruzzo is earthquake country. The landscape's odd and distorted contours are a constant reminder of the great disaster of 1915 when 30,000 people died and 400 villages were razed to the ground. You might want to avoid January, which is the month in which most earthquakes since the fourteenth century have occurred. "When the cold is at its strongest, the earthquake is at its greatest," runs an Abruzzo proverb.

Little Molise, sandwiched on the east coast between Puglia and the Abruzzo, is often seen as an appendix to Abruzzo. Although it was only officially created as a region in 1963, Molise has had a distinct identity, with its own dialect, since medieval times. It also has some of the most neglected hill country in Italy. People here are the rural hardworking folk they have always been, and proud of traditions that have been influenced by the arrival of Slavs and Albanians in the fifteenth and sixteenth centuries. Venture here and you will find one of the country's quietest and most charming corners.

GETTING THERE

By air: with excellent motorway connections between Rome and most centres in the Abruzzo and Molise, the capital's Leonardo da Vinci (or Fiumicino) international airport is as good a destination to fly to as any. Fly-drive deals from car hire firms such as Budget and Avis enable you to be in the Abruzzo within 2 hours of disembarking.

There is a provincial airport at Pescara, with charter flights and internal connecting services; Alitalia, T: (085) 26632. The nearest airports to most of Molise are Naples or Gino Lisa at Foggia in Puglia, T: (0881) 73959.

By rail: considering they are mountainous regions, the Abruzzo and Molise are well-served by railways, though the network is complicated and services can be slow. The main axis is the trans–Apennine Rome–Avezzano–Sulmona–Pescara line (for the Velino, Maiella and Simbruini). There are minor branches from the Sulmona–L'Aquila–Rieti–Terni line (for the Gran Sasso and Monti della Laga); Sulmona–Castel di Sangro–Carpinone–Campobasso (for the Parco Nazionale d'Abruzzo and Molise); Avezzano–Roccasecca; Vairano–Isernia–Carpinone.

WHERE TO STAY

Molise is little-known, and accommodation is scarce outside the main centres such as Campobasso. Abruzzo is better served, but again hotels are mostly in larger towns or ski resorts. For full lists of hotels consult local tourist offices, or write to the main regional offices (addresses below).

ACTIVITIES

Walking: the Abruzzo has the best walking in central Italy. The Gran Sasso and Abruzzo National Parks have numerous marked paths; the Maiella, Laga and Velino, by contrast, are virtually uncharted. Molise provides equally unknown countryside, more suited to low-level hikes, but with occasional high mountain environments. There are 2 unofficial long-distance paths: from the Sibillini to the Gran Sasso, and from the Simbruini to the Parco Nazionale d'Abruzzo (10 days). Shorter treks are listed in the relevant Exploration Zones, along with the CAI branches to contact for information.

Birdwatching: the lack of major wetland habitats is compensated for by mountain environments where most high-level birds can be seen. Extensive literature is available on these areas, particularly in the Abruzzo National Park. The main LIPU branches are: Via Svolta della Misericordia 2, L'Aquila, T: (0862) 27740; Via Ravasco 36, Pescara, T: (085) 72590. Both groups organize birdwatching courses in the Abruzzo National Park.

Fishing: FIPS branches for permits, conditions and information at: Via XXIV Maggio 5, Avezzano; Piazza Umberto I 7, Chieti; Via Rigopiano 65, Pescara, T: (085) 27740; (Molise) Via Monforte 16, Campobasso, T: (0874) 95025; Via Berta, Isernia, T: (0865) 3932.

Skiing: Gran Sasso has the best pistes in central Italy, and the most advanced and extensive facilities as a result. Other massifs have very minor resorts, though cross-country skiing is outstanding in all areas. In Molise there are small developments at Capracotta and Campitello Matese.

FURTHER INFORMATION

Regional tourist offices: Via Fabrizi 173, Pescara, Abruzzo, T: (085) 22707; Piazza Vittoria, Campobasso, Molise, T: (0874) 95663.

Monti della Laga

High, wooded mountain massif; proposed national park (50,000ha/123,500 acres)

Together with the Maiella, the Monti della Laga are some of Italy's remotest mountains. Although they are the lowest of the Abbruzzo's four colossal ranges, their highest peak, at Monte Gorzano, reaches 2,458 metres (8,064 feet), not high enough to attract down-hill skiers and thankfully also still free of development. Endless tracts of pine and beech forest cloak the eastern slopes, creating a marvellous aura of mystery, their silence broken occasionally by the play of streams and waterfalls.

Bounded by the mountain ranges of the Sibillini to the north and the Gran Sasso to the south, the Laga reaches its highest point from an unbroken scarp of some 1,500 metres (5,000 feet) from the Amatrice plain, to the west. A well-defined ridge some 30 kilometres (20 miles) long then

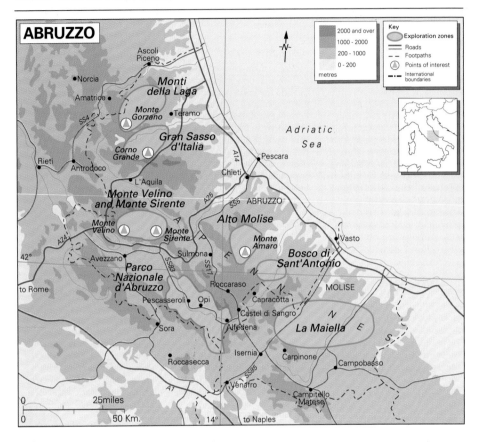

takes you through beautiful lush scenery that is unlike other parts of the Abruzzo.

The geology of the Laga differs from the other Abruzzese massifs in that it comprises mainly Miocene marls and sandstone. These less permeable rocks allow rainwater to collect, giving succour to vegetation; while streams, lakes and, above all, waterfalls (or *fossi*) appear in the mountains. Some of these waterfalls are up to 80 metres (250 feet) high, and all tend to emerge at around 1,500 metres (5,000 feet). At this height they can freeze in winter, creating one of the most magical sights in Italy.

If an Abruzzo winter is too daunting a prospect, a good time for a visit is between May and June. Then the meadows are in flower, the rivers in spate and the falls a torrent of crashing, muddied meltwater. On days such as these you might have stumbled

into the Alps. And if you *are* here at this time, pull on your boots and make straight for the valley of the Acero in the Laga's south-east corner.

The valley lies above the village of Crognaleto on the SS80, just before this lonely and lovely road begins its climb up to the ridges of the Gran Sasso. Follow the unmetalled lane to the hamlet of Cesacastina. Here a foaming abundance of water and a profusion of violets, buttercups and red and white orchids herald the region's highlight: the Valle delle Cento Cascate, the "valley of a hundred waterfalls". As you walk, the Himalayan profile of the Gran Sasso stretches across the near horizon, its snow-covered peaks contrasting with the exuberant foaming of white water.

Forests, however, and not water, are the Laga's main feature. In the woods of the

Martese, Langammella and San Gerbone trees grow in numbers greater than anywhere else in the Apennines. On the eastern slopes (those to the west being largely barren) dense beech and pine roll on indefinitely towards the Marche. In the Valle Castellana, by contrast, pride of place goes to mixed woodlands. In few parts of central Italy, except perhaps the Maiella, are you so lost in mystery, silence and utter solitude. The pines in these forests, especially those of the Martese, are centuries old, and largely untouched by human hand, unlike the forests in other parts of the Apennines. With few exceptions, these mountains and forests are still too inaccessible, and too far from the big cities, to be exploited.

Walkers in the Laga are well served by paths, mostly old mule-tracks, as well as by the tourist office at Amatrice. You might look into the mystery of the ancient track that traverses the massif from Amatrice to Montagna di Fiori. The stretch to Pizzo di Sevo (2,419 metres/7,936 feet) is known by tradition as the *tracciolino di Annibal*, "Hannibal's little track". The implication is that the great Carthaginian general, famous for his alpine crossing, traversed these mountains on his march to the Adriatic.

There is a one disappointment in the Laga: the scarcity of animal life, though you may, if very lucky, find traces of wolves. Some claim the brown bear survives and, given the secrecy of the mountains, they could be right. Deer are rare, and the only larger mammals are wildcats, badgers, hares and the odd fox. Birds prosper in the rougher country, and the Giaccio Porcelli region, in particular, is noted for its raptors.

Naturalists on the whole head south-west to the Lago di Campotosto, a man-made lake and a rather tawdry affair after the natural abundance of water in the Laga. For birds, however, it provides a rare inland resting place. The banks are a mixture of habitats, from marsh to woodland, and well-suited to a variety of wintering species, such as cranes, herons and the extremely rare *beccaccino*. Migratory birds include grebes, coots, terns, moorhens and many species of ducks and waders.

BEFORE YOU GO

For walking, climbing and skiing information contact CAI offices at: Via N. Sauro 46, Teramo; Corso Mazzini 81, Ascoli Piceno.

Maps: IGM 1:25,000 *Pietralto*, *Campotosto* and *Cortino;* CAI 1:50,000 *Monti della Laga*. For the Cento Cascate walk (see below) take IGM 139 1 NE *Monte Gorzano*.

Guidebooks: E. Ercoloni, *Appennino Bianco*; S. Ardito, *A Piedi in Abruzzo I/II*.

GETTING THERE

By car: the Laga are some way from major roads; from Rome use SS4 to Rieti, Antrodoco and Amatrice. From Pescara and the E take A14 (Teramo exit) and SS80 to Teramo, where minor roads spread into the Laga's eastern foothills. For the Lago di Campotosto continue on the SS80 beyond Teramo.

By rail: nearest stations are over 50km (30 miles) away at Antrodoco and L'Aquila. **By bus:** limited service to mountain centres from Amatrice, Teramo and L'Aquila.

WHERE TO STAY

Hotels at Amatrice, Campotosto, Acquasanta Terme and Leppo. Free camping is permitted. The hills are also scattered with huts and bivouacs belonging to shepherds and the forestry authorities.

ACTIVITIES

Walking: extensive hiking and trekking opportunities over scarcely frequented country. Highly recommended is the trek in the Valle delle Cento Cascate, with optional ascents of Gorzano and the Monti della Laghetta (6hr): it starts (and

finishes) at the bridge on the road above Cesacastina, a hamlet 6km (4 miles) SE of Gorzano. The path follows an obvious route along the stream and then climbs in open country to the main ridge at the Sella di Gorzano.

Other noteworthy walks include: the panoramic ascent of Monti di Mezzo (2,136m/ 7,007ft) above Lago di Campotosto from Frattoli or Campotosto village (4hr); to Monte Gorzano from Amatrice (via the Fosso di Selva Grande and Sella della Solagna). This walk starts at Capricchia, launching pad for several hikes.

FURTHER INFORMATION

Tourist information: Via Madonna della Porta 15, Amatrice, T: (0746) 85249; Via del Castello 10, Teramo, T: (0861) 54243.

ORSINI'S VIPER

Orsini's viper *Vipera ursinii ursinii* occurs in isolated populations in the mountains of France and Italy. It is a thickset, slate-grey snake with a black-bordered zigzag stripe down the centre of its back and a rather narrower head than most vipers. The smallest and least dangerous European viper, the adults are rarely more than a metre in length, rarely biting and with relatively weak venom. In Italy Orsini's viper has been recorded in the Monti Sibillini, Monti della Laga and the Velino Park. Of all these populations, the one that inhabits the Campo Imperatore at Gran Sasso is by far the largest.

Gran Sasso d'Italia

Spectacular massif of alpine grandeur; proposed national park (40,000ha/100,000 acres)

The Gran Sasso d'Italia ("Big Rock of Italy") is the highest and perhaps most spectacular mountain on the Italian peninsula. Although it appears as a single peak when seen from other massifs in the Abruzzo, a number of summits are visible from the Adriatic coast. At nearly 3,000 metres (10,000 feet), the most distinct summit is Corno Grande, a glorious free-standing pyramid overlooking the huge sun-baked plain of the Campo Imperatore ("Emperor's Field") to the south. On clear days both the Adriatic and the more distant Tyrrhenian coast can be seen.

Although much visited, the Gran Sasso does conceal corners of solitude. Once, indeed, there was nowhere as remote. In 1943, for example, it was used as a prison for the deposed Mussolini before German commandos in a daring raid took him north for a brief career as a puppet-ruler of the Salò Republic. The raid would not need to be nearly so daring today: a journey which could then only be made by light plane

can now be made every day by conventional traffic and cable cars, which serve an area hailed as Italy's finest, outside the Alps, for skiers and climbers.

To be alone you must climb high, rather like the mountain's beleaguered wildlife. For it is on the high ground, where many peaks are in excess of 2,500 metres (8,000 feet), that the Gran Sasso displays a dramatic combination of alpine and Apennine features. It has Europe's southernmost glacier, the Calderone, a modest area of only six hectares (15 acres); it has the highest spring in the Apennines, the Fonte Grotta (2,050 metres/6,700 feet); and rock walls rise sheer for anything up to 1,500 metres (5,000 feet). Perhaps the most striking feature is the Campo Imperatore which is the largest upland plain in the Apennines, 27 kilometres (17 miles) long and 8 kilometres (5 miles) wide. In the spring it is the grandest of all Italy's flower-filled meadows, yet in summer it becomes a desolate moonscape.

At the loftiest altitudes you can escape the masses and discover some of the secrets of this mountain. On the snowline of Monte Aquila, climbing towards the Corno Grande, grows one of the world's smallest trees: the dwarf willow (*Salix herbacea*). Its normal home is in the subarctic regions where the soil is exposed for barely three months of the year. To cope with such conditions it grows prodigious roots and pushes just a tentative couple of centimetres (one inch) above the ground. Elsewhere, Monte Brancastello is noted for its carpets of Apennine edelweiss; relict birch woods flourish at San Nicola and on Monte Preda; ancient yews thrive in the Angora valley; and at Ornano and Crognelato grow the best of the area's vast pine forests.

If the swish of ski and tramp of the tourist's boot have spared Gran Sasso's flora, however, they have frightened off what little of its native fauna has survived the hunters. A joint effort between the CAI and Parco Nazionale d'Abruzzo is trying to reintroduce the chamois for the first time since it was exterminated in the last century. Bear and deer are no longer here, though the wolf roams in the more remote areas (sightings have been reported in the suitably named Campo Pericoli, "Field of Dangers"). Generally, though, animals are limited to minor fauna such as Orsini's viper and the Italian newt (*Triturus italicus*), both typical of the high Apennines. The Italian newt is confined to southern Italy, living at heights of up to about 1,500 metres (5,000 feet). These tiny amphibians, the adults only seven and a half centimetres (three inches) long from head to tail, spend their lives in damp places, only venturing into still pools in the breeding season.

The more remote cliffs and crags provide nesting sites for a few pairs of golden eagles, lanner falcons and peregrines, as well as larger colonies of choughs, distinguished by their scarlet legs and beaks. It was here that I once disturbed a feeding peregrine, which flew across the valley in front of me trailing an awkward bundle of black feathers. When I reached the point on the path from which it had taken off, I found the neatly discarded head, feet and spinal cord of what had once been a chough. I was frankly amazed that such an aerial acrobat could have fallen prey to a bird that is only a little larger than itself.

For the most part, however, the Gran Sasso is the domain of man. Walking is superb, however social, with some of the most travelled trails in the Apennines. The Alpinist's handbook (CAI) lists over 700 routes in the Gran Sasso. Some are easy, and some call for stout heart and stout boots, but all, the authorities stress, should be treated with respect. Certain stretches require climbing skills, and in others the snow arrives early and stays long. Elsewhere areas are out of bounds because of avalanches. The rule is, stay on the trails.

An ideal day would be to go to the Gran Sasso in October when the crowds have gone and the snow has yet to fall. The refuges are still open, and the chair lifts get you off to a cracking start. There is also more high-level lodging here for treks that are longer than anywhere else in the Apennines. Some so-called huts are virtual hotels, others simple shelter for shepherds. The Rifugio Garibaldi was the first to be built, as long ago as 1884. Most are in the heart of the massif, but new huts are now planned in more peripheral areas.

BEFORE YOU GO
Maps: 1:50,000 *Carta del Gran Sasso* (CAI-L'Aquila) is the best single sheet.
Guidebooks: F. Antonelli, *Gran Sasso* (Zanichelli 1982); C. Landi Vittorj, *Gran Sasso d'Italia* (CAI-TCI 1972).

GETTING THERE
By car: L'Aquila, Gran Sasso's best base, is an hour from Rome on the A24. From Naples and the S use SS85 to Isernia and SS17 to Sulmona.

Northern and eastern routes on A25, SS150 and SS80 are laborious.

A24 (Assergi exit) for funicular to the Campo Imperatore. Small roads run E–W across the Gran Sasso, leaving the A24 at Assergi to cross the C. Imperatore.
By rail: L'Aquila is on the Sulmona–Rieti–Terni line (9 trains daily); rail information, T: (0862) 20497.
By bus: buses to L'Aquila from Avezzano, Sulmona, Teramo

and Rome. Services to local centres from L'Aquila's Piazza San Bernadino.

WHERE TO STAY
L'Aquila has accommodation in every category; on the massif's northern edge, Fano Adriano and Prato di Tivo are aimed at skiers, but have year-round hotels.
Refuges: CAI runs 5 huts; Duca degli Abruzzo and Franchetti are the most popular, both departure points for climbs and

walks on the Corno Grande and Corno Piccolo. The others are: San Nicola in the forest of the same name; Fonte Vetica, on the eastern edge of the C. Imperatore; and Del Monte, at the northern foot of Monte Corvo. Information: CAI, Via XX Settembre 99, L'Aquila, T: (0862) 24342.

Gran Sasso d'Italia

ACTIVITIES

Walking: the classic walk is the west wall ascent of Corno Grande from the Duca d'Abruzzi (there is a funicular from Assergi to 2,120m/ 6,955ft, 1km from the refuge). From the summit you can continue to Rif. Franchetti, cross the Valle delle Cornacchie and descend to Prati di Tivo, with another chair lift if required for the final descent; yellow and red markings (6hr). To repeat the traverse and return to the Duca the following day, take the trail via the Val Moane. (Snow may linger on the route as late as July).

Other noted hikes include: the climb to Pizzo Intermesoli (2,635m/8,644ft) from

Capanne in Val Moane (3hr); to Pizzo Cefalone (2,533m/ 8,310ft) from Passo della Portella (2hr).

Climbing: Gran Sasso is of exceptional interest to both summer rock- and winter ice-climbers. The Corno Piccolo's superb limestone provides over 100 established routes. Though the rock on the Corno Grande is less robust, it boasts further climbs including Paretone, longest route in the Apennines.

Skiing: resorts at C.

Imperatore, Fano Adriano and Prato di Tivo. Limited cross-country routes: the Tre Laghetti (16km/10 miles) on the C. Imperatore and the route up the Valle del Chiarino (12km/7 miles).

FURTHER INFORMATION

Tourist office: Via XX Settembre 8, T: (0862) 22306.

Ecology: WWF and LIPU local branches share an office at Via Svolta della Misericordia 2, L'Aquila, T: (0862) 28274.

Monte Velino and Monte Sirente

Mountain ranges between Gran Sasso and the Simbruini; proposed regional park (40,000ha/100,000 acres)

Climb to the top of St Peter's in Rome on a clear winter's day and you can see the snow-covered summit of Monte Velino on the eastern horizon. One of the most monu-

mental and magnificent of all the massifs in central Italy, it is known as *la montagna morta*, the "dead mountain", a mass of Mesozoic limestone with almost no vegetation. Across a vast tract of semi-desert you could walk from the Velino's northern foothills, cross the central peaks and then drop down by the ridges of the adjoining Sirente; a distance of 120 kilometres (75 miles), crossing just one tarmac road.

The highest point is Monte Velino itself (2,487 metres/8,159 feet), rising amid a cluster of other high peaks. Indeed, more peaks rise above 2,000 metres (6,500 feet) in the Velino than in any of the more famous Abruzzo massifs. The Velino merges with the Sirente in the south, and with the Monti della Duchessa in the north, even quieter and more remote mountains.

Despite having a classic limestone con-

The stark glacial grandeur of the Gran Sasso, the highest point in the Apennines (2,912m/9,554ft), attracts large numbers of hikers and climbers.

figuration, the Velino shows a degree of glaciation rare in the Apennines. There are tumbling screes, moraines, hanging valleys and even rogue rocks brought from distant mountains by the advancing ice. High on Monte Morane, in the Duchessa, for example, is the famous *pietra rosa* ("pink rock"), a huge, solitary boulder deposited during the last Ice Age.

Birds of prey nest in the moraines and rocky clefts. One of the most notable sites is the Murolungo ("long wall"). This towering cliff rises hundreds of metres high and is home to buzzards, lanner falcons, peregrines, short-toed eagles and a colony of alpine swifts. At the cliff base nestles the Grotto dell'Oro, a cave kept moist, even in summer, by the dripping of water through the rocks above, and where birds gather in the evenings.

Elsewhere you will find scooped-out tarns, tiny glinting lakes in an otherwise barren wasteland. The loveliest is the Lago della Duchessa, cradled in crags 1,772 metres (5,813 feet) high. It has no source, but is supplied simply by rain and meltwater, the spring and winter life-blood of visiting birds. Coots, teal, garganey and tufted ducks cluster here at dawn and dusk. Alongside gather hundreds of wheatears and water pipits, in a constant search for shore-side insects and larvae. It is a lovely spot, and can be reached in two hours from the hamlet of Cartore.

The most spectacular glacial features are the scoured valleys of the Val di Teve, Valle Majelama and Gole di Celano. The latter, situated on the southern side of the Sirente,

is perhaps the most majestic gorge in the Apennines and is easily accessible to walkers. Between the villages of Ovindoli and Celano the gorge drops 600 metres (2,000 feet) over 10 kilometres (6 miles), narrowing to a corridor the width of outstretched arms, and flanked by walls 100 metres (300 feet) sheer on either side. A magnificent track follows the entire gorge. Walk it in September before the rains make it dangerous and even impassable.

Grassy uplands such as the Piano di Pezza and Campo Felice enjoy brisk summer breezes and a brief but exceptional flourish of colour: buttercups, gentians, saxifrages, campions and toadflaxes are all too quickly snuffed out by either the sun or winter snow. Beech forests, with occasional oaks, shelter in the steeper valleys, but you have to descend from the beech's domain, anything up to 1,700 metres (5,600 feet), before reaching the mixed woodlands that harbour much of the Velino's wildlife. Wildcats and martens can be seen, and even wolves, which in the coldest winters have scavenged on the outskirts of Ovindoli.

Ovindoli itself commands the broad plateau between the Velino and Sirente massifs. Although some 1,200 metres (4,000 feet) high, this plateau is a break in the wilderness and supports considerable birdlife. Common birds, such as thrushes, blackbirds and woodcock, inhabit the fringes of the woodland. On the plateau itself quail, crows, shrikes and rock partridges thrive, and when heavy November rains turn it into a marshy bog, white wagtails, plovers and other waders appear.

BEFORE YOU GO
Maps: IGM 1:25,000 *Monte Sirente, Ciano di Campo Felice, Magliano de' Marsi, Celano*.
Guidebooks: E. Ercolani, *Appennino Bianco* (Iter 1985); S. Ardito, *A Piedi in Abruzzo I* (Iter, 1986).

GETTING THERE
By car: A24/25 from N, W and E (L'Aquila, Rome and Sulmona); A24 for the Duchessa and Lago della

Duchessa (Valle del Salto exit); Magliano exit for Massa and Monte Velino; Celano exit for the Golle del Celano. One minor road, the SS5, bisects the Velino and Sirente massifs; the SS578 winds W to skirt the outlying peaks.
By rail: the Rome–Sulmona–Pescara line hugs the southern edge of the park with useful stations at Cappelle (for Velino), Celano (for the gorge) and Avezzano. Branch lines

from Sulmona to L'Aquila and Terni (Umbria), both moderately useful for northern access to the massifs.
By bus: the Società ARPA runs extensive services to all towns and villages. Main termini at L'Aquila, Avezzano and Sulmona.

WHERE TO STAY
The mountain's borders have several centres with a wide range of accommodation.

L'Aquila is the best overall base, with rooms also available in the villages of Celano, Ovindoli, Rocca di Cambio, Rocca di Mezzo and Rovere. There is a single mountain refuge, the Sebastiani (2,100m/6,900ft) at the head of the Piano di Pezza. Information from CAI, Via Marconi, Avezzano, T: (0863) 20736.
Outdoor living: is permitted, and can be the only way of seeing much of the region.

ACTIVITIES
Walking: walkers on high ground can expect some of Italy's most exposed and gruelling outings. Local weather also has a reputation for being changeable. Try the superb traverse of the Celano canyon; the ascent of Velino from the Piano di Pezza (6hr); the Valle di Teve from Cartore (4hr); the Lago della Duchessa from Cartore. Longer ascents of Velino are possible from Cafornia and Massa d'Albe.
In the Sirente explore the relict beech woods at Anatella;

the Prati del Sirente and its tiny lake; and the lesser peaks of Faito, Serra di Celano and Pizzo di Ovindoli.
Climbing: surprisingly few possibilities, though winter snow and ice climbs are excellent; summit approaches to Velino, Sirente, Cafornia and Serra di Celano are Italian classics. Information from CAI at Avezzano (see above), and CAI, Via XX Settembre 15, L'Aquila, T: (0862) 24342.
Ponytrekking: the mountains will prove too much for all but the keenest riders and hardiest animals. The gentler terrain of the Altopiano delle Rocche is more suitable, and there are numerous trekking centres on the SS5 between Ovindoli and

Rocca di Mezzo.
Skiing: resorts at Ovindoli and Campo Felice, with cross-country circuits at Puzzillo and the Piano di Pezza. Alpine skiers head for Valle Majelama and the southern valleys of the Sirente. Further information from tourist offices and Società Campo Felice at Rocca di Cambio, T: (0862) 912 003.

FURTHER INFORMATION
Tourist offices: Cese, 15km (9 miles) E of Avezzano, T: (0863) 32291; Piazza S. Maria Paganica, T: (0862) 25149 and Via XX Settembre 8, T: (0862) 22306, both at L'Aquila; Rocca di Cambio, T: (0862) 918 107; Rocca di Mezzo, T: (0862) 91316.

SWIFTS
One of Italy's most common summer birds, swifts dart acrobatically around towns and cities from May to August. Their almost constant motion in search of insects has left their feet and legs shrunken. On the ground they can do little more than shuffle. They nest in roofs and under eaves, the same nesting sites often used from one year to the next.

Parco Nazionale d'Abruzzo

Classic Apennine massifs and major wildlife habitat: protection zones of 40,000ha/100,000 acres and 60,000ha/148,000 acres

The Abruzzo National Park is the last major refuge in central Italy for the wolf, bear and Apennine chamois, creatures that until this century had roamed the Apennines for thousands of years. In this model of good conservation, Italy for once has done itself proud, preserving its natural

heritage and producing in the process a park recognized as one of the most important in Europe.
The park claims 1,200 species of plants, 40 species of mammals, 30 species of reptiles, 300 different birds and 267 assorted fungi. It is, however, this degree of monitoring and control which can militate against the park's wildness. Wardens patrol, animals are kept in semi-captivity and signs instruct and implore at every turn. The park's symbol, a rather dozy-looking and domesticated bear can be seen everywhere in the park. All this, sadly, is the price of protection.
This state-within-a-state, however, is not just a wildlife park to the exclusion of

(Overleaf) Poppies blaze across a meadow in the Sangro valley, just one of 1,200 species of flora in the Parco Nazionale d'Abruzzo.

141

CHAPTER 6: ABRUZZO

The brown bear, Europe's most threatened carnivore, is represented in Italy by the subspecies *marsicanus*. About 60 bears remain in the Abruzzo, and between 10 and 15 in the Trentino Alps.

human civilization. It contains 18 towns and villages; the main centres — Pescasseroli, Opi and Villetta Barrea — are located along the Sangro valley. All are fully integrated with the park, an indication of a way of life in tune with an ancient landscape. National costume is sometimes seen, sheep farming still predominates, and you are as likely to encounter old men bringing firewood from the forests on donkeys as you are tractors and cars.

The park's treasures are jealously guarded and none more so than its fauna. The Abruzzo was once a royal hunting reserve, like many of Italy's present-day parks. Although the reserve was discontinued in 1877, its tradition of nurturing wildlife — albeit with a view to killing it later — was carried on by a smaller reserve between 1900 and 1912. By 1917 an embryonic national park had been formed; and by 1926 it had a central authority and care of some 30,000 hectares (74,000 acres) of land.

The area's central position has made it a natural gathering point for animals migrating to escape the summer heat of the south. It has also retained its inaccessibility, extreme even by the standards of the Abruzzo. Only one road, and that unclassified, serves the park, which, unlike the Gran Sasso, seems unaffected by weekend trippers from nearby towns.

Of the fauna that has survived here the most popular and now precious animal is the Apennine brown bear. It is the rarest and most reclusive of creatures, and though

you may find evidence of its presence, you will need the most enormous amount of luck to see one. However, it is exciting just to know that animals such as these are prowling the hills around you. The Abruzzo's bears are descended from alpine ancestors; but over the centuries they have evolved in complete isolation, such that they are now sufficiently different to merit the status of a subspecies *marsicanus*, named after Marsicano, the area in which they thrive. This is the generic name for much of the park region, deriving from the Marsi, the earliest known indigenous tribe of the Abruzzo.

Bears were common until the sixteenth century, when they were hunted and hounded almost to extinction. After a three-week hunting expedition with the King of Naples at the end of the eighteenth century, Sir William Hamilton, in a blood-satiated post-mortem on the trip, wrote: "We have been from morning to night without the least intermission persecuting bears, wolves, chevreuil and foxes, of which we have slain about one thousand." As late as 1915 a bounty was still being paid for every bear killed. About 35 to 60 bears are reckoned to have survived such treatment, and in the absence of a latter-day Sir William are now managing to increase their numbers at an encouraging rate.

The Abruzzo's wolves evoke the same instinctive fascination as the bears, though your chances of seeing one, alas, are probably equally remote. Here, where 15 to 20 individual wolves survive, they are a subject of local pride. Elsewhere they are harried by those who have no real motive other than base prejudice. Locals say the best time to catch a wolf's fleeting shadow is at dawn, when a few strays return to the forest after foraging in outlying farms. Because wolves now increasingly cross-breed with domestic dogs, the park maintains 20 wolves in a semi-liberated state at Civitella Alfedena, with the idea of preserving the genetic purity of the species.

Confrontation with the Abruzzese chamois is far more likely. Like the bear, these animals are descendants of an alpine strain now evolved into a distinct subspecies

(*Rupicapra rupicapra ornata*). Sporting a coat of uniform brown in summer, in winter they take on multicoloured tints that contrast with the white and black markings on the face and neck. About 400 chamois lead a carefree existence in the park, tolerant of humans, but able to run at 85kph (53mph) when the occasion demands. They are easily seen in the Valle delle Rose, and there is a reserve at Bisegna to train specialists in the care of the animals (many are released from here into other parts of the Abruzzo). Completing the picture are 400 red deer and 80 roe deer, mostly reintroduced during the last decade.

About two-thirds of the park is dominated by forests of beech and maple. The beech here is the choicest in Italy, especially on the highest slopes, where the cooler, moist conditions favour its growth. In few places will you see specimens of such magnificent height or colossal girth. However, the most striking feature of these forests is that they have trees of all ages: delicate striplings; fully grown, ramrod-straight giants; and gnarled veterans of 500 years or more, some of them growing out of the bedrock, others lodged among huge moss-covered boulders.

Interspersed with the beech are black hornbeam, ash and hawthorn, along with wild apple, pear, cherry and blackthorn, all trees with wonderful spring coats of blossom. Arboreal specialities include the black pine of Villetta Barrea, Lobel's maple, which is endemic to the mountain woods of central and south Italy, and *Acer obtusatum*. At Coppo Oscuro di Barrea there is even birch, an Ice-Age remnant of the cold-climate flora that once covered the Apennines. Stands of chestnut occasionally flourish, and on sunnier slopes the holm oak waves a reminder — for all the chill of the mountains — that here we are still in the Mediterranean.

With its wild flowers, too, the park enjoys the best of two worlds: the alpine and the Mediterranean. Spring, undaunted by the snow, which can linger until May, ushers in a splendid assembly of asphodels, crocuses, gentians and snowdrops. The park's proudest creation is the violet-flowered iris — the recently discovered

Among the many species of maple tree that occur in the Abruzzo are Lobel's maple (*Acer lobelii*), with leaves up to 15cm (6in) across (shown large); Italian maple (*Acer opalus*), with smaller toothed leaves (top, left); and Montpellier maple (*Acer monspessulanum*), whose leathery three-lobed leaves are less than 5cm (2in) across (top, right).

Iris marsica, endemic to calcareous rocky hillsides in the central Apennines. Other notables the park shares with neighbouring mountains, though in equally small numbers, are lady's slipper orchids, with splendid brown, yellow and purple flowers, gentians and columbines. These are followed by Apennine edelweiss later in the year.

Birdwatchers, too, will delight in the park. Two to three pairs of golden eagles are the stars among its many raptors (the park's own map suggests the best points to see these birds and also other animals). In two areas, the Camosciara and around Monte Pietroso, you might see the white-backed woodpecker, an extremely rare relict associated with ancient Apennine forests. Also scarce, but more widespread, is the Apennine rock partridge, very recently recognized as a sub-species (*Alectoris graeca orlandoi*) in its own right.

145

BEFORE YOU GO

Whatever your interest, visit Pescasseroli's park centre and museum (the town is also the best exploration base). The office is well-signposted (close to the town hall): Via Consultore 1, T: (0863) 91955; the museum, nearby, can answer queries on outdoor pursuits, refuges, camping, guided tours, wildlife and where to stay.

There are similar centres in Civitella Alfedena: Via Nazionale, T: (0864) 89170 (where the owner of the bar and a couple of ecology groups also have information); Barrea, Villavallelonga and at minor

The remote parts of the Parco Nazionale d'Abruzzo are home to some thirty wolves and the Apennines' last remaining brown bears.

centres during the summer.

The park has offices in Rome at: Viale delle Medaglie d'Oro 141, T: (06) 349 6993, and Via del Curato 6, T: (06) 654 3584.
Map: the park's own 1:50,000 map is all you need. It is available from park centres (L5,000).
Guidebooks: tourist offices and park centres issue numerous leaflets on a variety of topics. The park's energetic director, Franco Tassi, who takes much credit for the park's success, has written the definitive guide *Nel Parco Nazionale d'Abruzzo* (Martello 1985). Both volumes of S. Ardito's *A Piedi in Abruzzo* are useful for Italian-reading walkers.

GETTING THERE

By car: A25 (Pescina exit) E of Avezzano, then SS83 to Gioia dei Marsi, Pescasseroli and

The Gran Sasso shows its gentler sides. Whilst the eastern flanks of many Abruzzese massifs are glaciated, their western slopes are often rounded and grassy.

Opi. From Naples or Rome use A1 (Caianello exit), SS85 to Venafro and SS158 to Alfedena.
By rail: station at Alfedena on the Sulmona–Vairano line (connections from Rome and Naples), though the best approach from Rome or Pescara is by train to Avezzano and bus to Pescasseroli.
By bus: several buses daily between Avezzano and Castel di Sangro (at opposite ends of the park) via Pescasseroli, Opi, Civitella Alfedena and points *en route.* Services also to and from Pescasseroli from points outside the park (Sora, Scanno,

147

Cassino). For information, T: (0864) 556 220. ARPA services from Rome–Pescasseroli; CASNA buses from Naples to Castel di Sangro.

WHERE TO STAY
Hotels in all categories at Pescasseroli, but some closed off-season. The 2-star La Conca is central, warm and open all year: Via Vicenne, T: (0863) 91562. Also hotels at Opi, Alfedena, Barrea. Rooms and flats for rent in all villages.

Details from park centres or tourist offices.

Outdoor living: is forbidden, though the park sets aside 18 *campeggio-natura*, sites in remote areas without facilities; some are tended by forest rangers. Sites at Pescasseroli, Villetta Barrea, Barrea, Scanno and — one of the most pleasant — Le Foci di Opi near Opi, T: (0863) 912 233.

Youth hostels: La Tore, Civitella Alfedena, T: (0864) 89166; Le Vicenne, Barrea, T: (0864) 88348; Villetta Barrea, T:(0864) 89134; Opi, T: (0863) 91622.

Refuges: 1 park hut is open to the public, the Rif. dell'Orso; the other 8 are for study purposes. CAI run 2 huts at Valle Fischia and Prato di Mezzo.

ACTIVITIES
Walking: 150 numbered and well-marked trails of all standards. The most popular — avoid it during summer weekends — is trail 11 from Civitella Alfedena to the Valle delle Rose, sightings of chamois almost guaranteed (5hr).

Other favourites include: the climb from Barrea to Lago Vivo (2hr); the easy walk in the Camosciara valley to the refuge at Belvedere della Liscia (2hr); a variety of paths in the well-known Val Fondillo.

Marked treks include the

148

Parco Nazionale D'Abruzzo

Alta Via Est–Ovest from Roccaraso to Sora (3 days) and the *Alta Via Nord–Sud* from Villevallelonga to Civitella (4 days). Details from park centres and local CAI branches, but bear in mind that there is plenty of scope for linking trails and devising your own itineraries.

Ponytrekking: centres in Pescasseroli, Opi, Scanno and Villetta Barrea.

Skiing: at Pescasseroli, with cable cars to Monte Vitelle (1,945m/6,381ft), where there are 5 lifts, a beginners' slope and 20km (12 miles) of pistes. The best cross-country routes are N of the park at Scanno.

Canoeing: The River Sangro E of Opi has one of the classic Italian routes, an 8-km (5-mile) run through fast-running water to the Lago di Barrea.

FURTHER INFORMATION
Tourist information: Via Piave, Pescasseroli, T: (0863) 91461; Via S. Giovanni, Opi, T: (0863) 91622; Piazza Umberto 1, Alfedena, T: (0864) 87394.

Bosco di Sant'Antonio

Ancient tract of beech forest (300ha/740 acres)

If you had to pick a microcosm of the Apennines — its woods, hills and wildlife — it would probably be this most perfect of beech forests. Beech is the characteristic tree of central Italy: verdant in spring, fiery in autumn, it is the almost constant companion of walkers in the Abruzzo.

Sant'Antonio spreads over the Rio La Vera valley above Pescocostanzo, in the south-east corner of Abruzzo, just outside the borders of the national park. It is sheltered on either flank by Monte Rotella (2,127m/6,978ft) and Monte Pizzalto (1,969m/6,549ft). Together they form a perfect "V" of a valley, which cradles the wood and is overshadowed by high crags and surrounded by tranquil grassy meadows.

Some of the trees are a thousand years old, and most run to many hundreds of years. Certain gigantic specimens on the valley floor at Piano del Ceraso have trunks over 3m (10ft) in diameter. In modest contrast, spring sees common little eyelets of colour, peonies and narcissi, push through the forest floor.

The mood here alternates between a cathedral-like solemnity and the bird-filled chatter of stately, sun-washed branches. Sharing the glades are tits, woodpeckers, chaffinches, blackcaps, cuckoos and golden orioles. The sharp smell of fox is common, and wolves emerge from the forest, lured by the sheep in local meadows.

As so often, the wood owes its longevity to the care of monks, here based at the hermitage in nearby Sant'Antonio. However, it still came within a hair's-breadth of destruction 30 years ago, and it was as late as 1985 that a binding order was put on the area. Some 130ha (321 acres) of the total reserve comprise ancient woodland, a precious fragment that survives just kilometres from Roccaraso and Rivisondoli, two of the Abruzzo's most developed areas for holidaymakers.

Before you go Map: IGM 1:25,000 *Pescocostanzo*.

Getting there By car: most visitors make for Pescocostanzo, a lace-making village as appealing as the forest itself. It lies 5km (3 miles) N of Roccaraso, just off the SS17 between Isernia and Sulmona. From the village a lovely unclassified road runs for 20km (12 miles) up the Rio La Vera to Cansano.

By rail: stations at either end of the valley (at Cansano and Pescocostanzo) on the (slow) Sulmona–Carpinone–Isernia line (5 trains daily).

By bus: buses run to Castel di Sangro and Roccaraso from Avezzano, Pescasseroli, Isernia and Sulmona.

Where to stay: there is a rather ugly hotel on the margins of the wood itself (the Sant'Antonio, T: (0864) 67101); better options in Pescocostanzo, including a youth hostel, Ostello Le Torri, Via Roma 23, T: (0864) 66112. More luxurious hotels at Roccaraso, Rivisondoli and Campo di Giove.

Outdoor living: There is a campsite in the hills to the S at Piana del Leone, the Del Sole, T: (0864) 62532.

Further information *Tourist office:* Via Roma 60, Roccaraso, T: (0864) 62210.

La Maiella

Abruzzo limestone massif cut by deep canyons; proposed national park (35,000ha/86,500 acres)

Mystery and spirit of place are qualities as hard to account for as personal charm. The Maiella, the *madre montagna*, or "mother of mountains", in Abruzzese tradition, has both, along with the sort of wilderness that is found elsewhere in Italy only on Etna, Pollino and in the Sardinian interior. The name Maiella is probably derived from Maia, mother of the god Mercury (Hermes in classical Greece), who was widely worshipped in the Adriatic.

But to call the Maiella a mountain is to oversimplify it. It is a fantastically complicated massif of 61 peaks and 75 hills whose highest point is Monte Amaro (2,793 metres/9,163 feet), the "bitter mountain", second in height only to the Gran Sasso on the Italian peninsula. The main ridge runs north–south for 30 kilometres (20 miles). To the east spreads a labyrinth of valleys which are regarded as some of the most spectacular in Europe. To the west lies a series of lower hills, broad plains and finger-like crests that curl up towards the summits.

The Maiella is the great symbol of the central Apennines, more so than either the Velino or the Gran Sasso, from whose heights to the north it appears as a great bowed shield. It is a landscape that should be approached with caution. Distances are long, and the walks in the foothills laborious. Road and rail and the comforts of civilization are far away. Your exploration should be gradual, with time spent in the lower valleys before moving onwards and upwards.

The eastern, and more inaccessible, approaches are the best. The ancient tracks of brigands, monks and shepherds wend through dark, almost Nordic, forests. These are solemn places which from afar appear as a coarse blanket of furze over the mountains — a single intense green in which it is

Even among the Abruzzo's wild massifs, the Maiella, the "Mother of Mountains", remains one of Italy's most forbidding.

hard to discern individual trees. Under its mantle, invisible streams have cut deep fissures into the valley sides; their etched lines, which are apparent above the tree-lines, descend from amidst the many snow-covered summits.

On summer days there is nothing but an immense silence in these valleys. You may choose from several: the Fara San Martino or Santo Spirito, Selvaromana, Taranta Peligna, Tre Grotte, Fossato, Mandrelle or the ominous Vallone della Femmina Morta — the "Valley of the Dead Woman". Though most approaches are best made from the east, the most spectacular valley is, in fact, to be found on the north-western slopes of the Maiella above Caramanico, the Valle d'Orfento.

The forests of the Maiella valleys, with those of the Laga and Pollino, are some of Italy's grandest, and contain important

relict woodlands. The best of the many huge beech forests grow on the slopes of the Maielletta (1,995 metres/6,545 feet) and in the valleys of the Orfento and Valico di Forchetta. Gessopalena harbours colossal oaks, and on the Blockhaus ridge on the Maielletta grow clumps of dwarf pine that are found elsewhere in the central Apennines only in the Abruzzo National Park.

As well known as the valleys are the high plains above them. Here are some of the wildest meadows in the Apennines, vast areas of rocky grassland that give a wonderful sense of solitude and remoteness. Higher still, above 2,500 metres (8,000 feet), the plateaux turn into a severe barren landscape with hardly a tree or blade of grass in sight. The views are outstanding: they embrace the Gran Sasso, the Matese hills and the distant Tremiti Islands in the Adriatic Sea.

In the high plains flourish the wild flowers that have made the Maiella famous. The most scented meadows, heady with dozens of herbs, such as thyme, lemon balm, gentians, wormwoods and sage, lie on the massif's western fringes. There are rare alpines such as the Icelandic lichen *Cetraria islandica*, the *Papaver sendtneri* and a flood of endemics that include Apennine edelweiss, *Saxifraga italica*, Matilda's rock-jasmine and Apennine pheasant's eye (*Adonis distorta*).

Under these floral treasures lies the limestone that gave them birth, a rock as riddled with karstic quirks as it is in the rest of the Abruzzo. Where these have been emphasized by erosion, they have an extraordinary grandeur, shown, for example, by the sink holes in the Vallone della Femmina Morta and the Valle Cannella, and the famous cave system at Cavallone.

Many caves are to be found in the Maiella, particularly on its seaward side; but none compares with the one at Cavallone. Hidden beneath the slopes of the Taranta valley, its entrance is reached by 174 rock-hewn steps and guarded by bats and flocks of darting alpine swifts. The *galleria della devastazione*, a fantastic complex of fissures and fractured rock, provides evidence of major subterranean upheavals in the past. Piles of fallen stalactites lie on its floor, some massed like unicorns' horns, others starting to grow anew in bizarre and mutant forms. Lakelets, springs and waterfalls complete a highly theatrical effect.

The story of fauna in the Maiella is less encouraging: a century's impoverishment followed by a period of repopulation under the watchful eyes of conservationists. Wolves, bears and wildcats abounded until the nineteenth century; the last bear was killed in 1899 by gypsies, who offered it to the natural history museum in Florence. Now bears, wolves and otters, too, have reappeared of their own accord, while other species are being reintroduced. The Centro Studi Ecologici Appennini at Fara San Martino aims to bring the chamois to the Maiella, where it would join the red and roe deer returned by the efforts of state foresters. The biggest success story has been the protection from hunting of the wild boar.

Birds of the mountains are species typical of high rocky habitats, for instance alpine swifts, alpine choughs, jackdaws and the lovely wallcreeper — a gorgeous red and grey in flight. Raptors, including golden eagles, lanner falcons and peregrines are numerous, though it is the presence of the dotterel (*Piviere tortolino*) that establishes the Maiella's special place among Italian wildernesses. The bird was not discovered here until 1952. A handful of pairs nest 2,500 metres (8,000 feet) up on Monte Amaro, where they find conditions similar to their normal Arctic tundra habitats. As far as is known, this is the bird's southernmost breeding site in Europe.

The Maiella's proposed designation as a national park follows a history of attacks on its wilderness. At the end of the 1960s, in stories that made front-page news, it seemed as if the mountains were to be sacrificed to the great god of skiing. In the end the developers were held at bay, though traces of their preliminary activities — lifts and roads — still survive. Seven small reserves have protected the Maiella, the most important being those of the Orfento, Feudo Ugni, Fara San Martino, Quarto Santa Chiara and Piana Grande della Maielletta. The proposed national park will replace these reserves with an area under protection which will amount to ten times the coverage.

The wallcreeper's long-curved bill, its grey and crimson plumage and flight like a butterfly's belie its close relationship with the nuthatch.

CHAPTER 6: ABRUZZO

BEFORE YOU GO

Forest ranger offices, offering information and guided tours, are located at Fara San Martino, T: (0872) 980970, and Caramanico, T: (085) 92284.

For more advice contact the local CAI branches at: Palazzo SS. Annunziata, Sulmona; c/o Jacovella, Via Modesto Porto 13, Guardiagrele; Via Arniense 119, Chieti, T: (0871) 41313.
Maps: CAI at Chieti produce an invaluable 1:50,000 *Carta Turistica della Maiella.*

GETTING THERE

By car: the Maiella is more accessible from the E than from Rome: A14 to Pescara and then A25 to Sulmona, the main base if you have transport. Minor roads leave A14 at Alanno and Torre de' Passeri for the western slopes and valleys. Their eastern counterparts are served by SS84 and SS81 from Roccaraso to Chieti. There is a beautiful, though long, circumnavigation of the whole range on unclassifed roads; in the N, one lane climbs up to the Maielletta itself.
By rail: Sulmona is a busy junction on the Pescara–Rome, Sulmona–Rieti–Terni and Sulmona–Isernia lines.
By bus: Sulmona is well-connected by services from most surrounding towns. Centres in the N, like Lama and Casoli, are linked to Chieti and Castel di Sangro.

WHERE TO STAY

CAI operates several refuges and bivouacs; keys and information from local branches. The most useful are: Pelino, in the Valle on Monte Amaro; Pomilio on Maielletta; Manzini Cannella; Fusco on the Murelle. There are, in addition, forest cabins on Monte d'Ugni and dozens of shepherds' huts.

Hotels are thickest where there is skiing, unless you make

THE WILD BOAR

The boar was one of Italy's most prized mammals; not the boar of eastern Europe, but a slightly smaller indigenous race which was hunted to a hair's breadth of extinction by those seeking its huge-toothed head as a trophy. It has been persecuted since antiquity, as scenes on Etruscan vases make clear. There is even a panel showing a boar hunt on the Arch of Constantine in Rome.

Although the female produces up to 16 young in a single brood, this fecundity has not prevented a severe depletion in many of its old haunts. It is still found in its ancient heartland, the Tuscan Maremma, and in the Calabrian Apennines, Alto Molise, and parts of the Alto Tarvisio and Alpi Marittime. In both Alpine cases it is a refugee from other countries: Slovenia and France respectively.

The mating season begins on the 30th November, the feast day of St. Andrea, according to Italian tradition. Boars are shy, but seen relatively often. They are only vicious if wounded or cornered, especially females with young afoot. The marks of their passage — the furrows scooped as they dig for bulbs and tubers — are easily identifiable.

---

your base at Sulmona or Chieti.
Outdoor living: free camping is permitted, but possible mainly on lower slopes. All-year campsite at Passo Lanciano, La Maielletta, T: (0871) 896 132.

ACTIVITIES

Walking: often long and lonely walks; the key hike is the ascent of Monte Amaro (2,795m/ 9,159 feet) from the chair lift at Taranta Peligna (via the Valle

di Taranta), descending via Valle di S. Spirito to Fara S. Martino (10hr/2 days); also to Monte Amaro from either Blockhaus (6hr) or Campo di Giove (7hr); from Campo di Giove across Monte Porrara to the station at Palena (5hr); shorter walks in the Valle di S. Spirito (1–2hr) and from Blockhaus to Scrima Cavallo (1–2hr).
Climbing: mainly on the walls

of Monte Focalone, the Dea Maia at Pennapiedimonte and the Vallone di S. Spirito at Roccamorice (one of the Apennines' busiest walls). Noted are the Paretone on the NE Cima delle Murelle, the abseil after the Val Serviera and the winter routes on Morrone and Monte Porrara.

Birdwatching: the LIPU group at Pescara runs trips and has an observatory: Via Ravasco 36, Pescara, T: (085) 72590.

Skiing: resorts at C. Imperatore, Fano Adriano and Prato di Tivo. Limited cross-country routes: the Tre Laghetti (16km/10 miles) on the C. Imperatore and the route up the Valle del Chiarino (12km/7 miles).

FURTHER INFORMATION
Tourist offices: Via B. Spaventa 29, Chieti, T: (0871) 65231; Piazza Municipio, Rivisondoli, T: (0864) 69351; Via Roma 21, Sulmona, T: (0864) 53276.

Alto Molise

Wide limestone plateaux; proposed regional park (100,000ha/247,000 acres)

It is easy to treat Molise's high western borders as an extension of the Parco Nazionale d'Abruzzo and the runt of the Abruzzo mountain litter. In fact this is the least known corner of an undiscovered region: a timeless countryside of winding lanes, lazy rivers, soft valleys and lonely peaks.

High plains and pasture predominate and sheep farming is its principal activity. To the south, near the village

of Pescolanciano, runs one of Italy's great medieval sheep roads, used for centuries for the spring and autumn movement of flocks.

The area's capital is Isernia, a town that recent discoveries identify as the oldest settlement in Europe. Bones, evidence of fire and traces of a permanent camp suggest human activity going back 730,000 years. No human remains have been found, but the ghostly inhabitants have been given a name: *Homo aeserniensis* or Isernian Man.

Massive overhanging crags are typical of the peaks here, as at Monte Campo (1,746m/5,728ft), which is some 500m/1,600ft higher than the bulk of Molise's hill country. Views from these mountain tops reach as far as the Adriatic, the valleys of the Maiella and to the sea of hillocks that stretches unbroken to the plains of Puglia in the south. Walks are short and energetic, and never far from roads, the exception being the lonely, lake-dotted country around Frosolone.

The mildness of Molise's landscape, however, can belie a hard winter where depths of snow up to 7m (23ft) are known. Capracotta is one of the highest villages in Italy (1,421m/4,662ft) and holds the record for an urban snowfall. Wilder parts, too, can be found above the flower-speckled pastures, where wolves and wildcats may range for food.

Breeding birds in the mountains and hills between Capracotta and Rosello include honey buzzards, black and red kites, peregrines and maybe golden eagles.

The Alto Molise is Molise's only proposed park, still sadly very much a paper creation. The region's only genuinely protected spots are the reserves at Monte di Mezzo (291ha/719 acres) and Collemeluccio

(187ha/462acres).

Before you go *Maps:* IGM 1:25,000 *Frosolone, Carovilli, Vastogiradi, Capracotta, Agnone, Pescolanciano* and *Messer Marino.*

Getting there *By car:* the A2 takes you to within ½hr of Isernia (exits S. Vittoria and Caianello). The SS85 is then the main approach, though travellers from L'Aquila and the N will use the SS17; those from the E, the SS650 and SS652. There are many narrow and unclassified roads.

By rail: The area contains some of the most audaciously built railways in Italy. Change from Rome–Naples line for a direct ride through the Alto Molise via Isernia and Castel di Sangro, connecting at Sulmona for services throughout Abruzzo.

By bus: services run from Rome to Isernia, with connections to most local towns.

Where to stay: in Isernia, Agnone, Capracotta and Castel di Sangro; contact the tourist office at Isernia (address below). Rooms at Capracotta are aimed mainly at skiers. The hills are full of huts, still used by shepherds.

Activities *Walking:* the nicest areas are around Frosolone, and between Capracotta and Pescopennataro.

Climbing: limestone walls, especially at Colle dell'Orso and around Pescopennataro, offer striking and unclimbed routes. Information from CAI, Via Carderelli 59, Campobasso.

Ponytrekking: try the Centro Ippico Molisano in Brecelle (near Isernia), T: (0865) 3830.

Skiing: many possibilities for cross-country skiing, with established routes mainly around Capracotta.

Further information *Tourist information:* Via Farinacci 9, Isernia, T: (0865) 59590.

CHAPTER 7

The Mediterranean Coast

Both Lazio and Campania were once wild and very beautiful regions. Both, in parts, still are, but each has to support a major Italian city, respectively Rome and Naples. Rome, of course, came forth from wilderness, from the wolf that suckled the twins Romulus and Remus. And Naples stands at the edge of the *Campania felix* of the Romans, the "happy" region which Pliny described as "so blest with natural beauties and riches that it is clear that when nature formed it she took delight in accumulating all her blessings in one spot".

Campania's privileged position in many ways has been its own downfall. Good climate, soils and rich seas have always made it prosperous. Today the region has Italy's highest population density; Naples' figure of 80,000 people per square kilometre is rivalled only by cities such as Cairo and Calcutta. The verve and spirit with which Neapolitans live elbow-to-elbow is legendary, though there is little in the city or its hinterland for anyone who relishes air and space.

One continuing attraction is Vesuvius which looms over Naples ready one day to erupt and cover the city as it covered Pompeii and Herculaneum. Together with the Phlegrean Fields it forms the centre of a volcanic area that stretches along the coastal reaches of both Campania and Lazio. Less daunting and largely dormant volcanoes emerge in Lazio: the Frascati (or Albani) hills above Rome, the Tolfa hills and

The rock arch at Capo Palinuro, carved by wind and waves, is part of the Cilento coast, earmarked as one of southern Italy's future national parks.

tufaceous lowlands of the Roman Campagna (north of the city), and the old volcanic craters now filled with the lakes of Vico, Bolsena and Bracciano.

I have sat and slept through several minor earthquakes in Rome, but nothing to compare with the events of 23 November 1980, when for about two minutes Italy shifted very slightly towards the Balkans. Seventeen towns were destroyed and 4,000 people killed in the earthquake, whose epicentre lay 30 kilometres (20 miles) below ground just south of Naples.

Such malignancy makes Campania's other natural highlight seem part of another world. The Sorrento peninsula and the island of Capri form some of Europe's most fabled coastline, famed for its incandescent light and peacock-coloured seas. You will not find much in the way of wilderness here, but you will find some tiny enclaves of rare fauna, lovely areas for walking, and some of the most rapturous seascapes in Italy.

Further south lie the wilder and wetter shores of the Cilento, a mountainous area in Campania's south-east corner — as empty as Naples is full, and the first of the big southern massifs. By now you have crossed the invisible border into the south, the "other" Italy. Naples is the historical capital of this area, but where the frontier lies is anyone's guess. The Milanese say Florence, the Florentines Rome, and the Romans, who do not really care, say at the first petrol station south of Rome.

Inland from the Cilento lie the Apennines which run through both regions but do not form high, free-standing massifs like the Abruzzo, further north. The wildest and most distinct mountains are the Picentini, which though only a few kilometres from the

coast are the watershed for the Cilento peninsula. To the east lie the first of the southern badlands, the worn hills and exhausted soils that anticipate Basilicata's blighted landscape. To the west run short sharp rivers like the Sele, whose broad plain acts as one of only a few points of respite for birds migrating north up Italy's Tyrrhenian coast.

After this oasis the same birds put out to sea, likely as not to avoid Naples, and, by way of the Pontine archipelago, reach the territory of southern Lazio. For many centuries this would have been as tempting a place as any for them to settle. Prime agricultural land up till the end of the Roman Empire, this flat coastal strip then fell into disuse and reverted to lake, marsh and woodland, a landscape that used to stretch virtually unbroken up the coasts of Campania and Lazio into the Maremma of southern Tuscany.

Much of this land was malarial, uncultivable and uninhabited. What little could be used provided meagre grazing for sheep and cattle. Until the twentieth century it continued thus, with pastureland reaching up to, and often inside the gates of Rome itself. This scene changed completely with the vast Fascist reclamation projects of the 1930s. All but a fragment of this area disappeared in Mussolini's so-called "Battle for Grain". What remains today is the Circeo national park, a fascinating natural redoubt, and as important as any of the mountain parks of the Alps and the Abruzzo.

Elsewhere the draw of Rome over the past 30 years has left northern Lazio as empty of people as the southern half. What remains is an odd and somewhat foreboding area, made up of a complex succession of mountains, hills, basins and coastal lowlands. The coast is drab indeed, and inland the low volcanic uplands with their gloomy lavas do nothing to brighten the landscapes.

However, small pockets of green are to be found, principally in the sylvan hideaway that surrounds Lago di Vico. Moving east across the Tiber valley, you cross the Sabine hills and push into the forgotten part of Lazio that stretches an arm into the Apennines. Here the region claims its only mountains, the heights of Terminillo and the Ernici at the edge of the Abruzzo wilderness.

BEFORE YOU GO
Many organizations have their headquarters in Rome, and in some cases the "Useful Addresses" section at the end of this book will have details relevant to this chapter.
Maps: TCI 1:20,000. *Lazio* and *Campania-Basilicata* sheets.

GETTING THERE
By air: International flights to Rome's Leonardo da Vinci (Fiumicino) airport, T: (06) 651 4694; more limited international service to Naples' Capodichino, T: (081) 780 5763. Full internal connecting services from both centres. Charter flights to Rome's Ciampino airport.
By car: as befits a capital city, Rome is at the hub of central Italian communications. A1 from Milan and Florence. The SS1 (Via Aurelia), slow and only part motorway, connects to Pisa and Genoa on the W coast. A24 to L'Aquila, the Abruzzo, the Marche and Adriatic coast. A2 to Naples continues Italy's main arterial road. A3 from Naples to Reggio di Calabria. The minor road system in Campania is generally slower and of inferior quality.
By rail: Rome and Naples are both on international rail services from Paris, Vienna, Munich, Geneva and even Moscow. Internally they are at the heart of the national network, with trains to every corner of Italy. Rome–Florence–Milan is now a high-speed line on new track; Rome–Pisa–Genoa, Rome–

Pescara and Rome–Naples–Reggio–Palermo are other main links. Services in the S are considerably poorer. Numerous branch lines and minor routes from Naples: to the Cilento coast, Potenza, Ionian coast, Bari, Brindisi, Reggio, Caserta and Benevento.
By bus: Buses arrive at and leave from Rome and Naples to virtually all cities and major towns in Italy.

WHERE TO STAY
For details of rural accommodation contact: *Agriturist* at Corso V. Emanuale II 101, Rome, T: (06) 651 2342, and at Via A. Vespucci 9, Naples, T: (081) 225 250.

ACTIVITIES
Walking: accessible hills in northern Lazio such as Tolfa and the Cimini, middling mountain ranges in both regions (Picentini, Simbruini, Ernici) and the isolated Alburni and Cilento massifs in southern Campania. General information from: CAI, Via Ripetta 142, Rome, T: (06) 656 1011; CAI, Castell d'Ovo, T: (081) 404 421. Long-distance paths marked in the Picentini only.
Hang-gliding: major Italian centre at Rieti: details from Federazione Italiana Volo Libero, Via Rosatelli, Rieti, T: (0746) 43127.
Skiing: Resorts in Lazio at Terminillo, Campo Staffi (Arcinazzo) and Monte Livata (Subiaco); in Campania at

Although at first sight similar to many other wild roses, sweet-briar (*Rosa rubiginosa*) is easily distinguished by sticky russet glands beneath the leaves, which smell strongly of apples when crushed.

Piano Laceno (Bagnoli Irpino) and Campolaspieri. Excellent cross-country skiing in all mountain massifs.
Caving: important caves in the Alburni mountains (Cilento), marine caves on the Cilento coast and around Sorrento peninsula (Valle delle Ferriere). See Exploration Zones for details.

FURTHER INFORMATION
Tourist information: WWF, Via Salaria 290a, 00199 Rome, T: (06) 852 492; Friends of the Earth (*Amici della Terra*), Via del Sudario 35, 00186 Rome, T: (06) 687 5308; WWF, Via Mercadente 10, Rome, T: (06) 844 0108; WWF Riviera di Chiara 200, Naples (Villa Pignatelli), T: (081) 684 043.

Lago di Vico and Monti Cimini

Nature reserve of small volcanic crater and lake set in low mountains (3,300ha/ 8,200 acres)

Imagine a secret lake ringed on three sides by steep wooded mountains, and you have Lago di Vico, the most beautiful of northern Lazio's volcanic lakes. It is just 4km (2 miles) wide, and more intimate and rewarding for the naturalist

than the nearby lakes at Bolsena and Bracciano.

Like other volcanic mountains in Lazio, the Cimini are relatively low-lying: the highest peak reaches a mere 1,053m (3,455ft). However, they create a spectacular effect by forming a cone around the lake whose perfect symmetry betrays its volcanic origins. Monte Venere, on the inner slopes, is a later volcanic outcrop that has pushed up through the skin of its parent.

This landscape formed during an eruptive, rather than explosive phase of the volcano-building Quaternary period. Volcanoes burst into life with sudden, but quickly spent

force, spreading lava floods over a wide area, flows which then slumped into low mounds rather than building into the pyramid profiles of an Etna or a Fuji.

The nature reserve offers a small area of spectacular scenery in an otherwise drab region, and has largely managed to resist Rome's hunters and outdoor enthusiasts. Much of the reason is that it is hidden. The unspoiled woods above the lake shore, consisting of oak, beech and chestnut, are still wild and thick, a flourishing remnant of the mighty *Cimina Silva*. This forest was so impenetrable that for years it held back the

Roman advance into Tuscany and Umbria.

Soils around the Lago di Vico area are rich and acidic: a legacy of their volcanic origin. They support a luxuriant flora which ranges from anemones in spring to cyclamen in the autumn, together with more unusual species such as the yellow-flowered Gargano buttercup (*Randunculus garganicus*) and the foxglove *Digitalis ferruginea*, a splendid plant with yellow or reddish-brown flowers up to 3½cm (1½in) long, here growing in one of its westernmost stations in Europe.

The lake and its marshy surrounds support up to 40 breeding pairs of great crested grebes, a touching sight in early summer when the chicks can often be seen hitching a ride on their parents' backs, as well as the turquoise and chestnut kingfishers. Little bitterns skulk through the reeds in summer, their distinctive black and tan plumage and diminutive size serving to distinguish them from all other European herons.

Black kites and marsh harriers are the top avian predators here for most of the year, being joined by Egyptian vultures, peregrines and goshawks in winter. There are also reports that short-eared owls may be nesting in the area.

The region also offers a winter respite for a variety of wildfowl, including thousands of coot and pochard. A careful search among these birds may also reveal a few red-crested pochard, the bright red beaks and orange heads of the males being instantly recognisable. Otters have been reintroduced to the lake and wild boar roam the surrounding woods.

The scenery beyond the inner ring of the Cimini is worth seeing; dominated by countless thousands of hazelnut trees, and numbers of shallow, but steep-sided gorges which radiate from the crater in all directions.

Before you go *Maps:* IGM 1:25,000 137 III SE *S. Martino* and 143 IV NE *Capranica*. *Guidebook:* S. Ardito, *A Piedi in Lazio II* (Iter).

Getting there *By car:* A1 to Orte, SS204 to Viterbo and minor roads to the reserve; or SS2 from Rome to Sutri, then minor roads to Ronciglione. The scenic Via Cimini makes a circuit of the Cimini ridge with views on to the lake. *By rail:* there are infrequent connections on 2 rickety branch lines, with stations a long way from the villages they serve: Orte–Capranica (halt at

Ronciglione) and Rome (Stazione San Pietro)–Viterbo. *By bus:* ACOTRAL buses run from Rome to most centres, and from Viterbo to Ronciglione via the Via Cimina.

Where to stay: 2-star Bella Venere on SE of lakeshore, T: (0761) 646 453; 2-star Cardinale near Punta del Lago, T: (0761) 625 188. Accommodation also at S. Martino Viterbo, Ronciglione and Soriano. Free camping is prohibited.

Activities *Walking:* ascent of Venere (2hr) from Fontanile di Canale, reached by a lane on Vico's E shore from Punta del Lago (red waymarks). From the same departure point you can walk around the wooded northern rim of the crater on a medieval track, the Strada di Mezzo, finishing on the tarmac road at Fontanile della Vita (an area known as Le Pantanacce, "the wretched bogs").

Further information *Tourist offices:* Corso Umberto 22, Ronciglione, T: (0761) 625 460; Via S. Maria 28, Soriano, T: (0761) 729 001; Piazza dei Caduti 16, Viterbo, T: (0761) 234 795. *Ecology:* WWF, Viterbo, T: (0761) 263 120.

Limestone boulders litter the Camposecco, the aptly named "Dry field", one of several karstic plains dotted across the Monti Simbruini.

Monti Simbruini and Monti Ernici

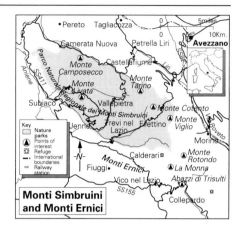

Nature park of two outlying Apennine massifs east of Rome (38,000ha/94,000 acres)

Monti Simbruini and Monti Ernici

East of Rome, beyond Tivoli and Hadrian's Villa, rise the Simbruini and Ernici mountains, two broad chains which lie almost parallel along the Lazio and Abruzzo borders. They are the foothills of the high Apennines, and the first genuine wilderness close to Rome, though often passed over in favour of the big Abruzzese massifs to the east. Both have several peaks in excess of 2,000 metres (6,500 feet), the highest being Monte Viglio (2,156 metres/7,100 feet) in southern Simbruini.

The Simbruini derive their name from the heavy rains (Latin *sub imbribus*) which year-round turn them into an area of gurgling streams and for centuries have provided Rome with water. These mountains are classic limestone creations of denuded slopes, beech forest and craggy ridges. The star-turn is the Zompo Lo Schioppo waterfall, one of the best falls in the Apennines, lost in the forest of a tiny valley above Morino. Also worth a visit are the karstic plains of Campaegli near Cervara di Roma and Camposecco ("the dry field") at Camerata Nuova.

The more southerly Ernici are wilder, their slopes less rounded and their valleys more incised. Sadly, they have yet to be included in the Simbruini's *parco naturale regionale*, though plans are underway for an all-embracing Parco dell'Appennino.

Both massifs offer forest walks — best around the Zompo waterfall and Vallone Sambucito near Basorano — as well as breezier excursions such as the traverse of the ridges between Monte Tarino, Cotento and Viglio. Rock walls are scarce, with the exception of the Tagliata at Vallepietra ("the valley of stone"). Valleys sometimes narrow into canyons, notably at Aniene between Jenne and Subiaco in the Valle d'Inferno at Collepardo.

The caves that dot the hillsides, especially around Collepardo, provide perfect haunts for foxes and are fine showcases of flora. Fragrant bushes of sweet briar (*Rosa rubiginosa*), rosemary and thyme guard the entrances. Clusters of maidenhair fern fall from ledges that are trimmed with tufts of the bellflower *Campanula fragilis*, its amethyst flowers found only on limestone rocks in central and southern Italy. And around Foss Fioio alone 20 species of orchid have been recorded.

The sparse beech forests of the higher Simbruini-Ernici provide an ideal habitat for white-backed woodpeckers, the largest of the black and white species in Europe, measuring 25cm (10in) from head to tail; further west, these impressive birds are found only in the Pyrenees. Eagle owls also inhabit these woodlands, while the remote cliffs and ridges above the tree-line support a few pairs of peregrines and choughs.

The whole area is a haven for mammalian carnivores. Wolves, wildcats and badgers are known to be present, and the occasional bear may wander across from the Abruzzo National Park. Where bears are thin on the ground, as in Italy and other parts of southern Europe, they do not form family groups. Instead the males lead a solitary existence, making long journeys in search of breeding partners; indeed, this lifestyle is

160

essential if the population is to survive. Research has shown that male bears can range over a phenomenal 2,700 square kilometres (1,000 square miles) in the course of a year, covering several females. Sporadic sightings of bears in the outlying Apennines can usually be attributed to the amatory wanderings of such lone males.

In winter the mountains, known as the Scandinavia of Rome, come into their own. Their snowy plateaus and grassy valleys provide central Italy with its best cross-country skiing. Key routes start at Camporotondo, Pereto, Campaegli and Marsia, with minor ski stations at Campo Catino, Campo Staffi and Marsia Livata.

BEFORE YOU GO
Maps: IGM 1:25,000 *Balsorano, Trevi nel Lazio, Sora, Vallepietra, Civitella Roveto, Subiaco, Pereto, Capistrello* and *Tagliacozzo.*
Guidebooks: E. Ercolani, *Appennino Bianco* (for skiers) (Iter, 1988); S. Ardito, *A Piedi nel Lazio I* (Iter, 1988).

GETTING THERE
By car: A24 from Rome and L'Aquila (exits Carsoli, Tagliacozzo and Vicovaro). For Simbruini take A25 to Avezzano and then SS82; southern fringes are served by A2 to Frosinone, SS155 to Alatri, and minor roads to Subiaco, Fiuggi and Collepardo. Pretty minor roads push into the Simbruini, especially to Vallepietra.
By rail: scenic but slow, Rome–Avezzano–Sora, runs along the Liri valley parallel to both chains.
By bus: ACOTRAL and ARPA buses serve most centres from Rome, Frosinone and Avezzano.

WHERE TO STAY
An easy day trip from Rome, but also a wide choice of hotels in Subiaco, Livata, Campo Catina, Tagliacozzo, Filettino, Carsoli, Marsia and Camporotondo.
Refuges: dotted over the hills, including old shepherds' huts, mostly in a state of picturesque squalor.
Outdoor living: is permitted throughout; organized sites at

Livata, Tagliacozzo, Marsia and Collepardo.

ACTIVITIES
Walking: numerous possibilities: best walk is up La Monna and Fanfalli from the huge abbey at Certosa di Trisulti (above Collepardo) via the Vado di Porca and the Vallone della Barca, yellow–red markings (5hr).
Try also the stroll to the Zompo waterfall from Morino (3hr); ascent of Monte Viglio from Valico della Serra (4hr); to Monte Tarino from SS Trinità; traverse of the Valle d'Inferno from Trisulti.
A perfect trek runs from Carsoli or Subiaco along the ridges of Tarino, Viglio and

Monna, descending through the Pizzo Deto and Val Roveto to finish in the Vallelunga. A recognized but unmarked trail runs from Camerata Nuovo to the Parco Nazionale d'Abruzzo via Balsorano (6 days); contact CAI, Via S. Simeone 5, Frosinone, T: (0775) 852 103; Via Borgo San Rocco, Sora.
Climbing: winter snow routes on Viglio and the Pizzo Deta; rock climbs around Liri, Tagliacozzo, Petrella and Castellafiume.
Skiing: there is plenty of opportunity available for cross-country skiing: routes start at Camporotondo, Pereto, Campaegli and Marsia, with minor stations at Campo Staffi and Marsia Livata.

The lanner falcon is the only member of its family known to attack flying birds head-on. Numbers in Europe are declining rapidly because of poaching and the shell-thinning effect on their eggs of pesticides in the food chain.

Birdwatching: LIPU branch at Sora for nature walks, courses and information; Piazza Risorgimento 17, T: (0776) 831 168.

Ponytrekking: Tagliacozzo is a major ponytrekking centre, but there are clubs and stables throughout the area. In Tagliacozzo contact the *Valle Verde*, Via Secondo Castello 8.

Canoeing: the spring runs down the Aniene between Subiaco and Trevi nel Lazio are the region's most renowned. Details can be obtained from the *Scuola Canoanium*, Via D. Alighieri 34, Subiaco, T: (0774) 83419.

FURTHER INFORMATION
Tourist offices: Via Gorizia 4, Fiuggi Fonte, T: (0775) 55446 (Apr–Nov); Via Cadorna 57, Subiaco, T: (0774) 85397; Piazza Argoli, Tagliacozzo, T: (0863) 6318.

Posta Fibreno

Nature park centred on lake in Liri Basin east of the Monti Ernici (400ha/1,000 acres)

Posta Fibreno is a haven for migrating winter birds and a pot-pourri of unusual natural phenomena; a soft sweet lake set in pastoral hills south of the Abruzzo and Ernici mountains.

Icy-fresh meltwater flows underground for 20km (12 miles) from the mountains before percolating into Fibreno. Fed both from these submerged sources and from the streams and waterfalls in the vicinity, the lake is like a huge spring. The volume and purity of its inflow results in a highly oxygenated body of water known for its crystal transparency and extraordinary red-green reflective tints. It is the only lake in Italy that has a visible underwater "forest" of algae and other water plants.

Outside the Circeo National Park, on the coast south of Rome, Fibreno is one of the few undrained areas of the Pontine marshes, preserving a lush vegetation that includes strange floating islands mentioned by Pliny in his *Naturalis Historia*. Beds of undergrowth supporting a whole range of marshland vegetation, they are like emerald rafts that drift aimless and windblown, moving gently under human weight like a listing boat.

The lake attracts birds such as mallard, marsh harrier and kingfisher and is home to carp, eel, trout and crayfish. Local people still fish in the traditional Pontine craft, flat punts known as *la nave*, "the navy". Once common all over Italy, those moored around

162

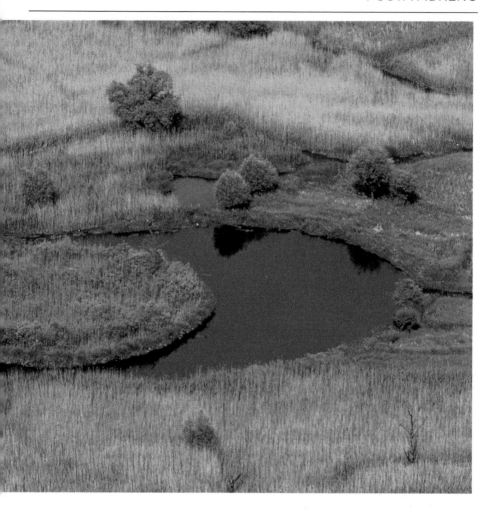

Fibreno's tree-shaded inlets are the country's last; probably descendants of primitive boats hollowed from tree-trunks.

This island of floating vegetation at Posta Fibreno is part of only a handful of protected areas of refuge for birds on Italy's Tyrrhenian coast.

Before you go: Avoid the NE part of the lake between Carpello and Codigliane which is spoiled by tourist development. *Map:* IGM 1:25,000 *Sora.*
Getting there *By car:* A2 to Frosinone, then SS214 for Isola and Sora. Follow signs for Madonna della Stella; the village of Posta Fibreno is 3km (2 miles) beyond. Station at Sora (9km/6 miles) on

Roccasecca–Avezzano line (5 trains daily).
By bus: buses to Sora and Posta Fibreno from Frosinone and Cassino.
Where to stay: at Sora and Isola; rooms and campsite at Posta Fibreno village.
Activities *Walking:* cultivated fields, marshes and occasional flooding can make walking difficult. Paths are very popular

in summer and at weekends.
Birdwatching: Sora's LIPU branch runs nature walks and birdwatching courses on the lake: Piazza Risorgimento 17, Sora, T: (0776) 831 168. Also contact second LIPU branch at Via Monteverdi 35, Frosinone, T: (0775) 81175.
Further information *Tourist information:* Il Comune, Posta Fibreno, T: (0776) 887 013.

163

Parco Nazionale del Circeo

Mixture of coastal habitats (8,622ha/ 21,305 acres), 100km/60 miles south of Rome

The Parco Nazionale del Circeo extends over a coastal region midway between Rome and Naples. Italy's smallest national park, and the only one not to feature high mountain landscape, it was created in 1934, designed to preserve a tract of incomparable coastal landscape at the time of Mussolini's huge drainage projects in the Pontine marshes. For centuries a malarial area of lake, forest and swamp, inhabited only by buffalo and fishermen, today this is one of the most productive and intensely farmed pieces of land in Italy. It was from this development that the Circeo was salvaged.

The park centres on the town of Sabaudia. Different architects were given the task of designing new towns that would be the standard-bearers of Fascist endeavour. Sabaudia was lucky. It escaped the grid-iron schemes of Latina and Pontinia, and was built as a garden town in keeping with the park.

Circeo's initial sense of compact uniformity is deceptive; it actually has many quite separate environments, and to explore them properly requires several days. You can wander in different types of woodland from mixed temperate to central European type, or among dwarf fan palms and more African vegetation; or you can explore the four coastal lakes with adjoining dunes, swamps and maquis. There are also 30 marine caves and, most strikingly, Monte Circeo, a knuckle of mountain (541 metres/1,774 feet) that overlooks the entire park.

If you like an overview of things, this mountain is the best starting point. From the interminable plain to the south it resembles a figure reclining on the horizon, the profile dominated by an abnormally large nose (though the locals' descriptions are a little more explicit) which is the peak of Monte Circeo. A mountain in a level country inevitably attracts myth, the main one, as the name suggests, being that it was the site of the Isle of Circe in Homer's *Odyssey*. It is Circe's form, according to legend, that is sculpted into the mountain.

On the southerly sea-facing slopes, known as the Quarto Caldo — literally, the "hot side" — the mountain drops to the waves in rocky precipices. (One, the Precipizio, plunges sheer for 200 metres/650 feet.) Maquis, cistus and cedar cling to dizzy ledges in this warm Mediterranean world, whose chief glory is the dwarf fan palm. Here flowers attract chafer beetles, hummingbird hawk moths, and butterflies such as cleopatras, green hairstreaks and long-tailed blues. Where the maquis grows under woodland cover, Sardinian warblers, sub-alpine warblers and woodchat shrikes are often found.

Such exotic species are missing from the north-facing Quarto Freddo, the "cold side", where a thick forest predominates instead, mainly holm oak, deciduous oaks and hornbeam. In places the base of the mountain cork oak has formed a natural hybrid with Turkey oak to produce *Quercus crenata*. Here you might hear the fluty song of the golden oriole, or glimpse great-spotted woodpeckers searching trunks and branches for insects.

The summit view is exceptional — turquoise seas, distant islands (the Pontine archipelago), patchworks of canal-bordered fields and woods, and, most lovely of all, a sickle-shaped bay spanning some thirty kilometres (twenty miles), almost lost in the haze of the far horizon. Along its curving shore lie four silvery lakes: Fogliano, Caprolace, Monaci and Sabaudia. Filigree canals connect all four to the sea, allowing marine and freshwater species to co-exist.

Once the whole Tyrrhenian coast as far as Pisa was like this. The atmosphere of this littoral is subtropical, magical. Forest creeps to the lakesides, umbrella pines giving elegant shade to the foreshore. The woods conceal old Roman remains, while on the infinite sandy crest of the dunes exists a world unto itself, the domain of bent grass, sea-spray and constant wind. It is all easily explored, courtesy of a scenic road, *Via Mediana*, which the authorities wisely keep closed to cars.

All manner of birds prosper in this heady environment. Some 230 species are recorded, many of them, even the rarest, remarkably easy to see. In autumn migrating wood-cocks arrive at the lakes; spring brings turtle doves, cuckoos and quail, but there are also black-throated divers, glossy ibis, spoon-bills, great white egrets, black storks, cormorants, even ospreys. There is also the ludicrously long-legged knight of Italy (black-winged stilt). Up on Monte Circeo, peregrine falcons circle and gyre.

Behind the lakes, however, lies the park's real jewel: the Selva di Terracina, 600 hectares/1,480 acres of primeval forest and swamp that form vestiges of the ancient Pontinia. When I first walked around this natural cornucopia, I was distracted by fences, yellow signs and things ominously called "didactic footpaths". In time these petered out, and I soon found the didactic notices telling me things that were a pleasure to know, such as that ivy can live for 500 years. Thereafter I was alone, and encountered not a soul in the course of a warm Friday afternoon. The rewarding part of the day was being presented with all that the guides had promised: the birds, boar, darting green lizards, macabre fungi, snakes, fallow deer and a huge range of trees.

The authorities give warning about the number of vipers around. Indian mongooses were introduced to keep them in check, but turned instead to less demanding prey such as birds and small mammals. As a result some of the smaller fauna are rather more scarce than they should be. In places non-native pines and eucalyptus were planted (eucalyptus for its supposed anti-malarial properties), species which are definitely at odds with Circeo's original oak forest. Nature is now putting things to rights, with slow recolonization by Turkey oak and European aspen (often the first trees to reclaim new territory).

Peals of thunder and a great deluge cut short my walk, turning the forest paths into steaming, puddle-filled bogs. By this time I had come to the edge of the reserve. It was strange to walk to a fence where the wood suddenly stopped. Ahead, the rich soil, the odd tree, the cultivated fields fading away to the horizon, had once all been wood, marsh and swamp. It was astonishing that anything as vigorous and fecund as the natural world in the Circeo could have been so irretrievably lost.

BEFORE YOU GO

The visitors' centre on the outskirts of Sabaudia has information on all aspects of the park, a small museum, even guides if required: Via Carlo 107, Sabaudia, T: (0773) 57251.
Map: the excellent if unwieldy 1:25,000 sheet available at the park centre (L5,000) marks trails, habitats and recommended areas for seeing particular birds and animals.
Guidebooks: P. Sottoriva, *Parco Nazionale del Circeo* (De Agostini 1979); S. Ardito, *A Piedi in Lazio I* (Iter 1988).
First aid: viper bites are serious; you should take serum within half an hour if bitten.

It is available in most Italian pharmacies.

GETTING THERE

By car: from Rome, and its southern suburb E.U.R., take the SS148 (often called the most dangerous road in Italy) under the *Anulare*, or ring road, towards Latina. South of the town follow the road to the coast at Capo Portiere and thence to Sabaudia (75km/46 miles). From Naples and the S, use the A2 (Frosinone exit) or SS7 to Terracina.
By rail: station at Terracina on a spur from the main Rome–Naples line; change at Priverno (7 trains daily). More frequent connections to Latina on Rome–Naples line (12 daily), but this requires a bus to Latina centre, and then an infrequent connection (from the sports stadium) to Sabaudia.
By bus: services from Latina and Terracina to Sabaudia and San Felice Circeo; information, T: (0773) 80647. ACOTRAL buses from Rome (E.U.R.) to Sabaudia, T: (06) 57531.

WHEN TO GO

Spring for wild flowers; late autumn amd winter for birds and changing colours.

WHERE TO STAY

Good accommodation in

Sabaudia and S. Felice Circeo. **Outdoor living:** is prohibited; official sites in Sabaudia at Sant'Andrea, T: (0773) 57757; and Europa at Acqua near Terracina, T: (0773) 726 523.

ACTIVITIES
Walking: trails are easy to plan using the park's own map. The recommended ascent of Monte Circeo (2hr) starts from Torre Paolo — after the bridge over the canal at the tip of Lago di Sabaudia; the path follows a knife-edge ridge and is well-trodden. All other paths are very gentle.
Climbing: the routes on the rock walls of Monte Circeo are the best in Lazio; the cream are on the Precipizio. Other itineraries (outside the park) exist on Monte Leano (676m/ 2,217ft), NW of Terracina.
Birdwatching: excellent, with well-placed observation point and many opportunities for sightings. For most information, nature walks, courses (spring and autumn) and summer cycling trips to birdwatch, contact: LIPU, Corso Matteotti 169, Latina, T: (0773) 484 993; try also LIPU at Terracina, T: (0773) 727 117.
Boat-trips: the Melacotogna co-operative runs trips on the lakes and around the Circeo promontory. Contact Sabaudia's tourist office.
Cycling: dune, forest and lake-side roads are all perfect for cycling. Bikes are also permitted on most of the park's marked trails. Take note that some roads, such as the one between Fogliano and Caprolace, are closed to cars. Bikes can be hired in Sabaudia.

FURTHER INFORMATION
Tourist offices: Piazza del Comune 18, Sabaudia, T: (0773) 55046; Piazza Lanzuisi 4, S. Felice Circeo, T: (0773) 527 770.

Monti Picentini

Limestone chain 40km/25 miles long and closest wilderness to Naples

"Misty and rolling mountains, like clouds on the extreme horizon; solitary heights whipped by the wind," wrote Giustino Fortunato in 1879, one of the first Italian ramblers in the Abruzzo and Campania mountains.

Then, as now, the Picentini were the wildest uplands within striking distance of Naples. They were also, wrote Carlo Levi in his famous novel, *Christ Stopped at Eboli*, the point at which Italian civilization ended. Directly east of Salerno, they are the first taste of the barren interior of Basilicata.

Self-contained mountains that seem high because they rise from the broad Sele plain, they look out from a lofty 1,783m (5,849ft) south to the Cilento, Campania's other wilderness, and east to the rolling hills of the interior.

Vast woods of beech and chestnut cloak sparsely populated slopes, with marvellous displays of wild flowers on the high meadows of Terminio (1,786m/5,849ft) and Montenero (1,142m/3,746ft), the "black mountain". Here you might see foxes, wildcats, badgers and even wolves, just 50km (30 miles) from Naples. Monte Terminio also supports breeding black and red kites, peregrines, eagle owls and black woodpeckers.

My favourite mountain here is the Accellica, not the highest in the range at 1,660m (5,400 ft) but, with twin peaks joined by a rocky crest, graced with the most elegant outline. Conquering the modest summit

provides the area's best walk, a 4-hour round trip from the Croci di Acerno.

Elsewhere the Picentini's numerous forest tracks offer cross-country skiing, notably around Cervialto (1,809m/ 5,934ft) and Polveracchio.

The year 1986 saw the birth of the first long-distance path in the south, the *Alta Via dei Monti Picentini*, a 3–5 day trek from Senerchia to Solofra.
Before you go: Acerno is a remote and lovely village, and a convenient base for local walks and drives.
Maps: IGM 1:25,000 *Solofra, Bagnoli Irpino, Cervialto* and *Montella*.
Getting there *By car:* A3 (Battipaglia exit), and then the beautiful SS164 through the heart of the Picentini via Acerna to Bagnoli. Minor and unmetalled lanes in this whole region are a delight. From the W use the Avellino–Salerno motorway link, exiting at Serino and following the high SS574 into the mountains.
By rail: railway branch lines in the area are slow, with infrequent connections; nearest stations: Eboli, on the Salerno–Potenza line; Bagnoli, on the Avellino–Bari line; Solofra, on the Avellino–Salerno line.
Where to stay: rooms at Acerno, Bagnoli, Lampolaspierto and the Piano Laceno ski-resort. *Outdoor living:* free camping allowed. Year-round campsite, Monte Raiamagra at Piano Laceno, T: (0827) 68057. For a comprehensive list of hotels contact the tourist office at Salerno, Piazza Ferrovia, T: (089) 231 432.
Activities *Walking:* Gentle walking in the Irpinia hills to the N; uncharted expeditions in the mountains E of the Picentini proper: Paratiello, Saracino, Eremita — all around 1,500m/5,000ft.

Tirone-Alto Vesuvio

Winter snow comes early to the Monti Picentini, a mountainous wilderness only a short distance from the urban clamour of Naples.

Nature reserve consisting of mountain, crater and cone of Europe's most famous volcano (1,027ha/ 2,538 acres)

Vesuvius is neither the largest volcano — a midget next to Etna's 3,323m (10,902ft) — nor the most dangerous, yet it entered the history books with the apocalyptic eruption of AD79. This particular maelstrom covered Italy in a thin layer of dust, and buried the cities of Pompeii and Herculaneum under 20m (66ft) of mud and ash. "Many a calamity has happened in the world, but never one that has caused so much entertainment to posterity as this one", wrote Goethe, on the destruction of Pompeii.

Though the last eruption was in 1944, today's steam is a reminder that a new outbreak is overdue; Vesuvius is expected to erupt every 30 years.

The volcano divides into two parts: the looming profile that dominates the Bay of Naples is Monte Somma (1,132m/ 3,713ft), otherwise known as the *nasone*, "big nose", named after the semi-circular residue of an ancient crater blown apart by the Pompeii eruption. Within this rises the Gran Cono, the main cone of Vesuvius: a barren, smooth-sided, perfectly circular crater formed by the same eruption.

A strange solitary place, the

167

crater is 300m (1,000ft) deep, 600m (2,000ft) across, and quite breathtaking. Sheer cliffs of pumice, dust and red-black lavas plunge to a chaos of scree.

This seemingly inert wilderness is what most people come to see, but for botanists, geologists and mineralogists, Vesuvius has more fascination. Over a thousand species of plants thrive on its fertile soils. Especially interesting are the pioneering varieties able to colonize the most inhospitable lava slopes — the ash-coloured endemic lichen, for example, *Stereocaulon vesuvianum*, which flourishes even on still-warm magma. On the southern slopes, oak, pine and birch woods have survived creeping urbanization. Foresters are replanting long-lost species like willow, alder and black pine, as well as the greenweed *Genista aetnensis*, a native of Sicily and Sardinia, that will complement the common broom. These woods and those above Ercolano, which are in part protected by the small Tirone reserve, make for an exhilarating area of green.

Equally captivating is the valley between Somma and the Gran Cono, the Atrio del Cavallo, called more aptly the Valle d'Inferno, the "Valley of Hell". Here you can see the jet-black lava flows from the 1944 eruptions, and lava bombs of up to a metre (3 feet) across. The view is spectacular, embracing the Bay of Naples, the islands of Capri and Ischia, the Sorrento peninsula and much of the central Apennines from the Alburni to the Monti Picentini.

Before you go *Map:* IGM 1:25,000 *Pozzuolo.*
Access: at all times, except for the Tirone reserve, where entry is by prior arrangement with, *Amministrazione delle Foreste* at Salerno, T: (089) 224 458.
Getting there *By car:* exits at Torre del Greco and Ercolano on the A3 have links to the *Strada del Vesuvio*. This climbs the volcano's western side to the Osservatorio Vesuviano (609m/1,998ft). Here the road divides; the left fork runs through the Atrio del Cavallo to a car park (1,017m/3,336ft). From here a path climbs the

NW slope of the cone to its rim, and thus to its highest point (20min). The right fork runs through the 1944 lava flows to a chair lift station. Here you can make a rewarding walk to the crater rim (1hr), or take the lift.
By rail: a picturesque railway, the Circumvesuviana, circles the entire volcano; trains are frequent and leave from Naples' central station.
By bus: A special bus leaves Ercolano station for the crater car park and chair lift.
Where to stay: at Ercolano, Pompeii and Torre del Greco, with campsites at Torre del Greco and Boscotrecase.
Activities *Walking:* a circuit of the main crater requires 2 hours. From the S side of the rim (by a small hut) a path leads to the woods and thus to Boscotrecase, where you can take the Circumvesuviana back to Naples or Ercolano.

Vallone delle Ferriere

Rugged coastal peninsula with rare wild flowers and birds of prey, containing small reserve (455ha/1,124 acres)

Though lauded as Europe's most beautiful coastline, the Sorrento peninsula is hardly off Italy's beaten track. Yet this small reserve, and the uplands above it, forms a haven of wilderness.

Behind the terraces and plunging sea cliffs at Amalfi, the peninsula rises to a high valley of ravines and dramatic rock faces until it culminates in the Monti Lattari.

Along the backbone of the peninsula there are plenty of windswept walks and panoramas, with some

The elegant avocet feeds by scything its flattened upturned bill through shallow water, trapping small invertebrates between the mandibles.

THE OTTER IN ITALY

The decimation of Italy's otter population is a damning indictment of the catastrophic — and ever-worsening — state of the country's rivers and, by implication, of the appallingly low priority that the Italian government gives to the environment.

Otters require specialized conditions, not least of which is clean water. Though numbers have been dropping all over Europe, the decline in Italy is particularly acute. In 1982 the WWF sounded the alarm, and commissioned two British experts to mount the country's first ever survey of the animal.

Their findings make depressing reading. Water was polluted at 92 of the 188 sites surveyed, with "gross organic industrial pollution" recorded at another 11. Only 26 were suitable for otters; animals were actually ·found at only 16, and at these, the report says, "the signs indicate the presence of isolated individuals with little chance of survival."

Researchers found only 2 sizeable colonies: at Serre Persano, and along the River Crati and its tributaries in Calabria. Many suitable sites were in "clean" upland areas, but sadly the otter is not an upland animal, and prefers the more productive lower reaches of rivers.

While pollution harms otters directly, and kills the fish on which they feed, dredging, gravel digging and the clearing of banks — removing the root system of riverside trees, the otter's preferred habitat — have made the decline more marked.

The report could not have been more discouraging, describing the overall situation as "bleak", and concluding that "the otter is on the verge of extinction in southern Italy."

---

surprisingly rugged peaks. You might try the climb at the western tip, best at sunset, from Termini to Monte Costanzo (497m/1,630ft) and to the Punta Campanella. Views to Capri are unforgettable.

Specialized micro-climates support a lush panoply of wild flowers, some of them also found in Africa and Latin America. Maritime warming, south-facing slopes and the steepness of the valley sides (which slows water evaporation from the soil) all help to reproduce tropical conditions. Rarities include *Woodwardia radicans*, a pre-glacial fern with leaves up to 2½m (8ft) long, discovered in 1710. Only ten plants now remain. Also present are the white-flowering grass-of-Parnassus *Parnassia palustris*, the pink or pale blue butterwort *Pinguicola hirtiflora*, and the scarce *Arisaurum proboscideum* of the arum-lily family.

Also enjoying the warm micro-climates are amphibians such as the diminutive Italian newt and the wonderfully named spectacled salamander (*Salamandrina terdigitata*).

Only 7-11cm (2¾–4½in) long, the adult salamanders are unmistakable with their blackish backs and bright red undersides; the "spectacles" take the form of a roughly triangular yellow-orange patch on the head which extends to the eyes. Kestrels, buzzards and peregrines haunt the crags and cliffs in large numbers.

Before you go *Maps:* IGM 1:25,000 *Amalfi* and *Nocera Inferiore* cover the area of the reserve. The Kompass 1:50,000 sheet of the whole Sorrento peninsula is excellent (sheet 682).

Guidebooks: Norman Douglas's *Siren Land* (Penguin) is a wonderful introduction to the Sorrento Peninsula, with many observations on its natural history.

Getting there *By car:* A3 Naples–Salerno (Vietri exit) and SS163 to Amalfi. All roads in this region are beautifully scenic.

By rail: Vietri is a halt on the Naples–Salerno line (trains hourly). Castellammare, on the N of the peninsula, is on the Naples–Sorrento line (trains every ½hr).

By bus: buses connect all centres, with most departures from Salerno's Corso Garibaldi.

Access: at all times to the lower valley, but the upper valley (the reserve proper) requires authorization from the Azienda per le Foreste Demeniali at Salerno, T: (089) 224 458.

Activities *Walking:* plenty of short sharp walks on the Lattari with marvellous views of Capri, Ischia and the Bay of Naples. You might try the Amalfi–Ferriere–Amalfi circuit (2hr), or the very popular hike from Faito to Monte S. Angelo a Tre Pizzi (1,443m/4,700ft), highest point on the peninsula (3hr). A funicular runs from Castellammare to Faito.

Oasi di Serre Persano

A WWF oasis protects the Serre Persano wetlands, a refuge for waterfowl and Italy's last major colony of otters. In the distance rise the summit ridges of the Monti Alburni.

Artificial lake and wetland habitat; WWF oasis (300ha/ 750 acres) and area of regional protection (4,000ha/10,000 acres)

Formed by the damming of the River Serre in 1934, the Serre-Persano's lake and marshland is a nature sanctuary of immense importance, and one of the prime birdwatching areas in south Italy. It is the only protected wet habitat, and the only resting place for birds on the Tyrrhenian migration route between Circeo and the Vendicari marshes in Sicily.

Two paths thread through the lovely WWF oasis. The first, on the right bank, resembles a long, shaded gallery, passing winding streams and thickets of willow and alder. On the left bank, the second path is more open, crossing vines, fields and maquis, and climbing a hill with views on to the lake and its green surroundings. A clearing at the end contains two hides and an observation post, the best spot from which to enjoy the landscape and its wildlife.

The Serre itself is that rare thing in Italy — a clean river. It rises in the nearby Picentini, with the oasis at the point where it breaks out on to the broad alluvial plain of the Piana del Serre. It supports some 50 otters, the *last* substantial colony of the animals in Italy.

Sightings are rare, though WWF guides take visitors to points where it is easy to find tracks and droppings.

Virulent poaching threatened the reserve until 1977, and only ceased after pitched battles occurred between hunters and conservationists. The latter won in the end, but are now forced to patrol the reserve 24 hours a day to keep the enemy at bay.

Their reward is the arrival of thousands of wintering birds, and the first-time breeding here of species like the black kite and great crested grebe. Mallard, pochard, tufted duck and teal are common visitors. Muddy islands harbour black-tailed godwit, ruff, snipe and wood sandpiper. Spring brings purple and grey, squacco and night herons, little egrets and cormorants. Among the reserve's rare visitors are ospreys, cranes, avocets, shelduck and red-crested pochard.

Getting there *By car:* SS18 Salerno–Paestum road has lanes branching to points on the Sele river and Piana del Sele. The reserve is 1km S of the Campagna exit on A3 motorway, 5km (3 miles) E of Eboli.

By rail: station at Serre-Persano on the Battipaglia–Potenza line.
By bus: from Salerno to Eboli to Postiglione; more convenient than by train.
Where to stay: Hotel Grazia at Eboli, T: (0825) 38038, is handy, but the village is not pretty. Free camping prohibited. Campsite Paestum at Foce del Sele on the coast, T: (0825) 691 003.
Access: 1 Sept–30 June, Wed and Sun only, Sat for groups.

Activities *Birdwatching:* one of the finest sites in S Italy, equipped with hides, nature trails and observation platforms. If the reserve is closed, sightings are possible all along the Serre and across the Piana del Sele.
Further information: from the Hera Argentina birdwatching centre at Paestum and LIPU branch at Somerset House, Via Diaz 53, Salerno, T: (089) 239 914. Both bodies organize tours of the reserve.

Cilento

Alburni and Cilento mountain massifs; proposed national park (100,000ha/ 247,000 acres)

The Cilento region is Campania's loneliest corner, hidden away in the south-west, little-known and rarely visited, yet a wilderness of great richness. It is to form a national park (one of only three proposed in the south), the main areas being the Alburni mountains in the north, the less distinct and more extensive Cilento to the south, and the coastline in the west that marks the Cilento's dramatic drop to the Mediterranean.

The coastal section is the best-known, climbing abruptly from the flat Piana del Sele at Agropoli to a series of huge cliffs, green valleys dotted with twisted olive trees and promontories that stretch southwards for more than 100km (60 miles). Much of this once deserted coast has now been spoiled by tourism, though there are still extensive tracts of wild seascape without road or village.

The remotest of these sections is the southernmost tip, the Punta degli Infreschi, designated a *parco blu*, or marine park, and still largely accessible only from the sea.

Peregrine falcons and seabirds in their thousands inhabit its coves and ledges. Sandier reaches support woods of aleppo pine, maquis and dune plants, including the

The Calore is one of few rivers in Monti Alburni. Many streams disappear into limestone sinkholes only to re-emerge several miles away.

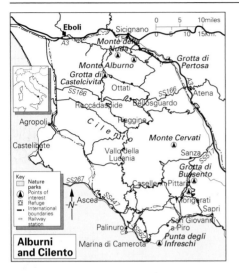

Alburni and Cilento

deep-yellow flowered Cilento or Palinuro primrose *Primula palinuri*, endemic to south-west Italy. Plans are afoot for a series of coastal trails, though at present the number of paths is small, and those marked on maps are often covered with undergrowth. The best walking, with reasonably visible paths, is on the Punta degli Infreschi itself, with the village of San Giovanni a Piro the main departure point. One track east from the village winds through the wild area known as the Ciolandra, dropping to the sea after three kilometres (two miles) at the Baia dei Francesci (4hr). Another walk from the village climbs to the colossal rock wall of Bulgheria (1,225 metres/4,020 feet), popular with climbers, and one of the most spectacular rock walls in the south.

Inland, the white limestone crests of the Alburni, spread on the horizon like an open fan, are as oxygen to a suffocating man after the murderous drive through the suburbs of Naples. Though only a small range of some 20 kilometres (12 miles) from east to west, the crests are nevertheless grand and imposing, rising to over 1,700 metres (5,600 feet) to become a serrated ridge, haunt of lanner falcons and peregrines.

Close up, the mountains reveal pillars of fractured limestone, deep-riven gorges and fantastic rock pinnacles like the Figliolo, "little son", a sheer face of 1,289 metres

172

(4,230 feet). Gigantic rock walls rear 400 metres (1,300 feet) on the mountains' magnificent northern side, culminating in Monte Alburno (1,742 metres/5,717 feet), also known as Monte Panorama for its sweeping views. Thereafter the Alburni tail off in a different vein altogether, fading away to the south as a vast slope famed for its cross-country and down-hill skiing.

At their core the Alburni are a huge slab of Cretaceous limestone, formed as an island in the sea during the Oligocene geological period. Today they have all the typical features of limestone country: sinkholes, dry valleys, limestone pavements and some of the finest caves in southern Italy. Caverns here vary in size from little more than shadowy cracks to great amphitheatres that could shelter a whole town's population. Often remote, they have been shelters for animals since time immemorial, in particular goats brought to graze on the Alburni's rough pasture.

The most celebrated cavern is at Pertosa, studded with stalactites and an underground lake of dark icy water. The best of the caves accessible to the non-specialist, are south of the Alburni near Castelcivita. Experts might want to tackle the Grava di Fra Gentile, a daunting vertical well 232 metres (761 feet) deep. Those interested in limestone effects might also want to see the enormous sinkhole that swallows the Bussento river near Caselle in Pittari. The waters reappear at Morigerati.

Dominant in much of Italy, limestone is a material that arouses deep passions. Southern peasants call it *pietra viva*, "living rock". Sandstone, however, far more scarce in the Apennines, is dismissed as *pietra morta* "dead rock". D.H. Lawrence, for one, took issue with this distinction, seeing limestone as a lifeless rock that "burns in the sun and withers". The granites of Sardinia, by contrast, he thought glowered and glistened with "a deep sparkle".

South of the Alburni, a series of low hills intervenes before the long, lateral ridges of the Cilento rear up beyond. The Cilento is some of the wildest and least inhabited territory in Italy. A huge area that extends for almost 100 kilometres (60 miles), one can walk most of it without coming across a single road. Paths and mule-tracks traverse a jumble of alternately sharp and blunt-nosed massifs, their summits ranging from about 1,000 metres (3,500 feet) in the west to the desolate Monte Cervati (1,899 metres/6,200 feet). The domain only of wolf, fox and wildcat, this is fine, uncharted wilderness — truly a trekker's paradise — but one where you are alone and where care, equipment and experience are required in equal measure.

BEFORE YOU GO
Maps: IGM 1:25,000 198 I SO *Sicignano degli Alburni* covers the Monte della Nuda walk described below; 209 II SE *Camerota* covers the walks around S. Giovanni a Piro.
Guidebooks: A. Gogna, *Mezzogiorno di Pietra* (Zanichelli).

GETTING THERE
By car: the Cilento is part-circled by the A3 motorway; exits at Sicignano and Petina for the Alburni. The Atena exit leads to the SS166, which divides the Alburni and the Cilento, radiating glorious minor lanes into the heart of both massifs. The Padula exit feeds into the SS517 for Sanza, best base for the central Cilento peaks and the ascent of Monte Cervati.
The SS267, SS447 and SS562 traverse the whole coastal region, forced inland only at the Punta degli Infreschi. The stretches S of Castellabate and around Palinuro are especially lovely.
By rail: the Naples–Reggio di Calabria line curves around the southern and western fringes of the Cilento promontory.
By bus: from Salerno, Sapri and Agropoli to most larger villages.

WHERE TO STAY
The single refuge in the Alburni, the Panoramo (1,233m/4,046ft) is reached by road from Ottati (contact CAI, Naples). There is a full range of mostly modern accommodation on the coast at Maiori, Massa Lubrense, Minori, Praiano, Sant'Agata

and Vietri, but the Cilento interior is ill-served; contact coastal tourist offices for assistance.
Salerno's tourist office (outside the railway station) has the most comprehensive listings for the Cilento: Piazza Ferrovia, T: (089) 231 432. The office at Paestum is also useful: Via Aquilia, T: (0828) 811 016.
Outdoor living: free camping is permitted, and in some places will be your only option. There are numerous year-round campsites on the coast, including Arco delle Rose at Agropoli, T :(0974) 824 885; Baia del Silenzio at Caprioli, T: (0974) 976 079; Trezene at Castellabate, T: (0974) 965 013. Marina di Camerota on the Punta degli Infreschi has 3 sites: Isola, T: (0974) 932 230; Mingrado, T: (0974) 931 391; and Sirene, T: (0974) 932 338.

ACTIVITIES
Walking: main departure point for walks in the Alburni is Campo Farina (1,340m/ 4,400ft), which you reach from Ottati (13km/8 miles), a village to the S of the main ridge. Here there is a new (summer only) refuge and restaurant.
The main climb is to Monte della Nuda (1,704m/5,590ft) via Piano Manzerra and Palombella. The descent (to the refuge) is by way of Colle Marola (1,482m/4,864ft) and the Piano di Vallescura (4hr). Another fine walk strikes off N from the refuge for the Vuccolo dell'Arena (1,450m/4,757ft) and from there to the Alburni's main crest.
Walks from the northern side include easy strolls around

Petina, and steep but striking climbs to Monte della Nude from Postiglione or Sicignano (5hr). These can be extended into 2-day treks by descending the ridge's southern flanks to Campo Farina.
Caving: Pertosa and Castelcivita caves are close together (cavers believe they are linked); Pertosa is open daily, except Mon, until 5.30pm. Serious spelunkers should contact CAI's Gruppo Grotte in Naples: Via Bonito 19, T: (081) 404 421; the Comitato Grotte Pertosa, T: (0975) 37037; the town hall at Castelcivita, T :(0828) 975 009; and the tourist office at Palinuro (for sea caves).
Boat trips: boats for rent from many villages, with or without crews, for diving, fishing, caving or casual looks at the coast. Palinuro is the main centre; contact tourist office, or go direct to the Co-operativa Pescatori on the harbour, T: (0974) 931 233.
Skin-diving: excellent at many points on the coast. Centres: Centro Subaqueo, Via Marina, Castellabate, T: (0974) 961 060; and Centro Santacroce, Via Verde 1, Sapri, T: (0973) 392 650. Further information from coastal tourist offices.

FURTHER INFORMATION
Tourist offices: Via S. Marco, Agropoli, T: (0974) 824 855; Via Oberdan, Marina di Ascea, T: (0974) 971 230; Marina di Camerota, Porto Piccolo, T: (0974) 93256; Piazza Virgilio 21, Palinuro, T: (0974) 931 121; Castellabate, Via Marina Municipio, Sapri, T: (0973) 392 460.

173

CHAPTER 8

The South of Italy

The Italian south is a world unto itself. It is known as the *Mezzogiorno*, "land of the midday sun", a region bedevilled by poverty, emigration and a harsh natural regime. Huge amounts of state aid have been pumped into the area, going some way to lifting it out of the social and economic doldrums it has laboured in for centuries. Too often, however, the changes have been only cosmetic and incapable of solving problems that are deeply rooted in the past. This constant political stone in the Italian boot will continue to cause trouble for a good while, and yet for the outdoor enthusiast the south offers some of the wildest scenery in the entire country.

The Apennines continue their march down the peninsula, becoming lower, but spreading range after range of hills in their wake. High massifs occasionally intrude, notably the Pollino, or the ranges of the Sila and Aspromonte in Calabria. The forests of the Sila and the spring green of the uplands are so verdant you might be in the Highlands of Scotland, but for the most part the landscape is a harsh Mediterranean ensemble of vines, olives and barren sun-scorched slopes. The rock-desert badlands of Basilicata have been likened to the Grand Canyon. Many of these areas are suffering the effects of soil erosion, resulting from deforestation — a centuries-old problem, much as malaria was a curse on the coast until recent times.

Over the whole area shines a quite unforgiving sun, yielding, in the words of the British writer Norman Douglas,

Despite attracting an ever increasing number of tourists, the Gargano peninsula remains the most outstanding natural feature on Italy's Adriatic coast.

"days of blistering summer heat, when the earth is burnt dry under a heavenly dome that glows like a brazier of molten copper". Temperatures can reach 40°C (100°F), and further torment comes from the *scirroco*, a scorching Saharan wind that can blow for days on end.

The south's arid centre is Puglia, a fascinating region that forms the narrow stiletto of the Italian boot. The Roman poet Horace never mentioned the area without the epithet *siticulosae*, "thirsty". The little rain that does fall is quickly lost in the local limestone. Puglia is Italy's longest region — 400 kilometres (250 miles) as the crow flies — and claims 750 kilometres (500 miles) of Italy's eastern coastline. Only a handful of primeval habitats, though, have survived the encroachment of man and the vine, which grows here in quantities unequalled anywhere in the world. The region produces a tenth of the wine drunk in Europe. Where the region does score is in its proximity to Greece, whence it enjoys stray species of birds.

West of Puglia, Basilicata is the neglected runt of Italian regions. Once it was the glorious heartland of the Greek-colonized area known as *Magna Grecia*. Today all the woes of the south gather here, little changed since they were encapsulated in Carlo Levi's *Christ Stopped At Eboli*, a marvellous evocation of this godforsaken land and its hard-pressed people: "a world apart . . . hedged in by custom and sorrow, cut off from history and the state, eternally patient . . . without comfort or solace, where the peasant lives out his motionless civilization on barren ground, in remote poverty and in the presence of death."

Basilicata's countryside is eerie and desolate. Ninety per cent is classified as upland, most of it stone and eroded clay, redeemed only by olives and the occasional patch of wheat. Abandoned farms stand as memorials to the tides of emigration that have made this the least populated region in Italy. How hard it is to believe that the region's ancient name, *Lucania*, derives from *lucus*, or woodland.

Relief from its almost hypnotic monotony comes only intermittently. The hills rise to about 1,000 metres (3,500 feet) and are branded collectively as the Appennino Lucano. The cone of the extinct volcano Monte Vulture and the deep gorges that run towards the sea in the east form a more enticing prospect, as do the mountain ramparts that rise on the southernmost border with Calabria, Italy's toe. The Pollino massif and its siblings fall as a mighty barrier across the country, severing Calabria from the rest of the country.

In the past Calabria was a byword for the south and its despair: emigration, crime, disease, illiteracy and malnutrition. Today Calabria is not as poor as Basilicata. Vast meadows of jasmine now make the region one of the world's largest exporters of the oil used in fine perfume; and horticulturists find conditions here ideal for growing the tiny bergamot orange. However, the price of advancement is evident along the coast, once one of Calabria's glories, where unsightly tourist resorts blight the scenery.

Inland, Calabria preserves something of Italy's real heart: rolling hills, streams, verdant pastures and vast woodlands, survivors of catastrophic deforestation caused by landslips and flash-floods. In the south-west corner of the country lies the harsher, daunting cape of the Aspromonte, wreathed in mist that swirls up from the sea. Here the immense granite Sila mountains are protected by the Calabria national park, teeming with wildlife.

GETTING THERE

By air: internal flights to Crotone's Capo Rizzuto (Calabria), T: (09620) 791 150; Bari Palese at Bari, T: (080) 374 654; A Papola at Brindisi, T: (0831) 412 141 (Puglia).
By boat: Sailings from Greece to Brindisi.
By road: fast motorway links to Puglia (A14, Foggia–Bari–Taranto) and Calabria–Basilicata on the A3 (or *Autostrada del Sole*). Otherwise there is a dense, but slow, network of minor roads in all 3 regions.
By rail: by inter-city lines on west and east coast linking all main centres to northern cities. There is a newly electrified Salerno–Potenza branch, and many scenic lines in Calabria, and a web of antiquated links in Puglia; but all of which have slow and infrequent trains. Travel by car if at all possible.

WHERE TO STAY

Accommodation has improved in recent years, but most hotels are new and functional, and outside the main centres (except on coasts) lodgings are still difficult to find. Prices, however, are mostly much lower than elsewhere in the country. For farm accommodation contact Agriturist at: Via Petroni 23, Bari (Puglia), T: (080) 365 025; Via XX Settembre 42, Catanzaro (Calabria), T: (0961) 45084; Via Settembre XX 39, Matera (Basilicata), T: (08350) 214 565.

ACTIVITIES

Walking: some of Italy's wildest and least known mountains are in Calabria (Sila, Aspromonte) and Basilicata (Pollino); numerous hill and forest walks in both regions, notably the Gargano in Puglia. There are as yet no marked trails in any of the regions. The GAEA agency in Reggio organize treks into the Sila and Aspromonte; Via Reggio Campi, T: (0965) 23328.
Ponytrekking: for list of approved centres contact IFE regional offices: Via Ferrarese 23, Bari (Puglia), T: (080) 211 799; Via Aschenez 140, Reggio di Calabria, T: (09650) 330 105.
Fishing: FIPS regional office: Corso Mazzini 286, Cosenza (Calabria), T: (0984) 21892.

FURTHER READING

Essential reading includes F. Pratesi, *The Blue Guide To Southern Italy*; *Guida alla Natura di Puglia, Basilicata e Calabria* (Mondadori 1979); Norman Douglas, *Old Calabria*; Carlo Levi, *Christ Stopped at Eboli*. Try also George Gissing, *By the Ionian Sea*; and Edward Lear, *In Southern Calabria and the Kingdom of Naples*.

Gargano and Foresta Umbra

Pronounced limestone promontory, spectacular coastline, salt lakes and virgin forest; proposed national park (29,000ha/ 72,000 acres)

The Gargano is the spur of the Italian boot, a peninsula of alien limestone that has its geological origins far from the central Appenines. Called by one writer "an island of Austrian stone stranded upon the beach of Italy", it is a dislocated piece of central Europe, left behind when two geological plates separated to form the Adriatic. For thousands of years thereafter it remained an island until silt deposited during the Ice Ages joined it to the mainland.

Now it is seen as a high tableland of limestone that extends some 30 kilometres (20 miles) into the Adriatic, bounded by sea and by the Puglian badlands to the south. The Conero promontory aside, it is the only piece of spectacular mountain scenery on the eastern seaboard between Venice and Calabria. In the east lies the Foresta Umbra — the "shady forest" — 25,000 hectares (62,000 acres) of some of the most beautiful mixed woodland in Italy. To the north are the lakes of Varano and Lesina; and to the south sprawl the plains of the Tavoliere. Along the coast there are some beautiful stretches of turquoise sea, wave-sculpted cliffs and sandy coves. Unfortunately tourism has brought its blight to many stretches of shore. Lovers of cliffs and wild seas should avoid the areas around Vieste and the Baia delle Zagare and concentrate on the south-east headlands.

The region's wilderness is now mainly found in the interior. The Foresta Umbra is

177

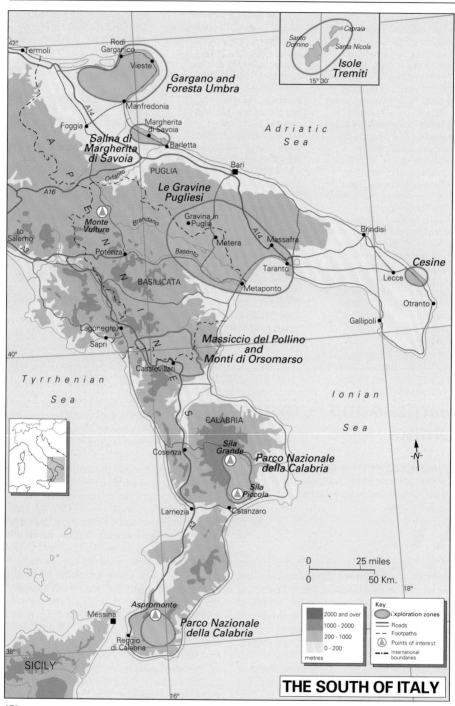

THE SOUTH OF ITALY

Scrub and woodland that are remnants of the ancient Foresta Umbra still cover vast areas of the Gargano's parched interior.

one of the south's most important natural enclaves, a primeval remnant of the woodland known as the *Nemus garganicum* that covered much of Puglia in antiquity. More than this, it has been described as the "botanical museum of the Italian peninsula", a floral showcase that contains more than 2,000 species of plant, tree and shrub. The reasons for this richness are various and disputed. Geographical remoteness has played its part, as has the physical isolation of species from the Apennines. The local climate is mild and severe by turns, the topography both sheltered and exposed. Fertile soils predominate, and the central area of the forest has been state-owned and protected since 1866, an unusual benefit in a country where 94 per cent of forest is in private hands.

Amid the profusion of flowers are numerous species more typical of the Balkans, including the bellflower *Campanula garganica*, the *Ranunculus garganicus* and the pink-lilac scabious *Scabiosa crenata,* sub-species *dallaportae.* All are best seen in the valleys around the hamlet of Pulsano, a solitary and abandoned place that should appeal to botanists and non-botanists alike. More common displays, such as the pink carpets of spring cyclamens *Cyclamen repadum* and white-leaved, golden-flowered bushes of Jupiter's beard *Anthyllis barbajovis,* are visible almost everywhere.

One of the most mysterious aspects of the Gargano's flora is the tendency of plants and trees to reach exaggerated proportions. The best-known examples are the beeches of the Baracconi in the Foresta Umbra, the oaks of the Bosco Quarto, the yews visible nearly everywhere and the Cappuccini holm oak at Vico del Gargano. Gargano also claims Italy's two largest aleppo pines, the taller of which stands on the road between Peschici and San Menaio. Known as the Zappino dello Scorzone, this 700-year-old monster has a girth of five metres (16 feet).

The forest fauna is equally fascinating, comprising various species common to the Apennines. It also has 138 species that have been identified as "transadriatic", that is, properly belonging to the Balkans, being distant ancestors of creatures that existed when Italy and the former Yugoslavia were joined during the Pleistocene epoch.

179

The most famous forest inhabitant is a small roe deer, a sub-species considered one of the few remaining examples of the original, pure-bred southern species. Wildcat and fox may be seen, along with the wild boar and fallow deer that have been reintroduced into the woodlands. Numerous birds, notably goshawks and eagle owls, relish the thick tree cover, while peregrines patrol the rockier sea cliffs.

For all its immense natural value, the Gargano is threatened less by tourism than by hunting. Even the rarest animals, including roe deer and wild geese, are slaughtered. Although the Foresta Umbra contains a number of reserves, their total area a risible 1,065 hectares (2,600 acres). This is not for want of trying by ecologists — the proposed national park has been on the drawing board since 1963.

One final surprise awaits in the Gargano: the salt lakes of the Varano and Lesina, stretched across the flat coastal margins to the north. Almost 30 kilometres (19 miles) in length, they are the largest lakes in southern Italy. Wind and waves threw up dunes to form Lesina, while Varano derives from an ancient gulf scooped out by the sea and isolated by silt from the nearby River Fortore. Plants suited to the mixture of sand, sun and salt line the banks, including the white-flowered *Cistus clusii*.

It is the huge bird population, though, that provides most interest here. Despite the effects of hunting, this is one of the most important waterfowl sites in Italy. Huge numbers of cormorants, shovellers, pochard, red-breasted mergansers and coots flock to both lakes. Breeding birds of the Gargano promontory include Egyptian vultures, honey buzzards, red and black kites, short-toed eagles, peregrines, eagle owls, rollers, middle-spotted and white-backed woodpeckers, Dartford warblers and lesser grey shrikes. Perhaps the loveliest bird of all is the stunning azure and turquoise roller, so called for its somersaulting courtship displays.

BEFORE YOU GO
Visit the forest centre for maps, information and museum (located at the junction of SS528 from Vico to Monte S. Angelo and the unclassified road to Vieste): Casa Forestale, Via V. Emanuele 39, Foresta Umbra, T: (0884) 91104.
Maps: available from visitors' centre and tourist office at Vieste (see below).
Guidebook: F. Pratesi, *Guida alla Natura di Puglia, Basilicata e Calabria* (Mondadori 1979).

GETTING THERE
By car: A14 from Pescara runs to the W of the Gargano, while the A16 crosses from Naples and the W to connect with the A14 below the peninsula at Canosa. From the Poggio Imperiale exit on the A14, approach the northern coast and pick up the SS272 for the central plateau.
By rail: access to the Gargano, using bus and train in tandem, can be very quick. Foggia is a halt for most fast trains on the main east-coast line, with a branch line connection to Manfredonia (7 trains daily). Fewer trains stop at San Severo, where a private line gives access to all towns on the N coast as far as Peschici.
By bus: an extensive local network links all local centres from Bari, Foggia and Manfredonia. Mon–Sat, 2 buses daily traverse the Foresta Umbra from Manfredonia to Vico del Gargano (2¼hr). July–Sept, 2 buses daily run from Rodi Garganico to the Foresta Umbra via Vico.

WHERE TO STAY
Accommodation in all categories on the coast (with Peschici the best base), less in the interior. See tourist information below.
Outdoor living: free camping is permitted outside the reserves within the forest. There are plenty of official sites on the coast; main centres include Peschici, Mattinata and Rodi Garganico.

Gargano Peninsula

ACTIVITIES

Walking: many marked trails in the Foresta Umbra, and some coastal paths around Vieste. Recommended forest hikes include: the visitors' centre to the forest's highest point, Monte Iacotenente (832m/2,729ft) via the Coppa dei Prigionieri (4½hr); from the SS89 to Monte Sacro (874m/2,868ft), one of the peninsula's loveliest spots (3hr); and the coastal path between Mergoli and Vignanotica near the Baia delle Zagare (1¼hr).

Caving: numerous coastal grottos, most accessible only by boat. Inland, the Grava di Campolato is one of Puglia's outstanding caverns, situated on the SS272 midway between S. Giovanni and Monte S. Angelo.

FURTHER INFORMATION

Tourist information: from offices at Via XXIV Maggio, Peschici, T: (0884) 94425; Piazza Garibaldi 4, Rodi Garganico, T: (0884) 95054; Corso Manfredi 26, Manfredonia, T: (0884) 21998; Corso V. Emanuele II 1, Vieste, T: (0884) 78806; Via E. Perrone 17, Foggia, T: (0881) 23650.

Isole Tremiti

Archipelago off the Gargano peninsula; marine reserve of 2,116ha/5,229 acres

The Tremiti take their name from "Tre Monti", the three mountains. In fact, they are three islands — San Domino, San Nicola and Capraia — that make up a tiny archipelago a dozen kilometres (seven miles) off the Gargano peninsula.

The islands are a miniature of all Puglia, graced with caves, bays, headlands, gorges, cliffs and dusty limestone interiors of luminous light and undulating hills. Marine life flourishes around their shores.

San Domino is the main island, and the Ripa dei Falconei is its natural highlight, a 90-m (300-ft) cliff that was used as a backdrop for the film *The Guns of Navarone*. As its name suggests, the cliff was once famous for its birds of prey, particularly peregrine and Eleanora's falcons. But the lower colonies have been depleted by nest-robbing and the seizing of birds for falconry. Manx and Cory's shearwaters, though, still nest at the top of the cliffs; their curious stiff-winged manner of flight (or "shearing" motion) can be seen as they skim the sea in search of fish.

Other seascape features include the Architiello, an arch formed by marine erosion, rock pillars like the Appicchio and the so-called *paliai*, majestic pyramidal bluffs named after the traditional hayricks they resemble. Sea caves are numerous; the most is famous the Bue Marino, the mauve-coloured Grotta delle Viole and the Grotta delle Murene.

Apart from a green carpet of maquis in summer, the treeless interior of San Nicola has a generally dry appearance. The crystal waters are rich in fish.

Capraia — little more than a large rock — takes its name from the caper bushes that cover it almost entirely. It has just two sandy coves, and a series of strange rock bridges known as *architelli*.

Getting there *By air:* daily flights with Alidaunia from Gino Lisa airport at Foggia, T: (0881) 71236.

By sea: In summer daily ferries cross to the Tremiti from Ortona, Manfredonia, Rodi Garganico, Vasto and Termoli; motor boats and hydrofoils run hourly from Termoli, daily from Ortona and Vasto.

Where to stay: hotels are all on San Domino.

Outdoor living: camping is allowed but difficult; ask permission and take supplies from the mainland (cheaper) and plenty of water. All-year camping at Villagio TCI on San Domino, with tents for hire.

Further information *Tourist office:* at the Municipio on San Nicola, useful for lists of rooms for rent and boat hire, T: (0882) 663 002.

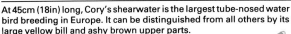

At 45cm (18in) long, Cory's shearwater is the largest tube-nosed water bird breeding in Europe. It can be distinguished from all others by its large yellow bill and ashy brown upper parts.

Salina di Margherita di Savoia

Ramsar site of salt flats and relict coastal marsh on the southern edge of the Tavoliere plain

The Salina di Margherita (named after the first Italian queen) is the largest salt-lake in Italy, its series of shallow evaporating pans accounting for three quarters of the country's salt production. It is at first sight a bleak treeless country, though salt-tolerant plants such as sea-blites and saltworts fringe the lagoons, grading into low fragrant garrigue in the drier areas.

The Salina lies between Manfredonia and the mouth of the River Orfanto. Until the drainage projects of 30 years ago, they were part of a huge area of marshland, periodically enlarged by the flooding of the rivers Candelaro, Celone, Cervaro and Carapelle. What remains today is but a tenth of the original habitat. However, this still amounts to 75,000ha (185,000 acres) of prime wetland, including not only the Savoia salt-lake (3,871ha/9,600 acres), but also the Alma Dannata lagoons and the basins of the Cervaro and Candelaro.

The shallow salt flats are a marvellous source of food for long-legged wading birds, the sediments containing a host of invertebrate life. Most birds are attracted to those pans where salinity is still fairly low, before too much evaporation has taken place. Because of its sheer size, variety of habitats and availability of food, this wetland is one of Europe's most important stopovers for migrating birds.

The salt flats attract small flocks of spoonbills on migration, unmistakable from their snow-white plumage and broad-tipped, spatula-like beaks, as well as huge numbers of waterfowl. Up to 10,000 wigeon and 3,000 or more shelduck can be seen here on occasion, together with as many as 5,000 avocets and large numbers of little egrets, curlew and slender-billed gulls. Some birds even manage to breed in and around the less heavily-worked salt flats. These include long-legged black-winged stilts and avocets, diminutive Kentish plovers and a large colony of little terns, by far the smallest sea tern and easily distinguished by their white foreheads and black-tipped yellow bills.

In the freshwater and brackish marshes of Candelaro and Cervaro, birdwatchers are treated to five species of breeding herons, including bittern, night, purple and squacco herons and little egrets. Even more remarkable is a handful of nesting glossy ibis that have recently made their home here; there is no mistaking this bird, half a metre (nearly two feet) in length, with a long, down-curved beak and purple-brown plumage tinged with metallic green.

Getting there *By car:* A14 via Foggia to Andrea-Barletta exit, then SS170 to Barletta, whence the SS16 takes you to the town of Margherita di Savoia. A coastal road runs across the northern perimeters of the salt flats.

By rail: station at Margherita di Savoia on the main Foggia–Bari line.

Where to stay: there is a campsite, the Tritone, at Canna Fresca: Via del Mare 130, T: (0883) 754 445.

Activities *Birdwatching:* contact the WWF in Barletta (Via De Nittis 15) and the forestry office in Margherita di Savoia, T: (0883) 656 278.

Further information *Tourist information:* Piazza Marconi 9, Margherita di Savoia, T: (0883) 754 012.

Cesine

Coastal saltwater and freshwater habitats of international importance; 1980 State nature reserve (640ha/1,600 acres) with WWF supervision

The Cesine are a pair of lakes, Salapi and the larger Pantano Grande, that lie behind the dunes along the coast between Lecce and Otranto. They are part of a region called the Salento at the southernmost tip of the Italian "heel".

This is one of the south's best birdwatching areas with a succession of habitats — beach, dune, swamp, maquis, lake and woodland — that preserves, uniquely in Puglia, the classic profile of southern Mediterranean littorals.

The lakes appear as two glittering turquoise lagoons, separated from the Adriatic by a narrow fringe of dunes. Inland, the landscape is dry and solemn, dotted with white farmhouses and carpeted to the far distance with centuries-old olive trees that have the reputation for providing Italy's best oil.

Cesine comes from *cese* (and the Latin *caedo*), meaning "to cut", here a reference to the thinning and burning of woodland to promote new growth. Vegetation cover is still substantial, the lake shores surrounded by a mantle of green that contrasts markedly with the sun-parched fields close by.

Dunal maquis, which has been windblown into a tangled barrier and reinforced by the planting of pines, provides a windbreak for more delicate flowers, allowing some 320 species to flourish here. Many burst into bloom in spring to provide a perfumed carpet over huge areas.

There is a notable presence of orchids, including Bertolini's ophrys, a subspecies of late spider orchid *Ophrys holoserica*, sub-species *parvimaculata*, endemic to Puglia and Basilicata and known locally as *Pantofola di Venere*, and the bug orchid *Orchis coriophora*, supposedly

smelling of squashed bed-bugs.

Small pockets of native oak survive among a large variety of replanted trees. And among the introduced trees, such as aleppo and maritime pines, are more unexpected exotica: acacia, Canary pine, elm, cypress and eucalyptus.

Birdwatchers can see up to 10,000 birds between October and April when the lakes are alive with their frenzied wheeling and the beating of wings. The great white egret is an occasional visitor from Greece. Equally unusual are the black stork, white-tailed sea eagle, red-crested pochard, red-breasted merganser, flamingo and glossy ibis that drop in from time to time on migration.

Map: IGM 1:25,000 *Acaia* and *Masseria Cesine.*

Getting there *By car:* by way of the SS543 from Lecce (8km/5 miles) to San Cataldo. From Otranto and the S, the SS611 to S. Cataldo touches the reserve's southern limit.

By rail: station at Lecce, with bus service to S. Cataldo.

Where to stay: at S. Cataldo, the Ostello Adriatico, Via Manelli 103, T: (0832) 650 026, and Lecce.

Access: Entry to the WWF reserve is possible as part of a tour on Thurs and Sun (15 Sept–15 May), T: (0832) 631 392.

Further information: the WWF, directly responsible for the reserve, has branch offices at the Franciscan Convent S. Maria delle Grazie, Via Tribuna 101, Manfredonia, and the Museo Missionario Cinese, Via Monti S. Michele 2, Lecce.

Le Gravine Pugliesi

*Canyons on the Puglia–
Basilicata border*

The Pugliesi *gravine* are some 25 gorges cutting through hills and limestone plateaux to the coast between Metaponto and Taranto. Dotted about the side of these canyons are the so-called *sassi*, or cave-dwellings, that are unique to Italy, and resemble the houses of Cappadocia in Turkey cut out of cones of rock.

The spectacular Matera gorge (10km/6 miles long, and up to 100m/330ft deep) is the best to explore (though the Laterza canyon is even more striking). Its soft tufaceous rock, which replaces the limestone of the other valleys, houses Greek Orthodox crypts.

The Madonna della Scala gorge above Massafra contains

Bertoloni's ophrys is a remarkable orchid whose flowers produce insect-like scents. These heady aromas induce bees and wasps to try to copulate with them, which enables pollen to be transferred from one flower to another.

caves mostly cut by hermits who survived by lowering baskets from their caves to solicit charity from passers-by. The best-known is the Farmacia del Mago Greguro, the pharmacy of Wizard Greguro, a mysterious series of hollows, in whose cool recesses the monks used to store medicinal herbs.

Getting there *By car:* the SS7 from Matera to Massafra bisects many of the ravines. To Matera from Potenza and the W, use the SS407/SS7.

By rail: stations at Massafra, on the Bari–Taranto line, and Matera, on a branch of the Bari–Altamura–Potenza line.

By bus: connections to centres from Taranto and Matera.

Activities *Walking:* short walks are possible in most parts, but many of the valley bottoms are blocked by thick vegetation. The best hikes are in the Laterza and Castellaneta gorges.

Further information *Tourist office:* Piazza V. Emanuele 3, Matera, T: (0835) 211 188.

Massiccio del Pollino and Monti di Orsomarso

Nature park (77,000ha/190,000 acres)

Pollino's colossal massif is the most impressive mountain region in the south, with landscapes comparable only to those of Sardinia, Etna and the Abruzzo. As the last major limestone massif of the Apennines, it is one of the highest points on the southern mainland, and one of the most daunting of mountains.

The heart of the range is a tortuous ridge that straddles the borders of Basilicata and Calabria. At 2,246 metres (7,368 feet) Monte Pollino itself is just lower than its neighbour, the 2,267-metre (7,437-feet) Monte Dolcedorme, "sweet slumber". However, it is not so much Pollino's height that astounds as its sheer vastness.

The scale of the mountains and massifs that radiate from the central heartland has kept the area's population density down to 60 people per square kilometre, one of the lowest in Italy. Most of them live in Castrovillari and the villages that line the *Autostrada del Sole*. This trunk road winds its way through the rocky mass that for centuries cut off Calabria from the rest of the country.

In typical Apennine fashion, Pollino's massifs present different faces to the world, depending on whether your approach is from the north or the south. The northern slopes that overlook the barren hills of Basilicata are gentle and green, containing some of the area's densest forests, notably the Magnano near San Severino, and the Cugno dell'Acero and Duglia above Terranova del Pollino. The south-facing slopes are much more Mediterranean in character. Steeper and more spectacular, they are an arid mixture of sun-bleached limestone and clinker-dry gorges. There is

none more imposing than the Ranganello, the south's greatest canyon, whose rocky wilderness supports numerous birds of prey. Access is from the solitary village of San Lorenzo Bellizzi. Other hidden corners include the dizzying Bifurto abyss, an unbroken drop of 683 metres (2,240 feet); the Caldenelle gorge; and the Grotta delle Ninfe, a thermal spring famous since Roman times for its curative waters.

The Pollino marks the southernmost extent of the ice-sheet in Italy during the last period of glaciation. Faint memories of this colder age remain only in the summit snows, which in some years fail to melt even in summer, when temperatures on the Calabrian plains can reach 40°C (100°F).

Nowhere is the solemn, silent dignity of the mountains better felt than on Dolcedorme, a peak whose intimidating pyramidal shape seems to promise a stiff climb but, in the event, lets the walker off lightly. Most hikers start from the Rifugio di Gasperi on the Piani di Ruggio, and are rewarded with breathtaking meadows of wild flowers before making the ascent of the Orrido di Malevento, "the pass of the bad winds". Here you may step with some trepidation as this is known to be a passage taken by wolves in their search for food.

The view from the pass is stupendous, but a final haul to the summit provides one of Europe's finest panoramas. Three seas, the Ionian, Adriatic and Tyrrhenian, are visible on clear days, along with a huge swathe of southern Italy: the Calabrian plains of Sibari and Castrovillari; the distant dark humps of the Sila; and to their right, more distinct still, the coastal spine of mountains that separates the Calabrian hinterland from the sea.

On the long climb to the summit you can see the thick and dense foliage of the majestic Bosnian pine (*Pinus leucodermis*). Intended as the symbol of the future national park, the tree is a "living fossil", a prehistoric relic that originated from and still grows in the Balkans, but is rarely seen in Italy. The tree is confined to the driest, rockiest heights, and only a thousand examples survive, sometimes in small groups, but more often in isolation. The advance of beech is constantly driving the Bosnian pines higher; their dead, white trunks everywhere provide evidence of their possible future extinction.

Pollino and Monti di Orsomarso

Other strange flora inhabit the Pollino: the Burning Bush *Dictamnus albus*, for example, is a mysterious plant which locals say shines by night, and actually is sometimes luminous; or the heavenly "manna", made famous by the erroneous accounts of nineteenth-century travellers such as George Sandys, who said that "it falls at night like dew on the mulberry leaves". He was referring to the sugary resin from the punctured barks of the manna ash *Fraxinus ornus*. This is still commercially cultivated in Sicily, where the dried resin is used as a mild astringent.

Pollino's wildlife is that of an undisturbed high mountain habitat, with the two great symbols of such terrain, the wolf and the golden eagle, both relatively prominent. Pollino offers your best chance of sighting the wolf, if you have patience and the sense of adventure demanded by these mountains. The wildness of this habitat is confirmed by the presence of such shy creatures as the otter, red squirrel, crested porcupine, wildcat and even the roe deer, which has vanished in the south except for the ancient nucleus in the Gargano and the group that has been reintroduced in the Sila.

Golden eagles are known to fly the thermals above Pianoro di Maselto, high in the Ranganello valley. Also visible are Egyptian vultures, black woodpeckers, black and red kites, goshawks, lanner falcons, peregrines, eagle owls and choughs. There has even been the odd sighting of the rare lammergeier, or bearded vulture, probably a vagrant from Corsica or the Balkans.

The Orsomarso massif, the south-western continuation of the Pollino, lies outside the boundary of the proposed national park, though it has its own 3,920-hectare (9,700-acre) reserve. It contains almost no signs of human presence, littered only with shepherds' huts that even shepherds have abandoned. Hardy and well-equipped walkers can make one of Italy's loneliest treks running for 45 kilometres (28 miles) along its main ridge, passing 12 rock peaks that are almost Dolomitic in character and over 1,700 metres (5,600 feet) high. Winter cross-country skiing is superb, as it is in much of the Pollino; the routes are long and the slopes free of hotels and ski-lifts.

As a footnote, many of the desperately poor villages on and around the Pollino (Civita, Eianina, Frascineto, San Paolo) are peopled with the *arberesh* — inhabitants of Albanian descent who preserve customs and a way of life brought with them when the Turkish invasions of the sixteenth century forced them to flee to Italy. In dress, manner, food, language, music and religion, they are still different from other Italians, even after some 500 years.

BEFORE YOU GO
If you want guidance — or company — use the Rif. di Gasperi on the Viggianello-Campo Tenese road (marked on TCI maps). Close to the mountains, it is open all year and is a fount of useful information. Or try the rangers' office (Corpo Forestale) at

the Municipio in Rotonda, T: (0973) 61005/61142.
Maps: Potenza's tourist office issues a free map with 11 walking and cross-country skiing itineraries. The IGM maps for Pollino itself are 221 IV SE *Morano Calabro*; and 221 I SO *Frascineto*.
Guidebooks: M. Tommaselli, *Il*

Massiccio del Pollino (BMG 1982); G. Braschi, *Sui Sentieri del Pollino* (Il Coschile 1987), for walkers.

GETTING THERE
Access to the Pollino is difficult without a car. Hitch-hiking is the other option and locals are usually obliging.

Hidden valleys and limestone uplands in the heart of the Pollino conceal the lairs of wolves, one of the symbols of the proposed national park.

By car: via the A3, both from the N (Naples/Salerno) and the S (Cosenza). For the Orsomarso use the Spezzano-Sibari exit and take the SS105 south of the mountains. There are no roads into the massif.

For the Pollino, exit at Campo Tenese and take either of 2 lanes, both very scenic, to Rotonda and the di Gasperi refuge.

By rail: the nearest station is Sapri on the main Naples–Reggio di Calabria line, where you can take a bus to Lagonegro (2 daily), and another to Rotonda.

By bus: between Salerno and Lagonegro (7 daily), and Lagonegro to Castrovillari (5 daily).

WHERE TO STAY

Best option is the di Gasperi refuge (see above), but there are rooms and hotels at Terranova di Pollino, Mormanno and Rotonda, and

186

further afield at Castrovillari, Campo Tenese and Lagonegro.

For guidance, booking and room-finding — often rooms are available even though they may not be advertised — contact local tourist offices.

Outdoor living: permitted anywhere in both the Pollino and Orsomarso; the latter also has many shepherds' huts suitable for bivouacs.

ACTIVITIES

Walking: many walks, often easy to follow because the ground is open and barren. Distances are long, however, snow is heavy from Oct onwards, and the mountains require care and adequate equipment. The classic walk is the ascent of Pollino from the Colle dell'Impiso (1,573m/ 5,160ft) on the road above the di Gasperi refuge (5hr). Variations on the route include a climb to the Serra del Prete (4hr) and a brief hike to the

Madonna del Pollino (1,537m/ 5,042ft) to the N (3hr).

More strenuous are the southern, mainly wooded ascent of Pollino (5hr) from Terranova di Pollino (take the road W from the village to the Lago della Duglia to start), and the long haul to Dolcedorme from the car park at the Vaccaro springs above the village of Civita (16hr).

The simplest stroll is up the Raganello gorge from S. Lorenzo; most demanding is an unmarked coast-to-coast walk through the Orsomarso and Pollino (7 days).

Canoeing: the Lao river on the northern edge of the Orsomarso has one of southern Italy's best runs, from the bridge at Papasidero 18km (11 miles) downstream to the SS18 coast road near Scalea.

FURTHER INFORMATION
Tourist information:
Municipio, Lagonegro, T: (0973) 21031; Via Alianelli 4, Potenza, T: (0971) 21812; Corso Calabria 45, Castrovillari, T: (0981) 27067.

Parco Nazionale della Calabria

National park of 15,894ha (39,274 acres) consisting of three distinct parks

Calabria's national park protects two massifs in the Sila mountains, which cover most of central Calabria, and the Aspromonte, a smaller knuckle of mountains that occupies the tip of the Italian peninsula — the rocky "toe" of the Italian boot.

Of all the mountains in the Apennines, the Sila come closest to the primeval wooded appearance of southern Italy before deforestation and cultivation took over. As for the Aspromonte, the "bitter mountain", there is a legend that until recently no one had ever crossed the mountains — indeed no one had ever *wanted* to cross them, so wild and inhospitable were they. Latter-day bandits and kidnappers are still liable to hide unfortunate victims in their empty wastes.

To visit either area is to find the wild Italy of old. This timeless landscape belies the image of the south as a sun-scorched desert, revealing instead spectacular and varied scenery: lakes, torrents, forests, deep valleys and frosted mountains which are the setting for a range of fauna from the Apennine wolf to a rare endemic dormouse.

The Sila mountains are divided from north to south into three ranges: the Sila Greca, the Sila Grande and the Sila Piccola. Of similar height, between 1,500 and 1,700 metres (5,000 and 5,600 feet), they are often described only as high plateaux, a put-down that does little justice to their grandeur. Any first-time visitor should see the Sila Grande; the Piccola are also lovely and a little more open; while the Greca (which are very inaccessible) are lower and less varied.

All three ranges are formed of crystalline rocks which only here begin to supplant the virtually unbroken chain of limestone running down the Appennines. Schists start to appear south of the Pollino, and by northern Calabria they are alternating with Triassic limestones. From the Sila southwards they dominate the geological picture, the only other rock-type being the occasional Tertiary sandstone. Much older than the Apennines, the Sila are the eroded summits of a range that continues into the sea off southern Italy.

In places these crystalline bedrocks crumble to form deep and fertile soils, which in turn support the huge forests from which the Sila take their name (Latin *silva*, "wood"). For a long time the lumber capital of Italy, the forests were felled from as early as the fourth century, when Pope Gregory IV used timber from the Sila to roof many of Rome's churches. Subsequently they were used for building ships and railways, and exploited in the nineteenth century to the point of exhaustion.

Spring brings an all too brief mantle of green to the Aspromonte, the "Bitter mountain", in the Parco Nazionale della Calabria.

Considerable replanting has since taken place, and the forests of the interior are still so vast that the Sila are considered one of Europe's most densely wooded areas. The principal tree is the Calabrian pine, a localized speciality with the long-winded title of *Pinus nigra*, subspecies *laricio*, variety *calabrica*. The most famous wood is the Bosco di Fallistro near Camigliatello Silano, where you can see the so-called *giganti della Sila* — "the giants of the Sila" — 56 trees over 500 years old, most two metres (six feet) in diameter and more than 40 metres (130 feet) tall. At the other end of the scale is the curious *ciciarella*, or needle-furze: a spiny shrub with yellow flowers growing far from its natural Atlantic habitat of moor and healthland.

As well as supporting a lush vegetation, the impervious granite bedrock also provides an abundance of surface water. Ancient writers counted 110 rivers in Calabria, a welcome respite from the south's general aridity. Together with the pines, the gurgling streams and waterfalls give the Sila a distinctly Nordic flavour, emphasized by the three immense reservoirs built on their western flanks in the 1930s. Of the three — Arvo, Ampollino and Cecita — Arvo is the most impressive, and strongly reminiscent of a Norwegian fiord.

The Scandinavian comparison continues through the winter, when Sila has freezing temperatures, despite being on a similar latitude to Tunis. The winter slopes can be snow-covered for as many as four months of the year. During the bleakest weeks, the Sila are transformed into Italy's finest and most severe cross-country skiing area.

The Aspromonte, a final burst from the Apennine range, shares the Sila's gifts of wood and water. Wilder than the Sila, it is a harsh country of valley and mountain, its geology a chaos of different rocks — including lava — torn and contorted by weather and earthquakes into one of Italy's most inaccessible landscapes.

By contrast, the even horizon of the sea that encompasses the Aspromonte on three sides can be seen from most of the area's 22 peaks. The highest point is Montalto (1,955 metres/6,413 feet), a vantage point which offers one of the best Italian views: Sicily stretches beyond the Straits of Messina; cloud-wreathed Etna is clearly visible; and the Aeolian islands appear as small spots in the azure of the Tyrrhenian Sea. Away to the east the Ionian Sea shines an equally vivid blue, lost only when the mist of Aspromonte, known as "the cloud-gatherer", swirls up to shroud the summit.

There are no roads to provide access to the region, only valleys, which radiate to the four points of the compass from the central massif. Most have water only in autumn and winter, when raging torrents replace summer's drought; in spring many of the dry beds are filled with wild flowers, one of the Aspromonte's celebrated highlights. This brief but rich flowering — all too soon snuffed out by the summer sun — includes hare's-foot clover, Carthusian pink, black bryony, long-spurred pansy, mountain cornflower and sweet vernal-grass that contains coumarin and has the smell of new-mown hay.

The western slopes fall seawards in broad steps, creating a series of plains of olive trees and meadows. The eastern slopes, by contrast, are barren, but have fantastic rock formations and spectacular gorges (known as *fiumare*) that drop as much as 1,500 metres (5,000 feet) to the sea.

Hunting has destroyed much of the area's larger fauna, and it is perhaps no accident that its most noted animal is a little dormouse (Italian, *dromio*). Usually found in the Alps, it is honoured here as a geographical sub-species *aspromontis*. The wolf is present, and Bonelli's eagles possibly breed here. The Sila mountains have the largest of the Apennine wolf communities, though individuals are difficult to see, given the size of the forests. The best place to try to spot them and other rarities is above the rangers' centre on Lago di Cecita. The hills, especially those of the Sila Grande, contain pine and beech martens, badgers, otters, deer and polecats. Notable birds include the short-toed eagle, goshawk, kestrel and sparrowhawk — best seen in the Arno-campo between Cecita and Germano, and in the Aspromonte above the Ferraghena meadows of the Ferraina valley.

THE GREY WOLF

The grey wolf is the largest wild member of the dog family still in existence, yet even so it is still considerably smaller than many would think, European individuals standing at about 75cm (30in) at the shoulder. Persecuted unmercifully for centuries as a symbol of evil and menace to livestock, it was not until 1972 that the wolf finally became protected by law in Italy. Yet even today animals are shot and poisoned illegally by farmers seeking to rid themselves of a largely imagined problem. In many areas where livestock losses are high, the real culprits are packs of wild dogs roaming the hills.

BEFORE YOU GO

Park headquarters: at Via della Repubblica 26, Cosenza and in the Aspromonte at Via Proiungamento Torrione, Reggio di Calabria.

There is a visitors' centre in the Sila Grande: Centro Visitatori, Cupone, T: (0984) 978 144; and forestry posts at Camigliatello Silano, T: (0983) 71141; Germano, T: (0984) 992 481; Buturo (Sila Piccola), T: (0961) 931 317.

In the Aspromonte there is a forestry post and information centre at Basilico, near Gambarie, T: (0965) 743 020.
Maps: IGM 1:25,000 *Lago Arvo, Lago di Cecita, Fossiata, Silvana Mansio, Spezzano, S. Giovanni in Fiore, Lago Ampollino* (Sila), *Plati, Montalto* and *S. Luca* (Aspromonte). The park issues its own map of the key area of the Sila Grande, available from bars, tourist offices and visitors' centres — 1:25,000 *Carta della Fossiata* (useful only as a basic guide to paths).

GETTING THERE

By car: the best base for touring is Cosenza, but the Sila cover an extensive area, and communications are long and difficult. You must have a TCI map and be prepared to do your own exploring; most of the roads are very beautiful.
By rail: change at Paola on the main Naples–R. Calabria line for connections to Cosenza. A fantastic railway operates between Cosenza and San Giovanni in Fiore (2hr), offering gorgeous views *en route* (3 trains daily).

A slightly less scenic line runs from Cosenza to Catanzaro (3hr), meandering through the western foothills of the Piccola.

WHERE TO STAY

The best choice of hotels is in Cosenza and R. Calabria.
Outdoor living: free camping is permitted in all areas bar a few small reserves (notably the Fossiata in the Grande). There is an all-year campsite, Lago Arvo, on the SS108 at Passo della Cornacchia, T: (0984) 997 060; other sites at Lorica and Camigliatello.

ACTIVITIES

Walking: the only marked paths are in the Bosco della Fossiata in the Sila Grande, but exploration is possible everywhere if you are properly equipped. Tree cover can be a handicap, especially in the Piccola, but many comfortable strolls are possible on the forest tracks in both the Sila and Aspromonte. Best base in the Grande is Camigliatello Silano; in the Piccola, Tirivolo and Villagio Mancuso; in Aspromonte, Gambarie.

The most strenuous walks are in the valleys of the Aspromonte, and on the slopes of Montalto. Tried and tested routes include the Aposcipo and Butramo canyons; ascents of Montalto from Gambarie (3hr) or Delianuova (5hr); the Amendolea valley-run from Roghudi. Further information from the CAI branch at Gambarie, T: (0965) 743 057.
Skiing: many centres mentioned above are first and foremost ski resorts — Villagio Mancuso (lifts at Cicicilla), Trepido Soprano (lifts at Villagio Palumbo), Lorica, Camigliatello Silano and Gambarie.

Cross-country skiing in the Sila is some of the best in Italy, with favoured routes around Silvana Mansio and Croce di Magara, and the run from Monte Curcio to Monte Botte Donato (16km/10 miles).

FURTHER INFORMATION

Tourist offices: Via Nazionale, Lorica, T: (0984) 997 069; Gambarie, T: (0965) 743 081; Via Tagliamento 15, Cosenza, T: (0984) 27821.

Sicily and Sardinia

Sicily and Sardinia are the largest islands in the Mediterranean. Steeped in myth and legend, they contain some of Italy's wildest scenery. The two islands are physically very different, but both are lands apart, inhabited by peoples of fierce pride and separated by history, culture and language not only from Italy, but also from Europe. D.H. Lawrence called Sicily the place where "Europe ends", and said of Sardinia that it is "unlike any other place on earth . . . inside the net of European civilization" but "not yet dragged ashore to join the rest of Europe". Visit both islands if you can, for to miss either, as Goethe said of Sicily, "is not to have seen Italy at all".

Sicily is the beautiful island of Persephone, the goddess of spring; a land traditionally associated with green and plenty that was once the granary of the Roman Empire. Yet it is also a land of contrasting moods and mixed identities, separated from the toe of Italy by just five kilometres (three miles) at the Strait of Messina and yet barely 150 kilometres (95 miles) from Africa at its south-western tip. Its northern mountains evoke the woods and hills of Central Europe; its desolate plains bring to mind the Spanish *meseta*; the olives and terracing of the east suggest Greece and the Aegean; the south's treeless hills and dunes foreshadow the featureless deserts of North Africa.

Besides the monumental presence of Mount Etna in the east, the island has

Dawn breaks over Lampedusa in the Pelagie islands, part of an archipelago between Sicily and the African coast. Their offshore waters, in which the rare loggerhead turtle survives, are protected by a marine park, one of seven proposed in Sicily.

one upland region: an unbroken chain of mountains that runs for 150 kilometres (95 miles) along the northern coast. Its massifs, the Peloritani, Nebrodi and Madonie, are a geological continuation of the mainland Apennines. Western Sicily is geographically more complex: a mixture of limestone outcrops, undulating clay plateaux and eye-stretching carpets of vineyards and olives on the plains of Trapani and Marsala. Along the coast, little bays, low hills and headlands of outstanding beauty, notably Monte dello Zingaro, are interspersed with lagoons that form the first landfall for many birds migrating northwards from Africa in the spring. In the east, the prosperous agricultural plains of Catania give way to the Iblean mountains in the southeast corner, a region of table-top uplands and steep-sided valleys.

The desolate rolling interior is what Giuseppe Tomasi di Lampedusa called "the real Sicily" in his novel *The Leopard*: "aridly undulating to the horizon in hill after hill, comfortless and irrational, with no lines that the mind could grasp, conceived apparently in a delirious moment of creation". This is monotonous and sun-baked landscape where dusty white roads vanish into a shimmering horizon. Under an African sun, crickets make the only sound, plodding donkeys and women in black the only movement. Farms and trees are almost unknown, while the poverty of slumbering hilltop villages still reeks of Sicily's feudal heritage.

Water is the great leveller in these regions, drought the normal condition. Mountains shut out most rain-bearing winds, and in summer the Sahara unleashes the *scirocco*, a scorching wind that can take temperatures up to 45°C (110°F), during which time people can die and the dry clay hills will bake to

a sickly yellow. A Sicilian proverb says that summer begins in January, winter in August, and that spring is a brief flicker when the fields are green and the flowers are in bloom. Flash-floods and short powerful rivers (or *fiumare*) pour off the northern mountains in this springtime interval. A greening of the landscape soon fades, however, after August; the cicada's song ceases and the furze returns to sun-burnt scrub.

Sardinia can, if anything, claim wilderness still more extreme — so extreme, in fact, that many declare it the finest in all of Western Europe. Only the luxury coastal developments of the Aga Khan, the so-called Costa Smeralda, and the capital Cagliari show determined efforts to welcome the twentieth century. Although lesser entrepreneurs have followed the Aga Khan, only a portion of the island's matchless seascape has been spoiled.

Two-thirds of the interior is given over to Sardinia's ancient pastoral way of life. Though it may be romantic to come across shepherds and their flocks, the reality is poverty and hardship. Not the poverty of the 1950s, when malaria flourished and only one tenth of all roads were surfaced, but the backwardness that shows itself in a small population and an illiteracy rate that is double Italy's average.

This is, of course, ironic good fortune for the landscape and its fauna. You can enjoy endless tracts of land unturned since the Romans: windswept uplands covered in dense scrub, vast forests of cork oak, which contribute three-quarters of Italy's cork production; and ten offshore islands.

It is hard to differentiate between one lonely spot in Sardinia and the next. The loneliest, though, is perhaps the proposed national park of the Gennargentu, granite and limestone mountains that sprawl across most of the island's eastern side. Italy's oldest rocks are here, and have been cut and thrust so many times that their structure is an almost indecipherable jumble.

As capricious as Sardinia's rocks are its rivers, which meander in vain along their courses, hostage to the summer droughts. Water, though, is too precious to be allowed to run away. There are several reservoirs created by dams, but only one natural lake on the island, Lake Baratz in the extreme north-west. There are, however, many natural *stagni*, or salt lagoons along the coast; those which have not been drained provide bases for most of the island's bird population. The most important of these lagoons are at Cagliari, and support thousands of flamingos despite being only a stone's throw from the city. At Sulcis on the western coast, a paradise of white sands

explains why half of Italy spends its summer holiday on Sardinian beaches.

Sardinia's island isolation has allowed a large fauna to thrive. In some instances endemic subspecies have evolved, such as those of mouflon, deer, fox, rabbit and wildcat. Insects, reptiles and plants also have large numbers of endemic species. The mountains of the interior are home to some of Europe's rarest creatures: the griffon and bearded (lammergeier) vultures, golden and Bonelli's eagles and the virtually extinct Corsican red deer. There are also interesting butterflies found only in Sardinia and Corsica, including the Corsican fritillary, Corsican grayling and the spectacular black and yellow Corsican swallowtail, as well as the Sardinian meadow brown (*Maiola nurag*), found only on this island, where it is common in the north.

GETTING THERE
By air: to Sicily: direct European charters to Palermo and Catania airports; up to 10 daily connections from Rome and 4 from Milan. Daily flights from Bologna, Pisa, Genoa, Naples and Cagliari.
To Sardinia: international and domestic flights to Cagliari, Alghero and Olbia, and internally between island airports.
By boat: to Sicily: daily boats from Naples to Palermo, Catania, Siracusa. Thrice weekly from Genova, Cagliari and Livorno. Very frequent car ferry crossings to Messina from Reggio di Calabria and Villa S. Giovanni (½hr). Summer hydrofoil services between all centres.
To Sardinia: sailings from many points on the Italian mainland but most convenient are state railway's ferries from Civitavecchia; sailings to Porto Torres, Cagliari (18hr), Olbia

(12hr), Golfo Aranci (8hr) and Arbatax.

WHEN TO GO
July and Aug are uncomfortably hot, African temperatures made worse by the *scirocco*. Hotels are also busier and prices higher. Spring is best, when the flowers are exuberant and the almond in blossom. Winter is mild, with frequent clear skies.

WHERE TO STAY
Sicily: Although accommodation is ample in cities and coastal resorts, it is often scarce and of poor quality in the interior. To obtain lists of rooms, or free camping booklet, *Sicilia Campeggi*, apply to main provincial tourist offices (see tourist information). For rural stays write to: Agriturist, Via Alessio Giovanni 14, Palermo, T: (091) 296 666.
Sardinia: Luxury hotels on the

Costa Smeralda; outside main towns accommodation is very limited. For rural stays contact Federazione Agricoltori, Via Trieste 6, Cagliari, T: (070) 668 330.

ACTIVITIES
Walking: Sicily: no long-distance paths, and just a few marked trails in the Madonie mountains, but walking opportunities on Etna, in the Nebrodi mountains and on the offshore islands. Details from the Club Alpino Siciliano (CAS), Via P. Paternostro 43, Palermo, T: (091) 581 323.
Sardinia: pioneering country for hikers, few paths but many shepherds' tracks; trekking and climbing information from CAI, Via Piccioni, Cagliari, T: (070) 667 877.
Caving: Sicily: numerous caves, including the Addaura at Mondello, Bue Marino at Filicudi and Cavallo on the Aeolian islands; many on

Ustica and Egadi islands, notably the Genovese on Levanzo, known for Neolithic cave drawings, details from Favignana tourist office, T: (0923) 921 704.

General assistance from the Gruppo Speleologico CAI, Via Mazzini 48, Palermo, T: (091) 250 875/581 323.
Sardinia: the agency, Sardegna da Scoprire, runs week-long trips to caves, with training and equipment provided if necessary: Via Dante 29, Nuoro, T: (0784) 30400.

Canoeing: Sicily: noted route on Alcantara river above Taormina; embark at Graniti for 9km (6 miles) run to sea

with some rapids.
Fishing: Sicily: FIPS offices at Via Terra Santa 93, Palermo, T: (091) 302 302; Via C. Vivante 24a, Catania, T: (095) 446 292.
Sardinia: FIPS branch at Via Elmas, Cagliari, T: (070) 290 077.

FURTHER INFORMATION
Tourist offices: Sicily: Piazza Castelnuovo 35, Palermo, T: (091) 583 847; Piazza V. Emanuele 33, Agrigento, T: (0922) 20391; Largo Paisiello 5, Catania, T: (095) 312 124; Via S. Sebastiano 47, Siracusa, T: (0931) 67710.
Sardinia: Piazza Deffenu 9,

Cagliari, T: (070) 663 207; Piazza Italia 19, Nuoro, T: (0784) 30083; Via Cagliari 276, Oristano, T: (0783) 74191; Viale Caprera 36, Sassari, T: (079) 299 544.

FURTHER READING
The best general guide is J. Brown, *The Rough Guide to Sicily* (Penguin 1993). M. Simeti, *On Persephone's Island* (Penguin) is fine and lyrical, with many accounts of flora and fauna. G. T. di Lampedusa, *The Leopard* (Collins Harvill), is one of Italy's finest post-war novels. Also see *Traveller's Guide to Sardinia* (Jonathan Cape).

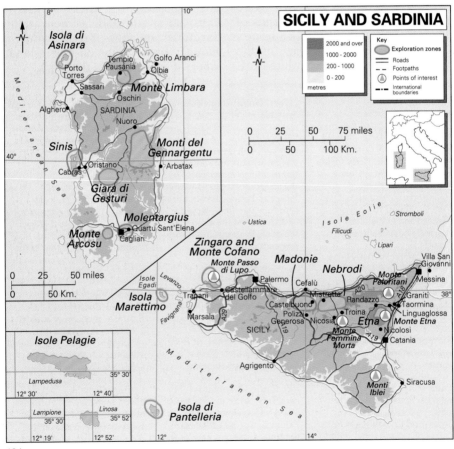

Etna

Smoke drifts from the snowy summit of Mount Etna during one of the volcano's quieter moments.

Europe's largest and most active volcano, partially protected by a nature park; proposed national park (60,000ha/150,000 acres)

♦♦♦

A ncient navigators believed Etna to be the highest point on earth. The Arabs called it Jebel, from which derives its alternative name, Mongibello, the "mountain of mountains". Pindar described it as the column that supports the sky. One of the world's greatest volcanoes at 3,323 metres (10,902 feet) high and over 200 kilometres (120 miles) in circumference, it is probably the single most monumental landform in the Mediterranean.

It is, however, a remarkably young volcano. Scientists believe it is only 60,000 years old. Magma wells up directly from the bowels of the earth, funnelled through a central crater which drops 50 kilometres (30 miles). One of Etna's chief characteristics is to split at the seams — eruptions tend to burst through the *sides* of the mountain. Over the years these ruptures have added over 350 minor craters to the main cone.

The first recorded eruption was in 475BC. There have been 90 major ones since, the last in 1992. The most catastrophic eruption on record was in 1669, when the mountain was rent apart leaving a chasm 25 kilometres (16 miles) long. Magma flowed for 122 days. Catania was engulfed and the castle surrounded by molten lava. The ash thrown up was carried for 100 kilometres (60 miles), and the lava took eight years to cool; local peasants, we are told, continued to

195

boil water on it long after the eruption.

Today Etna is always at least smouldering, if not actually erupting. This makes it a considerable tourist attraction. Jeeps and a summer procession of walkers make the pilgrimage as close to the volcano as the authorities, or the volcano itself, will allow. Away from the people, however, in the surreal atmosphere of the highest slopes, lies Europe's most extraordinary wilderness. "Alone! — on this charr'd, blackened melancholy waste," wrote Matthew Arnold. Everywhere seems an endless horizon of bare rock — not, to my mind, melancholy, but charged with the ethereal loveliness of desert landscapes. Views from the summit extend for 250 kilometres (150 miles), with Malta visible on a clear day. Pumice and clinker strew the barren slopes of lava — red, grey, green or black, depending on their age. Shifting sands and powdered ash drift across windblown hills, lunar and eerie; rivers of cooled lava lie like shrunken tentacles, black and macabre.

Apart from the summit the chief landmark is the Valle del Bove. A deep gash in Etna's eastern flank, it is an abyss 20 kilometres (12 miles) long, which accounts for about one sixth of the volcano's area. Lava walls plunge 900 metres (3,000 feet), their precipitous scarps pocked with small volcanic vents. It is thought to be the remains of an earlier crater, the Trifoglio, destroyed by the 1669 eruption. Etna otherwise rises in a relentless pyramid straight from the sea.

Despite the volcano's destructiveness, Sicilians continue to live on its fringes. After as little as a hundred years the lava can weather to a soil of great fertility. Locals plant prickly pear, whose powerful roots break up the rock, and follow up with hardy trees like almond and pistachio. Eventually they grow vines. As a result, Etna's lower slopes have one of the densest rural populations in Europe.

Botanists will find here one of the most fascinating floral enclaves in Italy. Colours and leafy profusions are almost tropical, and the variety of species, 1,500 in all, is exceptional. Coastal maquis comes at the lowest level, then a ring of fruit trees

(orange, lemon, carob, fig, olives), and up to 300 metres (1,000 feet), a thick belt of vines that almost encircles the volcano.

Holm oak, mixed with broad bands of chestnut and beech, flourishes at the lower levels; and the famous forests of Corsican pine lie around Linguaglossa in the northeast (though much of Etna's virgin forest has been felled). Predominant in the undergrowth and forest fringes is the greenweed *Genista aetnensis*, endemic to Sicily and Sardinia, with a profusion of golden flowers. Etna's most prodigious plants are its highmountain pioneering varieties. Most hardy is *Stereocaulon vesuvianum*, a silver-grey lichen able to grow on lava that is still warm. Most extensive is the endemic *Astragalus garanatensis*, subspecies *siculus*, or *spino santo*, "holy thorn". It creates a unique floral landscape covering huge areas of lava with its large hemispherical tussocks studded with delicate pink flowers. Other plants include the barberry *Berberis aetnensis*, the endemic Etna ragwort *Senecio aethnensis* and several species of violet, all adapted to life on lava beds 3,000 metres (10,000 feet) up Etna's gaunt slopes.

The volcano is most famous for its venerable individual trees, specimens that botanists think may be some of the oldest in Europe. Best known is the *Castagno dei Cento Cavalli*, "the chestnut of a hundred horses", so called from the legend that Queen Joan of Anjou sheltered under its branches with a hundred horsemen. The circumference of its trunk is a mindboggling 60 metres (196 feet). It grows near Sant'Alfio, due east of Etna's main crater.

After Etna, you might turn to the volcanic sideshows outside its immediate arena: the organ-pipe columns of basalt at Gole di Pretolo, for example; or the lava stacks at Aci Castello near Catania, rocks which the Cyclops hurled at the escaping Ulysses in Homer's *Odyssey*; and there is the spring at Fiumefreddo, which gushes 2,000 litres (440 gallons) of water a second; and the crater's lava "bombs"; the walls or *sciare* of solidified lava; and the minor craters such as the Salto della Giumenta (1852 eruption) and the Monti Rossi di Nicolosi (1669).

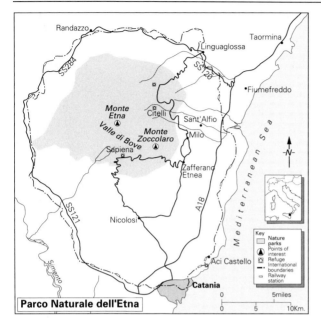

Parco Naturale dell'Etna

from Zafferana Etnea. The best walk of all is a 2-day trek from Sapienza curving around the NW edge of the crater and dropping to Linguaglossa.

Etna is an immense mountain, so take enough food and water, be prepared for snow and take adequate equipment. Walk only in hiking boots; anything else the lava will cut to ribbons.

Monti Nebrodi

Extensive and heavily wooded massif cut by ravines; proposed regional park (140,000ha/346,000 acres)

The Nebrodi mountains are one of the few areas to retain the appearance of virgin Sicily. They spread over a large part of the island's northern interior: a green belt between the urban ugliness of the Tyrrhenian coast and the baked earth of the central plains.

Huge tracts of ancient forest predominate, especially at Malabotta, Mangalaviti and Tassito. The most interesting trees are the yew, confined to higher mountains in the Mediterranean region, and the huge centuries-old beech trees of the Monte Soro and Pumeri forests.

Indiscriminate hunting has destroyed much of the larger fauna, although the thick forests still find favour with foxes which stalk through the thick undergrowth in search of mice and other small mammals, which they catch by rising on their hind legs and dropping, forepaws first, on their victims. These dog-like predators are

BEFORE YOU GO
Park headquarters in the Municipio, Piazza V. Emanuele, Nicolosi, T: (095) 914 588.

GETTING THERE
By car: The SS120 and SS284 encircle the massif, whilst 2 minor "sea to snow" roads run up to its lower slopes: one to the Rif. Sapienza in the south, another to the Rif. Citelli and Linguaglossa woods in the north-east. Both are starting points for climbs to the summit.

By rail: a 114-km (71-mile) private line, the Circumetnea, one of Sicily's most scenic, runs round the base of Etna. It starts from Catania, with many stations *en route*, and a connection from the state line from Messina at Randazzo.
By bus: a single AST-run bus leaves Piazza Giovanni XXIII in Catania first thing in the morning for the Sapienza refuge; it returns in the late afternoon. From here you can walk or take one of the SITAS

minibuses to the crater.

WHERE TO STAY
The closest shelter to the summit is the Sapienza refuge, T: (095) 911 062. Also hotels in Randazzo, Catania, Zafferana, Linguaglossa and Taormina.
Outdoor living: is possible (a fine way to see Etna's stupendous dawns, and her frequent firework displays). Sites open all year at Milo, Linguaglossa and Nicolosi.

ACTIVITIES
Walking: the most popular ascent is from the Rif. Sapienza, using the rough track taken by jeeps and minibuses. To avoid crowds start the ascent 1km E of the refuge, following the Schiena d'Asino to La Montagnola (2,644m/ 8,674ft), with breathtaking views of the Valle del Bove. You can also climb from the Rif. Citelli on a rough track via Serra delle Concazze. A difficult path takes in the Valle del Bove via Monte Zoccolaro

generally unfussy eaters and will consume snails, beetles, frogs, small birds, blackberries and carrion. There is little competition, therefore, for the Nebrodi's other main carnivore, the wildcat which, although about half the size of the fox, is a much more aggressive predator, taking mammals up to the size of a roe deer fawn.

Nebrodi is justifiably proud of its breeding birds of prey, which include a few pairs of golden eagles and Egyptian vultures, both of which are extremely rare birds in Sicily today; their nests are guarded round the clock by LIPU volunteers. The area is also thought to support a few individual griffon vultures, birds which have not bred in Sicily since 1965.

The proposed park will be enormous, covering even more ground than the Stelvio National Park in the Alps. Forest walks here seem infinite. You can wander for days without seeing a soul, enjoying unexpected views, as the tree cover breaks, across to Mount Etna and the Aeolian islands. Summits here are a little lower than those of the Madonie to the west, averaging about 1,500m (5,000ft) and culminating in Monte Soro and the Serra del Re.

Lakes are dotted among the woods, notably at Biviere di Cesarò (near Monte Soro) and L'Urio Quattrocchi (near Mistretta). South of the massif sprawls the huge new reservoir at Ancipa. All three provide resting and refuelling stops for birds on migration.

Before you go *Maps:* IGM 1:25,000 *Colle del Contrasto, Monte Soro, Serra del Re, Capizzi, S. Teodoro, Cesarò* and *Pizzo Luminaria.*
Getting there *By car:* A20 from Messina and the NE; A19 and SS117/575 from Etna, Catania

Rugged limestone uplands such as these near Mezzojuso dominate the Nebrodi and Madonie mountains on Sicily's northern seaboard.

and Palermo. The SS120 takes in much of the Nebrodi.
By rail: public transport reaches local villages but not the mountainous interior. Stations on the north coast, with bus services to Nicosia from Mistretta, Palermo and Leonforte.
Where to stay: at Nicosia, Mistretta, Randazzo, Troina and Portella di Femmina Morta. Numerous forest refuges; apply to the rangers' office at Randazzo, T: (095) 921 124; or to CAI in Palermo, T: (091) 581 323. Good opportunities for free camping.
Activities *Walking:* an adventurous 4-day trek across the massif from Mistretta to Maniace, plus routes from Passo Femmina Morta to the summit ridges, and through the Foresta Vecchia from Trearie or Randazzo.

Madonie

Nature park containing westernmost massif of Sicily's northern coastal mountains (35,000ha/ 87,000 acres)

Second in height only to Mount Etna, the Madonie mountains soar above the northern coast, commanding views eastwards across the Sicilian interior to Etna, and over the Tyrrhenian Sea to the Aeolian islands.

Stepping out on the *Alta Via dei Monti di Sicilia*, the long-distance path that runs from here to Etna, you can experience dramatic scenery that in places resembles the Apennines on mainland Italy, including deep canyons such as the Gonato near Geraci, towering crags at Quacella and Piano Zucchi, and huge *quarare*, or sink holes, on high plateaux.

Although these mountains are still swathed in woods of pine, beech and chestnut, they were once more densely forested and graced with an endemic fir, *Abies nebrodensis*, more akin to African firs than to its Apennine counterparts. Today a mere 25 examples survive, concentrated near Polizzi Generosa and the Madonna degli Angeli valley. Other woods cluster around Castelbuono, Monte Quacella and the Piano Battaglia. Characteristic of these high limestone enclaves is the violet *Viola nebrodensis*, its dark violet flowers oustanding against the pale rock in high summer.

The lofty peaks of Madonie, of which the highest is Pizzo Carbonara, at nearly 2,000m (6,500ft), are undeniably wild. Birds of prey, such as Egyptian vultures, golden and Bonelli's eagles and peregrines, may be spotted. However, the area is not free of tourism; proximity to Palermo and lingering summit snows have been its downfall.

Sadly, any efforts to enforce conservation in the park seem to be confined to the special reserves: Monte Quacella (1,900ha/4,700 acres) and Faggeta Madonie (3,000ha/7,400 acres).

Maps: IGM 1:25,000 *Pizzo Carbonara, S. Mauro Castelverde* and *Polizzi Generosa*.

Getting there *By car:* A19 from Palermo or Messina; exits at Cefalù or Buonfornello (for Campofelice) provide 2 good access roads to the nature park. Minor roads from Collesano lead to Piano Zucchi (15km/9 miles) and Piano

The cliffs and coastal margins of the Zingaro reserve, Sicily's first protected area, provide a foothold for dwarf palms and eyries for raptors, such as Bonelli's eagles, lesser kestrels and griffon vultures.

Battaglia (25km/16 miles). *By rail:* station at Cefalù on Palermo main line, with buses on to Castelbuono; direct services from Palermo and Termini Imerse to Collesano. **Where to stay:** at Cefalù, Petralia Sottana, Polizzi Generosa and Piano Zucchi. Solitary refuge in Milocca forest, Crispi, T: (0921) 72279; other huts: Marini (Piano Battaglia), T: (0921) 49994; and Orestano (Piano Zucchi), T: (0921) 62159. Many opportunities for free camping (take ample water).

Activities *Walking:* best from Piano Battaglia and surroundings; ascent of Pizzo Carbonara (1,979m/6,493ft, 2hr), with optional circuit to Antenna Grande; climb to Monte dei Cervi (3hr). Marked trail from Piano Battiglia to Rif. Marini and the Piano Zucchi.

Further information *Tourist offices:* Via Amendola 2, Cefalù, T: (0921) 21050; Via Carapezza 10, Petralia Sottana, T: (0921) 41680; Via Carlo V, Polizzi Generosa, T: (0921) 49932; CAI, Via Garibaldi 252e, Petralia Sottana; LIPU, Via P. Paternostro 43, Palermo, T: (091) 581 323 (organized trips).

Zingaro and Monte Cofano

Nature reserve of cliffs on the north coast of Sicily with rugged mountainous hinterland (1,600ha/4,000 acres)

As oases of solitude and silence, and some of Sicily's most beautiful coast, the neighbouring headlands of Cofano and Zingaro, located between Trapani and Castellammare, owe their survival to perhaps the bravest battle against developers in Italy's history.

A mass demonstration in May 1980 halted a road-building scheme and led to the foundation of Sicily's first ever reserve a year later. It also prompted the creation of a further three parks and 19 reserves, giving protection to 100,000ha (250,000 acres) across the whole island.

The zone covers just 7km (4 miles) of coast. Vertiginous limestone cliffs rise from a rugged, if flat, shoreline fringed with bays and shingle beaches. Behind are mountains culminating in Monte Cofano, which is a miniature Dolomite, and the more inhospitable Passo del Lupo.

The rocks, caves and thick vegetation of the landscape are well-suited to birds, present in ever greater numbers since the creation of the reserve. Especially notable are peregrines, Egyptian vultures and a pair of golden eagles, which are now largely safe from being traded to Arab markets as hunting birds. Some rare birds have been sighted by local shepherds, including griffon

vultures, lesser kestrels and Bonelli's eagles. The best spot for a sighting is on Monte Monaco. Seabirds include Cory's and Manx shearwaters, and Europe's smallest seabird, the storm petrel.

Tracts of dwarf fan palm take pride of place amid the Zingaro's 670 plant species. This is the one area in Italy where Europe's only indigenous palm can be said to form woods. The trees reach heights of about 2m (7ft), and together with a wealth of maquis, bay laurel, wild fennel and caper, the reserve displays distinct characteristics of northern Africa.

Among the immense diversity of lesser plants which thrive here are bladder vetch, *Anthyllis tetraphylla*; friar's cowl, *Arisarum vulgare*; sea squill, *Urginea maritime*; sowbread; tree germander; hare's tail, *Lagurus oratus*; and blue-hound's tongue, *Cynoglossum creticum*.

Strict conservation measures are in force: boating, building and camping are banned, and there is a 300-m (1,000-ft) exclusion zone for boats around the shoreline.

Before you go *Maps:* IGM 1:25,000 *Castelluzzo* and *Monte Cofano*.

Getting there *By car:* A19 from Palermo to Castellammare del Golfo and SS187 to Scopello, which is the most convenient base for the reserve. Minor roads from Trapani to Custonaci (via Bonagia) for access from the W.
By rail: station at Castellammare, with buses from Trapani and Palermo to local centres.

Where to stay: handful of hotels and *pensioni* at Scopello, San Vito lo Capo, Castelluzzo, Castellammare and Custonaci.
Outdoor living: Free camping prohibited; sites at the Baia di Giudaloca, T: (0924) 596 022

(3km/2 miles from Scopello); and the Nausica (4km/3 miles from Castellammare), T: (0924) 31518 (both Apr–Sept).

Activities *Walking:* the coastal walk is relatively easy (2½hr); try also the hike from Scurati to Tonnara di Cofano; and the rewarding ascent of Monte Cofano (659m/ 2,162ft) from Baglio Cofano (2hr).
Birdwatching: excursions to the reserve are organized by the local branch of LIPU, Via Ugo Manno 71, Alcamo, T: (0924) 20542.

Further information *Tourist office:* Trapani, Piazzetta Saturno, T: (0923) 29000.

Isola Marettimo

Island of the Egadi archipelago off western Sicily, regional reserve (12,000ha/29,700 acres)

Marettimo, rugged and sacred to the ancient Greeks, is by far the most spectacular island off Sicily and, some say, the wildest island in the Mediterranean. Much of it is inaccessible, even by boat. The white shimmering cliffs and wave-beaten headlands are entrancing, especially the rocky cape at Punta Troia. On the western coast you can explore numerous tiny bays, the most secret being those at Cala Bianca, Cala Nera and Cala Spalmatore.

Caves are scoured into the steep hills of limestone which cover most of the island; the most famous are Tuono, Presepe and Passo Marino. Many can be visited on the demanding 3-day trail round the island. Outcrops of marble and crystalline layers intrude, mostly as a crown to the hogsback central ridge. Paths are hard to follow into the hinterland, but a couple ascend to the rocky heights of Monte Falcone (686m/2,251ft), a lovely vantage point, especially on clear winter days.

By Sicilian standards, there is abundant water, with the result that local vegetation is immensely luxuriant despite the fact that only one patch of woodland has survived: a stand of aleppo pines at Fonte Pegna. All told, however, there are 515 lesser plant species.

Garrigue dominated by rosemary and stunted maquis is widespread, especially on the high rock ledges, known locally as *orru*, out of reach of the nibbling of goats. Here too flourish species which are found nowhere else in the world, including the thorow-wax *Bupleurum dianthifolium*, a member of the carrot family which has found its niche on

the calcareous rock ledges on the northern face of Marettimo, as well as the white-flowered scabious *Scabiosa limonifolia*, endemic to Sicily.

An attractive stopping place for many thousands of migrating birds, the island is also a nesting ground for birds such as storm petrels, an extremely rare bird in Sicily, but here forming a colony of up to 400 pairs, as well as Cory's and Manx shearwaters. Cliff-nesting raptors include peregrine falcons, while a single pair of Bonelli's eagles, otherwise known as the partridge eagle on account of its preferred prey, breeds regularly inland.

Before you go: the Azienda delle Foreste at Trapani has responsibility for the reserve; T: (0923) 807 111.
Map: IGM 1:25,000 *Isola di Marettimo*.
Getting there: A29 or rail from Palermo to Trapani (or by air to Birgi airport, 15km/9 miles S of Trapani). Then ferries (3hr) and hydrofoils (1hr) run daily from Trapani (more frequent in summer), also calling at Favignana and Levanzo.

Where to stay: no hotels on the island, though rooms and houses can be rented in the port; ask at the café in the main square. Camping is possible, but water and suitable pitches are in short supply.
Activities *Walking:* is the only way to see much of the island. Walks are not demanding, but can require some scrambling. There are 2 main paths: to Punta Troia on a track that runs the island's length close to the sea; and to the lighthouse (Italian, *il faro*) on a stony track S from the port, passing Cala Sarde and Cala Nera. A diversion from the track climbs to the main ridge via Punta Ansini.
Climbing: many limestone routes, particularly up walls on the island's west side.
Fishing: for sea fishing enquire at the port, or contact FIPS branch in Trapani: Via Martogna 45.
Snorkelling: boats for hire, or crewed 3hr trip round the coast.
Further information *Tourist offices:* at the station, harbour and Piazzetta Saturno in Trapani for room and ferry information, T: (0923) 29000.

Bonelli's eagle, with its long-tailed silhouette and dashing flight, is also known as the partridge eagle on account of its favoured prey.

Isola di Pantelleria

Fourth largest of the Italian islands and an unspoiled Mediterranean enclave

Early Phoenician settlers on Pantelleria called it Hiranini, the "island of birds", after the migrating flocks that still cross from Tunisia just 70km (45 miles) to the south. The present name derives from the Arabic for "daughter of the winds", after a constant maddening breeze that relents only in high summer. One of the wildest of Sicily's islands, Pantelleria, is a refuge of solitude. Indeed, in Roman times it was a place of banishment, though it is less of a natural wonderland than, say, Isola Marettimo to the north.

The island is volcanic and still a hotbed of activity. Although the last eruption was in 1835 and the original crater at Montagna Grande is now extinct, the island hisses and steams from 24 minor craters, known as *cuddie* in the local dialect, and from blow holes called *favare* or *mofete*.

You pass the best of these, the Stufe (ovens) de Khazeri, on the climb to the old crater from Siba. They form a famous natural sauna where you can sit and sweat in a dark cave; take a towel and expect to last about ten minutes.

Elsewhere you might explore the hot springs that boil into the sea at Sataria, or the thermal pools at Gadir. Lovely, too, is the Specchio di Venere (Venus's mirror), a murky volcanic lake that lies in an old crater, constantly warmed from below.

Walks are lonely, through sparse and darkened landscapes that are scorched by the sun and whipped by the incessant salty wind. The tang of mint, sage and oregano fills the misty air. It is an eerie place, especially the Dietro Isola in the south-east.

Occasionally you come across white cuboid houses, Arabian in appearance, or the traditional *dammuso*, dwellings that date back to Neolithic times. More mysterious are the *sesi*, 57 giant funeral mounds made from rough-hewn volcanic blocks. These again are Neolithic, probably built by early settlers from Tunisia.

Some of the island, however, is fertile and supports oases of orange groves known as the "Arab gardens", surrounded by high walls to keep out the wind; or the special *zibbibo* vines, planted for centuries on small ridges to catch what little rain falls on the parched island. **Getting there** *By sea:* daily sailings (5hr) from Trapani (not Sun off-season); 3 daily hydrofoils (2hr) summer only. Weekly sailings from Marsala. *By air:* daily flights from Palermo, twice daily from Trapani, to Pantelleria airport, T: (0923) 911 172. For Alitalia on the island, T: (0923) 911 078. **Where to stay:** ample accommodation, but hotels can be expensive, and many close during winter. Contact the port tourist office (see below). You can also rent a *dammuso* house: dome-roofed and thick-walled for coolness; contact Dammuso, Contrada San Vito, T: (0923) 911 827. **Further information** *Tourist information:* Via San Nicola, T: (0923) 911 838.

Isole Pelagie

Islands of Lampedusa, Linosa and Lampione; proposed marine park

The three islands of the Pelagie archipelago (Greek, *paligia*, "sea island") are among the most primitive and isolated in Europe. The most southerly part of Italy, they are closer to Africa in distance and appearance than to the Italian mainland.

Lampedusa and Linosa are geologically linked to Tunisia

by a limestone platform which is never deeper than 100m (350ft) below the sea. Linosa is the last link in a volcanic chain that extends to Vesuvius and the Pontine islands away to the north.

All three islands were deforested long ago, and little more than a dust-bowl and scrub remain today. On Lampedusa there is a joke about the contents of the island's "national park": two trees withered by the lack of water and incessant wind. Utter solitude, however, and some of the cleanest water in the Mediterranean make up for any scenic shortcomings.

White limestone hills and rugged cliff faces form the typical scenery of Lampedusa. High precipices fall sheer to clear cool grottos filled with fish. Gentler inlets on the south coast have sardines, sponge and coral, the island's economic mainstays.

Linosa has four craters to explore, a few lavic beaches, and is as remote from civilization as you will find in western Europe. The ashy soil, strewn with coke-like boulders, is dry and black, adding to the cauldron effect which, in summer, makes the island one of the hottest places in Italy. Paths thread the interior, leading to caves which provide nesting sites for hundreds of Cory's shearwaters.

Lampione is the smallest island and barren. Like the others it is populated by itinerant sub-aqua fishermen and numerous reptiles, including the western whip snake, geckoes, even marine turtles. Sub-aqua opportunities are particularly good off Lampione where the sea-bed slopes gently and the fish grow to huge proportions.

The whole archipelago presents fascinating birdwatching. The wailing cries of Cory's and Manx shearwaters haunt the night in early summer, bringing to mind the legendary shrieks of the death-heralding banshee. A small colony of shags is the pride of Lampedusa; and phalanxes of Eleanora's falcons form offshore in early autumn in some of nature's most organized hunting expeditions, designed to trap young migratory birds as they cross the Mediterranean to Africa. **Getting there** *By sea:* daily ferries (9hr) from Porto Empedocle on the Sicilian mainland (hourly connecting buses to the port from Agrigento railway station).

Tickets from Siremar on the harbour, or agents in Agrigento. Daily connections between Lampedusa and Linosa. *By air:* flights (1hr) from Palermo to Lampedusa's airport. Details from ATI, T: (0922) 970 299. **Where to stay:** single hotel on Linosa, The Algusa, T: (0922) 972 052 (book in advance), and an unofficial campsite. Many rooms in Lampedusa; call the tourist office, Agenzie le Pelagie, Via Roma 155, T: (0922) 970 170. Campsite at Cala Greca, La Roccia, T: (0922) 970 055 (open all year).

The carob, or locust tree, has thick leathery pods which contain 55 per cent sugar and may be used as animal fodder and a chocolate substitute.

MAQUIS

Maquis, a Corsican word, refers to a type of dense vegetation found frequently in the Mediterranean. Its composition varies considerably, but is usually considered to consist of a low shrub and tree community that reaches heights of anything between one and three metres. Normally it is found on more moist, thus western, slopes on coasts and low-lying hills.

In its pristine form it is now comparatively rare. Burning, grazing and land clearance over the centuries have either removed or reduced its cover. At a more degraded stage, where cover consists of vegetation up to 50cm (20in) high, maquis is more properly known as *garrigue*.

This boasts aromatic and shrub evergreens such as thyme, rosemary, savory (satweja), lavender, wild garlics and sage, though there is an immense degree of variety, much bare and rocky ground, and considerable debate between naturalists over the precise definitions which separate dwarf shrub or *garrigue* from maquis and secondary maquis.

Maquis itself is not too contentious. There are three basic types, each typical of different climatic zones. The most common in Italy is the evergreen oak maquis, descended from ancient holm oak woodlands. The tree layer, low as it is, might typically consist of holm, kermes, and cork oaks, sometimes laurel, manna ash and Montpellier maple, plus a scrub community of myrtle, mastic tree, sage, and narrow-leaved cistus, ivy, blackthorn, strawberry tree, laurustinus, tree heath, prickly juniper, tunic, broom and, especially on coasts, Christ's thorn and chaste tree. In the field or plant layer you might find spurges, wild madder, butcher's broom, cyclamen, bee orchids, comfrey, violet limodore, yellow centaury and quaking grass.

The second type of maquis is the higher-occurring montane maquis. This occurs where the climax vegetation would otherwise be deciduous oak woodland. Confusingly — and maquis and *garrigue* are nothing if not confusing for the naturalist — evergreen species like kermes oak, box and prickly juniper also occur. Here you might expect to come across hornbeam, hawthorns, Turkey oak, wild cherry, wall germander, holly, jasmine, cyclamens, asphodels, irises, arum lilies, black bryony, orchids, bracken and many more.

In the driest areas of Sicily there occurs olive-carob maquis. This derives from olive and carob woods cleared in the very distant past. Man's long settlement, soil erosion and summer heat in such areas means that this is a rare and often a very degraded form of maquis. Its chief components are holm oak, clematis, mastic tree, myrtle, dwarf palm, buckthorn, tree spurge, spiny broom, wild madder and Juniper's beard.

Monti del Gennargentu

Sardinia's wildest mountain scenery; proposed national park (100,000ha/ 247,000 acres)

N o invader, not even the Romans, has ever succeeded in penetrating the remote heights of the Gennargentu. No Christian voice was heard in its pagan wilderness for seven centuries. Today it is crossed by just two roads and is still virtually uninhabited. Such shepherds as dwell on its lonely slopes are people of fierce dignity, sustained by ancient traditions. This is the true Sardinia, say the Sards, its customs, dialects and superstitions intact, its people the pure-bred stocky islanders of old.

The Gennargentu massif itself forms only the central core of the whole region, a granite dome that rises to Sardinia's highest point, the Punta la Marmora (1,834 metres/ 6,017 feet). The massif is surrounded by the Barbagia mountains which divide into four separate bastions: the Ollolai, Seulo, Mandrolisai and Belvi. To the north lies the most primordial area of all, the famous limestone mountains of the Sopramonte. Where these fall to the sea in the Golfo di Orosei they create a coastline considered by many to be without equal in Europe.

In many ways the coast has determined the fate of this area. The sea was always the way of the invader, and centuries of islanders retreated from it simply to be free of danger. Moving inland from the east, however, they found only poor winter grazing, and so they continued with their flocks to the richer pastures of the west. The Gennargentu, uneconomic and inhospitable, was left as they had found it — solemn and deserted.

The area's most distinctive scenery lies in the encircling Barbagia mountains, particularly in the Barbagia di Belvi in the south and west. Among steep valleys and sweeping forests of oak, rise the so-called *tacchi* or *torroni*, high limestone tors, isolated and splintered, which rise from the schists and granites of the surrounding hills. The most impressive tors are Sadali, Si and Ricci, which appear on Monte Arcueri and Monte Tonneri, near Seui. Other interesting examples are found near Aritzo, Irgini and Tonara. The most famous is the mighty obelisk of Piana Liana at an altitude of 1,293 metres (4,242 feet). Visible from a great distance, its name is linked to the Oliesi, an ancient tribe of which traces have been found (at Oliena) dating back 14,000 years.

The sturdy rustic villages of shepherds in the Barbagia are a joy after the monotony of the urban eyesores on the Sardinian plains. These communities, however, are no ordinary mix of families. Each village, or hamlet originally, was founded as the clan

The world population of the Mediterranean monk seal has fallen to less than a thousand. The seals used to breed in Sardinian waters, but are thought to have stopped since tourism encroached on their birthing beaches.

headquarters of a different clan. The village of Desulo, for example, in the Mandrolisai region, consists of three cantons: Asuai, Issiria and Orolaccio, each founded by a separate family. One bred cattle, another pigs and the third, sheep. Many families are replacing their picturesque houses with functional concrete boxes. Others, though, still lead the traditional way of life, with the menfolk disappearing into the hills for six months of the year to tend their sheep.

The Sopramonte, by contrast, has had no communal settlement since prehistoric times. Its dry empty scenery is considered the most spectacular of its kind in Italy. Silent and sun-beaten, with griffon vultures circling on high, this is a vast and featureless desert of dazzling limestone. Sparsely inhabited by taciturn shepherds, it is still the haunt of bandits whose sense of honour — luckily for the tourist — usually forbids the seizing of foreigners.

At the heart of this wilderness lie unforgettable trips for the determined walker. The remote prehistoric rock village under Monte Tiscali is one example of many: the Gorroppu canyons are the grandest in Italy, 500 metres (1,600 feet) wide and 200 metres (650 feet) deep, with relict woods containing yews many hundreds of years old; the so-called *codule* of Luna and Sisine are only slightly smaller gorges, filled with oleanders and surrounded by some of the Mediterranean's largest oak forests. Elsewhere there are caves such as the Su Sterru, the Donanigoro's karstic plateaux and the sink hole at Su Sercone.

Spring rains nurture foxgloves and red peonies, as well as more precious endemics such as the redcurrant, *Ribes sardoum*, and a sea-thrift, *Armeria sardoa*. Spring flowers, indeed, are outstanding everywhere, each of the regions yielding its own indigenous varieties. The Gennargentu boasts a crucifer, *Iberis pruitii*, and white- or lilac-flowered thyme, *Thymus herbabaroa*, which gives its scent to scrubby summer pastures. Walkers everywhere will learn to rue the thickets of spurge and the dense tangle of maquis that impedes progress at every turn.

In many cases, animals and birds in this wilderness include some of the last Italian survivors of particular species. Between 100 and 200 mouflon shelter in forest areas such as the Montarbu di Seui. This lovely animal, distinguished in the male by scimitar-curved horns, is related to the Asiatic wild sheep and has been present on the island since classical times. Although colonies exist in Corsica and Cyprus, zoologists believe them to be of different provenance to the Sardinian variety. Far more rare — perhaps just two or three birds — are the bearded vultures, almost certainly extinct in Sicily and on the mainland.

Of similar scarcity are the monk seals, *Monachus monachus* (Italian, *bue marino*, "sea elephant"). Only ten to fifteen, at most, survive in Sardinian waters today. The most likely places for a sighting are the coves sheltered by cliffs that plunge to the sea around Capo di Monte Santu.

Similarly rare is the huge black vulture, the largest of all Old World vultures, with a wingspan close on three metres (ten feet); only a handful of individuals survive in Sardinia today. More abundant are golden eagles. The Gennargentu harbours ten or twelve pairs of these magnificent birds, as well as Bonelli's eagles, red kites, peregrines and goshawks. The cliffs bordering the Golfo di Orosei are renowned for their breeding colonies of Audouin's gulls and Eleanora's falcons which choose to rear their young on these lonely precipices.

CHAPTER 9: SICILY AND SARDINIA

BEFORE YOU GO

Maps: IGM 1:25,000 208 IV SE *Grotta del Bue Marino* and 208 IV NE *Dorgali* (for the coastal walks); 208 IV NO *Cantoniera Manasuddas* and 208 IV SO *Monte Oddeu* (for the Sopramonte).

Guidebooks: A. Gogna, *Mezzogiorno di Pietra* (Zanichelli) and F. Tassi, *La Natura della Sardegna* (Mondadori).

GETTING THERE

By car: this is a large area with few roads; best approaches are the SS125/131 from Olbia (airport) and the N; SS128 via Mandas from Cagliari and the S. Especially lovely stretches of road are Dorgali–Baunei (SS125) and Desulo–Fonni (highest village in Sardinia) in the Gennargentu; Oliena–Baunei in the Sopramonte.

By sea: Arbatax is the nearest ferry port.

By rail: the spectacular Arbatax–Cagliari line bisects the S of the region, with halts at Seiu and Villagrande (1 train daily); the Cagliari–Sorgano branch is useful for the W, with stations at Aritzo and Desulo (2 daily); for the Sopramonte the nearest station is Nuoro (6 daily).

By bus: buses run to the bigger villages from Nuoro and Olbia; timetable information, T: (0784) 30155 (Nuoro) and T: (0789) 21453 (Olbia).

WHERE TO STAY

Hotels and rooms (many closed Oct–Mar) in Nuoro, Dorgali, Cala Gonone, Su Cologne, Fonni,.Tonara, Arbatax, Sorgono and S. Maria Navarrese.

Outdoor living: feasible everywhere, but take plenty of water; organized camping sites at Lotzorai, Cala Gonone, T: (0784) 93165 (Apr–Oct) and Tortoli (near Arbatax), T: (0782) 622 774 (June–Sept).

ACTIVITIES

Walking: enormous scope, though most walks are not for the faint-hearted. Paths are few, navigation difficult and water scarce; but the rewards are huge. Roads take car drivers to remote spots, ideal for short hikes; for example above Oliena in the Sopramonte and from Fonni to Bruncu Spina (1,829m/6,000ft) in the Gennargentu.

A fine walk in the Sopramonte runs S from the Su Cologne spring (signposted from the Oliena–Dorgali road) along the Corrojos valley to Tiscal (518m/1,699ft), returning via the parallel valley, the Dolovere di Surtana, some blue markings

(4hr). Other routes possible from Oliena (some marked) and Su Cologne.

Most popular hike is the coastal traverse from Cala Gonone to Cala di Luna, with the possibility of taking a boat back to Cala Gonone (summer only, check times, 8hr walk, 3hr with boat). One of Italy's finest treks takes in this stretch and the rest of the coast, from Cala Gonone to Baunei (4 days).

Climbing: dozens of superlative climbs on coastal cliffs and Sopramonte limestone, including: Vie della Poltrona (Cala Gonone), Gorruppu and Surtana canyons (Dorgali) and the Punta Cusidore (Oliena).

Ponytrekking: ideal country,

The Giara di Gesturi's basalt plateau provides a belvedere for views across Sardinia's harsh interior.

but facilities are limited; contact the small tourist office at Sadali (on the SS128 from Arbatax): Piazza Chiesa, T: (0782) 59094. Also call CAI at Cagliari for organized treks from Oliena to Orosei (4 days) and from Cala Gonone across the island to Capo Mannu (12 days).

FURTHER INFORMATION
Tourist offices: Via Lamarmora 181, Dorgali, T: (0784) 96243; Piazza d'Italia 19, Nuoro, T: (0784) 30083.
Ecology: in the absence of a park office, the WWF is especially useful: c/o A. Congiu, Via Potenza 10, Oliena; Via Gramsci 6, Nuoro, T: (0784) 30206.

Giara di Gesturi

Isolated plateau of meadows and cork woods

Gesturi is a singular basalt plateau (known as *giure* in Sardinia) that rears up 600m (2,000ft) above the plains and pastoral hill country in the island's central-southern heartland.

From afar the 12-km

(7-mile), flat-topped plateau appears unexceptional. On its top, however, spreads one of Sardinia's oddest landscapes, as eerie and mysterious as that of Conan Doyle's *The Lost World.* Plains of herbs and maquis are interspersed with outcrops of pinky-black basalt and vast woods of cork oak (an estimated quarter of a million trees). Prehistoric settlements — the *nuraghi* — add to a feeling of otherworldliness. So, too, do the wild horses that roam the heathland, shy and tiny creatures resembling Shetland ponies.

Trickling streams and areas of marsh form on the plateau after rain, rich in spring flowers and host to occasional migrating birds. The largest areas of marsh are Pauli Maiori and Pauli Minori.

The little bustard is present in some numbers, along with other birds such as buzzard and rock partridge. Animals that you may see, especially close to Gesturi's wooded springs or *mitzas,* include the fox and wildcat, here a distinct Sardinian race (*Felis silvestris sarda*).

Before you go *Maps:* IGM 1:25,000 *Genoni* and *Barumini.*
Getting there *By car:* take SS131 N from Cagliari (40km/ 25 miles), and branch on to SS197 following signs for Barumini; Gesturi village is 5km (3 miles) beyond, with a rough road on to the plateau.
By rail: station at Nurallao (10km/6 miles) on the Cagliari–Sorgono line (2 trains daily). Bus service from Cagliari to Gesturi.
Where to stay: 1 hotel at Barumini, with the possibility of free camping on the plateau.

Molentargius

Wetland nature reserve of international importance on the outskirts of Cagliari

The 500-ha (1,200-acre) salt marshes just 1km east of Cagliari are among the largest in Europe, and one of the continent's finest birdwatching areas. One third (170) of all European species are recorded

here, with many thousands of birds present in the winter, among them the huge flocks of flamingos that bring the reserve its fame.

These birds have visited the marshes for centuries, and were noted in medieval records. They congregate in groups of hundreds and sometimes thousands. Day and night, flamingos can be seen with their heads submerged trawling the marshes for small aquatic invertebrates whose high level of carotinoids give the flamingo its distinctive colour. They are an unforgettable sight, whether flying or simply feeding in shallow water, heads dipping, necks gracefully curved, the ordered pink ranks living up to the local name for the bird — the *esercito inglese*, the "English army".

Other birdlife is also exceptional. Over and above thousands of ducks, coots, terns and gulls, the brackish marshlands support numerous warblers, avocets, purple gallinule, black-winged stilts, marsh harriers, collared pratincoles and slender-billed gulls; and even ospreys and Bonelli's eagles have been sighted. In 1986 the cattle egret and glossy ibis bred here for the first time.

These birds are locked on to one of the Mediterranean's key migration routes, passing over the Cape Bon promontory in Tunisia and dividing into two on its way north over Sicily and Sardinia.
Before you go: contact Cagliari's tourist office and the local LIPU branch (which provides guided tours of the lagoons); LIPU, Via L. Alagon 21, T: (070) 494 971.
Getting there *By car:* from the city centre take roads for either Quartu Elena or the lane parallel to the Spiagga di Quartu.
Access: free at all times.

Monte Arcosu

WWF oasis and State reserve in the Sulcis mountains (3,000ha/ 7,500 acres)

Arcosu occupies a place in conservation folklore, having been bought with a quarter of a million pounds raised wholly by public subscription.

One of the largest and most splendid WWF reserves in Italy, its chief purpose has been to ensure the survival of the extremely rare Sardinian red deer. This dark and petite creature — little more than 90cm (3ft) tall — was once common all over Corsica and Sardinia. Adapted to the vagaries of life in harsh Mediterranean climes, it forms a distinct sub-species of the European red deer (*Cervus elaphus corsicanus*).

Today it is listed as an endangered species, one of 12 distinct races (or subspecies) of red deer in the world. It is now extinct in Corsica, and in Sardinia some 200 to 300 survive, either in Arcosu or as part of two herds kept in semi-captivity by the WWF and the Sardinian Forest Guard.

The reserve is in a mountain environment of exquisite beauty, tucked into a corner of the Sulcis massif. The centre is the Guttereddu valley, whose crystal-clear river sparkles over polished granite pebbles and through shadowy, tree-lined pools. At dawn and dusk, the deer come down to drink, edging around tiny beaches of brilliant white sand.

Above rises a tangle of maquis and forest — 50,000ha (124,000 acres) devoid of human habitation — without parallel

Although the Corsican red deer has almost disappeared from Corsica, about 300 still roam the maquis of Sardinia.

in Sardinia. At the valley head rises a spectacular ring of pink granite mountains. Splintered tors and crags are the homes of peregrines, goshawks and the majestic Bonelli's eagle (two breeding pairs).

Before you go: get permission, and confirmation of opening times, from the WWF at Cagliari: Via del Mercato Vecchio 15, T: (070) 662 510. There is a warden's office in the Guttereddu valley, with

information on nature trails, forest hides and ponytrekking, T: (070) 493 778.
Map: IGM 1:25,000 *Monte Arcosu.*
Getting there *By car:* the massif is on Cagliari's doorstep, due W of the Stagno di Cagliari; access is by minor roads, a total of 25km (16 miles) from the city.
When to go: autumn for mushrooms, the mating of deer and a vegetation refreshed by

October rains; spring for the wild flowers and breeding of birds.
Where to stay: Cagliari, with free camping near the massif itself; contact the tourist office, Piazza Deffenu 9, Cagliari, T: (070) 663 207.

Sinis

Nature park in coastal region of vast dunes, lagoons and spectacular cliff scenery, known for its raptors and flamingos

Sinis is at the heart of Sardinia's wildest coastline. To the south lie the Arburese mountains and the "Costa Verde", towering cliffs and inlets unspoiled by roads or villages. To the north around Bosa — part of a proposed natural park — stretches one of the ultimate redoubts for some of Italy's rarest raptors, including griffon vultures, Bonelli's eagles, golden eagles, red kites, peregrine falcons and sparrowhawks.

Sinis itself, which has been called Sardinia's only desert, contains 2,000ha (5,000 acres) of dunes and lagoons, the largest flat surface on the island. With the Oristano gulf to the south, this Caribbean wilderness of white sand and turquoise water is also one of the country's chief birdwatching areas, its lagoons,.

(Overleaf) The shore of the Sinis peninsula is strewn with a curious shingle made from seaweed. Strands of this alga, *Posidonia oceanica,* are brought to land and formed into "pebbles" by the action of the waves.

marshes and estuary on a par with Orbetello and the Po Delta.

The area is best known for its flamingos, which have recently colonized Sardinia. The most important breeding areas are the five lagoons: Cabras, Mistras, Sale Porcus, Is Benas and Pauli Murtas. All are immensely rich in fish — eels, grey mullet, bass, giltheads — a total of 600kg (1,320lbs), it is estimated, for every hectare of water.

Here you will find four of Europe's 20 most threatened birds: the flamingo, Audouin's gull, peregrine falcon and white-headed duck. You should also see birds only a little less rare, like the garganey, red-crested pochard, purple gallinule, purple heron, bittern, white-tailed eagle and osprey (both now wintering birds only), little bustard and Eleanora's falcon. More common aquatic birds by the thousand also make this their breeding ground, including slender-billed gulls, marsh harriers, little bitterns, avocets and black-winged stilts.

Before the summer sun turns Sinis into a scorched and shimmering plain, the dunes are carpeted in a tapestry of scented maquis and flowers, including gorgeous violets, the endemic *Limonium lausianum*, rock-roses and the splendid barbary nut *Iris sisyrinchium*, whose blue flowers mirror the azure of sea and sky.

Before you go *Map:* IGM 1:25,000 *Capo Mannu, Capo S. Marco* and *S. Salvatore*.
Getting there *By car:* SS131 to Oristano, and then via a web of minor roads west of the town (10km/6 miles).
By rail: station at Oristano.
When to go: spring is best for the flowering of orchids and maquis, the breeding of birds, and large flocks flying off the sea.

Where to stay: wide range of hotels in Oristano, S. Giovanni di Sinis, Cabras and S. Caterina di Pittinuri. Ample scope for free camping, with many commercial sites, including the Is Arenas N of the promontory, T: (0783) 57584. Try also the youth hostel, Ostello Eleonora, Via dei Pescatori 31, Torre Grande, T: (0783) 418 066.
Access: free, except to the small WWF reserve. For visits here (accompanied, or in groups) contact Giancarlo Fantoni, Via Canalis 20, Oristano, T: (0783) 71447. For details of the LIPU reserve (and for guided tours) call LIPU, Via Deledda 2, Oristano, T: (0783) 73375.
Activities *Ponytrekking:* contact the tourist office at San Vero Milis (Via Eleamora 51), or Sanverese, Via S. Barbara 31, San Vero Milis.
Windsurfing: contact ARCI Vela, Via del Bianco, San Vero Milis.
Further information *Tourist office:* Via Cagliari 278, Oristano, T: (0783) 74191.

Monte Limbara

Highest mountains of northern Sardinia

Monte Limbara (1,359m/ 4,459ft) is a remote and forbidding massif in northern Sardinia, typical of much of the island's long, rugged ridges and broad, boulder-strewn valleys.

Throughout the region, but especially on the plateau above Aggius, there stand high granite tors, wind-sculpted into fantastic shapes. Many are covered in gorgeous golden lichens, dazzling against the red of the underlying granite.

This is the territory of hunting birds, peregrines in particular, on the lookout for prey such as the blue rock thrush (known in Italian as the "solitary sparrow").

Patches of pine and cork oak push through the scrubby

The night heron can be identified by its hunched silhouette when stalking fish and amphibians, and its erratic moth-like flight when disturbed.

wilderness, and in the south farmers scratch a living from odd patches of cultivated land. This follows the habit of isolated farms, or *stazzi*, adopted by Corsican settlers over the centuries.

Otherwise all is empty and silent. Tempio Pausania is the only town, a mountain resort where the air is crisp and where some of the Costa Smeralda's tourists are accommodated.
Getting there *By car:* SS127 from Olbia to Tempio Pausania, and then a choice of minor roads into the hills.
By rail: stations S of the massif on the Olbia–Cagliari line at Monti and Berchidda (8 trains daily).
By bus: buses from Olbia to local centres.
Where to stay: 3-star Petit Hotel, Piazza de Gasperi, Tempio Pausania, T: (079) 631 134. Rooms in Olbia and Oschiri.
Further information *Tourist office:* Piazza Gallura 2, Tempio Pausania, T: (079) 631 273.

The narrow rocky isthmus is covered in craggy hills which culminate in Punta di Scomunica (408m/1,339ft), and the coast is cut by bays and sandy creeks, with large surviving reefs of pink coral just offshore.

Little wildlife prospers among the tamarisk and close-cropped vegetation inland; the greatest oddity is an endemic white donkey.

The northernmost bays at Cala Arena and around the lighthouse at Punta Caprara are breeding grounds for thousands of screeching seabirds, especially Audouin's gulls, shags, common terns and possibly Cory's shearwaters and storm petrels.

The curving peninsula on mainland Sardinia which swings round to meet the island is irresistible, with sea views and sublime sunsets across dunes and salt-flats. The Li Puzzinusi marshes here are the domain of rails and night herons. The most famous sites are the Casaraccio and Pilo lagoons, haven for winter ducks and coots, and a breeding ground for the rare red-crested pochard. To my mind this is one of the loveliest of all ducks, the males unmistakable with their vermillion heads, black necks and scarlet eyes and bills.
Getting there: by boat, road or rail to Sassari or Porto Torres, SS131/291 W, and then minor roads to Capo del Falcone, crossing point for ferries. Access to lagoons from Stintino and local unclassified roads. Station at Porto Torres.
Where to stay: at Sassari, Porto Torres and Stintino on the mainland; a few rooms to rent at Fornelli and La Reale on the island. Free camping is a possibility. Youth hostel, the Ostello Balai, at Porto Torres: Via Lungomare 91, T: (079) 502 761.
Further information *Tourist office:* Piazza d'Italia 19, Sassari, T: (079) 233 751.

Isola di Asinara

Rugged island and curving peninsula at Sardinia's north-west cape

The second largest of Sardinia's offshore islands, Asinara preserves the wilderness sacrificed to tourism by the Maddelena archipelago to the east. For years it was a penal colony and, more ominous, a quarantine zone.

USEFUL ADDRESSES

World Wide Fund for Nature (WWF), Via Salaria 290a, 00199 Rome, T: (06) 852 492.

Lega Italiana per la Protezione degli Uccelli (LIPU), Vicolo San Tiburzio 5, 43100 Parma.

Lega per l'Ambiente, Via Francesco Carrara 24, Rome, T: (06) 35791.

Italia Nostra, Via Nicola Porpora 22, Rome, T: (06) 852 333.

Club Alpino Italiano (CAI), Via Ugo Foscolo 3, Milan, T: (02) 864 380.

Friends of the Earth (Italy), Amici della Terra, Via del Sudario 35, 00186 Rome, T: (06) 687 5308.

Greenpeace (Italy), Viale Manlio Gelsomini 28, 00153 Rome, T: (06) 578 1173.

FURTHER READING

Ardito, S: *Andar per Sentiero* (De Agostini)

Ardito, S: *A Piedi in Umbria* (Iter)

Ardito, S: *Backpacking and Walking in Italy* (Bradt)

Arnold and Burton: *A Field Guide to the Reptiles and Amphibians of Britain and Europe* (Collins)

Arrighi, A: *A Piedi in Toscana* (Iter)

Corbet and Ovenden: *The Mammals of Britain and Europe* (Collins)

Davies, P and Huxley, A: *Wild Orchids of Britain and Europe* (Chatto and Windus)

Farneti, G: *Guida alla Natura d'Italia* (Mondadori)

Gooders, J: *Where to Watch Birds in Britain and Europe* (Christopher Helm)

Heinzel, Fitter and Parslow: *The Birds of Britain and Europe* (Collins)

Higgins and Riley: *Field Guides to the Butterflies of Britain and Europe* (Collins)

Polunin, O: *Flowers of the Mediterranean* (Oxford University Press)

Polunin, O and Walters, M: *A Guide to the Vegetation of Britain and Europe* (Oxford University Press)

Pratesi, F: *Oasi d'Italia* (Musumeci)

Price, A: *Walking in the Dolomites* (Cicerone)

Schauer, T: *A Field Guide to the Wild Flowers of Britain and Europe* (Collins)

Tassi, F: *Aree Protette d'Italia* (De Agostini)

Wilson, C G: *Alpine Flowers of Britain and Europe* (Collins)

GLOSSARY

Agriturismo: This is an increasingly popular accommodation option allowing you to spend the night in a rural setting, usually on a working farm. Most landlords offer good home cooking and a range of outdoor activities, predominantly ponytrekking. Prices are low and you can usually negotiate long-stay agreements. Most regional and local tourist offices have lists of *agriturist* operators.

CAI: Club Alpino Italiano is more a climbing organization than an environmental body, but it takes a strong interest in all issues affecting the mountains. It also runs mountain refuges and marks trails, as well as offering support and information for walkers and climbers. Many towns have branch offices.

FIPS: Federazione Italiana per la Pesca Sportiva is a national body with local branch offices devoted to fishing in Italy. It advises on local conditions and regulations.

FISE: Although chiefly concerned with equestrian events, **Federazione Italiana Sport Equestri** and its branch offices also provide information on ponytrekking and on recognized riding centres throughout Italy.

GEA: Grande Escursione Appenninica is a path crossing the Apennine mountains from Tuscany to Umbria.

GTA: Grande Traversata delle Alpi is a long-distance path running through the Piedmont region of the Alps.

IGC: Instituto Geografico Centrale produces a series of 23 contour maps covering north-west Italy.

IGM: A series of military maps produced by **Instituto Geografico Militare** covers the whole of Italy.

Italia Nostra: One of the longest-established and most highly respected of Italy's pressure groups, it concerned itself first with urban problems, in particular the conservation of Venice, but is now turning to outdoor environmental issues.

Kompass: This series of contour maps covers most parts of northern Italy, usually on a scale of 1:50,000.

Lega per l'Ambiente: One of the youngest and most dynamic environmental groups, the Lega was initially concerned with pollution and anti-nuclear campaigns but is increasingly addressing wildlife conservation as well.

LIPU: Lega Italiana per la Protezione degli Uccelli is Italy's leading society for the protection of birds. Most towns have a branch office, many of which organize working parties or birdwatching trips. Contact local officers through tourist offices or the addresses given in the Fact Packs.

WWF: The Italian branch of the **World Wide Fund for Nature** (formerly the World Wildlife Fund) was established in 1966.

INDEX

Species are indexed only where information is provided in addition to general description and location, and where they are illustrated. Emboldened page references denote relevant chapters and italicized page references denote illustrations.

Abetina Reale valley 92
Abetone 92–3
Abisso Roversi 112
Abruzzo **130–53**
   national park 8, 141–9
Accellica mountain 166
accommodation 215
   see also Fact Pack Sections
Acerno 166
Aci Castello 196
Acqua Bianca waterfall 16
Acquerino 92
activities *see* Fact Pack Sections
Adamello 50–3
adder 70
Adige 40–1, 43, 47, 64, 88
Adriatic Sea 88, *174–5*
Alagna 17
Albani 154–6
Alberete peak 88
Alburni mountains 157, 172
algae 52, 87, 97
algyroides 81
Alma Dannata lagoons 182
almond trees 196
Alpe delle Tre Potenze 92
Alpi di Siusi 54, 55
Alpi Maritime *see* Maritime
alpine grayling 28
Alps *see* Apuan Alps; Carnic Alps; Central Alps; Eastern Alps; Julian Alps; Maritime; Western Alps
Alta Via I 59
Alta Via II 14, 20
Alta Via II Delle Dolomiti 58
Alta Via Est–Ovest 148
Alta Via Nord–Sud 148
Alta Via dei Monti Liguri 110
Alta Via dei Monti Picentini 166
Alta Via dei Monti di Sicilia 198
Altissimo mountain 112
Amalfi 168
Amaro mountain 149, 151, 153
amber 40–1
Ambro gorge 100
Ampollino reservoir 188
216

Anatella 141
ancient forests and woods
   see forests and woods
ancient king (saxifrage) 29
Ancipa reservoir 198
Anemone baldensis 67
Angeli valley 199
Angora valley 137
Aniene 160
Ansini peak 201
Antro del Corchia (cave) 112
Aosta valley 10, 14
Apennines 32, **82–105**, 156, 160
apollo butterfly 20, 28
Appennino Lucano 176
Appicchio 181
Apuan Alps 106, 109, 110, 111–16
Apuane Trekking 110
Aquila mountain 136
arberesh 185
Architiello 181
Arcosu 208–9
Arcueri mountain 204
Ardo 70
Argentera 26, 28, 30, 32
Argentario 124–5
Aritzo 204
Arnica montana 56
Arnold, Matthew 196
arctic hare 60
arum lily 169
Arvo reservoir 188
Asinara, Isola 213
asp 70
Asphodeline liburnica 97
Aspromonte 187–9
Assisi Bird Campaign 108
Atrio del Cavallo *see* Valle d'Inferno
Audouin's gull 127, 205, 212
Aurina valley 40
avens 41, 48, 67
avocet *168*, 171, 182

badger 76
Badia valley 57
Badia Prataglia 93, 95
Baia dei Francesci 172
Baia delle Zagare 177
Baldo 42, 66–8
ballooning *see* Fact Pack Sections
Baratz lake 193
Barbagia mountains 204
barberry 196
Bargetana valley 92
Bartolo valley 76

bats 151
Battaglia 199
bean geese 88
bearded vulture 205
bears *see* brown bear
beccaccino 135
bedstraw 67
beech 72, 92, 93, 104, 128, *130–1*, 132, 135, 145, 148–9, 150, 158–9, 179, 184–5, 196, 197
beech marten 33
bee-eater 109, 124
Bellevalia dubia 97
bellflower 52, 56, 67, 160, 179
Bellunesi 8, 69–71
Belluno 64, 65, 71, 72
Belvi 204
bergamot orange 176
Bertoloni's ophrys *183*
birch 137, 145
birdwatching *see* Fact Pack Sections
Bifurto abyss 184
Bisegna reserve 145
bittern 159
Biviere di Cesarò lake 198
black grouse 25, 44
black kite 70, 153, 166, 180
black vulture 205
black-winged stilt 124, *125*, 182
black woodpecker 25, 166
bladderwort *87*, 90
blind ringlet butterfly 28
Blockhaus ridge 150
blues (butterflies) 28, 104, 164
bluethroat 119, 124
Blyth's reed warbler 119
boar *see* wild boar
boat trips 35, 79, 81, 90
   see also Fact Pack Sections
Boccaccio 35
Bolgheri 119
Bologna 84
Bolsena lake 156
Bolzano 57
Bondinaio 92
Bonelli's eagles 188, 200, 201, 209
bora 7, 90
Bormio 49, 50
botanical gardens 20, 66, 72, 80, 81
Bove valley 196, 197
Bracciano lake 156
Braies 59–60
Brancastello mountain 137
Brembana valley 42
Brenta 50–3, 64, 88

Brentonico 66, 68
brown bear 25, 47, 51–2, 141,
  144, 151, 160–1
Bulgheria 172
Burano lagoon 108, 124–5
Burning Bush 185
Bus de la Lum (cave) 72
Bus della Genziana (cave) 72
buttercups 101, 134, 140, 159
butterflies 20, 28, 36, 104, 125,
  164, 193
butterwort 169
buzzards 153, 180

Cabras lagoon 212
Cacciatore mountain 76
Cagliari 192, 193, 209
Cala Arena 213
Cala Bianca 200
Cala di Forno 123
Cala Maestra 126
Cala Nera 200
Cala Rossa 126
Cala Spalmatore 200
Calabria national park 8, 169,
  187–9
Caldenelle gorge 184
Calderone 136
Calore river *171*
Camaldoli 93, 96
Camogli 33, 35
Camosciara 145
Campaccio lake 57
Campaegli 161
Campanella peak 169
Campania 154–7
Campanile Basso 52
Campiglio 53
Campigna 93
campion 41, 127, 140
Campo mountain 153
Campo Catino 161
Campo Farina 173
Campo Felice 140, 141
Campo Imperatore 136
Campo Pericoli 137
Campo Staffi 161
Camporotondo 161
Camposecco *159*
Campotosto lake 135
Canale valley 76
Canali valley 55
Candelaro river 182
Cannella valley 151
canoeing *see* Fact Pack Sections
Cansiglio 64, 72
Cantagallo 92
Caorame valley 70

Caorle lagoon 77–8
capercaillie 44
Capo di Monte Santu 205
Cappuccini holm oak 179
Capracotta 153
Capraia 125–7, 181
Caprara peak 213
Capri 156
Carnia 64
Carnic Alps 76, 77
carnic lily 76
Carniche 64, 73–7
Carex buxbaumii 101
carob tree 8, *203*
Carsanica 81
Carso 80–1
Casaraccio lagoon 213
Cascata di Nardis 50
Casentinesi forests 93–6
Castagno dei Cento Cavalli 196
Castelbuono 199
Castelcivita 172, 173
Castellana valley 135
Castellaneta gorge 183
Castello mountain 54, 126
Castelluccio *82–3*, 100, 101, 103
Castelnuovo 116
Castrovillari 184
Catania 195
Catino plain 161
Cavallo mountain 72
Cavallone 151
Cave del Predili 76
cave salamanders 36
caves 72, 100, 112, 128, 140,
  151, 172, 200–1
  see also Fact Pack Sections
Cecina 119
Cecita reservoir 188
Celano 140, 141
Celts 41
Cento Cascate 134, 135
Central Alps **38–61**
Centro Studi Ecologici
  Appennini 151
Cephalia arvensis 72
Cervaro river 182
Cervati mountain 173
Cervialto 166
Cesacastina 134
Cesine 182–3
Cevedale 46–7, 50
chamois 16, 19–20, *22–23*, 31,
  44, 47, 57, 59–60, 76, 137,
  141, 144–5, 151
Charaxes jasins 36, 125
charcoal 120
chestnut 93, *111*, 158–9, 196

Chianti hills *118*
chickweed wintergreen 48
Chioggia 88
Chirocephalus marchesonii 101
Chisone valley 25–6
chough 60, 101, 137
Ciapit 54
Ciardonnet lake 25
Cilento *154*, 156, 157, 171–3
Cima Fiammante 44
Cima Scotoni 59, 60
Cima Telegrafa 66
Cima di Terrarossa 54
Cima Tosa 52
Cima Valdritta 66
Cimina Silva 158
Cimini 157, 158–9
Cimone 87, 92–3
cinquefoil 20, 67, 101
Ciolandra 172
Circeo national park 8, 156,
  164–6
Cistus clusii 180
Civago 92
Civetta massif 62
Civitella Alfedena 144, 147,
  148
cleopatra butterfly 164
clematis 48
climbing *see* Fact Pack Sections
Club Alpino Italiano (CAI) 14,
  137, 214, 215
  see also Fact Pack Sections
Cofano 200
Cogne 20, 21
Col della Sone 57
collared pratincoles 89
Colle dell'Impiso 186
Collemeluccio 153
Collepardo 160
columbines 29, 76, 145
Comacchio 85, 88, 89, 90
Comelico valley *59*
common terns 89
Como lake 41–2
Conero 85, 96–8
conservation 8–9, 51, 72, 200
  see also ecology
coots 88
cork oak 120, 164, 207, 192, 212
cormorants 89
Corniglia 35–7
Corno Grande 136, 139
Corno Piccolo 139
Cortina d'Ampezzo *38–9*, 60
Cory's shearwaters 181, 202–3
Coscerno mountain 129
Cosenza 189

Costacciaro 128
Costanzo mountain 169
country code 213
crab, freshwater 36
cranes 171
Crati river 169
Crespeina lake 57
crested porcupine 33, 95, 101, 119, 120
Cristallo massif 62
Croci di Arcerno 166
Croda Rossa 59
Crognelato 137
Crosson 52
crustacean 101
Cucco 109, 110, 127–8
cuckoo 124
Cugno dell'Acero forest 184
curlew 124
Cusna mountain 92
cyclamen 179
cycling see Fact Pack Sections
  see also mountain biking

dammuso 202
Dante Alighieri 35, 113
Dartford warbler 127, 180
deer see fallow deer; red deer; roe deer
Desulo 205
Dietro Isola 202
dog, domestic 144
Dogna valley 76
Dolcedorme mountain 184
Dolomites 38–61
Dolomiti Bellunesi e Feltrine national park 8, 69–71
Donanigoro 205
donkey, white 213
dormouse 188
dotterel 151
Duchessa 139, 140, 141
Due Sorelle 97, 98
Duino 80
dwarf palm 123, 200
dwarf pine 150
dwarf willow 136–7

eagle owl 25, 93, 101, 166, 180
eagles 70, 119, 180
  see also Bonelli's eagles
earthquakes 156
Eastern Alps 62–81
ecology 78, 151
  see also Fact Pack Sections
edelweiss 15, 25, 52, 56, 65, 69, 76, 101, 137, 145, 151

eels, Commacchio 85
egrets 77, 78–9, 124, 125
Egyptian vulture 180, 198, 200
Elba 125–7
Eleanora's falcons 181, 203, 205
Emilia–Romagna 84, 87
Emmanuel, Victor 28
Ernici 157, 160–2
erosion 57, 80, 91, 174, 181
Etna 193, 195–7
eucalyptus 165
eyed lizard 37

Fabbrica 121
Faggeta Madonie 199
Falcone mountain 201
falcons see Eleanora's falcons; lanner falcons; peregrine falcons
Fallistro wood 188
fallow deer 70, 95, 180
Fanes 59–60
Farina plain 173
Farmacia del Mago Greguro 183
Fate cave 100
Felice plain 141
Feltre 71
Feltrine 69–71
Fema mountain 104, 105
Ferentillo 129
ferns 113, 160, 169
Ferrara 89
Ferrata 128
Fibreno 162–3
Figliolo 172
figwort 41, 52, 76
fir 199
fishing see Fact Pack Sections
Fiumefreddo 196
flamingos 123, 208, 212
Florence 156
flowers and plants 20, 33, 59, 67, 68, 70, 80, 87, 90, 94, 97, 102–3, 113, 127, 144, 150–1, 157, 159, 169, 172, 176, 179, 180, 185, 188, 196, 199, 200, 201, 205, 212
  see also botanical gardens; edelweiss; gentians; grasses; orchids
Fontanile di Canale 159
Fonte Pegna 201
Foresta valley 59, 60
forests and woods 7–8, 15, 48, 49, 62–3, 79, 117
ancient 25, 29, 64, 89, 93–6,

104, 148–9, 197,
primeval 24–5, 55, 165, 179
relict 72, 137, 150, 205
  see also beech; birch; chestnut; fir; Foresta valley; larch; manna ash; maple; oak; pine; Umbra forest; yew
Fortunato, Giustino 166
Foss Fioio 160
Fosse valley 44, 45
Fossiata wood 189
fox 101, 197–8
foxglove 159, 205
Francis of Assissi 104, 108
Frignana 92
fritillaries 29
fritillary butterfly 193
Friuli 64, 65
Fumana arabica 97
Funes valley 57
Fusine lakes 62–3, 76, 77

Gadir 202
Galino 121
Garda lake 41–2, 66, 67, 68
Gardena valley 58, 59
Garfagnana valley 112, 113, 116
Gargano 174–5, 177–81
garrigue 8, 201, 203
Gat plain 71
geckoes 36, 37, 202
geese see wild geese
Gennargentu 192, 204–7
Genova valley 50, 51
gentians 15, 24, 25, 41, 48, 76, 140, 145
geology 7, 38–9, 44, 49, 50, 54, 91, 95, 97, 125–6, 134, 187
karstic terrain 27, 55, 69, 72, 80, 160, 205
  see also caves; glaciation; marble; sinkholes; volcanoes
Gessopalena 150
Gesturi 207–8
Ghiacciaio dei Forni 46, 47
Giannutri 125–7
Gigante 81
giganti della Sila 188
Giglio 125
Giudicarie Fault 50
Giulie–Carniche 73–7
Gizmo 128
glaciation 16, 20, 46–7, 50, 51–2, 57, 59, 67, 70, 100, 139–40, 184
Glenodinium sanguineum 52
glossy ibis 182

Gnifetti 16
Gola del Corno 128
Gola di Fromm 54
golden eagle *16*, 48, 57, 70, 76, 96, 137, 145, 153, 198, 200
goldeneye 79
Gole di Celano 140
Gole dell'Infernaccio 100
Gole di Pretolo 196
Golfo di Orosei 204, 205
Golfo Paradiso 33
Gonato canyon 199
goosander 124
Gorgona 125–7
Gorroppu canyons 205
gorse 84
Gorzano mountain 133
Grado lagoon 78–9
Gran Cono 167
Gran Paradiso national park 8, *10–11*, 14, 18–24, 45
Gran Sasso d'Italia 132, 134, 136–9, *147*
Gran Zebrù 50
Grande plain 102–3
Grande Escursione Appenninica (GEA) 87, 92, 96, 110, 215
Grande Traversata delle Alpi (GTA) 12, 14, 24, 25, 26, 28, 32, 215
grasses 8, 32, *54*, 79, 97, 169
Grava di Campolato 181
Grava di Fra Gentile 172
grayling butterfly 193
great crested grebe 159
great spotted cuckoo 124
great spotted woodpecker 48
great white egret *77*, 124
grebe 159
green hairstreak 164
green lizard *68*
greenweed 196
grey heron 124
grey wolf 189
griffon vulture 76, 198, 200, 209
Grohman (path) 60
grouse 44
Gusela del Vescova 70
Guttereddu valley 208, 209

hang-gliding *see* Fact Pack Sections
hare, arctic/blue 60
harriers 79, 81, 89, 124
hazel hen 44
Herculaneum 167

Hermann's tortoise 37, 116
herons *77*, 81, 89, 124, 182, *212*
hiking *see* walking
Hiranini 201
holm oak 164, 179, 196
honey buzzard 153, 180
horses *see* wild horses
Horvath's rock lizard 81
hunting 5, 19, 36, 44, 47, 57, 59, 144

ibex 19, *20*, 24, 25, 31, 47, 76
ice sheets *see* glaciation
Imperatore plain 136
Infernaccio 100
Inferno valley 113, 160, 161, 168
Infreschi peak 171
Iôf di Montasio 76
Irgini 204
iris 70, 145
Irish spurge 113
Is Benas lagoon 212
Isernia 153
Isola 163
Isonzo river 64, 81
Italian Alpine Club *see* Club Alpino Italiano (CAI)

jasmine 41, 151, 176
Julian Alps 64, 76, 77
Jupiter's beard 179

karstic terrain 27, 55, 69, 72, 80, 160, 205
kestrels 200
knapweed 33, 80
Kotschy's gecko 37

La Lamia 93
La Stagnone 126
lady's slipper orchid 29, 52, 56, 145
Laga 133–5, 136, 150
Lagazuoi valley 60
Lago peak 159
Lama forest 95
Lama Lite 92
lammergeier 185
Lampedusa, Giuseppe Tomasi di 192
Lampedusa 37, *190–1, 202–3
Lampione 202–3
Langammella 135
lanner falcon 137, *161*
Lao river 186
lapwing 119

larch 20, 24, *30*, *38–9*, 57
Laterza canyon 183
Lattari mountain 168
Lazio 154–7
leaf-toed gecko *36*, 37
Leano mountain 166
Lega Italiana per la Protezione degli Uccelli (LIPU) 9, 90, 214, 215
see also Fact Pack Sections
leopard snake 37
Lesina lake 177, 180
lesser grey shrike 180
lesser kestrel 200
lesser spotted eagle 119
Lessini 64, 69
Levi, Carlo 166, 176
Li Puzzinusi marsh 213
lichen 41, 151, 168, 212
lilies 25, 70, 76, 97, 169
see also martagon lily
Limbara mountain 212–13
Linguaglossa 196
Linnaea borealis 20–1
Linnaeus, Carl 20–1
Linosa 202–3
little bittern 159
little egret *78–9*, 124
lizards 33, 36, 37, *68*, 81, 125
locust tree *203*
loggerhead marine turtle 37
Lombardy 41–2, 47
long–eared owl *48*
Lora 69
Lugano lake 41–2
Luna 205
Lupo pass 200
lynx 19, 29–31, 72

Macchia di Migliarino 117
Macinare valley 128
Macugnaga 16, 17
Madonie mountains 193, 198–9
Madonna degli Angeli valley 199
Madonna della Scala gorge 183
Maggiore lake 41–2
Magnano forest 184
magredis 64
maidenhair fern 160
Maiella 149–53
Maielletta 150
Majelama valley 140, 141
Malatina tors 91–2
Manarola 35–7
Mandrolisai 204
Manfredonia 182
Mangart 76, 77

manna ash 185
Manx shearwater 181, 202–3
maple 15, 104, 145
maquis 8, 203
Marano lagoon 78–9
marble 36, 66, 111–12
Maremma 106–8, 120–4
Maresca 92
Marettimo 200–1
Margherita di Savoia 182
marginated tortoise 37
Marguareis 27, 32
Marittime 12, 26–32, 152
Marmolada massif 62
Marmora peak 204
Marmore waterfall 129
marmot 19, 45, 47, 92
marsh harriers 79, 81
Marsi 144
Marsia 161
martagon lily 15, 48, 69, 101
Martello valley 47
Martese 135
Massa Marinelli 76
Massa Pirona 76
Massaciuccoli 92, 117
Massafra 183
Matera gorge 183
Matterhorn 16
meadow brown butterfly 193
medicinal plants 25, *56*, 67
Mediterranean Coast **154–73**
Merlin 25
Mesco peak 35
Mesola woodlands 88, 89
Messner, Reinhold 57
mezereon 67
Mezzo mountain 135, 153
middle spotted woodpecker 25, 180
Migliarino 117
milk vetch 20
Miramare 80, 81
Mistras lagoon 212
Misurina lake 60
Mnestra's ringlet 28
Molentargius 208
Molise 132, 133, 152, 153
Mongibello *see* Etna
mongoose 165
monk seal 127, *204*, 205
monk's hood 67
Mont Blanc 8, 18
Montagna Grande 202
Montagu's harrier 124
Montarbu di Seui 205
Montecristo 125–6
Montecristo viper 126

Montenero 166
Monterosso al Mare 35–7
Montpellier snake 37
Moorish gecko 37
Morane mountain 140
Morigerati 172
Morino 160, 161
Moso 61
mouflon 31, 70, 95, 205
mountain biking 55, 59
    see also Fact Pack Sections
mountain clouded yellow 28
mountain safety 61
Murolungo 140
musk thistles *94*
Muzzerone 35

Naples 154, 156
narcissi 25, 67, 69, 151
Nebrodi mountains 193, 197–8
Nemus garganicum 179
Nera river 129
newts 67, 70, 137, 169
night heron *212*
Ninfe 184
Nivolè lakes *18–19*
Northern Apennines **82–105**
Nuda mountain 173
nuraghi 207

oak 89, 150, 158–9, 164, 165, 179, 196, 205
    see also cork oak; holm oak
ocellated lizard 33, 37
ocellated skink 37
Oliesi 204
olives 121, *122*, 182, 188, 192
Ollolai 204
olm *80*, 81
Ombrone river 123
Opi 144
Orbetello lagoon 108, 124–5
orchids 36, 48, 134, 160, 183
    lady's slipper 29, 52, 56, 145
Orecchiella 109, *111,* 112
Orfanto river 182
Orfento valley 150
Ornano 137
Oro cave 140
Orobie massif 42
Orrido di Malevento 184
Orrido di Val Clusa 70
Orsiera 25–6
Orsini's viper 136, 137
Orsomarso 184–6
Ortles 46–7
osprey *119*, 123, 171
otters 79, 119, 151, 159, 169, 170

Ovindoli 140, 141
owls *48*, 70, *93*, 101, 159, 166
oxen 123

Padano toad *89*, 90
Palanfrè 26, 28, 32
Pale 55–6
paliai 181
Palmaria, Isola 36
Panaro valley 91
Paneveggio 55–6
Pania della Croce 112
Pania Forata 112
Panorama mountain *see* Alburni mountain
Pantano Grande lake 182–3
Pantelleria 201–2
Paradiso *see* Gran Paradiso national park
Parnassia palustris 169
Parnassius phoebus sacerdos (butterfly) 20
partridge 101, 105, 127, 145
partridge eagle *see* Bonelli's eagle
pasque-flowers 25
Pasubio 69
paths 9, 20, 35, 42, 52, 58, 59, 60, 77, 148, 166, 198
    see also Grande Escursione Appenninica; Grande Traversata delle Alpi
Patino valley *94*
Pauli Maiori 208
Pauli Minori 208
Pauli Murtas lagoon 212
Pavione mountain 69
Pelagie 202–3
Pelobates fuscus insubricus 89, 90
peregrine falcon 91, 101, 123, 137, 153, 166, 180, 181, 200, 212
Pereto 161
Pericoli plain 137
Pertosa 172, 173
Pescasseroli 144, 147, 148
Peschici 180
Pescocostanzo 149
Pescolanciano 153
Pesio valley 26, 27, 29, 32
Petrarch 35
petrels 200, 201
pheasant's eye 67, 151
Phlegrean Fields 154
Physoplexis comosa 52, 56
Piana Liana 204
piani 100–1, 199

Piani di Ruggio 184
Piani Eterni 69, 70
Piano del Ceraso 149
Piano di Pezza 140
Pianosa 125–7
Piave 64, 69, 70
Picentini 156, 157, 166, *167*
Pietra di Bismantova 91
Pietroso mountain 145
Pilate lake 100
Pilo lagoon 213
pine *10–11*, 29, *34*, 72, 88, 135,
   136–7, 145, 150, 164–5, 179,
   187–8, 196
pine marten 55
Pis del Pes waterfall 26, 32
Pisanino mountain 112
pistachio trees 196
Pistoiesi forests 92
Pizzalto mountain 148
Pizzo Carbonara 199
Pizzo del Diavolo 100
Pizzo di Sevo 135
Pizzo d'Uccello 116
Pizzocco mountain 70
plants *see* flowers and plants
Po river 5, 64, 87–8, *90–1*
   delta **82–105**
Poggio Scali 95
Polizzi Generosa 199
Pollino 150, 174, 176, 184–6
pollution 5, 52, 64, 87–8, 169
Polveracchio 166
Pompeii 167
Pontebba 77
Pontine craft 162–3
Pontine marshes 164
ponytrekking *see* Fact Pack
   Sections
poppies 52, 56, 76, 101, *142–3*
porcupine *see* crested
   porcupine
Portofino 33–5
Portoro marble 36
Portovenere 35, 36, 37
Pracchia 92
Prada 68
Pramallo pass 76
Prato mountain 92
Prato Piazza 59
pre-Alps 64, 76
Precipizio 166
Preda mountain 137
Pretolo 196
prickly pear 196
primeval forests *see* forests and
   woods
primrose 52, 56, 67, 172

Procinto 112, *111*
Pruner's ringlet 28
ptarmigan 44
Puez–Odle 57–9
Puglia 176
Pugliesi *gravine* 183
Pulsano 179
purple heron 81, 124
pygmy cormorant 89

Quacella 199
quarare 199
Quarto wood 179
Quattrocchi lake 198

Raganello gorge 186
ragwort 196
Ramsar Convention 78, 119
Ranco valley 128
raptors *see* black kite;
   buzzards; eagles; falcons;
   harriers; kestrels; osprey;
   owls; red kite; vultures
Ravenna 88, 89
reclamation of land 64, 88
red-crested pochard 159, 171,
   213
red deer 24, 47, 55, 57, 72, 76,
   95, 117, 145, 151, 208, *209*
red kite 153, 166, 180
red-legged partridge 127
red squirrel 76
relict woods *see* forests and
   woods
Rendena valley 51
Reno river 88
Retiche massif 42
Ricci tor 204
Rienza valley 60
ringlet butterfly 28
Rio La Vera valley 148
Riomaggiore 35–7
Ripa dei Falconei 181
Riviera **10–37**
Rivisondoli 149
Roccaraso 149
Rocciavrè 25–6
rock jasmine 41, 151
rock partridge 25, 101, 105, 145
rock rose 97
roe deer 24, 47, 57, 72, 76, 95,
   101, 117, 119, 145, 151, 180
roller 180
Romans 41, 84, 126, 129
Rome 154, 156, 160
Ronchi valley 69
Rosa mountain 16, 18
Rosa rubiginosa 157, 160

Rosandra valley 81
Rose valley 145, 148
rosemary 160
Rossi di Nicolosi mountain 196
Rotella mountain 148

Sabaudia 164, 165, 166
Sabine hills 157
Sadali tor 204
salamanders 36, 70, 112, 169
Salapi lake 182–3
Salbertrand 24–5
Sale Porcus 212
Salerno 173
Salina di Margherita di Savoia
   182
Salto della Giumenta 196
San Candido 60
San Classiano Formation 57
San Domino 181
San Gerbone 135
San Giovanni a Piro 172
San Lorenzo Bellizzi 184
San Martino 55–6
San Nicola 137, 181
San Pietro abbey 129
San Rabano 120
San Rossore 117
San Stefano church 70
Santa Caterina Valfurva 47
Santa Margherita Ligure 33, 35
Sant'Alfio 196
Sant'Anatolia di Narco 129
Sant'Anna 12
Sant'Antonio 148–9
Sangro *142–3*, 144, 148
Santo lake 92
Sardinia 37, **190–213**
Sargasso Sea 85
sassi (stones) 91–2
sassi (cave dwelling) 183
Sasso *see* Gran Sasso d'Italia
Sassofratino 93–5
Sataria 202
Savoia 182
Savoy, House of 12, 19
saxifrage 25, 29, 33, 41, 67, 76,
   140
scabious 67, 179, 201
Scala gorge 183
Schiara 69, 70, 71
Sciliar 54–5
scirroco 7, 176, 192, *193*
Scoglietto 121
Scomunica peak 213
scuba diving *see* Fact Pack
   Sections
seal, monk 127, *204*, 205

sedge 67
Seeber valley 44
Sele 166, 171
Sella Nevea 77
Selva di Terracina 165
Sentiero Azzuro 35
Sentiero dei Franchi 26
Sentiero delle Odle 58
Sentiero Sersaret 24
Sentiero dei Signori 58
Seriana valley 42
Serra Santa 128
Serre river 170
Serre-Persano lake 169, 170–1
Sesi (funeral mounds) 202
Sesto 40, 60
Seui 204
Seulo 204
Sgonico 80
sheep farming 132, 144, 153
shelduck 171, 182
short-eared owl 159
short-toed eagle 25, 70, 180
shrikes 33, 180
Si tor 204
Siba 202
Sibillini 8, 87, 136
  mountains *94*, 99–104
Sicily **190–213**
Sila 187–8, 189
Silva palatina 117
Silva pisana 117
Simbruini 157, 160–2
Sinis 209–12
sinkholes 27, 172, 199, 205
Sirente 139–41
Sisine 205
Sistiano 80
Siusi 54, 55
skating *see* Fact Pack Sections
skiing 55
  see also Fact Pack Sections
skin diving *see* Fact Pack
  Sections
skink 37
Slovenia 64–5, 80
smew 124
smooth snake 37
snakes 37, 70, 81, 126, 136, 137,
  165, 202
Sole mountain 69
Somma mountain 69
sooty ringlet butterfly 28
Sopramonte 204, 205, 206
Sora 162, 163
Sorrento peninsula 156, 168–70
sottobosco 84
Southern Italy **174–89**

spadefoot toad *89*, 90
Specchio di Venere lake 202
Spoleto 129
spoonbills 182
spur-thighed tortoise 37
squacco heron 89
squirrels 76
Staffi plain 161
Stella river 79
Stelvia 57
Stelvio national park 8, 45,
  46–50
stilts 124, 182
stoat *17*, 76
storks 124
stone curlew 124
storm petrel 200, 201
Strada di Mezzo 159
Stua lake 70
Su Sercone 205
Su Sterru 205
Sulcis 193, 208
Summano mountain 69
Susa valley 25–6
swallowtail *28*, 193
sweet briar 157, 160
swifts 140, 141, 151

Tagliamento river 64
Talamone 123
Tana dell'Olmo Selvatico 112
Taranta valley 151
Tarvisio 64, 77, 152
Tavoliere plain 177
Tazza valley 104
Termini 169
Terminillo 157
Terminio 166
terns 81, 89
terracing 35
Tessa 44–5
Tetti Niot 31
Teve valley 140
thistles *28*, *94*
thorow-wax 201
thyme 160
Tiber valley 157
Timavo river 81
Tinetto lizard 36
Tires valley 54
Tirone reserve 167–8
Tiscali mountain 205
Titian (path) 60
toad flax 127, 140
toads *89*, 90
Tofane mountain *58*
Tognola 55, 56
Tonara 204

Tonneri mountain 204
Torricchio 104–5
Torrile 90
tortoises 37, 116
Tovel lake 52
Traversata Carnica 77
Tre Cime 61
Tre Cime di Lavaredo 60
Tre Potenze 92
tree spurge 97
trekking *see* walking
Tremiti 181
Trentino–Alto Adige 47
Trieste 80, 81
Trifoglio 196
Troia peak 200, 201
trumpet gentian 25, 48
Tschigat mountain 44
Tuckett refuge 51–2
tulip 15
Turkish gecko 37
Turtles, marine 37, 202
Tuscany 95, **106–29**
twinflower 20
two–tailed pasha 36, 125

Uccellina hills 120, 123
Umbra forest 177–81
Umbria **106–29**
Uque valley 76
Usseaux 25

Val Foresta 59, 60
Val Gardena 58, 59
Valbruna 76, 77
Valasco 12, 27, 28
Valgrande 15
Valico di Forchetta valley 150
Valle d'Aosta 10, 14
Valle d'Inferno 113, 160, 161,
  168
Vallescura 173
Vallone della Femmina Morta
  151
Vallone Sambucito 160
Vallunga 57
Valnerina 109, 129
Valnontey *10–11*, 20, 21
Valscura lake 29
Valsesia 16–17
Valsorda 128
Varano 177, 180
Velino 136, 139–41
velvet scoter 124
Venere mountain 158, 159
Venetian Plain **62–81**
Vento cave 112
Verna 95

Vernazza 35–7
Vesuvius 154, 167–8
Vette Feltrine 69, 70
Vettore mountain *82–3*, 100
Via delle Bocchette 52
Via Emilia 84
Via Mediana 165
Vico lake 156, 157, 158–9
Vico del Gargano 179
Vieste 177, 181
Viglio mountain 160, 161
Villetta Barrea 144
vines 196
violets 134, 196, 199
vipers 37, 126, 136, 137, 165
Vitelle mountain 148
volcanoes 154–6, 167–8, 176, 193, 195–7
voles, alpine 113
Voragine Boccanera 128
vulcanelli 91
Vulture mountain 176
vultures 76, 180, 185, 198, 200, 205, 209

walking 12–13, 20, 33, 46–7, 55, 68, 137, 160

see also paths; Fact Pack Sections
wall lizard 81, 125
wallcreeper *151*
Walser 17
warblers 127, 180
war remains 47, 61, 62, 69
water sports *see* Fact Pack Sections
Western Alps **10–37**
wetlands 8, 77–9, 87–90, 117, 180, 182
see also World Wide Fund for Nature
whip snake 37, 81, 202
white alpenrose 15
white donkey 213
white-backed woodpecker 101, 145, 160, 180
white-headed duck 212
wigeon 182
wild boar 76, 117, 119, 151, 152, 180
wild geese 180
wild horses 123, 207
wildcat 24–5, 101, 198
windsurfing *see* Fact Pack Sections

winter sports *see* Fact Pack Sections
wolves 95, 101, 137, 140, 141, 144, 151, 185, 188, 189
"Wood of Oars" 72
woodpeckers 25, 48, 101, 145, 160, 166, 180
woods *see* forests and woods
Woodwardia radicans 169
World Wide Fund for Nature (WWF) 9, 79, 80, 81, 88, 104, 108, 119, 124, 170–1, 182–3, 208–9, 214, 215
see also Fact Pack Sections
Worndle caverns 57
Wulfania carinthiaca 76

yew 137, 179, 197, 205

Zanseralm 57
Zebrù valley 46, 47, 50
Zenobito peak 126
Zibbibo vines 202
Zingaro *199*, 200
Zompo Lo Schioppo 160
Zucchi 199
Zuvletti 126

PICTURE CREDITS

Front Cover – FLPA/Marka. 10/11 – T. Jepson. 18/19 – FLPA/Marka. 22/23 – FLPA/Marka. 27 – T. Jepson. 30 – T. Jepson. 34/35 – FLPA/Marka. 38/39 – Woolverton Picture Library. 46/47 – T. Jepson. 51 – FLPA/Marka. 54 – FLPA/ Marka. 58 – V. Tomaselli, Panda Photo. 59 – FLPA/Marka. 62/63 – G. Cappelli, Panda Photo. 71 – FLPA/Marka. 74/75 – FLPA/Marka. 68/69 – R. Mattio, Panda Photo. 79 – R. Ricci, Panda Photo. 82/83 – D. Walsh. 90/91 – FLPA/Marka. 94 – T. Jepson. 98 – FLPA/Marka. 99 – FLPA/ Marka. 102/103 – D. Walsh. 106/107 – J. Cleare, Mountain Camera. 111 – T. Jepson. 114/115 – FLPA/Marka. 118 – J. Cleare, Mountain Camera. 122 – S. Benn. 126/127 – FLPA/Marka. 130/131 – FLPA/Marka. 138 – Italian Tourist Office. 142/143 – E. Parker, Hutchinson Library. 146 – J. Sutherland, Nature Photographers Ltd. 147 – FLPA/Marka. 150 – Sheldrake. 154/155 – FLPA/Marka. 159 – A. Mongiu, Panda Photo. 162/163 – A. Mogiu, Panda Photo. 167 – A. Nadri, Panda Photo. 170 – A. Nadri, Panda Photo. 171 – A. Nadri, Panda Photo. 174/175 – FLPA/Marka. 179 – S.Benn. 186 – FLPA/Marka. 187 – N. Birch. 190/191 – FLPA/Marka. 195 – N. Birch. 198 – R. Francis, Hutchinson Library. 199 – FLPA/Marka. 206/207 – FLPA/Marka. 210/211 – FLPA/Marka.

ACKNOWLEDGEMENTS

The contributors and editors wish to extend their grateful thanks to the following people for their assistance:

Piers Burnett, John Burton, Julia Farino, IUCN, Jane Judd, David Stubbs.